THE CURE
for CATASTROPHE

ALSO BY ROBERT MUIR-WOOD

The Dark Side of the Earth

Earthquakes and Volcanoes

THE CURE
for CATASTROPHE

How We Can Stop Manufacturing Natural Disasters

ROBERT MUIR-WOOD

BASIC
BOOKS
NEW YORK

Published by Basic Books,
An imprint of Perseus Books, a division of PBG Publishing, LLC, a subsidiary
of Hachette Book Group, Inc.

DESIGNED BY LINDA MARK

Library of Congress Cataloging-in-Publication Data

Names: Muir-Wood, Robert, author.
Title: The cure for catastrophe : how we can stop manufacturing natural
disasters / Robert Muir-Wood.
Description: New York : Basic Books,
    [2016] | Includes bibliographical references and index.
Identifiers: LCCN 2016004281 (print) | LCCN 2016016150 (ebook) |
    ISBN 9780465060948 (hardcover) | ISBN 9780465096473 (ebook)
Subjects: LCSH: Natural disasters—Planning. | Natural disasters—Prevention.
    | Environmental risk assessment. | Hazardous geographic environments. |
    Hazard mitigation.
Classification: LCC GB5014 .M85 2016 (print) | LCC GB5014 (ebook) | DDC
    363.34/07—dc23
LC record available at https://lccn.loc.gov/2016004281

10 9 8 7 6 5 4 3 2 1

To my wife Elizabeth: writer, teacher, and muse

CONTENTS

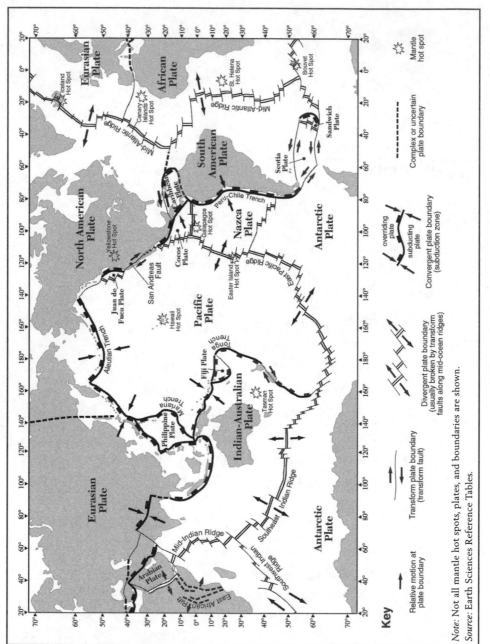

Tectonic plates

Key

Relative motion at
plate boundary

Transform plate boundary
(transform fault)

Divergent plate boundary
(usually broken by transform
faults along mid-ocean ridges)

overriding
plate

subducting
plate

Convergent plate boundary
(subduction zone)

- - - - Complex or uncertain
plate boundary

☆ Mantle
hot spot

Note: Not all mantle hot spots, plates, and boundaries are shown.

Source: Earth Sciences Reference Tables.

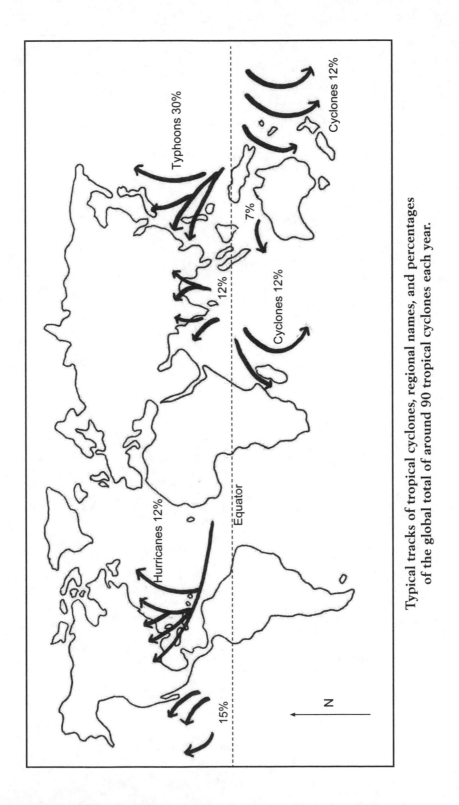

Typical tracks of tropical cyclones, regional names, and percentages of the global total of around 90 tropical cyclones each year.

INTRODUCTION

I T WAS NIGHT IN THE EARTHQUAKE-RAVAGED CITY OF EL ASNAM, Algeria. Arc lights illuminated the rubble pile. The steel bucket of the excavator screamed as it clawed at the concrete slabs. Soldiers stood listlessly, waiting to retrieve another body.

The dust swirled as the drills bored into the pancaked concrete slabs. I brushed the crumbled concrete and plaster off my clothes. I could taste the dust, feel it in my lungs. (I would taste it again the day after 9/11 on the streets around the World Trade Center.)

Next morning all was ugliness and despondency. Ruins spilled into the street. Second-floor rooms missing a wall, wallpaper torn, a child's artwork flapping, a bed covered with debris. Clothes, a saucepan, school bags, family photographs strewn in the dirt—banal and poignant mementos of ordinary lives, interrupted.

Over the years I would go on to visit towns newly blitzed by hurricanes, storm surges, tsunamis, and more earthquakes. (Don't get me wrong, this is not an obsession with destruction. I much prefer my medieval Italian hill village to be crumbling gently with age.) But you learn many things from seeing natural disaster for yourself, on the ground. Sometimes, as in New Orleans, the people have all gone. More often, as in coastal Dichato, Chile, or Bhachau, Gujarat, the survivors are camped on waste ground, their desperation palpable.

Several first questions arise in a newly ruined town: What happened? What was this destructive force? How far did it penetrate? What made some structures fall while others remained standing?

The follow-up questions emerge more slowly: Why? Why this town at this time? Was anyone aware of what lay in wait when they built the houses next to the beach? Did anyone question the idea of constructing concrete apartment buildings without an engineer? Did the villagers know what could happen when they settled high on the slopes of the volcano?

I first became intrigued by the forensics of disasters while working as the science writer on a Royal Geographical Society expedition to the Karakoram Mountains of northern Pakistan. Wanting to get deeper into the science, I volunteered to help pursue the next big disaster. Two months later came the Algerian earthquake. The first headline death toll was 20,000. The call from Cambridge seismologist Geof King came through early that evening to drive a jeep down to the port at Marseilles and take the ferry to Algiers to join a small team of research seismologists.

After the adventure of the journey, we arrived in the late evening to walk the sad ruins of the city of El Asnam. Next morning we set off to install seismic recorders far away from the principal roads and towns. Each day we did the "milk-round"—driving 80 miles of rutted dirt tracks to replace the car batteries powering the recorders and lift out the paper-lined drum, swarming with the "butterfly wing" traces of the aftershocks. (Fixed with a concoction made from crushed beetles, the paper records would be analyzed back in Cambridge.)

All the visiting researchers slept on the floor of an abandoned schoolhouse located out of the damage zone, high above a ravine. The outhouse latrine was a seat suspended over the void. In the evening we got together with French geologists and structural engineers from California, Skopje, and London who also "did science" after a disaster—in this case, rapidly surveying why half the concrete structures in the El Asnam city center had collapsed. The buildings in the city—which had been reconstructed following an earthquake twenty-five years before— were all relatively new. Why had so many of them fallen?

I went back to El Asnam on behalf of UNESCO a couple of years later to inspect trenches dug at the base of the hills. On the walls of the trenches I could trace the "smoking gun": a tongue of white limestone thrust three meters over the red earth of the valley. The tongue revealed the surface trace of the fault movement that generated the vibrations that destroyed the city. Underneath was another white limestone band on top of the red soil—the fault break from the previous earthquake, radiocarbon-dated to sometime in the fourteenth century.

It seemed easy. Geologists would identify and map the dangerous faults. Trenches would be dug to reveal the incriminating evidence of the fault's last shift in a big earthquake and whether it was primed for a repeat. Buildings in the vicinity of dangerous faults would be designed by engineers to remain upright through the wild earthquake ride. As the geologist Martin Capelletti said after the 1944 San Juan (Argentina) earthquake: "It is within the power of builders, architects and engineers to erase earthquakes from the list of human scourges if they wish it."[1] With the application of all this scientific knowledge, cities could be safe from disasters—or so it seemed—within a generation.

We were of course naive. Engineers still go out to study the latest catastrophes in Haiti or Pakistan. The lessons they bring back are no different than those learned from the collapsed buildings at El Asnam. We know how to make buildings that resist strong shaking or hurricane winds. We can tell where the land will flood from a river or a tsunami, or where it will lose its strength in earthquake liquefaction. Yet a chasm yawns between this knowledge and its application.

As with the tribes of scientists and engineers in the El Asnam schoolhouse, every disaster draws researchers from a range of disciplines, each of whom takes a piece of the puzzle back to his or her institution. Disasters lie at a bewildering crossroads where science, engineering, social sciences, geography, economics, and history intersect. No single discipline captures the whole picture. Even the science is splintered into specialties with their own terminology and tools: seismology, volcanology, hydrology, meteorology. As informed by my coordinating lead authors on the 2011 *IPCC Special Report on Extremes*, earthquakes, tsunamis, and eruptions were strictly off-limits.[2]

Meanwhile, since the year 2000 more people have died in sudden "natural" disasters than in any equivalent period in history. Most of them were victims of negligence: bright schoolgirls killed by collapsed concrete school buildings in Pakistan, or the Karen delta people of Myanmar abandoned by their military rulers as a vast cyclone storm surge flood barreled toward them.

Disasters consume wealth, depreciate land values, and threaten governments. Disasters are political. From Simón Bolívar to Fidel Castro, leaders have understood the need to outwit catastrophes in order to maintain their authority. Disasters have both promoted (Herbert Hoover) and derailed (George W. Bush) US presidents. Faced with an existential threat from catastrophic floods, the Dutch tamed the "Water-Wolf" with a potent mixture of regulation and landowner responsibility, which then framed their "polder model" of collaborative governance.

Everyone questions why money should be diverted to protect against a disaster that may not happen in their lifetime. Politicians prefer the photo opportunities of being seen to dispense money amid the ruins. Twenty-five years ago, insurers learned the hard way how dangerous it is to let a catastrophe teach you the price of risk after the fact. Nine insurers went out of business following Hurricane Andrew in 1992, and the Lloyds of London reinsurance market came close to dissolution following years of unremitting catastrophe losses.

On the back of the crisis, catastrophe models, with their 100,000 years of synthetic catastrophe histories, were developed to quantify the price of insurance and determine how much an insurer needs to keep in reserve to withstand an extreme year of losses. The technology that protects the markets can also protect people. Catastrophe models are now being adapted to design the most cost-effective ways to reduce disaster risk. Political leaders will increasingly be expected to account for latent disaster deaths and losses before they happen.

Meanwhile, in a thousand cities, from booming Dhaka to greater Miami (the hurricane hazard hot spot of the Western world), mountains of new risk are being quietly created. As if attracted by danger, the world's most valuable technology companies have congregated in Silicon Valley—a tectonic rift in the middle of a plate boundary. The world's largest city, Tokyo, is itself uniquely underlain by three tectonic plates. And whether from sea level rise or stronger storms, climate change is brewing some unprecedented future floods.

It can sometimes feel as though we are at war—up against a cunning disaster enemy who ambushes our complacent sleeping cities. While it was a catastrophe that launched the age of reason, in the law of contracts unforeseen calamities are still labeled "acts of God." And yet the call for "resilience" has gone out, some countries are deep into containing their risks, and we are approaching the day when a great earthquake or hurricane will hit a coastal city and nobody will die.

This is the story, across continents and history, of the search for the cure for catastrophe.

1 • TRUST IN THE WALLS

THE SHAKING CAME IN VIOLENT BURSTS, STRONGER THAN ANY-one had felt before. Periods of slow regular oscillation followed by sharp grinding vibrations. Buildings were cracking open, and tools hurtled to the floor in the fishermen's sheds by the wharf. To stay standing, you had to hold on to a wall or doorway. Dust rose from little landslides along the cliffs. It was 2:48 p.m. on a cloudy Friday afternoon in March. The shaking, which lasted six grueling minutes, felt as if it would never end.[1]

As the violent tremors faded away the tsunami sirens sounded their mournful cries, whooping from low to high. People already outside started to clamber up the cliff-side staircases from the port. In the lower town, seniors glanced out of their windows at the ugly concrete tsunami walls that separated them from the sea and hunkered down. Five years before, the sirens had sounded but no waves had arrived. This was probably another false alarm. It was a cold afternoon, with snow flurries, and venturing outside, standing around, had no appeal.

Among those who climbed up above the lower town, all eyes were on the sea, on the water in the harbor, and on the distant horizon seen between the headlands. As the minutes passed and nothing happened, they began to relax.

Kamaishi is a former steel town, situated in a drowned valley inlet on the remote mountainous coast of northeast Japan. In the 1970s, 12,000 people were employed in the steelworks and the town's population was close to 100,000. The mill closed in 1988, and now the population was down to 40,000. The economy depended on fishing. In 2009 the government spent $1.5 billion on a 1.25-mile (2-kilometer) breakwater, rising up from the seafloor 200 feet (60 meters) below. Said to be the deepest and most expensive in the world, the breakwater was intended to revive the town by providing shelter from the Pacific swell for moored container ships. Yet no ships had come to call.

Kamaishi was known for having a "tsunami problem." In 1896 the town had been wiped off the map in a deadly and unforeseen night-time tsunami. The triggering earthquake, 180 miles offshore, was felt by ships out at sea but scarcely noticed on land. Two-thirds of the town's population of 6,500 died when 1,800 houses and warehouses were washed away. The memory of that calamity preserved the lives of the survivors thirty-seven years later, on March 3, 1933, when they felt a strong nighttime earthquake and fled inland in their nightclothes. Even though the tsunami destroyed more than 7,000 homes and in some places lapped as high as 70 feet (20 meters), this time only 164 were killed out of a population of almost 32,000.

Now, in 2011, the older residents remembered the stories told by their parents of hiding on the edge of the forest in the night and hearing the tsunami demolish the town.

———

AS SOON AS THE SHAKING CALMED, THE TEACHING STAFF AT KA-maishi East Junior High School attempted to muster their students into the school yard. They tried to take a roll call, but the electricity was out and the microphone didn't work.[2] Meanwhile, some students had already started running out of the school gate and uphill toward the preplanned evacuation site almost half a mile away (700 meters). Among them was fourteen-year-old Aki Kawasaki. He had just started

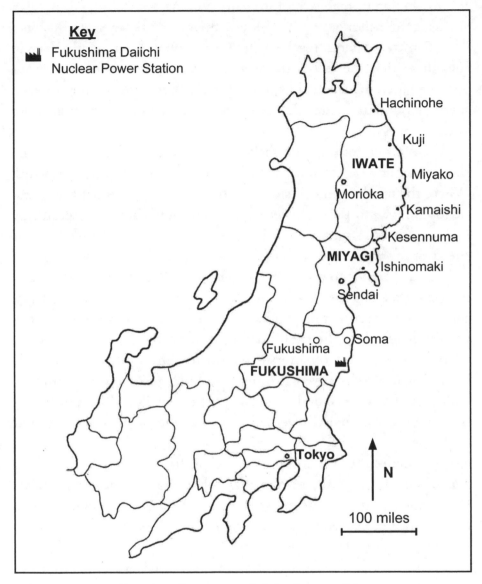

Key

Fukushima Daiichi
Nuclear Power Station

Hachinohe

Kuji

IWATE

Miyako

Morioka

Kamaishi

Kesennuma

MIYAGI

Ishinomaki

Sendai

Fukushima

Soma

FUKUSHIMA

Tokyo

N

100 miles

Japan prefectures and cities impacted by
the 2011 Tohoku earthquake and tsunami

baseball practice and was terrified that a tsunami was coming. Many
others, however, like his classmate Kana Sasaki, only ran because everyone around them was running.

At the neighboring Unosumai Elementary School, the teachers had
begun evacuating children to the third floor of the school building.

Seeing the junior high school students running, they changed the plan and sent the children to run alongside their older brothers and sisters.

When the children reached the evacuation site, an elderly woman told them that she feared the worst, that the earthquake was stronger than anything she had experienced. So they kept running to even higher ground, the older children holding the hands of the frightened younger ones.

Twenty minutes after the shaking ended, the watchers on the cliffs saw a dark line on the horizon that soon became whitened with surf. Where the breaking line of surf met the great breakwater at the steep-sided entrance to the open sea, furious currents could be seen raging between the concrete walls. Then the white water was bursting over the crest of the breakwater itself.[3]

The first water to arrive in the harbor boiled up over the quays, floating off some parked cars. Water in the streets moved sluggishly, but as the level rose it flowed like a fast river. The wooden two-story buildings, lifted off their foundations even when the water was little more than one or two meters deep, turned into battering rams that demolished warehouses and other buildings, which collapsed in on themselves in great clouds of dust and plaster. The clock on the gable of the Unosumai village hall stopped when it was immersed at 3:25 p.m.

The children turned and looked back at their schools. The tsunami was surging through the buildings, smashing houses and cars, and rising so high as to overwhelm the third floor of the elementary school; eventually it deposited a car on the roof. If they had waited another ten minutes, they would have drowned.

Weeks later, after the bodies had been pulled out of the piles of debris, after the unaccounted for were listed as "missing," the tally for Kamaishi was 1,200 fatalities, or one person in thirty. Many of the victims were older people who had lived in the low-lying port area.[4]

Remarkably, however, every single student who was in school that day survived: all of the 212 junior high and 350 elementary school students. In other nearby coastal towns, there had been tragedies. In eleven out of the twenty-one schools inundated by the tsunami, the children had stayed in the building.[5] At the Okawa primary school, 74 out of 108 children died.

The headlines proclaimed "The Miracle of Kamaishi."[6] Yet the story at Kamaishi was no miracle. Its children survived because of one maverick Japanese professor who had set out to teach them a completely different narrative about disasters and survival.[7]

———

WHO AT THE START OF THE NEW MILLENNIUM KNEW WHAT TO DO in a tsunami? The Boxing Day Indian Ocean earthquake on December 26, 2004, changed everything. This was the first oceanwide tsunami in forty years. In resorts along the west coast of Thailand, the tsunami surged into the beachside hotels midmorning. Tourists pointed their cameras and captured the first-ever movies of a great tsunami. One sequence shot from a headland shows the water draining out of a wide bay before a great wave rolled back in, overwhelming a man who had gone down to collect stranded fish and now stood spellbound as the gray-brown water surged over the beach.

Another movie captures the water flooding over the swimming pool and into the ground-floor patio of a hotel, rising slowly at first and then much faster. Guests are caught trying to hold on to railings as the water seethes around them, but the camera moves away before we see who managed to escape.

In Banda Aceh in northern Sumatra, a video cameraman was filming a wedding party on a second-floor rooftop balcony in the heart of the city. The scene starts with a call to watch a trickle of water arriving along the neighboring street. As the water grew deeper the current accelerated, filling with floating cars, until the tsunami came close to overwhelming the cameraman.

A tsunami has many different guises: sometimes a great wave breaks, but more often the water rises and rises, more and more alarmingly, for five to ten minutes. The original English term "tidal wave"—half tide, half wave in character—failed to evoke this monstrous terror; thus, in 1896, a more compelling word was borrowed from the Japanese: "tsunami," or "the wave in a small village harbor," is the local name for the kind of sudden rise in the sea that destroyed Kamaishi.

After the visceral experience of watching these movies, you can never again walk along a sandy shoreline without experiencing some subliminal mistrust of the ocean. On a malevolent whim, it seems, the benign waves can rise up and pounce far inland, dragging their spoils out to sea.

Tilly Smith, a ten-year-old English girl, was on holiday with her family in a beachfront hotel in Thailand. She had been taught about tsunamis by her geography teacher at Dane's Hill School in Surrey only three weeks before.[8] She had learned that when the sea mysteriously drains away far below low tide and the water streaks with rising bubbles, a tsunami is coming. Seeing the water slowly recede, and not waiting to ask an adult, Tilly took it upon herself to scream at all those around her to move to higher ground. Almost 100 people on that stretch of Mai Khao Beach followed her lead, and as a result, it was one of the few beaches on the island where no one drowned.

Toshitaka Katada, a professor of civil engineering at Gunma University in central Japan, visited the tsunami-ravaged coastlines of Thailand and Sumatra and considered the lessons to take back to Japan.[9] On Sumatra he saw how tens of thousands had felt the strong earthquake shaking but had not thought to evacuate in the twenty to thirty minutes before the tsunami arrived. He saw the consequences of passivity. Everyone had waited for official instruction, but no order came. He marveled at the story of Tilly Smith. Children, he observed, can possess a fearless authority.

On Katada's return to Japan, he was shocked to discover how little people worried about tsunamis. Even in the coastal towns along the Sanriku coast—the birthplace of the term "tsunami"—memories of the last great disaster, seventy years before, had faded. Through the 1980s, the government had constructed concrete tsunami walls to protect the low-lying ports, but as a result many coastal towns had given up their annual tsunami evacuation drills.

When Katada visited the schools in Kamaishi to talk to the children, he found that they had total confidence in the walls. Their sense of obedience was strong. If the adults did not run to higher ground, the children would not think of doing so themselves.

A story about a tsunami known to all children in Japan highlights this desire for official instruction.[10] The story tells of how the wise village headman saved all the lives in his coastal village after a tsunami in late December 1854.

Hamaguchi Gohei lived up the hill from the bayside houses in the exposed Wakayama Prefecture town of Hirogawa, on the Kii Peninsula of southern Honshu. Late in the afternoon one day close to the end of 1854, he felt a long-lasting vibration. Within a few minutes, the sea began to recede, while on the distant horizon he saw a dark line growing thicker as it approached. Recalling a story told by his grandfather, he realized that a tsunami was on its way. How could he get the villagers below to evacuate inland? Running inside to bring out a burning log from his winter hearth, he turned the year's precious harvest of rice stalks into a crackling, smoky bonfire. Seeing the wanton destruction, and believing that their feudal lord had gone mad, the villagers all rushed up the hill, then turned to watch the tsunami destroy their houses down below. It took another tsunami in 1933 for the Japanese to accept their tsunami affliction, after which the story was mainstreamed into the culture in the national schoolbook for fifth-graders.

Motivated by the story of Tilly Smith, Katada explored how to inspire children to take action in a future disaster and came up with "Tsunami Tendenko"—a policy that cut hard against the grain of conservative, "follow the instructions" Japanese culture.

Katada chose to focus on the frontline city of Kamaishi. Initially, the local teachers claimed that there was no time in the curriculum for disaster education. Then, in 2006, a tsunami scare followed a great earthquake off the Kuril Islands to the north. Fewer than one in ten of the children in the low-lying schools most at risk from tsunamis were evacuated. Each of the fourteen schools in Kamaishi subsequently agreed to Katada's request to allocate ten hours a year to disaster education.

In March 2010, working with the teachers, Katada produced a manual in which he emphasized his three principles:

Don't believe in preconceived ideas.
Do everything you can.
Take the lead in evacuation.[11]

Katada recognized that, when dazed and confused, people search for instruction:

> Even though you know you should escape, you convince yourself that you are safe. When the alarm bell sounds you don't want to believe that there is a fire. . . . You often need a second piece of information to make you flee—a smell of smoke—someone shouting "fire." After an earthquake everyone looks around to see if their neighbors are responding. They feel reassured if their neighbor has not run. A temporary network of security is established—people convince themselves they have made the right decision. And then the tsunami attacks and everyone dies.

What Katada had seen in the 2004 Indian Ocean tsunami had taught him to distrust official hazard maps, "because no one can predict nature's power." He encouraged the children to trust in their instincts: "It takes a lot of courage to be the first person to run out of the room when the alarm bell sounds," he wrote. "You have to be the first to run. And others around you will be inspired and will also make their escape . . . and you will save many people." The children could not have known then how soon they would be called upon to turn these principles into action.

On the afternoon of March 11, 2011, Katada was in Hachinohe, a town near Kamaishi, to deliver a talk. When he was rocked by five minutes of intense shaking, he knew that this was a giant earthquake out in the ocean on the subduction zone and that a tsunami would inevitably follow. He was consumed with worry about all the children he had taught. Would they evacuate high enough? The live TV coverage from Kamaishi showed horrific scenes. When he heard the news later that all those who had been at school had survived, he was filled with emotion: "From the bottom of my heart I wanted to thank them."[12] Yet not everyone had heard his message. Some parents lost their lives waiting for their children to return home.

Those who chose to drive toward higher ground initially overtook those on foot, but then got blocked by congestion.[13] In some towns the tsunami arrived before drivers could escape onto the embanked highway. (After an earthquake in Samoa only eighteen months before, for fear of the expected tsunami, everyone got into their cars. As a result, the principal coast road became blocked, and almost 200 people were drowned, many of them washed out to sea in their vehicles. To escape people only needed to walk to higher ground.[14])

After the 2011 tsunami, the Ministry of Education authorized the return to school textbooks of the story of the village headman setting fire to the rice stalks. Yet there was some ambivalence about promoting Katada's real-life lesson on the merits of civil disobedience.

———

WHETHER TO TRUST THE FLOOD WALLS OR EVACUATE WHILE THERE is still time—what information do people need so that they can take the right action? Is it education or concrete defenses that provides the greatest protection? We come to another extraordinary disaster of the new millennium: Hurricane Katrina and its storm surge.

In a storm surge the flood is driven by fierce winds blowing toward the coast. The stronger and more persistent the winds the higher the surge, which can last for hours—the time it takes a big windstorm or hurricane to pass. The wind-whipped waves of a storm surge ride inland, smashing everything fragile in their path; a tsunami, which drains faster and takes most of its debris out to sea, is said to be "tidier."

Confined by the coast, the winds bulldoze a mound of water ahead of the storm, but if the water is deep or the storm front is narrow, the mound drains away, under or around the storm. Off the coast of Mississippi, you can wade out to sea for miles because the North American continent's greatest river has filled the sea with sediment. And that is where the biggest of all Atlantic storm surges roll inland.

There is only one flood-walled city along the US coast, and that is New Orleans. Without its levees, the surf would break on Bourbon Street every day. Apart from the original city (the French Quarter) built on the natural river levee, the average elevation in New Orleans is six feet below sea level. The city was founded by the French in the eighteenth century, a palisade on the first dry land up the Mississippi River. Fur trappers could tramp through the bayou swamp between the river and sea-level Lake Pontchartrain a few miles to the north. From the late nineteenth century, as the city expanded, the swamps were pumped dry and the land sank like a desiccated sponge.[15]

By the start of the new millennium, Kamaishi had been flooded by tsunamis twice in little more than a century, while New Orleans was already on its third storm surge inundation since 1900. Yet residents of the Big Easy preferred not to dwell on the city's watery history.

The first lesson from New Orleans is that flood defenses follow big floods. The damage demands some action. Wait too long, however, and politicians find something else to do with the money. New flood defenses need to be built high enough to withstand the latest floods, and then a little bit higher, depending on how much money can be found.

The second lesson for a sinking city is that, as sure as night follows day, big floods will eventually follow the flood defenses. And because the city is sinking, the next flood tends to be even deeper than the last.[16]

In 1915 a hurricane passed over New Orleans, driving a 6-foot surge in Lake Pontchartrain. Water flowed into the city, reaching 8 feet (2.5 meters) deep in some downtown areas. The city invested in some bigger pumps, built walls by the sides of the drainage canals, and created an embankment along the lake shoreline.

In 1947 a hurricane passed right over the city, breaching the embankment along Lake Pontchartrain.[17] When the western wall of the Seventeenth Street drainage canal collapsed, thirty square miles of land in neighboring Jefferson Parish were inundated. Fifteen thousand people were evacuated. Holes had to be dug and blasted in the defenses to let the water escape back to the sea. The flood defenses were then raised, and land was reclaimed from the lake, inspiring a postwar boom in house building to the northeast of the city.

By the early 1960s, the city's population was 625,000. In 1965, in a fit of grandiose geo-engineering, the US Army Corps of Engineers dug a shipping channel, linked with the Industrial Canal, to approach New Orleans from the open sea to the east.[18] The channel, known as the Mississippi River and Gulf Outlet (MRGO, or "Mr. Go"), was cut 36 feet (11 meters) deep and 650 feet (200 meters) wide.

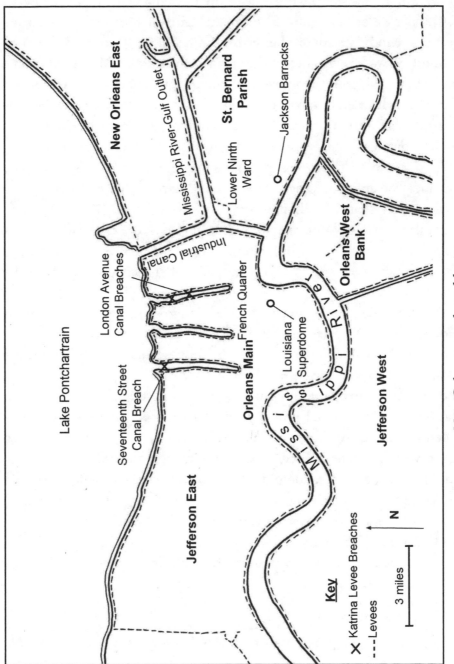

New Orleans canals and levees

Within months of the opening of the new channel, Hurricane Betsy, a Category 3 storm, came in from the Gulf of Mexico.[19] The strong easterly winds ahead of the storm funneled a 12-foot (3.6-meter) mound of water straight up the newly constructed Mr. Go shipping channel to spill over the low embankments of the Industrial Canal and flood the whole eastern part of the city. Thirteen thousand houses were immersed in water up to nine feet deep, more than 60,000 people were made homeless, and 58 died. The defenses along Lake Pontchartrain held, so if not for the Corps of Engineers' gift of the "Mr. Go" shipping channel, the city would have stayed dry. Betsy was the first US disaster to cost more than $1 billion.

Following Betsy and years of "white flight," New Orleans never recovered its early 1960s population. The middle classes, unable to sell their properties in the lowest-lying parts of the city, left them to be rented to the poor.

In the same year as Betsy the US Congress passed the ambitious Flood Control Act, designed to flood-proof New Orleans and prevent a repeat of the flood disaster.[20] Yet the money and the will behind the plan began to drain away as the memory of Betsy faded. In 1977 a federal court barred the construction of a proposed Lake Pontchartrain dam, on environmental grounds. With a reduced budget and diminished ambition, the Corps of Engineers began a long slow program to improve the defenses. Faced with homeowners unwilling to sacrifice any part of their waterside plots, the Corps had to construct very thin concrete flood walls along the drainage canals. In 2004 the city ran a "fire drill" for a direct hit from Category 5 "Hurricane Pam" with water up to 25 feet (7.5 meters) above sea level.[21] According to the simulation, one-quarter of those who remained in the city would die.

ONLY A YEAR LATER, THE KATRINA TRACK FORECASTS WOULD PROVE remarkably consistent and accurate: the actual track was only 15 miles (24 kilometers) east of the track forecasted fifty-six hours earlier. On Sunday, August 28, 2005, the day before landfall, when the storm was at maximum Category 5 intensity, the National Weather Service

(NWS) stated apocalyptically: "Most of the area will be uninhabitable for weeks . . . perhaps longer . . . human suffering incredible by modern standards." The NWS office in New Orleans predicted the "partial destruction of half of the well-constructed houses in the city."[22]

That would be warning enough, you might think, to get people to flee inland. Indeed, more than 90 percent of the city's population had left following Mayor Ray Nagin's mandatory evacuation order on August 28, when he warned that "the storm surge most likely will topple our levee system." Yet tens of thousands either chose not to leave or had missed the available transportation options. Some wanted to protect their property from looters. Some had been discouraged by the evacuation terms, which forbade pets on the buses. Some who dismissed the order were remembering the false alarm evacuation for Hurricane Ivan the previous year. And many stayed through inertia, not really believing their lives were at risk, trusting in the flood walls.

As is often the case, the wind forecasts had indeed been hyped. Like a pirouetting dancer stretching out her arms, the original Category 5 storm had both grown in size and weakened. In the middle of the morning of Monday, August 29, the weaker western sectors of Hurricane Katrina passed over the city of New Orleans. As the wind died down, reporters came out of their hotels and walked the streets, filming images of twisted roof metal and shifted tiles in the older buildings of the city's French Quarter. The story in the main news feeds was that the city had once again "dodged a bullet," escaping both major wind damage and the long-feared citywide flooding.[23]

Officials from the Orleans Levee District were responsible for monitoring the flood defenses. As the weather conditions deteriorated, the inspectors were withdrawn to hurricane shelters. The telephone system was almost completely dead, the mobile transmitters having been disrupted by power outages.

Ahead of the storm, the circulating winds had blown from the east, exactly as in Hurricane Betsy, pushing the storm surge straight up the Mr. Go channel. On the south side of the channel to the east of New Orleans, between 4:00 and 6:00 a.m. on the morning of August 29, 2005, the 18-foot (5.5-meter) surge overwhelmed the piled defenses and poured into impoverished St. Bernard Parish.[24] Many houses were lifted off their foundations. At the Murphy Oil Corporation refinery, a massive, partly filled oil tank floated, broke, and spilled its contents over the town. The surge was still 16.5 feet high where it came into the Industrial Canal in eastern New Orleans. The first breaching occurred at 4:45 a.m.: the water spread over the 14-foot defenses into the lowland to the north of the city's French Quarter as well as into the Lower Ninth Ward to the east of the canal. These were the areas flooded during Betsy—but now the water was three to four feet deeper.

The district commander of the Army Corps of Engineers, which was ultimately responsible for the defenses, ventured out at 3:00 p.m., but finding his path blocked by strong winds and debris, he returned to his bunker. He had encountered enough water to know that some key defenses must have failed.

The surge had not completed its mischief. The second phase of the flooding came from the north—from Lake Pontchartrain, as in the floods of 1915 and 1947. The three drainage canals, originally dug to allow water to be pumped out of the city, now turned the city into a lake. The flood walls along the canals were a minimum of 12.5 feet (3.8 meters) above sea level, and the surge coming in from the lake only reached 11 feet, so the concrete walls should have held; at around 9:00 a.m., however, the first thin concrete panels fell over.[25] Once one panel had gone, the water surged through with such force that it tore out the neighboring panels, eroding chasms tens of feet deep.

The drainage canals passed through the lowest areas of the city— land that lies several feet below sea level—so water continued to flow into the city long after the hurricane had disappeared over the horizon. The operators of the city's pumps had been evacuated for fear of the strongest hurricane winds. No one had considered how critical the pumps would be in the midst of an intense hurricane. In a circular irony, later that afternoon the pump house operators were unable to return to their pumps *because* the city had flooded.

The first that the New Orleans Police Department heard of their city's inundation was late on Monday evening, when off-duty police officers called in from their flooded homes. That evening a private helicopter flew over the city and fed images to a local TV station. Only at 9:00 the following morning was the local commander of the Corps of

Engineers able to get into his own helicopter to see that 90 percent of the city was underwater.

It had taken more than twelve hours for people to realize that New Orleans was flooded, and a whole day before the city could be inspected and mapped by emergency officials. One in six New Orleans police officers abandoned their post. Untold numbers of people died because of the delays in initiating rescue.

With water depths reaching 10 to 15 feet, twenty times more people died in Katrina than in Betsy in 1965. This was a disaster that had been well forecasted, a catastrophe of a kind that people believed was no longer possible in a developed country. The majority of the 1,464 Katrina fatalities listed for Louisiana were drowned in New Orleans. Of those who died, 56 percent were black and 64 percent were over sixty-five. (In the Japanese tsunami, 65 percent of those who died were over sixty.) Those who stayed in their single-story houses first had to climb into the attic space and then attempt to break through to the roof in the hope that they would be rescued. In some areas, however, even roofs became submerged. Almost two-thirds of the 147,000 properties in the city were flooded by more than four feet of water. When a large hospital complex was left without power after the ground-floor generators became submerged, doctors were forced during the chaos of helicopter evacuations to make decisions about who would live and who would die.[26]

———

HURRICANE KATRINA WAS A HUGE HURRICANE. WITH ITS NORTHerly track passing to the east of New Orleans, the city missed the worst of the storm surge, which tore into the Mississippi coastal towns of Biloxi, Gulfport, Pass Christian, and Bay St. Louis. The land rises gently from the beachfront in those towns, with their streets of grand Southern houses nestled among oak shade trees. This coast took the full force of the hurricane winds. Like the citizens close to the port at Kamaishi, Mississippi Gulf coast residents made a calculation about their own safety. Over the previous fifty years, the worst storm to hit this coast had been the notorious Hurricane Camille in 1969. That storm had been at maximum intensity, Category 5, at landfall and driven a terrible 21-foot surge that scoured houses off their foundations for the first three blocks inland. Katrina had reduced to Category 3 intensity, so anyone whose house had survived Camille assumed that they would be safe to stay indoors for the duration of the storm. They knew that because the Saffir-Simpson Hurricane Wind Scale told them so. They created in their minds an invisible wall beyond which the storm surge would not advance.

The Saffir-Simpson scale was designed two years after Camille to trigger evacuations ahead of deadly storm surges.[27] The five-level scale tied together the central pressure of the storm, the speed of the accompanying winds, and the height to which the sea would rise: thus, according to the scale, a Category 3 storm with a 950-millibar central pressure and 120-mile-per-hour wind speeds would drive a 12-foot surge flood. The scale had become the standard currency of the hurricane season, but the link with water height was dangerously oversimplified.

Hurricane Katrina was a much larger storm than Camille. Even after becoming less intense, the storm was still pushing a Category 5 storm surge—a huge mound of water. The waves reached five feet higher than Camille all along the Mississippi coast, sweeping away all the houses four or five blocks in from the coast and killing 200 people who had thought they could sit out the storm. "Camille," it was said, "killed more people in 2005 than it did in 1969."[28] The linked surge and wind Saffir-Simpson scale was officially retired in 2009.

The hundreds of home movies shot on December 26, 2004, and March 11, 2011, have dramatically expanded our understanding of tsunamis. However, a big storm surge arrives with the fiercest hurricane winds, blowing 120 miles per hour or higher, making it impossible to hold a camera steady, let alone stand. So the most savage storm surges have only been filmed through smeared windows streaming with rain.

In 2013, when Supertyphoon Haiyan was bearing down on the city of Tacloban in the Philippines, as civil defense personnel were attempting to get the low-lying residents to evacuate, the common response was, "Why should we be frightened of a storm surge?" People stayed to look after their homes, believing themselves protected by the invisible wall.

The surge rose to 20 feet (6 meters) in the city, even flooding the cyclone shelters. After the storm had passed and civil defense personnel were collecting the bodies of the 6,000 people who had drowned, the survivors asked: "Why didn't you call the surge a 'tsunami'? Then we would have evacuated."[29]

———

ANYONE WHO STUDIES DISASTERS WILL REMIND YOU THAT, WHILE the agents of destruction—the tsunami or the storm surge—are natural, the outcomes are all too human and "unnatural." Disasters are determined by what we build, where we choose to live, how we prepare, and how we communicate warnings. Before 2005, there was no maverick educator like Katada in New Orleans or Gulfport, Mississippi, to teach people to distrust official hazard information and to escape on their own initiative.

The flood wall is the simplest of all catastrophe remedies. It also exemplifies the challenges in searching for a cure. The remedy works only as long as the water level does not rise too high. Once overtopped, or breached, all those people who believe themselves and their property to be protected are in jeopardy. We call this the "cliff-edge effect." Take one step further and you will fall off the cliff. Should the water rise another foot, the whole town goes underwater.

How high shall we build the flood wall? The construction engineers tell us that every extra unit of height means multiples of additional costs—the structure will need to be broader, the foundations deeper. Raising the wall has to be justified by economics. Imagine that the flood wall does not exist—what would be the costs of the flood damage? Yet the flood wall and what it protects are not independent of each other. Flood protection acts as a honeypot for developers. You only have to look at the growth of New Orleans through the 1970s and 1980s as thousands of homes came to shelter behind the walls. While the wall protects against ordinary floods, when one day an extreme water level overwhelms the defenses, the consequences are much more catastrophic than if the wall had never been built.

There is a broad spectrum of potential floods to be considered, from the high water levels that arise every year or two to the catastrophic extremes that happen once every century. For these extreme events, inevitably we will not have perfect information. The flood wall cannot protect against every eventuality. And then if we build a wall, the displaced water may flood some other worse-protected downstream town. Should we add that cost to our equation?

The benefits are all in the future. How do we scale their value in terms of today's money? What is the time frame over which we are looking to earn back our original investment? Thirty years? Fifty years? What discount rate shall we use for future costs? It makes a big difference in how we calculate the benefits of flood protection.

Imagine a giant set of antique weighing scales. In one pan we put all the costs of building the flood wall. In the other pan go all the savings of the floods that will not happen. We need to adjust the scales for the number of years of the comparison, move the weights in and out, and raise and lower the flood walls until the scales are balancing at our target—the maximum benefit for the least cost. For example, we may want the benefits of flood losses saved to be three times the costs of building the flood walls. Then we can determine how high to make the flood walls.

Fifty years ago, when flood walls were being designed for New Orleans and Kamaishi, it was beyond the state of knowledge—and computing power—to evaluate the full spectrum of possible floods. Both projects instead focused on a single "design flood." For Kamaishi, it was the tsunami from an offshore earthquake that was considered credible.[30] For New Orleans, it was the storm surge from the Standard Project Hurricane (SPH), an idealized fast-moving Category 3 storm.[31] The description of the Standard Project Hurricane was vague and arbitrary: "the most severe storm that is considered reasonably characteristic of a region." In 1969 Hurricane Camille was a Category 5 storm at landfall just to the east of New Orleans, but it was conveniently ignored—dismissed as "too far outside the norm."

No one asked too many questions about where these scenarios came from or how they could be improved. Once you had the scenario, all the engineering questions suddenly became a lot easier. You built the wall to protect against that particular flood.

New Orleans is surrounded by flood walls. Before 2005, there had never been a risk assessment to identify the weakest links. After Katrina, puzzled as to why the walls had been built so low, surveyors discovered that the benchmarks used to level the city's flood defenses had themselves sunk 16 inches (400 millimeters) unnoticed.[32] The whole southern Louisiana delta region, it turns out, including New Orleans, is slumping steadily into the deep waters of the Gulf.[33]

Compare the attention given to flood protection in New Orleans before and after Katrina![34] The irony of a catastrophe is that the funds to prevent it only become available after it has happened. The horse has to bolt for the stable door to be closed. After the flood, the Corps of Engineers was invited to develop a plan to protect the city and had no problem in obtaining $14.45 billion (more than the cost of all the Katrina flood damage in the city) to raise the level of protection enough to ensure that the annual chances of a flood would be below one in 100.[35] And the much-cursed Mr. Go shipping canal was finally dammed with thousands of tons of rock and ship gates, so that it could never again direct the flood into the heart of the city. The Corps of Engineers built flood walls to withstand another storm like Katrina. However, in a direct hit from a Category 5 storm—considered the "500 year event"—the surge flood could be another 6 to 10 feet (1.8 to 3 meters) higher. The Corps claimed it would cost at least $70 billion to protect against that eventuality—five times what Congress had authorized.[36] Even in the national political crisis that followed Katrina, the check was not completely blank.

In Kamaishi, the national government announced that it would spend $650 million to rebuild the broken breakwater in the harbor. Not to repair it would have implied that the original decision was wrong, and that is not the Japanese way.[37] The government also announced that it would spend one trillion yen (almost $10 billion) on more tsunami walls in the three prefectures that were the worst hit in 2011.[38] At Koizumi, south of Kamaishi, a $14.7 million wall is planned, even though the village has now been relocated three kilometers inland. Not prepared to give up fighting disasters with concrete, the government remains committed to extending the ugly coastal "Great Wall of Japan."

Kamaishi and New Orleans, two coastal cities in decline, lavished with money after their floods, and doomed to be on perpetual life support, challenge us to ask a fundamental question. Does having a flood wall increase the numbers drowned? This may sound like a ridiculous question—of course a wall to prevent flooding should save lives. Yet what if more people come to live in harm's way behind the flood wall? What if, faced with the choice of evacuating inland ahead of an impending storm surge or tsunami, people choose to stay because they believe the wall will protect them and then, as happened in Kamaishi and New Orleans, they are wrong in their judgment? What if the "cure" causes more casualties than no intervention?

There are no tsunami walls along the Pacific coast of Chile. In the great nighttime Chile earthquake and tsunami of 2010, some 200 people were drowned. In the daytime 2011 Japan tsunami, despite (or because of?) the tsunami walls, the toll was 20,000.

2 • CATASTROPHE YEAR ZERO

EVERYONE AFTERWARDS REMEMBERED THE WEATHER ON THAT fateful morning. At first light the town was covered by a thick sea fog, which quickly burned off as the sun rose, leaving a cloudless sky. It was going to be a beautiful, warm autumn day.

Home to 235,000 people, Lisbon was the fourth-largest city in Europe.[1] Sprawled over seven hills, it was framed by a perfect harbor in the estuary of the River Tagus. A parade of waterfront pink-and-white-marble palaces lined the north side of the estuary from Belém to Lisbon, displaying the pecking order of the Portuguese aristocracy. Behind the facade, 20,000 buildings, many four or five stories high, spread over the hills, crowded along winding medieval alleyways. One hillside was covered with rising smoke from the open fires of an African shanty-town. Unlike any other place in Europe, Lisbon was a world city, racially diverse, pungent with spices from India and Brazil.

Lisbon was also the most obsessively religious city in Christendom. One in six of the local population was said to have some official religious role. The streets were filled with *religiosos:* priests, monks, and friars in their colorful costumes. The old King John V (who reigned from 1706 to 1750) had set up a church hierarchy in Portugal to rival that in Rome; at its head was a patriarch, flanked by twenty-four prelates in their crimson vestments. The king allowed the army and navy to dwindle as he diverted the copious Brazilian gold to fund the largest building complex of its time—palace, monastery, basilica, and library—at Mafra, 19 miles (30 kilometers) northwest of Lisbon.

The Jesuits had near-total control of education. The head of the Colégio das Artes in Coimbra in 1746 forbade reference to the new ideas of Newton and Descartes. The Inquisition maintained its secret courts, prisons, and torture chambers to root out apostates and Jews. Almost all the largest buildings belonged to the Church and housed thousands of monks and nuns.

Since the empire building of the sixteenth century, Portugal had grown lazy, relying on the Royal Navy for protection. British merchants were allowed to run Portuguese commerce in exchange for Brazilian gold. In 1750 the new king, Joseph I, more worldly than his father, ordered a magnificent new opera house—"the finest in Europe"—which opened five years later, in the spring of 1755.

November 1, 1755, was a Saturday, but more importantly it was *Dia de Todos-os-Santos* (All Saints' Day), one of the six holiest days of the religious calendar. In the traditional All Saints' Day ritual, groups of young children were out in the streets banging on their neighbors' doors to demand *Pão-por-Deus* (small cakes or sweets).

On this most pleasant of mornings, on this most revered of holy days, what was about to happen was completely beyond the thoughts of every duke, nun, African slave, or English merchant in the city. What was about to happen was not only inconceivable but would serve to press the reset button on philosophical argument, challenge the church to its foundations, and taint the name of "Lisbon" for more than 100 years. It would also launch the idea that disasters were fit for scientific investigation.

For all of human history, sudden destructive interventions in the world had been attributed to the gods. Take the example of an eruption. Three thousand years ago, in the lands stretching from the eastern Mediterranean to Arabia, there was no concept of a volcano. A mountain suddenly bursting into fire, its rocks melting, was nothing short of miraculous.

At least two eruptions (or two perspectives on the same eruption?) appear in the Old Testament.

Psalm 18 follows all the phases of the eruption, beginning with the characteristic tremor: "Then the earth shook and trembled. The foundations also of the mountains quaked and were shaken, because he was angry." The eruption of a red-hot cloud of ash blocked out the sun: "Smoke went out of his nostrils. Consuming fire came out of his mouth. Coals were kindled by it. He bowed the heavens also, and came down. Thick darkness was under his feet. The Most High uttered his voice: hailstones and coals of fire. He sent out his arrows, and scattered them; Yes, great lightning bolts, and routed them."[2]

The account has the firsthand stench of sulfur about it. What we would now attribute to eruption physics was the work of an irascible God.

Was this also Moses's "Mountain of God"? First, the eruption on the far horizon served as a direction finder for the children of Israel: "the pillar of cloud by day and fire by night." Two days after they reached the mountain, they witnessed an eruption: "There were thunders and lightnings, and a thick cloud upon the mount, and the voice of the trumpet exceeding loud; so that all the people in the camp trembled. And Mount Si'nai was covered in smoke, because the LORD descended upon it in fire: and the smoke billowed up from it like the smoke from a furnace, and the whole mount trembled violently" (Exodus 13:17–22).

Meanwhile "the LORD called Moses up to the top of the mount" to witness the eruption from the crater rim; he returned bearing the Ten Commandments, written with the "finger of God" on slabs of (freshly chilled?) lava.

The volcano's summit is where God intersects with man.

WHAT HAPPENS WHEN A DISASTER ARRIVES IN THE MIDDLE OF A religious war? Does God take sides?

In the twelfth century, two large earthquakes occurred along the Crusader front line between the coastal Christian territory known in

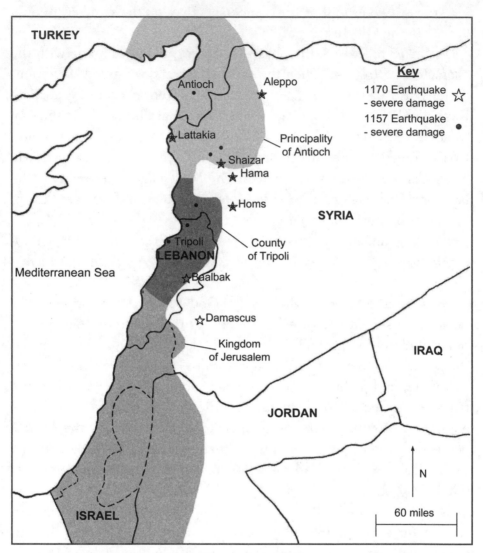

**Cities severely damaged by two twelfth-century earthquakes;
Crusader territories are shaded.**

contemporary Arab sources as Bilad al-Sham and the inland Muslim sultanate of Syria. The earthquakes became an extra agent in the territorial religious war. Yet on whose side was God intervening?

The first, a strong regional (Magnitude 7+) earthquake, struck in late summer 1157, after some months of foreshocks, along the northern frontier between the Levantine Crusader states and Syria.[3] The principal axis of damage ran to the north-northwest for 62 miles (100 kilometers) from Hama in the south (where "few survived") to Aleppo in the north (where 100 people died).[4] The damage to towns and cities was almost all on the Muslim side of the border.

The Crusaders made a halfhearted attempt to take advantage of this intervention by God in their favor. A combined force marched north from Jerusalem to attack the weakest point in the earthquake-damaged defenses 12 miles (20 kilometers) north of Tripoli.[5] However, as a result of a dispute among the Christian commanders and a strong defense by the Isma'ili defenders, the campaign was abandoned.

Then, in 1170, a second, larger earthquake occurred to the west of the 1157 shock. This time the devastation was much more evenly distributed.[6] Fortifications along both sides of this border suffered massive damage. The coastal city of Tripoli was said to have been reduced to a heap of stones and to have become a burial place.

Neither side was in any state to mount offensive action, but more than this, both Muslims and Christians perceived that God had destroyed their fortifications to stop them fighting. William of Tyre writes: "Both in our territories and in those of the enemy were found half-ruined fortresses, open on every side and freely exposed to the violence and the wiles of the foe. But since each man feared that the wrath of the Stern Judge might descend upon him individually, none dared molest his fellow man. . . . Peace brought about by the desire of all, ensued, albeit for a short interval, and a truce was arranged through fear of divine wrath."[7]

IN THE EARLY THIRTEENTH CENTURY, THE PHILOSOPHER AND THEOlogian Thomas Aquinas, while a child, shared a room with his younger sister and their nurse—until one night, alongside him, they were both killed by a lightning strike. Throughout his life he sustained a deep thunderstorm phobia. Perhaps influenced by this early trauma, Thomas believed the world to be populated by demons and bad spirits that brought lightning, mischief, and misfortune. And so the Church created prayers and rituals to combat their influence, whether it was witches in the mountains ruining the crops or devils causing floods and hailstorms.

How could the Church combat the deafening lightning demons? By harnessing the loudest weapon at its disposal: bronze, tower-hung bells.

Multiple powers were ascribed to church bells, which became widespread in the sixteenth and seventeenth centuries. For instance, one clanging rhyme proclaims:

> *Funera plango fulmina frango sabbata pango*
> *Excito lentos dissipo ventos paco cruentos*
> (At obsequies I mourn, the thunderbolts I scatter,
> I ring in the sabbaths;
> I hustle the sluggards, I drive away storms,
> I proclaim peace after bloodshed.)[8]

Of all the functions of the bells the most mysterious was this ability to ward off thunderstorms. At the consecration of new bells, the priest would pray that their chimes might "temper the destruction of hail and cyclones, and the force of tempests and lightning, check hostile thunders and great winds; and cast down the spirits of storms and the powers of the air." Bells were sometimes inscribed when they were cast: FULGURA FRANGO (I break up the lightning).[9]

It was general practice in Catholic countries to ring tower-hung church bells during thunderstorms. At the first murmur of thunder, villagers would rush to the church to pull on the bell ropes. The clamor of the bells, so it was said, dispelled the demons riding the storm, while the sonorous chords of sound disrupted the jagged lightning. In an article on thunder in Diderot's trusted *Encyclopédie* (compiled in 1756), it was said that "one can break up and turn aside thunder by the sound of several large bells, or by firing a cannon."[10]

Scholars in Protestant Sweden first questioned the practice.[11] In Lower Brittany on Good Friday 1718 (as Diderot also mentioned), all the bell-ringing churches had been struck by lightning. French regional newspapers started to carry sensational stories, like that of the church at Albigny on June 11, 1775, when lightning struck the tower as the bells were rung to disperse the storm, killing three bell ringers along with four sheltering children.[12] In 1784 a scientist in Brussels demonstrated that the sound of a bell had no influence on electrical discharges.[13] Eventually a German researcher searched back through the French newspapers and took a tally. From 1753 to 1786, lightning struck 386 French church towers, discharging down the bell ropes to kill a total of 103 bell ringers.[14] Not only did bell ringing fail to scare off storms, but it put the life of the ringer in great jeopardy. In 1786 the custom was outlawed in France. Yet in remote corners of Europe at the beginning of the twentieth century they were still ringing the bells to quell the storms.[15]

THE FIRST GLIMMERINGS OF DISASTER SCIENCE CAN BE FOUND AT the end of the sixteenth century in Protestant England. The early-century invention of printing, allied with expanding literacy, gave spontaneous citizen journalism its first opportunity for expression. In an age before newspapers, if you had something to say and could convince a printer, you published and sold a pamphlet. The public was eager to read tales of calamity and stories of amazing preservation.

On a fine spring evening on April 6, 1580, an earthquake shivered the whole of southeast England and northern France. In London pinnacles and stones fell off the roofs of churches and public buildings and two people died. "Queen Elizabeth I and those present with her at White Hall noted 'the strangeness of the occasion.'"[16]

The earthquake triggered more than twenty pamphlets (the sixteenth-century equivalent of the blog), authored by clergymen, poets, and archivists—all competing for the public's pennies. Some of these publications sought to extract religious lessons from the experience.[17] Other pamphlets simply treated the subject as a natural phenomenon.[18] Almost contemporary, when a puffed-up Glendower claims that "the earth did shake when I was born," we hear through Hotspur Shakespeare's skeptical voice: "Why, so it would have done at the same season if your mother's cat had but kittened."[19]

In January 1607, a storm surge arrived on top of an extreme spring tide and flooded all the protected polders for 250 miles (400 kilometers) surrounding the Bristol Channel in western England.[20] The main ports of Bristol and Cardiff were inundated, much cargo was ruined, and hundreds died. The publishers in St. Paul's Churchyard in London (who also printed Shakespeare's latest plays) vied with each other to issue rival pamphlets. With titles like "God's Warning to the People of England," their authors described the details of what had happened, knowing their readers would want to be chastised *and* informed.

A disaster above all provided a "taster" of the Day of Judgment, an argument to bring sinners back to God. The first two verses of *"Dies Irae"* in the Requiem Mass reference the ashes or cinders (*favilla*) of an eruption or conflagration (*dies illa solvet saeclum in favilla*—that day will dissolve the world into ashes), along with an anticipated monster shake (*quantus tremor est futurus*). After the London earthquakes of 1750, in a widely published sermon, the preacher John Wesley famously commented, with relish, "There is no divine visitation which is likely to have so general an influence upon sinners as an earthquake!"[21] He was echoing Increase Mather, from Cambridge, Massachusetts, who preached in 1706: "There never happens an earthquake but God speaks to men on the Earth by it: And they are very stupid, if they do not hear his Voice therein."[22]

———

WHICH BRINGS US BACK TO LISBON ON THE MORNING OF November 1, 1755.

The bells were ringing across the city, not to suppress lightning, but to summon the faithful. The famously devout people, dressed in their finest, were either on their way to morning church services or already in church. The king had attended a special early matins and was in his palace at Belém, to the west of the city. It was just before 10:00 a.m. when the earth started to shake. The vibrations continued for six minutes, in phases of a rolling sensation broken by terrible shuddering. By the time the earth had finally calmed, almost all the buildings in the city center had collapsed, including all but five of the forty city churches. Within an hour, a tsunami had surged through the riverside streets and squares, while fires sparked by tumbled church candles took several days to consume most of the central city, including the royal library and national archives.

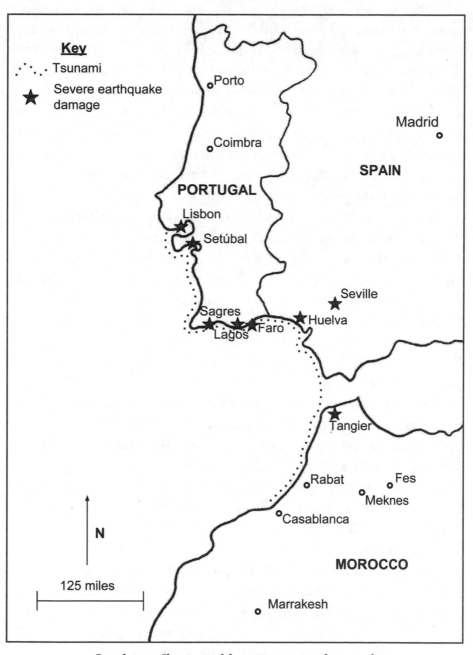

Key

∴·. Tsunami

★ Severe earthquake damage

Porto

Coimbra

Madrid

SPAIN

PORTUGAL

Lisbon

Setúbal

Seville

Sagres

Huelva

Lagos Faro

Tangier

Rabat

Fes

Meknes

Casablanca

N

MOROCCO

125 miles

Marrakesh

Southwest Iberia and locations most damaged
by the 1755 earthquake and tsunami

The people of Lisbon were not to know that while the earthquake originated beneath the sea southwest of Lisbon, its six-minute duration reveals that the source spanned hundreds of miles.[23] By all measures it was an enormous earthquake, causing damage from Morocco to south-west Spain and even into northern Portugal. Lisbon was not even the worst-affected city. The towns at the western end of the Algarve coast were flattened by the shaking.[24] The powerful vibrations set lakes and ponds violently oscillating across the whole of northern Europe. The sudden changes in bathymetry caused a tsunami that was still 15 feet (4.5 meters) high in the northeast Caribbean.

This was the largest European earthquake of the past 1,000 years; it released more energy than all the other European earthquakes since 1755 and was comparable in size to the March 2011 earthquake in Japan. Even with our latest knowledge, we still don't understand why an earthquake this big occurred beneath the sea southwest of Portugal. If it hadn't in fact happened, we would not consider it conceivable that this location could generate such an earthquake. At the time the ca-tastrophe was utterly mysterious. Unique and iconic among historical catastrophes, it has preserved its mystery.

The earthquake intersected with the career of the fifty-six-year-old prime minister Sebastião José de Carvalho e Melo, who, on the king's instruction, stepped up to the Churchillian challenge of becoming the original urban disaster manager. Born in 1699, he was the oldest child of a family of modest gentry, but was a natural and charismatic leader. He had been sent as ambassador to London and Vienna in the 1740s and then, in 1750, was appointed by the new king one of four ministers to run the country.

According to de Carvalho's mythologizing biographer, as soon as the shaking stopped the king asked his minister what was to be done, to which de Carvalho replied: "Bury the dead and feed the living!" before leaping into his carriage and hurrying to the ruined burning city. "Wherever his presence was required," it was said, "there he was to be found."[25] De Carvalho lived in his carriage, issuing orders day and night—200 decrees covering the maintenance of order, lodging for the survivors, the distribution of food, and the disposal of bodies at sea.

He also knew the benefits of suppressing the news. In Lisbon's sole newspaper, the official weekly *Gazeta de Lisboa*, the lead article on November 6 was only 50 percent longer than a tweet.[26]

De Carvalho placed an embargo on ships leaving Lisbon, for fear they would be carrying wealth looted from the city. For several days the whole postal system in and around Lisbon had collapsed: stables had tumbled, horses were crushed, and the riders had dispersed. Two days after the catastrophe, Abraham Castres, the British special envoy to the king of Portugal, located a Spaniard who was anxious to return home and who promised to carry a letter to the border city of Badajoz, where he would put it into the Spanish post-house system.

The news from Lisbon radiated out across Europe at the speed of the postboys, riding horses in relay, reaching Paris on November 22–23, London on November 25, Cologne on the 28th, and Hamburg on the 29th before continuing its advance by sea and land to Copenhagen, Stockholm, and Saint Petersburg in early December and by ship to the New World colonies in early January. The first London account in the *Whitehall Evening Post* on November 25 claimed that 60,000 had died. By the 29th, this figure had almost doubled and the story had gained further embellishment: A "dreadful earthquake . . . continued about eight hours, . . . and upwards of 100,000 persons [were] buried in the ruins. [T]he remains of the city was set on fire . . . by flames which issued from the bowels of the earth."[27]

The news was so extraordinary that at first many refused to believe it. The sage Samuel Johnson considered the account "inconceivable." On December 2, the *Caledonian Mercury* (from Edinburgh, Scotland) published a letter claiming that "the whole Story was invented at Paris, to disconcert the London Merchants, and that by this time it is looked upon there as a Piece of French Finesse."[28]

The newspapers became filled day after day, week after week, with fresh accounts of the disaster from private letters and stories copied from gazettes across Europe. Increasing numbers of people across northern Europe convinced themselves that they too must have felt the shock.

On November 11, de Carvalho authorized an official account, published in December in Paris; that report, while admitting that "nobody knows, nor will ever know," the number killed, proposed that one-tenth of the population (25,000) died.[29] A month and a half after the first news, on January 16, 1756, the *Gazette de Cologne* reported "the earthquake is still on people's lips."

Across many arenas, 1755 became "Catastrophe Year Zero."

———

BIG CATASTROPHES AFFECT AN ENORMOUS AREA, FAR LARGER THAN any single researcher can survey. One of the principal innovations in developing a catastrophe science would be to harness the experiences of hundreds or thousands of people as the observing system. It was Daniel Defoe, the London satirist and dissenter, who, days after being released from prison for seditious libel in 1703, first employed "crowdsourcing" to make sense of a catastrophe. He'd had scarcely time to return home before being battered by the most destructive windstorm to hit southern England since at least 1500. The streets were filled with tiles and other debris, and scores were killed by falling trees and chimneys. The experience gave Defoe the idea for a publication freed from politics or controversy.

He placed advertisements in the two principal daily newspapers requesting firsthand observations of the storm, then published all the letters in a book.[30] He articulated the wisdom of crowdsourcing: "Every Circumstance is a Sermon and everything we see a Preacher. Individual eye witness account are so 'speaking' that their Testimony is not to be question'd."[31]

On November 8, as King Ferdinand II of Spain read the letter from his brother-in-law, the king of Portugal, he realized that the ruined city of Lisbon was closer to Madrid than the outlying cities of Spain—Barcelona, Cádiz, Almería, and Corunna. The Spanish king needed to be a spider at the center of a web of inquiry about what had occurred in his own dominion. He asked his secretary, Ricardo Wall, to order the viceroys (provincial governors), general captains, and magistrates of the towns and cities of the kingdom to respond to a set of questions that were dispatched by messengers to all the provinces of Spain.[32] Many replies were returned within seven days of receipt of the request. The king learned that there had been 5,300 deaths across the towns and villages of Spain. Many buildings had collapsed in villages near Seville, not far from the Algarve coast of Portugal. In January 1756, de Carvalho launched a comparable survey of earthquake effects throughout Portugal, quizzing every parish priest.[33]

THE RESPONSE TO WHAT HAPPENED AT LISBON ON NOVEMBER 1, 1755, marked an intellectual watershed: the view of catastrophes as some supernatural mystery outside the ordinary workings of the world yielded to attempts to develop a scientific understanding of these events. Yet no one knew at the time the specific characteristics of an earthquake or volcanic eruption, so no one could see any contradiction in the idea that fire came out of the earth to incinerate the city or that the tidal wave lasted for eight hours.

At the time there was no understanding of what happened in the atmosphere as separate from what happened underground. Great hurricanes, it was said, could be born from earthquakes or spun out of volcanoes. In the middle of an intense hurricane, as houses were rocked to their foundations, many observers concluded that they were experiencing an earthquake.[34] Volcanic eruptions and landslides could both be termed "earthquakes," while earthquakes even far from volcanic mountains might be labeled "eruptions."[35] A Spanish playwright in 1668 wrote that "a hurricane was an earthquake in the air, and an earthquake was a hurricane beneath the ground."[36] Even great floods might be caused by "earthquakes."

De Carvalho maintained the line, strongly and repeatedly, that the November 1 earthquake had natural origins and should not be interpreted to imply any providential malice against Lisbon. Many of the city's *religiosos* strongly disagreed. In October 1756, a charismatic and barefoot Jesuit preacher, the Italian-born Gabriel Malagrida, who had tended the king's father on his deathbed, wrote "Judgment on the True Cause of the Earthquake," in which he lashed out against the wicked "heresy" that such a catastrophe could have a natural cause. The city's destruction was punishment from God for the wickedness of the *alfacinhas* (the colloquial term for the people of Lisbon)—for their decadence, their love of fashion and theater, their wanton dancing and flirtation, their playing cards and licentiousness.

The first anniversary of the earthquake was looming. Malagrida now predicted an even greater disaster on All Saints' Day 1756. The city was still in total ruin. Fear took hold among the survivors in their broken houses and temporary wooden shelters. On October 29, 1756, two days before the fated anniversary, de Carvalho issued a proclamation banning anyone from leaving the city.[37] After the day had passed without incident, he exiled Malagrida to the ravaged coastal town of Setúbal and banned all Jesuits from the Royal Court, where they had held such influence over the young king in the years leading up to the earthquake. In September 1759, de Carvalho confiscated all Jesuit property in Portugal and expelled the entire order. When the pope complained, de Carvalho expelled the papal nuncio. Malagrida, who continued his preaching against the state and its heresies, was arrested in the summer of 1761 and then subjected to an auto-da-fé in September 1761, where he was publicly garroted and burned at the stake.

———

ACROSS NORTHERN EUROPE THE EARTHQUAKE INSPIRED A SHIFT from a philosophical "best of all possible worlds" optimism, ruled over by a beneficent God, to a new, darker world order of rational skepticism. The contrasting old and new worlds are captured in the original meanings of the terms "disaster" and "catastrophe." "Disaster" derives from the Greek for an ill-fated, or "bad" star—in Italian, the *dis-astro*. "Disaster" captures the essence of astrology. A conjunction of planets, or the passage of a comet, triggers a calamity on earth. "Catastrophe" describes the final resolution of the story in a Greek drama. In a tragedy by Aeschylus or Euripides, within the "catastrophe," one or more of the main characters will die. The catastrophe is the inevitable consequence. The catastrophe is the moral.

In their original meanings, we are powerless to affect a disaster, an act of fate. In a catastrophe, on the other hand, we have the potential to intervene.

Making sense of "disasters" has been at the core of ancient myths and religious rituals from the earliest times. Such extraordinary interventions in the world must be manifestations of a higher power capable of summoning boundless strength, laying waste, and destroying cities. Why would the higher power want to cause such devastation? Sodom and Gomorrah were destroyed, not because they were hazardously situated, but because their inhabitants were deemed (after the fact) to be "bad." All that men could do was speculate on what motivated the anger and explore how to pacify the deity with sacrifices and rituals.

In polytheism, the gods could simply be fighting among themselves, and then the destruction on earth was no more than collateral damage—as in the epic volcanic eruption interpreted in the ancient Greek myth of the Titans doing battle with the gods.[38] Periodically, the Mayan storm god *hurakán* was seen to be in the ascendant against *cabrakán* (the capricious god of earthquakes) and *chirakán* (the choleric god of volcanoes). Humans simply needed to keep out of the way.

In monotheism there is only one possible target of God's anger— the humans, us, mankind. But why was the rage directed at Lisbon in particular? Francisco Xavier de Oliveira, a former Portuguese diplomat living in London, voiced the thoughts of many outside Portugal when he blamed the earthquake on the twisted form of Catholicism that had created the Inquisition. Privately, de Carvalho may have held the same position.[39]

The largest earthquake in Europe for a thousand years occurred at the most religion-obsessed capital city in Europe, in the middle of church services on one of the holiest days of the year, the day to commemorate the souls of the departed, now a day on which tens of thousands more souls had joined the dead. To see how improbable that is, we can calculate that there are six principal holy days in the Catholic church calendar, on each of which church services might span three hours. That makes around one chance in 500 for the catastrophe to hit a "holy day" and "church services" combined. This coincidence seemed at the time beyond chance.

As with the 2001 World Trade Center attacks, the wave of news was met by a mixture of incredulity and incomprehension. In a small German town, a precocious six-year-old, Johann Wolfgang von Goethe, recalled that accounts of the Lisbon earthquake had been the first disturbance to perturb his sheltered world. "Perhaps the 'Daemon' of fear," he later wrote, "has never spread so rapidly and so powerfully its terror on earth."[40] The fear—that the old religion was flawed, that God had become vengeful, that no city and no one was safe—was existential. The king of Portugal believed himself a marked man and refused ever again to sleep in a stone building. Fear arose that there was some cosmic terror afoot, that other cities would be next. "Lisbon" became the code word of the age, just as "9/11" is the code in our age for something diabolical, a deadly "bolt out of the blue" catastrophe directed at one of the world's leading cities.

With 9/11, once the smoke had cleared, there was a perpetrator to be identified, pursued, and finally assassinated. Yet where was the perpetrator at Lisbon? God appeared to be playing at both ends of the pitch, as both creator and destroyer, playing against himself.

One could, of course, recount the story of Sodom and Gomorrah. Protestant clergy in northern Europe relished such finger-wagging sermons. Yet why should the pious churchgoers of Lisbon have been singled out? A whole row of brothels in the city, it was reported, was left unscathed while all around the churches collapsed.

The person who came to articulate most cogently the horror and doubt engendered by the earthquake was the sixty-one-year-old French writer and philosopher Voltaire. Within weeks he had penned and published (in January 1756) the 180-line "Poème sur le désastre de Lisbonne." In brilliant, excoriating language, he articulated how inexcusable it was to argue that God had some role in what had happened, that the response to the tragedy should above all be humanitarian. In the preface he wrote caustically, satirizing the philosophy of Optimism, which had ruled the age: "All is well, the heirs of the dead will increase their fortunes, masons will make money rebuilding the buildings, beasts feed off the bodies buried in the debris."

> *What crime, what sin, had those young hearts conceived*
> *That lie, bleeding and torn, on mother's breast?*
> *Did fallen Lisbon deeper drink of vice*
> *Than London, Paris, or sunlit Madrid?*

In these men dance; at Lisbon yawns the abyss.
Tranquil spectators of your brothers' wreck,
Unmoved by this repellent dance of death,
Who calmly seek the reason of such storms,
Let them but lash your own security;
Your tears will mingle freely with the flood.

In early 1756, Voltaire sent his poem to the forty-three-year-old Jean-Jacques Rousseau, who was in the midst of his ruminations on social ills (the *Discourse on Inequality* of 1754 and his *Social Contract* of 1762—"Man is born free and is everywhere in chains"). Rousseau wrote to Voltaire in August 1756, complaining of the poet's cynicism and proposing to find the rational cause of the disaster in social conditions.[41] Lisbon contained 20,000 precarious houses of six or seven stories. Had the people been more widely distributed, or living in shorter houses, then there would have been far fewer casualties. Rousseau, a critic of private property, saw how materialism had worsened the tragedy—the fleeing victim pausing, and thereby perishing, while trying to take "his clothing, another his papers, a third his money." He was dismissive of the publicity, speculating that the "earthquake" could have "happened in the middle of some desert. . . . But no one talks about those, because they have no ill effects for city gentlemen."

Rousseau's perspective contains the seeds of the modern social understanding of disasters and the practical scientific approach to disaster risk reduction.[42]

The philosopher Immanuel Kant, in 1756, wrote three essays on the earthquake, condemning those who blamed the earthquake on the behavior of the people of Lisbon.[43] The solution, he argued, was to build at locations and in styles to withstand earthquakes. Science would have to explain why terrible catastrophes happened and how their impacts could be prevented.[44] In the *Journal Encyclopédique* of 1756, it was said that "all scientists are occupied today in searching for the true cause of earthquakes," that the academies had offered a prize for such discovery, and that brilliant men should no longer waste their time on frivolous quests. "Everyone wants to solve this terrible secret of Nature."[45]

What if the catastrophe was not inevitable? With this question, we arrive at the liberating and radical potency of the little word "risk."[46] Risk acknowledges that the world is playing dice, but asserts that harm is not predestined. There is some randomness around the bad outcome, but risk is not simply unforeseeable, "bolt out of the blue" misfortune, and randomness can be reduced through better knowledge. Some places and times are particularly risky. (Even lightning bolts are more likely to strike if you stand high up in a church tower and tug on a rain-sodden bell rope in a thunderstorm.) Before "risk," there was only fate. With "risk," there was something that could be forecasted and influenced. It is not too far-fetched to state that the idea of risk made the modern world. Yet that story—how science turned the "act of fate" disaster into the "controllable" catastrophe—is a subject for later.

TO APPRECIATE HOW THE LISBON EARTHQUAKE CHANGED EUROPEAN culture, first listen to Handel's *Messiah*, written in 1742, an enthusiastic, chanted, baroque glorification of a beneficent God. Such language would not have felt appropriate in the decades after 1755. Born within eight weeks of the earthquake, Wolfgang Amadeus Mozart was much more interested in writing sensuous operas—like *The Magic Flute* or *Così fan tutti*—than works of religious fervor. For some after Lisbon, "faith and morality gave way to the pleasure principle."[47] For the majority, God was vengeful, punishing, more to be feared than glorified.[48]

In case you might think that the argument was now settled, that catastrophes were no longer blamed on divine intervention, a half-century after "Lisbon" another catastrophic earthquake intercepted church services in a capital city on a holy day. Republican Venezuela, liberated from Spanish rule for two years, was hit by two large earthquakes on the afternoon of the Maundy Thursday before Easter, March 26, 1812.[49] The first caused the collapse of most buildings in Caracas and the neighboring coastal cities. Three or four thousand died, many in the churches, "crushed by the fall of their vaulted roofs." La Trinidad and Alta Gracia, both more than 150 feet high, collapsed into piles five to six feet deep.

Soon after the shock, Simón Bolívar, father of the revolution, was spotted by a Royalist clambering onto the impromptu pulpit provided by the rubble summit of a collapsed church in Caracas and proclaiming: "If Nature opposes us we will struggle against her and force her to obey"—words his witness considered "extravagant and impious."[50]

Unlike the situation in Lisbon, the Church's narrative that this earthquake was a "punishment from Heaven sent to the infidel citizens of Caracas" gained ascendancy over the Republic's attempt to argue that the earthquake had natural causes. Many Republican troops had been killed in the collapse of their barracks.[51] On July 25, the Royalists and the Spanish, assisted by the aftershocks of an apparently partisan earthquake, had recaptured Caracas, and the first Republic in South American was over. On October 19, the image of Nuestra Señora del Rosario, patroness of earthquakes, was carried through the ruined city. The processions were followed by three days of fasting.

In the battle with the Catholic Church, the Republicans in Caracas had the last word. In 1874 the Venezuelan president ordered that the reconstructed church of La Trinidad should be appropriated as the National Pantheon mausoleum to house the sarcophagus of the Liberator, Simón Bolívar.[52] Bolivar's defiant words, proclaimed from the summit of the ruined church after the 1812 earthquake, came to define his legacy. In 1967, SI LA NATURALEZA SE OPONE LUCHAREMOS CONTRA ELLA Y HAREMOS QUE NOS OBEDEZCA was carved in foot-high letters on a monumental wall in the Plaza San Jacinto, erected to celebrate the 400th anniversary of Caracas.[53]

Once again the primacy of science had been asserted.

Yet the earth provided the coda. Four days after the city's 400th anniversary—on July 29, 1967—Caracas was shattered by a Magnitude 6.5 earthquake in which 240 died.[54]

———

SOMETIMES "CATASTROPHE" STILL SEEMS TO LIVE UP TO ITS ORIGInal meaning as a dramatic plot device in a Greek tragedy, as though this world is magical realist fiction.

In Japan, even today, people do not believe that their disasters arrive by chance alone. After all, didn't the weather gods protect Japan against not one but two marine invasions of Kyushu by the Mongol armies in 1274 and 1281?[55] On both occasions the invaders were dispersed and destroyed by the intervention of typhoons celebrated as divine winds—*kamikaze*.

Between February 1853 and November 1855, Japan was bombarded by devastating earthquakes, culminating in the destruction of the city of Edo (modern Tokyo) by earthquake and fire. In November 1854, the emperor attempted to escape the demons by declaring a new era—the *Ansei* Era (meaning "tranquil government")—but within two months came the largest earthquakes of all.[56] In the middle of this fusillade, Commodore Matthew Perry arrived at the entrance to Tokyo Bay in a convoy of four vessels, including two black steamships—"giant dragons puffing smoke," as though arriving from another planet—to force the Japanese to agree to American terms of trade.[57] When the Russians sent a fleet to emulate American treaty-making, their flagship *Diana* was spun around by a tsunami to its eventual destruction.[58] Gabriel García Márquez could not have made this stuff up!

A decade later, after losing a war and two-fifths of its territory to Prussia, Denmark agreed to the sale of the Danish West Indies islands of St. John and St. Thomas to the United States, in exchange for $7.5 million in gold. On October 24, 1867, both sides signed the terms of sale. The treaty was to be ratified by the US Congress a month later. What could go wrong?

Five days after the signing, on the afternoon of October 29, an intense hurricane passed directly over St. Thomas with winds of 130 miles (210 kilometers) per hour, "surpassing in destructiveness . . . anything hitherto known at the island."[59] Before all the shipwrecks could be cleared, three weeks later, on the afternoon of November 18, a strong (Magnitude 7.5) earthquake struck in the subsea rift between St. Thomas and St. Croix, tumbling hundreds of tall brick chimneys off the bagasse boiling houses on the old sugar estates. The shock was followed by a 20-foot (6-meter) tsunami that flooded the town of Charlotte Amalie on St. Thomas and sent the 2,000-ton USS *Monongahela*, a US Navy screw sloop of war, into the main street of Frederiksted on St. Croix.

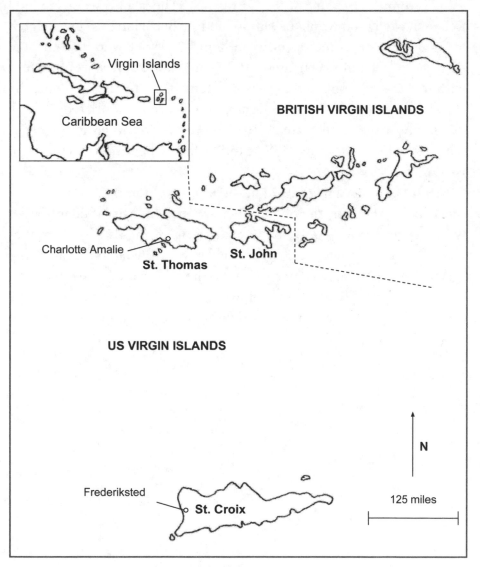

Danish West Indies

It took three weeks for the local newspaper article from St. Thomas giving details of all the hurricane damage to reach New York, where it was reprinted in the *New York Times* on November 24. The following day the US House of Representatives threw out the deal.[60] News of the earthquake and tsunami took a month to arrive, only getting published in the *New York Times* on December 20 while confirming the prejudice gained from the account of the hurricane.[61] The islands were assumed to be wrecked (and would be lampooned by Bret Harte as "just a patch of muddy water, in the open ocean lying").[62] What were the chances that these two unprecedented "100-year" catastrophes would occur within this key month—between the agreement to the deal and the congressional vote?[63] For the Danes, spooked and infuriated, it took nearly fifty years, until March 1916, before they returned to the negotiating table and the Danish West Indies finally became the US Virgin Islands.

After being shaken wildly in his bedroom at Stanford University by the 1906 earthquake, the philosopher and psychologist William James wrote: "I realize now . . . how inevitable were men's earlier mythologic versions of such catastrophes, and how artificial and against the grain of our spontaneous perceiving are the later habits into which science educates us. It was simply impossible for untutored men to take earthquakes into their minds as anything but supernatural warnings or retributions."[64]

3 · CATASTROPHYSICS

AFTER 1755, WHO WERE THESE SCIENTISTS WHO WOULD IN-vestigate and solve the problem of disasters? It could take five months for news of a Peruvian earthquake to reach Paris, and then another five months for a Parisian philosophe to voyage back to Peru. How could anyone hope to study what had happened?

The first disaster to receive the scientific treatment was the hurricane.

For a nineteenth-century sailing vessel, there was nothing—no giant squid or great white whale—to be feared so much as an encounter with a hurricane. The strength of the winds and waves rose inexorably. Riding with the wind, ships were lured into the heart of a hurricane, never to reemerge.

Hurricanes, like tomatoes and tobacco, had been surprise New World discoveries. Before they were first encountered by Columbus, Europeans had had no idea that storms could be of such size and violence. As the colonists cut down the jungle forest to plant their crops, *huracán* (as the locals called these storms) returned to wreck their walls, houses, and fields.[1] By the end of the sixteenth century, Spanish settlers in the Caribbean were reciting the Latin prayer for deliverance—"to repel tempests"—at every Sunday mass throughout the hurricane season.

Some naval commanders, like Captain Langford of the Royal Navy, who had long experience in the Caribbean, developed an appreciation for the warning signs and learned how to dodge an impending storm. In 1667 an English fleet attacking the French island of Nevis put to sea before a great hurricane and then returned four to five days later, unscathed, to the great "admiration" of the hostile French inhabitants. A French capuchin friar said in a sermon: "You may now see your wickedness in praying for a hurricane to destroy the English fleet, when you see they all come back safe—and we do not have a house left to serve God in, nor for our own convenience, nor forts, nor ammunition left to defend ourselves against these our preserved enemies."[2] In 1698 Langford wrote that the storms of the West Indies were counterclockwise "whirlwinds."[3] No further progress would be made in understanding the structure or tracks of these storms for more than a century.

The man who came to pioneer hurricane research, William Redfield, was a storekeeper from Middletown, Connecticut. In the early evening on Monday, September 3, 1821, a fast-moving hurricane passed over New York City heading rapidly north-northeast through the western end of Connecticut and on into Massachusetts. A few days after the storm, Redfield set out on horseback to Stockbridge, in the southwest corner of Massachusetts, to inform his parents-in-law that their new-born grandchild had just died, followed to the grave by their daughter. On this tragic journey he found himself in a surreal devastated landscape of fallen coppice and orchard trees, all pointing northwest toward his destination—that is, until he reached Litchfield County in the northwest corner of Connecticut, where he noticed that trees had been "prostrated *towards the south-east*." How could two locations within the same state have experienced opposite winds? Close to the end of his return journey, Redfield suddenly gained illumination: "This storm was exhibited in the form of a great whirlwind."[4]

While this intuition was profound (if not actually original), he did not do what even any first-year geography student would instinctively have done: try to "crowdsource" the direction of treefall across the counties of Connecticut. It would have been impossible to prove any "whirlwind theory" when trees were felled in only two directions (why not in all directions around the compass?) and when there was only circumstantial evidence that the treefall was synchronous.[5]

Redfield mulled over this idea for nine years. During that time he became a successful steamship owner and captain on the Connecticut River. One day on the voyage to New York, he encountered Dennis Olmstedt, a professor of physics and mathematics at Yale University. After hours of scientific conversation, he confessed his interpretation that the Great September Gale of 1821 had been a gigantic whirlwind. Olmstedt encouraged Redfield to write up his theory (and later helped him get it published in the *American Journal of Science and Arts*).[6] Recognizing that his evidence was weak, Captain Redfield had an inspired idea. Ships carried chronometers so as to locate their longitude. On a well-run ship, every hour "the first lieutenant should report the vessel's speed as well as the prevailing waves and winds." By collating news of the 1821 hurricane from ports and from ships' logs, he was able to retrace the hurricane's path all the way back to its first reported appearance at Grand Turk Island southeast of the Bahamas.

In ships' logbooks Redfield had uncovered a rich source of scientific observation. By piecing together synoptic weather maps hour by hour, he found that he could reconstruct the counterclockwise rotating hurricane structure and track. Based on his 1831 paper, Redfield launched an influential career in amateur storm research (which culminated in 1848, when he became the first president of the American Association for the Advancement of Science).[7]

Why would the atmosphere develop intense whirling storms? Maybe like the maelstroms around tidal races, Redfield proposed, storms were whirlpools generated by "atmospheric tides." In this view Redfield found himself mercilessly lampooned by James Pollard Espy, "the storm king," who in 1842 became the chief meteorologist in the US War Department. Espy followed the latest European work on thermodynamics, which posited that the rise of warm moisture-laden air powered storm formation.

However, Espy believed that winds should move straight inward from all directions to the convection at the heart of a hurricane. In

1835 Espy said of Redfield's whirlpool proposal that it was "anomalous and inconsistent with received theories," to which Redfield riposted: "I did not anticipate so complete an evasion of all the distinguishing points at issue."[8]

In his official naval role, Espy debunked the rotational theory of storms, meriting a repudiation from Redfield, who was concerned that this "could pose deadly risks to mariners who might come into contact with them."[9] We now understand, as Redfield showed, that the surface winds of a hurricane are a whirlpool, but there is also a chimney of rising air at the center, as Espy identified.

In 1831 a devastating hurricane struck Barbados in which almost 1,500 died. A British army officer, Colonel William Reid, came to supervise reconstruction.[10] Reid had been commissioned a lieutenant of engineers in 1809 and had fought in many campaigns, including the 1815 British attack on New Orleans. He knew nothing about hurricanes, but as he surveyed the damage upon his arrival in Barbados, he came across Redfield's 1831 paper, which inspired him "to procure as many logs from ships in these storms . . . as possible."[11]

Over the next few years, through collecting ships' logbooks, Reid became an avid storm-chaser. He found that nine ships had intercepted a sequence of hurricanes in the summer of 1837. The most graphic descriptions came from vessels that narrowly survived, like a brigantine bound for Kingston from Cork, the *Judith and Esther,* which had been thrust over on her beam-ends, having lost all sail. Reid published his findings in a book boldly titled *The Law of Storms.*[12]

From researching the marine archives, Reid also reconstructed some of the most notorious storms of the previous century. Four ships of the East India Company had been sunk by the March 1809 "Culloden's Storm" in the southwest Indian Ocean.[13] Reid plotted the course of each surviving ship and reconstructed the recurring path of the hurricane, which had twice intercepted the flotilla. He also accessed Board of Admiralty logs for the surviving ships of the two great October hurricanes of 1780, the second of which had devastated the island of Barbados at maximum intensity before blitzing St. Lucia.[14]

Although Reid never met Redfield, they exchanged logbook entries from British and American ships, while Reid championed Redfield's work in Britain. Reid's research career ended in 1839 when he was appointed governor of Bermuda, an island colonized (in 1609) by a hurricane.[15]

On the other side of the globe was a third self-taught student of hurricanes, Henry Piddington, a former ship commander who had lost his mast and nearly his life in a storm. In 1839 he was appointed to organize the meteorological services of the East India Company, and he would go on to become president of the Marine Courts of Enquiry in Calcutta.[16] He coined the term "cyclone" (meaning the coil of a snake) for these circulating storms wherever they occurred, leaving the label "hurricane" for storms around the Atlantic.

Piddington set out his stall of knowledge of cyclones.[17] He mapped a near-tenfold range in storm sizes and showed how deep the central pressures could fall in the vortex at the heart of the central "lull" (what we now call the "eye") of the storm. He saw how the forward speed of the storm typically increased with latitude. He understood how the cyclone's winds could drive a sea flood to inundate a coast; some of the most deadly surges had drowned ports in the River Ganges delta.

Piddington also mapped the global geography and seasonality of cyclones, as best as this could be retrieved from where ships sailed the early-nineteenth-century seas. Ships sailing west across the Atlantic at the twentieth parallel north, following the all-year trade winds, provided a rich survey of hurricanes. Clippers bound for India sailed round the Cape of Good Hope and in the southern summer intersected the southwest Indian Ocean cyclones. However, few ships sailed into the Pacific and by the mid-nineteenth century he knew of only a single (1804) report of a typhoon close to Japan, for Europeans one of the least-traveled parts of the ocean.

In 1848 Piddington published the universal *Sailor's Horn-book for the Law of Storms*.[18] Writing in what he called "the familiar terms of common sailor-language," he declared his readership to span from the midshipman's hammock to the admiral's desk. His mission was to teach sailors not to delay "running away from a fair wind"—that is, pointing the ship away from a hurricane to make good her escape. (It is the advice from a later edition of Piddington's *Sailor's Horn-book* that Captain MacWhirr chooses to ignore when he keeps his steamship on course toward the center of a northwest Pacific cyclone in Joseph Conrad's 1902 novel *Typhoon*.[19])

From Redfield to Reid and on to Piddington, in little more than fifteen years, cyclones had been named, their tracks had been surveyed, their wind fields had been defined, and all this knowledge (Piddington termed it "cyclonology") had been turned into instructions for sailors to avoid being consumed by the storms. Yet once ship's captains understood the "law of storms" and learned to avoid them, they became much less interested in reporting the conditions of the wind. Moreover, the new steamships had no need to divert through the favorable trade winds of the tropics to voyage from Europe to North America. By the mid-nineteenth century, the peak period of crowdsourcing hurricane observations was coming to an end. As a result, hurricane research stalled for almost a century.

In 1948 the Finnish meteorologist Erik Palmén discovered that tropical cyclones only form where the sea surface is warmer than 26–27 degrees Celsius (80 degrees Fahrenheit) and that it takes hotter water to spin up stronger storms.[20] Piddington had believed that Indian Ocean tropical cyclones emerged like smoke rings from "Sumatra Volcanoes." It would take satellite observations to reveal how a vortex can spontaneously emerge out of a group of thunderstorms or an atmospheric wave.

CAPTURING A WILD EARTHQUAKE

Making sense of earthquakes proved far more difficult than unraveling cyclones. Short-lived and destructive, earthquakes were all over long before a scientist could find anything to come and measure. It was not even clear what constituted the impulse, the "quaking," through the ground. After 1755, many scientists believed that this was some kind of electrical shock, although the Rev. John Michell at Cambridge, author of works on astronomy and geology, in 1760 proposed that earthquakes comprised a spreading wave of vibrations.[21]

Yet unlike the arriviste New World hurricanes, since ancient times earthquakes were familiar to all those who lived in Italy and around the eastern Mediterranean. Across this region the accepted explanation for earthquakes remained unchallenged for 2,000 years since Aristotle first announced it in the middle of the fourth century BCE. Earthquakes were caused by farts of wind bursting out of underground tunnels, probably triggered by cavern collapse.

When a theory is so completely accepted and ingrained, every observation is reconciled to support it. After the Ferrara earthquakes of 1570–1571, the biggest fear of the inhabitants was that the city would fall into a gigantic hole.[22] Shakespeare references an earthquake caused by "the teeming earth . . . with a kind of colic pinched and vexed by the imprisoning of unruly wind."[23] Immanuel Kant believed that the 1755 Lisbon shock radiated across Europe through vast subterranean caves.[24]

Based on Aristotle's explanation, it even became possible to advance practical steps to prevent earthquakes. In 1721 the Persians successfully "ended" a sequence of damaging earthquakes at the city of Tabriz (Tauris) by cleaning out all the wells surrounding the town, so that the "exhalations" could escape without causing tremors.[25] As described in Francesco Milizia's 1781 work on *Principii di Architettura Civile*, a truly antiseismic house should be surrounded by caverns, cisterns, and wells to relieve a buildup in the underground winds.[26]

As if proving the point, there was the notorious 1692 catastrophe in Port Royal, Jamaica, the largest earthquake disaster on British territory. After the English captured Jamaica from the Spanish in 1655, they founded Port Royal on the great Palisadoes sand spit, which protected the best anchorage in the Caribbean. By 1690 Port Royal was said to be the wealthiest town in the world—the Dubai of its age. Privateers captured gold and silver from ships sailing back to Spain, stole goods from Spanish ships resupplying their colonies, and then sold the goods back again. The original Spanish buildings in the town had been wooden and single-story, but in a mad imitation of London after the Great Fire, the English constructed three- and four-story brick buildings encircled by a brick city wall. By 1692 Port Royal had 6,500 inhabitants and 2,000 buildings, concentrated in 50 acres. Port Royal was a party town: there were far more gambling dens, taverns, and brothels than churches.

The newly arrived rector, Rev. Emmanuel Heath, gave morning prayers on June 7, 1692, so as "to keep up some shew of Religion among a most Ungodly Debauched People."[27] Three hours later, at 11:43 a.m., a strong earthquake caused the saturated sands beneath the city to liquefy.[28] Landslides, weighted by the brick buildings, set off into the lagoon along the whole inland side of the sand spit. Between 1,000 and 3,000 were killed, most of them by drowning.[29]

Stories of the 1692 earthquake at Port Royal made a terrific tale, with all the ingredients of sin, divine punishment, and comeuppance. As described by the preacher John Wesley almost sixty years later: "In many places the earth would crack, and open and shut quick and fast, of which openings, two or three hundred might be seen at a time; in some whereof the people were swallowed up; others the closing earth caught by the middle, and squeezed to death; and in that manner they were left buried with only their heads above ground; some heads the dogs ate!"[30]

This lurid reportage convinced generations of Britons (on both sides of the Atlantic) that what was to be feared most of all in an earthquake was the ground opening up and swallowing you as you fell into one of Aristotle's subterranean caverns.

The Port Royal story still pervaded how people made sense of earthquakes in 1770 when accounts of a devastating earthquake in Port au Prince, Haiti, arrived in Boston, Massachusetts. "A Village called Croit De Bouquets" (containing about 100 families, two leagues from Port au Prince) "had wholly sunk & disappear'd," and "a huge Inn, about a mile from Leogane, with a number of people in it, was instantly taken in by the opening of the earth, so that no remains of it could be seen." "The trembling of the earth," it was reported, "lasted about two days, all which time great numbers of people, who had escaped out of the towns, continued sitting and walking on the hills and sides of the mountains in continual fear of being swallowed down."[31]

Whether it was how people expressed their fear or how they reported episodes of engulfment, all seemed to lend support to Aristotle's theory of collapsing caverns. And yet, with an earthquake on the scale of Lisbon in 1755—the duration, the number of cities devastated—the question arose: just how big was this cavern? Aristotle's theory was getting stretched to the breaking point.

THE FIRST TO INVESTIGATE AN EARTHQUAKE CATASTROPHE "SCIEN-tifically" was an Irish civil engineer and inventor named Robert Mallet.[32] Born in Dublin in 1810, Mallet had developed a passion for earthquakes while running his father's foundry business, and in 1846 he boldly de-fined a new science, carving from the Greek root for "earthquake" two new words: "seismic" and "seismology." Together with his son, he com-piled a catalog of reported earthquakes, and in 1852 he produced the first world map showing the narrow corridors of the earthquake-ridden zones girdling the continents.[33]

At the end of December 1857, following accounts of a destructive earthquake in the interior of the Kingdom of Naples, Mallet obtained £150 from the Royal Society of London to undertake a field investi-gation of the disaster.[34] Equipped with two Admiralty chronometers, a barometer, a theodolite, and a compass, along with provisions, a tent, and his own riding saddle, Mallet acquired horses, mules, and a local guide who knew the dialects of this wild and impoverished area of southern Italian hill villages and set off to investigate the ruins. He was lucky not to be taken for a government spy.

Mallet was in the field for two weeks in the middle of winter and was "wet through from morning to night." Believing that the orienta-tion of fissures in buildings could reveal the source of the earthquake, he mapped the "focus" of the earthquake "explosion" as lying beneath the epicenter, between two and nine miles underground.[35]

Mallet's method of locating the epicenter from cracks in buildings was copied by other earthquake investigators for the next two decades before it was discovered that the method was highly subjective and unworkable.[36]

———

IN THE 1870s, JAPAN OPENED TO THE WEST AND SET ABOUT LEARN-ing to imitate the Victorian industrialized world. To nurture a new generation of Japanese technocrats, in 1873 the emperor established the College of Technology in Tokyo under the control of the Ministry of Public Works. The ministry appointed a twenty-five-year-old En-glish principal, who hired bright scientists and engineers, also in their twenties, mostly from Britain, on three- to five-year contracts, tempting them with handsome salaries and the lure of the Orient. In 1876 the college hired John Milne, a twenty-six-year-old from Liverpool, educated at King's College London and the Royal School of Mines, to become professor of geology and mining.[37] For the expatriate scientists in Yokohama, "earthquakes are as much talked about as the weather in European countries," Milne reported. "We had earthquakes for breakfast, dinner, tea and supper."[38]

In the early morning hours of a February night in 1880, Milne was shaken awake by the most powerful vibration of his tenure, followed by the sound of crashing chimneys. This earthquake reset Milne's destiny. He published a proposal in the English-language *Japan Gazette* to found the first-ever Seismological Society in Japan. The society was quickly established, with Milne as its enthusiastic vice president. The first mission was to develop a working seismic recorder, a competition won by James Ewing, professor of mechanical engineering at Tokyo University.[39]

By the mid-1880s, the majority of the foreign lecturers at the college had completed their tenure and returned home, and a new generation of talented Japanese scientists and engineers had matured to take their places. In 1886 one of Milne's former students was appointed to be the world's first professor of seismology at Tokyo University.

Early in the morning of October 28, 1891, a large earthquake occurred on-land beneath the Nobi plain to the north of Nagoya; though closer to Osaka than Tokyo, it caused some damage in both cities. The earthquake galvanized the Japanese earthquake research agenda, and Milne's students took the lead. One geologist mapped a surface fault that had cut through the Nobi plain for more than 40 miles (60 kilometers), displacing fences and roads by several meters.[40] It was the two sides of the fault grinding against one another, he argued, that had generated the vibrations.[41] Another of Milne's students, Fusakichi Ōmori, monitored the smaller earthquakes that continued for months after the original shock.

In an editorial, the *Japan Weekly Mail* exalted "Japan's prospects of establishing a scientific reputation" in seismology. The government established an Imperial Earthquake Investigation Committee to direct research funding, with Milne as the only foreign member.[42]

In 1894 Ōmori published a scientific paper showing that aftershock activity decays "exponentially": it reduces at a consistent rate through time, so that, if the number on the second day is 80 percent of the number on the first, the third day will have 80 percent times 80 percent to equal 64 percent of the first day's activity. This extraordinary characteristic of the earth recovering from an earthquake still bears its author's name: "Ōmori's law."[43] (The reduction in aftershock activity was intuitively understood in medieval Italy, where people would move out of their houses for a week after a great earthquake.)

After the premature death of the former incumbent, in 1896 Ōmori was appointed professor of seismology at Tokyo University and head of the Imperial Earthquake Investigation Committee. By 1899 he had designed and built his own "Ōmori" seismograph (manufactured after 1909 by the Bosch instrument makers in Strasbourg, Germany).[44]

In 1905 Ōmori traveled to northern India to study the great Kangra earthquake in Himachal Pradesh. In place of Mallet's barometer and chronometer he brought with him portable seismograph recorders to measure and locate the succeeding earthquakes. In early April 1906, he was investigating a destructive earthquake in Formosa (modern-day Taiwan, which was then a Japanese colony) when he heard news of the great Californian earthquake. By May 1, he was on a boat to San Francisco at the head of a group of leading Japanese architects and engineers.

AN INCONVENIENT TRUTH

On arrival in California on May 18, Ōmori was astonished to discover that while there were leading science and engineering universities around the San Francisco Bay, there were no earthquake researchers. California was an increasingly sophisticated society, and fast losing its frontier and gold rush mentality, but it retained a deeply held prejudice that engaging in earthquake research would imply that there was a tangible "earthquake problem."[45]

The late-nineteenth-century Californian scientists whose work in some way touched earthquake science all observed the requirement to play down the threat. The astronomer Edward Holden wrote: "The earthquakes of a whole Century in California have been less destructive than the tornadoes or the floods of a single year in less favoured regions."[46] This assessment was not much less rhetorical than the newspaper that proclaimed after the 1868 disaster: "Earthquakes are trifles as compared with runaway horses, apothecaries' mistakes, accidents with firearms, and a hundred other little contingencies which we all face without fear."[47]

In 1885, while waiting to take up his post as head of the mountaintop Lick Observatory, Holden was appointed interim president of the University of California. He managed to divert some money intended for the Observatory to support earthquake monitoring— under the unconvincing argument of being "able to control the positions of astronomical instruments"—and ordered from Scotland two vibration-triggered smoked-glass-plate seismographs made by James Ewing, which arrived in 1887.[48] Holden encouraged other astronomical observatories in northern California and Nevada to acquire reproductions of the Ewing recorder fabricated in San Francisco and discreetly organized eight stations to function as a "California System" (managed from the Lick Observatory), which operated for the next decade.[49] Holden eventually fell out with his staff at the Lick Observatory so badly that in 1897 he had to step down, after which coordinated seismic monitoring fell apart.[50]

By 1906, scientists in Russia, Japan, and Germany had advanced the technology to a whole new generation of seismic recorders. While the latest recorders were installed in Mexico, in Canada, and at three institutions on the US East Coast, there were no modern recorders within 1,000 miles of San Francisco. The primitive and obsolete Ewing smoked-glass seismographs were sustained in the observatories of northern California, only because no government funds were available for replacements. In 1895 John Milne wrote that "Siberia and America are regions of seismic darkness."[51]

After the April 18, 1906, shock, with the Stanford University library in ruins, John C. Branner, the professor of geology, sent out his research assistants to survey reports of a "line of disturbance" along the

San Francisco Peninsula. Like the trace of a huge plowshare dragged through the ground, the rupture followed the course of the San Andreas Fault, first identified and mapped in 1895. Along the Pacific coast north of San Francisco, the fault intersected peninsulas for a total end-to-end length of 275 miles (443 kilometers). Ōmori spent eighty days in California, inspecting the whole on-land fault break and visiting all the damaged towns and cities. Where the fault cut tracks or fences, the west side was consistently shifted to the north, by up to 8 feet (2.4 meters) along the San Francisco Peninsula, but by 16 feet (4.9 meters) and in one place 20 feet (6.1 meters) to the north of the bay.

On July 11, inspired by Ōmori, a conference was held in Berkeley "for all those interested in seismological equipment on the Pacific coast." They talked of establishing a US national seismological survey, based on the Japanese model, and the meeting passed a resolution to set up the Seismological Society of America.[52] Revered as "the world's greatest authority on seismology," Ōmori assured San Franciscans, in a newspaper interview on June 6, that based on his studies, "there will be no more serious earthquakes in this vicinity in the near future."[53] He brought with him a gift for the University of California at Berkeley—one of his own design seismic recorders. The equipment was gratefully received, for the university had no hope of obtaining a recorder through state funding. By June 15, the new Ōmori seismograph was recording the aftershocks.

However, fieldwork in California proved a challenge for a dapper Japanese gentleman: Ōmori was stoned by a gang of children on Mission Street in San Francisco and assaulted for being a suspected strike-breaker in Eureka.

Ōmori returned to Japan in August. Why wouldn't the legacy of the 1906 earthquake in California be like the legacy of the 1891 earthquake in Japan—with a professor of seismology, active earthquake monitoring programs, and an American equivalent of the Imperial Earthquake Investigation Committee to coordinate and fund research? Yet the 1906 earthquake had only served to intensify and popularize the culture of "earthquake denialism," led by the "boosters" intent on suppressing any earthquake research or publicity that might threaten Californian prosperity or discourage immigrants from relocating to the state.

Within a week of the April 19 earthquake, the San Francisco Real Estate Board passed a resolution to rebrand the "San Francisco Earthquake" as the "San Francisco Fire." The California State Board of Trade (the future Chamber of Commerce) would reference the San Francisco "disaster" or "catastrophe" but never uttered the dreaded "e-word": earthquake.

No memorial was erected to commemorate those who died in the disaster, not even at the site of the greatest loss of life: twelve brick buildings collapsed at the "mental asylum," the State Hospital in Santa Clara, killing staff and 117 patients, many of whom were buried in unmarked graves.[54] Even a century later, in 2003, when an attempt was made to erect a brown commemorative historical sign at Daly City, the closest land location to the epicenter (and a community founded by refugees from the disaster), the initiative was twice rebuffed by the mayor, who explained: "We don't need to put a blemish on Daly City's shine."[55]

However, in the days immediately following the earthquake, and before the denialist response had taken root, Andrew Lawson, a professor of geology at the University of California at Berkeley, badgered the governor into commissioning eight scientists to author a report on the disaster. Only one of these, the geologist Grove Karl Gilbert of the Western Geological Survey, had any previous experience relating to earthquakes.[56] The goals were narrowly defined: to record what had happened, to collect observations of landscape change, to explore the timing of the earthquake waves, and to map the earthquake intensities. While Ōmori was in California, he was made an honorary member of the commission. Having appointed the commission, the state then offered no money to support its work, a situation labeled "an embarrassment" in the preface to the commission's eventual report. Professor John C. Branner wrote of this time: "There was a general disposition that almost amounted to concerted action for the purpose of suppressing all mention of that earthquake. . . . There hasn't been an earthquake [was] the sentiment we heard."[57]

Fortunately, American wealth had created new sources of progressive funding remote from Californian political sensibilities. Lawson appealed to the Carnegie Institution in Washington, DC, and received the promise of almost $6,000 to support field research and publication costs.[58] The two-volume Lawson Earthquake Commission report, published in 1908, was by far the most detailed and scientific study of an earthquake ever made.[59]

The most valuable of all insights on the earthquake came from trigonometric survey data: measurements of the precise angles between monuments located on hills and cliffs across coastal northern California. These angles had first been surveyed in the 1850s; the measurements were repeated in the 1890s, and now once more after the earthquake. It was as if a giant net had been set decades earlier and then the largest possible earthquake 'fish' had landed right in the middle of it. Harry Fielding Reid, from Johns Hopkins, analyzed the data and found that since the first survey the western edge of the coastline had moved persistently north relative to the remainder of California. Like bending a stick, this crustal warping had finally led to a breakage at dawn on April 18, 1906, when the San Andreas Fault ruptured and became permanently displaced. In 1910 Reid termed this the "elastic rebound theory." It remains the explanation for earthquake generation today.

Yet despite the profound importance of Reid's discovery—it would certainly have won the prize offered by the French after the 1755 earthquake—the 1906 earthquake had no immediate scientific legacy. No chair in seismology was funded. No Earthquake Research Institution was established.[60] The Lawson Earthquake Commission's report carefully avoided saying anything at all about the prospect for future earthquakes in California.

A thirty-two-year-old associate professor of civil engineering at the University of California at Berkeley, Charles Derleth Jr., was a lone voice in speaking out against the boosters: "Rather than try to tell outsiders that San Francisco was visited by a conflagration . . . it will do San Francisco and California in general more lasting good to admit that there was an earthquake and that with honest and intelligent construction and the avoidance of geologically weak locations our losses would not have been so great."[61] The following year he was made head of engineering at UC Berkeley and ever after became mute on the subject of earthquake research and education, as though under pressure not to "rock the boat" of reconstruction. Only thirteen people turned up to inaugurate the Seismological Society of America in San Francisco on August 30, 1906.[62] Even after they had been widely mapped, no faults were shown on the 1916 "Geological Map of the State of California" issued by the state mining bureau.

(The prejudice was not uniquely directed at earthquakes. Before 1900 the leaders of Galveston, Texas, were heavily invested in denying that the city had a hurricane problem, even after the rival port city of Indianola on Matagorda Bay, only 100 miles away, had been destroyed twice by hurricane storm surges in eleven years.)

The culture of earthquake denialism spread far beyond California. In 1907 the head of the US Geological Survey, Charles Walcott, was appointed to run the independent Smithsonian Institution in Washington, DC, and immediately made it his principal mission to establish a US Bureau of Seismology. While stars can be mapped from a single observatory, little can be learned from one seismograph; a regional network of instruments is needed to locate earthquakes. On May 23, 1907, Walcott wrote brazenly to Charles R. Bishop, Vice President of the Bank of California, enclosing an endowment form, with the offer to set up the Charles R. Bishop Foundation for Seismological Research.[63] Walcott admitted that "there has never been a dollar appropriated by any State or by the National Government for systematic research in this direction. . . . [In] all this broad land we have scarcely any seismologists." The proposal was not taken up.[64]

In April 1909, the American Philosophical Society passed a resolution calling for a National Bureau of Seismology, followed in March 1910 by motions of support from the US Geological Survey and the Seismological Society of America, and then in May 1910 from the National Academy of Sciences. All it now required was the government to authorize the proposed $20,000 annual funding (equivalent to around $500,000 in 2015). Roger Penrose, geologist, mining tycoon, and now scientific philanthropist, proposed to work through his brother, Boies Penrose, a senator from Pennsylvania and a conservative Republican lawyer.

After learning of opposition to a Bureau of Seismology, Walcott reduced his ambition to creating a Seismological Laboratory at the Smithsonian.[65] On March 1, Boies Penrose introduced an amendment for the establishment of a National Seismological Laboratory—including an "expeditionary corps" to investigate earthquakes in the field. On April 6, the Geological Survey Committee voted to recommend the amendment to the Senate. Walcott and Reid set about lobbying senators. However, in early May, the proposal was rejected by the Senate Standing Committee on Appropriations and then on June 10 by the whole Senate.[66]

At the start of 1911, having seen the failure of the Smithsonian initiative, the Weather Bureau made a move to become the official national earthquake monitoring agency and asked Congress for a small appropriation to host seismographs in some of its offices.[67] The government was determined, however, to quash earthquake monitoring: in August 1911 the US Treasury Department blocked the initiative because "what happened underground was not weather"—a posture lampooned on the front page of the *New York Times*.[68] By January 12, 1912, Walcott had run out of ideas and was writing plaintively to the well-known East Coast philanthropist Mrs. Russell Sage to ask her to fund a seismological laboratory.

Three years before, in February 1909, recognizing the political difficulty of getting the government to support earthquake research, Father F. L. Odenbach from St. Ignatius Jesuit College in Cleveland, Ohio, wrote to all the Jesuit colleges of North America proposing that they should each buy a standard Weichert seismograph for $112 and create a recording network.[69] By early 1911, fifteen colleges in the United States and one in Canada had signed up. (It was a curious irony that the same organization that had been thrown out of Portugal in 1759 for its despotic activities and refusal to countenance a scientific explanation for earthquake disasters was now proposing to perform a key role in scientific earthquake monitoring.) Meanwhile, the Weather Bureau offered to pay Jesuit colleges to switch over to be part of its own network. At the end of 1911, Odenbach, fed up with the intrigue (and probably under political pressure), told all the Jesuit colleges that they were now on their own, wherein coordinated monitoring collapsed.[70]

So by 1912 the United States was back to where it had started—the only advanced nation without earthquake monitoring.

This stubborn American refusal to acknowledge or research the earthquake threat was still active in 1927 when the president of the

California Institute of Technology, Robert Millikan, received a letter from Henry M. Robinson, a Caltech trustee and bank president, reflecting: "I wonder if you have any idea how much damage this loose talk [on earthquakes] is doing to the [property] values in Southern California" and threatening, "I for one am going to see what I can do about stopping the whole seismological game."[71]

Earthquakes proved an earlier American "inconvenient truth." If promoting earthquake research—like acknowledging climate change—could conceivably damage the economy, the science should be censored and sidelined.

However, then as now, the private sector contained a wide spectrum of business activities not all of which shared a denialist perspective. First of all, the press was keen to sell newspapers. With both the state and federal government not prepared to fund a single Californian seismic recorder, in stepped the press mogul William Randolph Hearst, who was eager to emulate the deal that John Milne (now based on the Isle of Wight in England) had with the *Daily Mail* in London to provide news scoops on faraway earthquakes. In 1910 Hearst gifted three of the latest German seismic recorders to UC Berkeley and the Lick Observatory.[72]

Another sector with no interest in hiding risks was insurance. Against all attempts to label the San Francisco disaster a "fire," in July 1906 the insurance industry journal *The Standard* was pleased to report that, after intense questioning, the California insurance commissioner "admits there was an earthquake."[73] John R. Freeman, a distinguished civil engineer and president of the leading company Manufacturers Mutual Insurance, operating out of faraway Rhode Island, later wrote: "There seems to have been a local attempt to suppress information about earthquakes, lest it hurt California business, and rumors of this suppression have reacted unfavourably by increasing the apprehension of Eastern underwriters."[74]

EARTHQUAKE GEOGRAPHY

By 1912, there was only one man in America, himself little more than a technician, to keep the flame of earthquake monitoring alive: Maine-born and Harvard-educated Harry Oscar Wood. Since 1904 an instructor in geology and mineralogy at the University of California, after 1906 he taught himself to interpret the earthquake records. From these inauspicious beginnings, "Mr. Wood," as he was denigrated by the "doctored" professors around him, was to become the principal agent of change around American attitudes to earthquake research.[75]

In 1912, after two years teaching the first course on seismology offered anywhere in the United States, and frustrated by his inability to get an academic position without a doctorate, Wood left UC to run the Ōmori seismographs at the Volcano Observatory in Hawaii.[76] At least Hawaii did not deny that it had a volcano problem! In late 1917, Wood joined the US Army Corps of Engineers Reserve Corps to employ seismic recorders to locate enemy guns.[77] In the nerve center of applied physics in Washington, DC, he developed a web of connections between the Carnegie Institution and the newly formed California Institute of Technology.[78]

Wood worked with an astronomer based at the Mount Wilson Observatory, north of Los Angeles, to develop a new portable "Wood-Anderson" earthquake recorder, first deployed in southern California in 1923.[79] The Carnegie Institution and the National Research Council were now spending an annual $20,000 supporting seismology (the amount requested by Walcott back in 1910). In 1925 Carnegie paid for a Spanish Mission–style building to house a seismological laboratory (so as not to attract objections from the wealthy neighbors), embedded in the granite bedrock of the San Rafael Hills of western Pasadena. For Wood, Carnegie had become his career-saving patron—a relationship reciprocated when decades later Wood left his entire estate to the Carnegie Institution.

———

CHARLES RICHTER, BORN IN 1900, WAS AN ACCIDENTAL SEISMOLOgist. In 1928, as he completed his thesis on the spinning electron, he was advised by his supervisor, Robert Millikan, to end his ambitions in physics and instead become a part-time research assistant in the seismology lab. Richter set out to learn how to decipher the traces inscribed on a seismic recorder.[80]

At 5:54 p.m. on March 10, 1933, Richter felt the building shake and went to watch the amplified trace of the seismograph's needle. Radio news reported that the damage was strongest in the Long Beach area of western Los Angeles. Richter was sent out with a portable seismometer to record the aftershocks, following the practice pioneered by Ōmori.

It was left to Harry Wood to remain in the seismology lab and handle the newspapermen who had discovered the number to call and were clamoring for information. He found, to his cost, that his casual remark that "one could not exclude another larger earthquake" would become hyped by the press as a forecast of an imminent calamity. After this experience, Richter was assigned to manage communications.

Newspapermen always had one question he could not answer: "How big?"

The size of the recorded vibrations could vary enormously. In the 1933 Long Beach earthquake, the pen had moved off the chart, while unfelt local earthquakes gave the tiniest recorded squiggle. Richter converted the size of the vibration on the Wood-Anderson recorder into its logarithm and then corrected this measure to a standard distance—100 kilometers—from the focus of the earthquake. In 1935 Richter published his "instrumental magnitude scale."[81]

The scale quickly got picked up by the radio and newspapers and soon (to the chagrin of his boss and colleagues) became known as "Richter Magnitude." Richter, a geeky, eccentric loner, proved adept at talking to the local and national press. Journalists relished the simple intuitive way he had devised to reference the size of an earthquake, and so "Richter Magnitude" became part of the vocabulary.[82] The "Richter scale" can be abstracted to describe any set of ranked calamities or hyperbole: "The government crisis is a '7' on the Richter scale," or, as heard on a London street in 2015, "She was off the Richter!"

On February 9, 1971, a Richter Magnitude 6.7 earthquake occurred at San Fernando not far from Caltech itself. Although by now retired, Richter came into the seismology lab and found himself talking to reporters. Amazed to rediscover the famous Dr. Richter, the press made him the go-to expert on any earthquake news story. In a 1974 book on famous figures of the age, Charles Richter found himself in a pantheon alongside the folk singer Joan Baez, the Black Panther activist Huey

Newton, the author of the Dr. Seuss books, Ted Geisel, and the publisher of *Playboy*, Hugh Hefner.[83] At seventy-four, Richter had become a celebrity.

———

JESUIT EARTHQUAKE MONITORING FINALLY TOOK OFF IN THE mid-1920s. In 1954 Father Frank Rheinberger, reader of records at the Jesuit Riverview College observatory in Sydney, Australia, noticed a "blip" on the record that appeared to correspond with a hydrogen bomb test explosion at Bikini Atoll, as reported in the news.[84] The director of the observatory contacted other Jesuit observatories and together found the signatures of four such explosions—each at five minutes past the hour.

If seismic recorders could detect H-bombs, they could be used to police a nuclear test ban treaty. In late 1958, President Dwight Eisenhower commissioned an investigation of ways to improve the detection of nuclear tests using seismic recorders; the subsequent report was highly critical of the Balkanized state of international earthquake monitoring. Based on this report, starting from 1961, the US Defense Department spent $250 million to build and run a worldwide network of 120 monitoring sites.[85] Big money had finally arrived to track earthquakes.

The output of this worldwide earthquake monitoring was plotted by early-generation computers. As the earthquakes arrived year by year, a pattern was emerging. The outer shell of the earth consisted of broad regions with few earthquakes, bounded by narrow earthquake-ridden corridors, a geography first identified by Robert Mallet—although now new chains of earthquakes could be detected far from land, running along the centers of the oceans.[86]

At the end of the 1960s, the global geography of earthquakes could finally be explained. Stable areas largely without earthquakes are rigid "plates," and their relative movements of a few centimeters each year are "plate tectonics."[87] Earthquakes occur at the plate boundaries, where the plates move relative to one another along "active" faults. In some continental regions, it is hard to discern a simple boundary, and infrequent large earthquakes are distributed over a broad region, but in many zones around the oceans earthquakes are narrowly confined. At the midocean plate boundaries, the crust is being pulled apart. In California the Pacific plate is moving to the northwest, past the North American plate, and in Alaska the Pacific plate is sliding underneath North America—as when it suddenly moved more than 20 meters to generate the great Alaska earthquake of 1964. In Japan four plates meet—and three of them underlie the city of Tokyo.

The longer the fault that breaks, the bigger the magnitude of the earthquake generated. The largest of all faults are the subduction zone plate boundaries where the oceanic plate dips down at shallow angles beneath the continent of South America and the islands of Japan. This is the site of the largest of all earthquakes—such as the 1964 Alaska earthquake and the 1960 earthquake in south Chile, where 620 miles (1,000 kilometers) of the subduction zone fault ruptured in a single episode. The height and geography of the tsunami are driven by the area and size of the change in seafloor elevation that accompanies the subsurface fault movement, so that the largest regional tsunamis follow the biggest of all earthquakes.

EARTHQUAKE SCIENCE WAS ENABLED BY TECHNOLOGY. IN 1755 IT took four weeks for accounts from Lisbon to reach London at the speed of the post-horse. A century later, news of the 1857 earthquake in the mountains of southern Italy reached London in seven days, moving slower along the cart tracks of Basilicata, then faster as the Morse code electrical pulses traveled along the under-Channel telegraph wire, first installed in 1851. Mallet was then able to travel by train (only fully opened the previous year) from the Channel coast to Marseilles to pick up a steamer for Naples. Today, with instant worldwide news, we can be at the site of any disaster within a day.

A half-century after Mallet's first global map of reported earthquakes, John Milne had returned to England from Japan and installed himself at the center of an international "web" of earthquake recording stations. At each station the operator reported the time every earthquake was recorded and sent the information back to Milne, who would laboriously calculate the epicenter. By the 1960s, earthquake locations could be calculated by the latest mainframe computers and the tens of thousands of earthquake dots were merging into plate boundaries.

Mallet was so intent on proving that his 1857 shock was caused by a chemical explosion that he did not notice a raw fault scarp slicing through the hills of Basilicata—later identified as the source of the earthquake.[88] Even after the extraordinary photographs of horizontally offset roads and fences in the 1891 and 1906 earthquakes, midway through the twentieth century there were a few seismologists who still believed that at least some shocks were the product of Aristotle's cavern collapse. In the new millennium, satellite radar data (full name: "interferometric synthetic aperture radar"[89]) can now reveal the complete pattern of elastic rebound around each new earthquake fault rupture.

——◆——

IN SPITE OF THESE ADVANCES, ANY SURVEY OF EARTHQUAKE SCIence would have to conclude that the subject merits only a "C" grade for its communications.

First, there is the Richter scale of magnitude, a scale sometimes derided as having been created only to satisfy journalists. Despite having become the universal currency, what proportion of the population has an intuitive understanding of the logarithms on which the Richter scale is based?

The Wood-Anderson instruments are long retired. Richter's original scale was found not to work for the largest earthquakes, which simply went off scale, or all appeared to have the same magnitude, like a car speedometer with a nail through the dial.

In the late 1960s, Japanese seismologists produced a superior size measure of the "seismic moment" based on the dimensions and displacement of the fault rupture.[90] Yet in acknowledgment that Richter's scale had become the undisputed currency, the new measure was then converted back to be consistent with that scale in moment magnitude (Mw).

It suits the media to elevate the significance of every tiny tremor (currently to the annoyance of the fracking industry), but seismologists have failed to impress on the public that a Magnitude 7 earthquake is 1,000 times bigger than a Magnitude 5 earthquake. The huge difference in the size of the tsunami from a Magnitude 9 earthquake as compared with a Magnitude 8 earthquake is what condemned three of the Fukushima nuclear reactors to melt down. For earthquakes, as for eruptions, it would make better sense to have a scale based on energy release—as in tons of TNT equivalent. (Or why not label the phenomenon according to size? Below Magnitude 2: "microtremor"; Magnitude 2 to 4: "tremor"; Magnitude 4 to 6: "temblor"; Magnitude 6 to 8: "earthquake"; and over Magnitude 8: "megaquake.")

And then there is the question of what to call the process that generates the shaking. As identified by Michell back in 1760, the "quake" in the earth is the equivalent of thunder—a low-frequency noise that passes through the ground and is so loud that it can make buildings fall down. Thunder is the noise from the phenomenon lightning. What is the name for the phenomenon that generates the shaking in the earth? There isn't one. Like a vast steel spring, or a giant crossbow, the crust that has been slowly loaded with strain over decades and centuries is suddenly discharged into fault displacement. Thus, "lightning" is to "thunder" as "X" is to "earthquake." The word (X) would need to combine the concepts of fault rupture and elastic rebound. (My entry would be "faultspring"; send your own suggestions to the director of the Global Earthquake Model.)

In the last two decades, we have gotten better at observing both halves of this process. From satellite observations we can monitor the slow strain accumulation and observe its dramatic release.[91] We can also map the sudden movement along the fault—even when it does not break the surface.[92] As long as we focus only on the earthquake shaking, however, we miss all the other consequences of the sudden release of stored elastic strain.[93] Much to the dismay of *onsen* owners, hot springs switched off across northern Japan after the 2011 Tohoku earthquake.[94] The crust had been squeezed horizontally for centuries, and when this force was suddenly taken away, vertical cracks opened and began to fill with water, diverting the springs for weeks.

Sudden strain release can raise or lower land levels; the coastal city of Valdivia sank 8 feet in the 1960 Chile earthquake, leaving streets and houses underwater.[95] Beneath the ocean it is the sudden change in the level of the seafloor—which leads to the instant raising or lowering of the sea surface—that generates the tsunami as the water tries to recover its elevation in a great radiating series of waves. Reposition yourself in the bath and you generate a tsunami.

Typically a new scientific theory brings new concepts and language. For Mallet in 1857, earthquakes were underground explosions. The point at the surface above the site of the explosion was the epicenter. When, around 1900, the underground explosion theory died, the terminology might have been expected to die with it, yet strangely, the "epicenter" had a second life. At each seismic recorder, the seismologist measures the time when the first vibration arrives. Knowing the speed at which the vibrations travel, the seismologist traces time backwards from each recorded vibration to the point where these times intersect; that is the location where the rupture *began*. The epicenter is no longer the point above the explosion but instead the point above where the fault *started* to break.

However, the vibrations experienced in an earthquake are radiated all along the fault rupture, not just from the point where the rupture starts. And a big earthquake is generated by a very long fault. For a Magnitude 8 earthquake, the fault may stretch for 125 miles (200 kilometers), taking perhaps 50 to 100 seconds to break. Some faults break in two directions, starting from the middle, so the epicenter might at least be in the center of the fault, but many faults break from one end, so the epicenter is not even in the middle of the vibration-radiating fault. The bigger the earthquake the more the location of the epicenter will misrepresent from where the shaking is being generated.

For a long time it was impossible to determine quickly the overall extent of the fault rupture, so seismologists were happy to provide news media with the location of the epicenter. Now, using powerful computer algorithms, seismologists can quickly identify the pulses of vibration radiated all along the breaking fault, not just the point where the rupture started. And so they can now provide a map of the fault rupture. But no one in the news media seems to know what to ask for, and they continue to request the location of the epicenter. Then their graphics departments dress up the epicenter as though it were one of

Mallet's underground explosions, by locating a point on a map and drawing neat (but completely fictitious) rings around it, like the waves from a stone thrown into a pond.

The bigger the earthquake the more misleading this becomes. The epicenter of the 2008 Wenchuan earthquake in China was at the southwest end of a fault rupture almost 160 miles (250 kilometers) long. In the 1995 Kobe, Japan, earthquake, the epicenter was far to the southwest, even though the fault rupture ran right through the city. In the great Magnitude 9 Japan earthquake in 2011, the fault rupture extended for around 250 miles (400 kilometers). In each case, TV news showed a point with rings around it.

In the Kathmandu earthquake in April 2015, television news showed the epicenter as located 60 miles (100 kilometers) to the west of the city, but in fact the rupture had passed right underneath Kathmandu and continued another 60 miles to the east. The BBC even helicoptered a correspondent to the epicenter in the belief that the center of the fictitious bull's eye would exhibit the greatest damage. The focus on the epicenter can even become a dangerous distraction: the biggest aftershocks of that earthquake were occurring 125 miles from the epicenter, at the eastern end of the rupture, close to Mount Everest.[96] My niece, a doctor specializing in emergency medicine, was close to Everest Base Camp and texted me to ask whether she was at risk. While the media's epicenter fixation implied that she was out of danger, I urged her to avoid exposed sections of the trail and sleeping in masonry buildings.

Yet seismologists have also come to appreciate that disaster consequences are determined by neither the size of the earthquake nor even the strength of the shaking. "It's not the earthquake that kills you," became the slogan. "It's the buildings."

4 • THE STORY OF THE THREE LITTLE PIGS

A T THE END OF NOVEMBER 1836, THE FIERCEST WINDS FOR more than 100 years swept southern England. At Horsham, Sussex, midway between London and the south coast, "there raged the most tremendous storm that ever happened in my life . . . the streets were strewn with chimney pots, bricks, and all sorts of debris. . . . Outside the Town trees were dismembered and uprooted by the score, by the hundred."[1]

Privately educated in Brighton, Sussex, James Orchard Halliwell was an impressionable sixteen-year-old at the time of the storm.[2] He went on to study at Cambridge and in 1843, when he was twenty-three, produced his first publication, a compilation (possibly for the entertainment of a younger cousin or sibling) entitled *Nursery Rhymes and Nursery Tales*. Among the traditional nursery tales was an original composition, "The Story of the Three Little Pigs and the Big Bad Wolf."[3]

In case this story was not read to you as an impressionable five-year-old, I will summarize.

The three little pigs are exploring resilience in building materials. The first little pig acquires the materials to build a house out of straw. "Huff and Puff and Huff and Puff and Blow Your House Down," says the Big Bad Wolf, who demolishes the house of straw and eats the little pig. The second little pig, having seen the culinary fate of his brother, builds his house out of sticks, but again the Wolf blows down the house and consumes the pig. Then the third little pig selects bricks as his building material, which proves beyond the power of the Wolf's huffing and puffing. The third little pig not only thwarts the Wolf but leads him a merry dance until, inverting the food chain, pig eats wolf.

Hurricane-force exhalation is not a characteristic of timberwolves.[4] It is a windstorm that huffs and puffs at a house, which, if built out of straw, would quickly disintegrate, as happened to the thatched roofs of the Horsham cottages in that November storm of 1836. In contrast to Holland's "Waterwolf"—the name given to the rapacious power of rivers and the sea[5]—the force that terrorizes the three little pigs is the "Storm-Wolf": the destructive power of windstorms.

"The Three Little Pigs" is a powerful fable of risk management, employing the modern idea of alternative futures.[6] The tale identifies the key to upward mobility at the start of the Victorian period and contains the most shameless (but presumably unsponsored?) example of product placement in children's literature, at least until *Willy Wonka and the Chocolate Factory*.

The moral is blatant. To keep "the wolf" from the door, a prudent pig should live in a brick house. Brick equals resilience in the face of local vicissitudes. Brick, by enabling the urban Victorian to rise above a savage world in which poor people live in huts made of sticks or thatched cottages roofed with straw, is civilization.

The little pigs acquire their building materials by imperiously demanding them off carters. While straw and sticks could plausibly be valueless waste, a load of bricks would require real money. Brick therefore also means capitalism.

In the seventeenth and eighteenth centuries, brick was an expensive and high-status building material. Mechanical brick-making started in the 1820s. Even as mass production kicked in and brick production doubled, the price of bricks scarcely budged from the 1820s to the

1890s, remaining at £6 per 1,000 high-quality bricks for building railway arches.[7]

———

AS THOUGH PART OF AN ORCHESTRATED MARKETING CAMPAIGN, soon after the story of the three little pigs was composed, the British began exporting industrialized brick construction around the world with a missionary zeal. Brick was the epitome of Victorian modernity. Brick was not only wind-resistant but fireproof—a principal concern of the Victorians. Two places where climatically the British felt particularly welcome to sustain this mission were northern California and Japan.

At the height of the California gold rush, San Francisco suffered six big fires in eighteen months.[8] The largest destroyed three-quarters of the wooden buildings in the new city. With the population exploding (from 200 inhabitants in 1846 to 36,000 in 1852), speculative builders, after each fire, erected wooden stores and rooming houses at even higher density on all the vacant lots. In a town filled with reveling gold prospectors, a volunteer fire brigade, and no effective water supply, resources for checking the fires were few. Among the buildings, a small number were made of brick, and those largely survived the fires, confirming their Three Little Pigs superior status (as a Big Bad Wolf armed with a blowtorch would have much the same impact as the Storm-Wolf who "huffed and puffed").

Industrialization had brought fire for manufacture and warmth into the heart of the city. In 1852, San Francisco established a city center "fire district" and imposed a building code requiring "fire-resistant" (i.e., brick) construction. By 1853, San Francisco had acquired 626 brick buildings, half of them constructed that same year; the number had risen to 1,500 brick buildings by 1860. The San Francisco city center was starting to look like Liverpool.

The thirty-year-old Londoner George Gordon arrived in San Francisco in 1849 intent on making his fortune.[9] By 1850, he had constructed a wharf, and in 1852 he established the third iron foundry in the city, providing the materials for a city block of iron buildings.

In 1851, he set out to make South Park the smartest address in the city—an imitation London "square" with a central garden surrounded by brick and stone Italianate houses.

On October 8, 1865, the new city was shaken by a strong earthquake. The shock was centered close to San Jose, 30 miles south of San Francisco, where, it was said, "a very slight increase in violence would have thrown every brick building in the city into a mass of ruins." Meanwhile, in San Francisco the local *Alta California* newspaper reported reassuringly that "brick buildings should no longer be considered hazardous during the prevalence of earthquakes." Instead, the story focused on the influence of geology, noting that "in those parts of the city which were formerly part of the Bay, and have been filled with earth, few of the foundations are firm and there the most damage has been done."[10]

Three years later, on October 21, 1868, there was an even stronger earthquake; we now know that this one was located on the Hayward Fault, along the flank of the mountains on the eastern side of the bay.[11] Again, the most serious damage in San Francisco was on filled ground. This time it was more difficult to claim that brick buildings had a clean bill of health. Yet the tally was modest: seven buildings had been wrecked, and thirty-five seriously damaged. Six people died in the city, killed by falling cornices and a runaway team of horses.

At the instigation of "Lord" George Gordon, the San Francisco Chamber of Commerce set up the Joint Committee on Earthquakes; Gordon was the committee's president.[12] As a prominent developer of brick buildings in the city, he had a personal interest in the findings. The committee established seven specialist work groups to research everything from building materials to past earthquakes to testing apparatus. By December, the subcommittees were collecting Spanish mission records of earthquakes and devising a simple shake table for testing brickwork. This agenda was on the way to seeding the world's first earthquake research institution in California.

And then . . . nothing. The committees all stopped meeting. None of them produced a report. It was as if a plug had been pulled. We only know that the Committee on Bricks, Stones, and Timber planned to champion wood as the most earthquake-resistant material, proposing that it could somehow be made fireproof "through electrical or chemical means."[13]

After the 1906 earthquake, the only surviving member of the committee, George Davidson, admitted that the 1868 "report was suppressed by the authorities, through the fear that its publication would damage the reputation of the city."[14] In fact, it seems that Gordon the businessman also colluded in the report's suppression, after reflecting on what it implied for the commercial future of San Francisco. Following a family scandal, he died in February 1869.[15]

The transcontinental railroad was completed in May 1869 and reached Oakland in November of that year. Behind the scenes, "booster" financial interests not wishing to deter immigration or to blight the economy, actively sought to discourage raising the specter of earthquakes.

Although nothing came out of the experience of the 1868 earthquake, some lessons from the 1865 earthquake were incorporated into an 1866 revision of the San Francisco fire code: iron anchors were to be used to fasten brick walls to each tier of beams and to secure the front and rear walls, while beams and girders were to be strapped together with wrought iron.[16] San Francisco set out to make its largest brick buildings both fireproof *and* earthquake-resistant, through laying horizontal strips of "bond-iron" in walls, or inserting vertical reinforcing rods through holes drilled in the brickwork. During the 1880s and 1890s, however, as the large earthquakes stayed away, unreinforced brick once again became widely used for downtown stores and municipal buildings throughout the towns and cities of California.

———

AMONG THE SEVEN DEPARTMENTS IN THE NEW TOKYO COLLEGE OF Technology was the Architecture Department, led from 1877 by an Englishman, Joseph Conder, who would stay in Japan for his entire lifetime and become revered as "the Father of Japanese Architecture."[17]

The architecture students' education in the history of world architecture culminated in the use of brick and masonry. In an 1879 diploma examination, they were allowed to choose from a range of potential building materials—"brick and stone," "brick and terracotta," "entirely brick," or "entirely stone"—as the subject of their drawing.[18] Japanese students proved receptive to learning about these materials. Fire had been the curse of the capital Edo (Tokyo) for hundreds of years. There had been forty-nine great conflagrations in the wooden city between 1601 and 1867, some killing tens of thousands.

The first students of architecture graduated from the Tokyo College of Technology in 1879 to begin rich and successful careers. During the 1880s, Japanese architects took over the design of the principal brick buildings and industrial factories for the ministries, in a style that was indistinguishable from that of their British teachers. One of the new generation of Japanese architects wrote in an architectural journal in 1888: "Gradually we should make every building in Japan completely brick or stone. . . . This is the basis of a strong nation."[19]

One key obstacle in imposing brick construction on the builders of Japan, however, was the hierarchical relationships among Japanese craftsmen. At the top of the craftsman pyramid were the high-status *daiku* who worked in wood on the finest buildings, while those naturally suited to become workers in brick were the lowly plasterers, as they possessed mortar trowels. One compromise was a "hybrid" design in which a wooden building was faced with brick so that it had the appearance of modernity (and therefore preserved the relative status of the artisan craftsmen). In fact, the only buildings being constructed fully of brick were those sponsored by the ministries, banks, and new industrial corporations.

In 1872, several city blocks in Ginza, in the center of Tokyo, became cleared after a fire, and the Council of State instructed the government of Tokyo city to rebuild in brick and stone.[20] "No matter how much money it costs we should do it for the sake of our honour." And so a neighborhood of wide-columned brick shops was built, a symbolic first step in the long-term goal of re-creating the whole city of Tokyo in brick and stone, just like London after the Great Fire. Yet seeding a new architecture was not as easy as it sounded. By 1883, the brick shops had been largely abandoned when they failed to find Japanese tenants.

Moreover, some of Tokyo College's architecture students were questioning whether their teachers really knew Japan. One wrote fatalistically in 1883: "Our great enemy—*Earthquake*—is glaring at us incessantly, with its fiery keen eyes, to dash upon our houses, suddenly and unexpectedly."[21] The Japanese were becoming less willing to assume the merits of European learning, and the tenure of foreign professors was coming to an end. Many of their contracts expired in 1886 when the Tokyo College of Technology became the Engineering Department of the newly formed University of Tokyo.

On the morning of October 28, 1891, the arguments about the relative merits of European and Japanese buildings became tested by the Great Nobi earthquake.

The first reports to reach Tokyo were from the city of Osaka, where only one building had been completely destroyed: the Naniwa cotton textile mill, "a three storey redbrick structure in the usual English factory style" that had "only been standing for a few months."[22] Twenty-one people had died in the collapse. On November 3, the first news arrived from closer to the center of the earthquake in Nagoya. Headlines focused on the dramatic collapse of "those magnificent brick buildings," the symbols of modernity, including the post office, the divisional headquarters of the army, a large spinning mill (in which more than 200 women workers died), the police headquarters, the prison, an electricity company, and certain hospitals and schools. The newspapers quickly got into their groove around what was "the Story" of this earthquake: the failures and collapses of the brick buildings developed in the European style and imposed on Japan by the Meiji government.[23] Falling brick was said to have caused more grievous and life-threatening wounds than falling wooden Japanese roofs. Editorials thundered in condemnation of "the negligence of the architects and engineers" and of the government for having allowed these foreign practitioners to operate without controls. As more information emerged it became clear that Japanese buildings had also fallen, more than 1,000 in the city of Nagoya, and that in rural areas the fall of temples had in some places killed as many as the collapsed brick mills. (The city of Gifu had caught fire and burned down after the earthquake, for entirely Japanese reasons.) However, "the Story" of the Great Nobi earthquake was already established.

The Association of Japanese Architects—whose membership was almost entirely the new professionals educated either at the Tokyo

College of Technology or the University of Tokyo—met fifteen times in the aftermath of the 1891 Nobi earthquake to learn from what had happened and set a new direction.[24] Their first response was to consider how brick could be refashioned to resist earthquake shaking. Maybe bricks could be made in shapes that interlocked (like Lego pieces). Maybe vertical iron bars could be inserted through holes in the brick work, as pioneered in California. Architecture meant brick. There was no possibility for giving up the whole project and admitting that only wooden buildings were viable.

Brick buildings—welcomed in the 1850s as the answer to the fire dangers of San Francisco and expected by the 1870s to take over all the cities of Japan—had encountered headwinds stronger than those of the Storm-Wolf. Following the 1906 San Francisco earthquake, one observer reported that "streets on all sides were filled with brick and mortar buildings either completely collapsed or brick fronts had just dropped completely off."[25] Jon D. Galloway, a San Francisco engineer, summarized the situation: "Brick buildings are a menace to life."[26] New buildings made of unreinforced masonry (i.e., brick) would finally be banned by law in California after the 1933 Long Beach earthquake.

In Tokyo, the earthquake of September 1, 1923, provided the toughest test. Brick buildings designed by the first generation of European architects, or their original students, were shattered and demolished at Ginza, Ueno Museum, and Tokyo University, including those that housed the seismological laboratories. However, some reinforced masonry buildings designed after 1891 performed quite well; for instance, the Tokyo Main Railway Station building, which looks like something from a provincial town in Sweden, survived the Great 1923 Earthquake, proving that, with suitable reinforcing, brick construction could be made safe.

What if we transpose the Three Little Pigs to the "climate" of California, where seismic "storms" are more troubling than windstorms? In "The Story of the Three Little Pigs and the Quake-Wolf," once again the little pigs go about their investigation of resilient building materials, but now, instead of huffing and puffing, the Quake-Wolf shakes and quakes. For the little pig in the house built of straw, the vibrations prove uneventful, as is also true for his brother in the house built out of sticks. However, for the house built out of bricks, the tremors prove catastrophic, and the walls collapse on its smug little pig owner. The moral has been transposed: there is no universal set of threats, and you should build according to your hazard climate.

Other cities at other times have discovered the folly of brick in earthquake country by not knowing what is "earthquake country." The city of Seattle, rebuilt in brick and stone after a great fire in 1889, still does not think of itself as a city on the earthquake frontline.[27] The brick city of Tangshan, China, population 1 million, had not seen a big earthquake for 2,000 years when it was entirely destroyed in 1976.[28] The brick towns in the Po Valley of Italy had not experienced a strong earthquake before May 2012.[29] In 2006 a modest-sized earthquake led to 5,700 deaths in the brick city of Yogyokarta on Java.[30] In some places, earthquakes happen less frequently and therefore the challenges of brick take longer to emerge. London has had tremors, as has New York City. The brick city of Charleston, South Carolina, was shattered by a surprise earthquake in 1886.[31]

One-third as energy-intensive (weight for weight) as concrete and 6 percent as energy-intensive as steel, clay brick remains a vital building material and lives on, even in earthquake country, where it is transformed into lighter concrete blocks with internal holes so that reinforcing rods can be run through a wall—whatever it takes to prevent the bricks in the wall from moving out of alignment when shaken. In "confined masonry," panels of bricks or blocks are sealed tightly between cast-in-situ concrete pillars and beams, so that the bricks are locked in permanent compression.[32]

———

WHERE AND WHEN DID PEOPLE FIRST LEARN HOW TO BUILD earthquake-proof houses? Let's return to that second little pig: the one who built his house out of sticks. Faced with the Quake-Wolf, timber is an excellent material from which to construct resilient dwellings.

Hundreds of years ago, before engineering, before science, before builders were even literate, the people who first had this insight were practical and observant. If the original shock was experienced as a unique punishment from the gods, never to be repeated, no one would have felt a need to take any action, so these early observers must have lived in an earthquake-prone area. In a town with a mix of housing styles, it would have been possible to see how different buildings responded, which structures survived intact, and which collapsed. We can see how the natural selection of the buildings (and of their owners) might have come about.

Big earthquakes are triggered somewhere along the braided North Anatolian fault boundary through northwest Turkey several times each century, and the most earthquake-afflicted large city in Europe is Istanbul (formerly Constantinople). The Ottomans captured Constantinople from Christian Byzantium in 1453. To make the city their capital they went on a building spree in stone. On a late summer evening in 1509, the city was shaken by the most violent earthquake for hundreds of years, what we now know to have been an estimated Magnitude 7.5 earthquake on the east-west plate boundary that runs underwater through the Sea of Marmara, 6 miles (10 kilometers) south of the city.[33] Thousands of buildings collapsed, and not a structure in the city, it was said, was left undamaged. An estimated 5,000 people died in "the Little Day of Judgment."

In 1542 another great earthquake killed 4,500 in the city. More destruction and damage followed in 1556.[34] The Ottoman Empire was at the height of its power and glory, having conquered the Mamluk Empire of Egypt in 1517 and marched to the gates of Vienna in the late 1520s. The city of Constantinople was the cultural and economic center of a great empire stretching into three continents, yet the Ottomans' new capital was wracked by earthquakes. In reaction, architects switched to building out of timber, whether palaces with flamboyant turrets, mansions with large paneled bay windows, or simple peasant houses.

At the start of the seventeenth century, a visiting Italian nobleman reported what he had learned from Constantinople builders: "They first build a timber frame as in the ships and then cover it from the outside in wooden boards. The filling is of mud brick or simple adobe."[35]

The architects of sixteenth-century Constantinople had discovered how to construct earthquake-resistant buildings: copy the boat builders. To withstand the shocks as it crashes over the waves, a boat has a strong and flexible wooden basket frame that links the keel, ribs, and canopy.[36] If house construction had been left to boat builders, the problem of earthquakes would have been solved centuries ago. From the early seventeenth century, it was boat builders who designed the wooden churches on the island of Chiloe at the earthquake front line in southern Chile.[37] Two years after the latest 1868 earthquake disaster, and at the end of the era of timber ships, San Francisco's wood-frame Grand Hotel advertised its safety, the result of "having been built like a ship."[38]

The boat builders' method is called "timber lacing," or *hımış* in Turkish. In Kashmir, the old Persian *dhajji dewari* translates as "patch quilt wall." A framework of beams is latticed together, with diagonal members creating triangles that maintain their form and cannot be skewed. The spaces between the beams are in-filled with insulating rubble, weak brick, dried mud, lime, or a mixture of plaster and horsehair—material that is not rigid and therefore does not prevent the wooden beams from flexing. The design is strong, light, and easy to construct using the timber offcuts, thick branches, or twisted beams unsuitable for cutting planks.[39]

This is a very ancient building style. There were timber-laced structures in Knossos on Crete, older than 1600 BC.[40] The AD 79 eruption of Mount Vesuvius preserved a complete two-story timber frame house in Herculaneum as well as many timber-laced walls.[41] By the eighth century, *hımış* had become a standard style for Turkish village houses, and it was still the standard into the twentieth century.

Known in England as "half-timbered," in France as *colombage*, and in Germany as *Fachwerk*, timber lacing was also common in northern Europe. In Port au Prince, Haiti, there were even old late-Victorian half-timbered *pan de bois*, or "gingerbread" building styles.[42] After 1910, following city fires, such timber-frame houses were banned by the mayor of Port au Prince.[43] However, these imports from Normandy survived the 2010 shaking better than ordinary rubble stone masonry structures, and far better than the downtown concrete buildings, of which more than one-third fell.[44] None of these northern European styles were built to withstand earthquake shaking, but rather to resist the force of the wind and the load of a heavy snowfall. The presence of half-timbered houses in Istanbul seems to have become a teachable moment in the life of the sixteenth-century city. Following an earthquake in 1688 in Izmir, a visitor noted that the upper stories of buildings were constructed of timber frames in-filled with panels of brick and that this "technique . . . proved resistant in the earthquakes that followed."[45]

By the late seventeenth century, it was general knowledge that wooden buildings offered protection from earthquakes. After half the brick-built streets of Port Royal Jamaica sank into the sea in 1692, the surviving colonists would not relinquish "that fatall spott," as they called it, but rapidly rebuilt in timber on the remaining land. (In January 1703, the wooden town was almost entirely destroyed by a fire lit by a disgruntled pirate captain.[46]) When, in 1766, an earthquake damaged the Topkapi Palace, the Ottoman sultan relocated to temporary wooden buildings, just as timber structures had housed the king of Portugal after the Lisbon earthquake eleven years before.

Yet the timber building stock of Istanbul, notable for its earthquake resistance, was only a toppled oil lamp away from a conflagration. In a fire on April 7, 1588, 22,000 houses, 15,000 shops, and 28 mosques were destroyed.[47] With ready supplies of timber, the wooden buildings were reconstructed. Paul Lucas, a Frenchman, witnessed another bonfire of the vanities in 1715 that destroyed 15,000 houses. The great fire of 1755 burned so close to the Ayasofya mosque that lead from the cupola melted and ran down the drainpipes. Then an earthquake in 1766, the most destructive since the sixteenth century, ruined many stone houses in the city, killed 880, and served to ensure that the builders' yards would remain well stocked with timber.

For the next 150 years, while the fires spread, the strong earthquakes stayed away. The fire of 1782 destroyed 7,000 buildings.[48] During a visit in 1852, the French traveler Théophile Gautier witnessed a whole neighborhood of the city consumed in an enormous fire—"this spectacle of disastrous magnificence." There were twenty-nine great fires in the city between 1853 and 1906.[49] The 1865 Hocapasa fire burned thousands of houses in a broad zone from the Golden Horn in the north all the way to the Sea of Marmara. By the second decade of the twentieth century, as Turkey was fighting alongside Germany in the Great War, 16,000 buildings were lost to fire, half of them in a single conflagration in 1918.[50]

With the earthquake threat long forgotten, the city government wanted to be rid of the timber city. From 1865, each mass burning provided the opportunity to replan and widen the main streets and line them with brick and stone apartment buildings.

A DIFFERENT THEORY OF THE EARTHQUAKE-PROOF HOUSE EMERGED independently at the other end of Asia. The city of Manila was founded in 1571 on the banks of the River Pasig, in a magnificent natural harbor. Streets were laid out in the standard Spanish colonial grid, with the main government buildings and cathedral arranged around a central plaza. Spanish residents (the *intramuros*) lived within the city walls, while beyond the walls lay a community of Chinese merchants and a smaller Japanese settlement. Within fifty years after its founding, the city's population had reached 40,000.

In the beginning, all buildings were constructed out of the plentiful timber, bamboo, and palm, even the grand cathedral. Then, in 1583, almost the whole city burned down.[51]

In 1587 a new governor-general, Santiago de Vera, outlawed further wooden construction and commanded that buildings within the walls be constructed out of volcanic stone sourced from a new quarry opened up river. Roofs were to be made from locally fired tiles. Just as Istanbul was switching from stone to timber, Manila was swapping timber for stone.[52] In the first year after the decree, twenty new stone buildings were built. The rebuilding was accelerated when another fire, in 1603, destroyed half the remaining wooden city; by 1609, Manila had 600 stone buildings. At eight o'clock in the evening on November 30, 1645, a great earthquake demolished 150 of the principal buildings of the city, including the palace, the royal Audienzia, and the cathedral, and left the rest in such a perilous state that many had to be abandoned. Joseph Fayol, the royal chaplain in Manila, wrote that "the inhabitants of Manila, while avoiding in their buildings the activity of fire, fell into the terrible power of the earth."[53]

And so the search was on to find some compromise, to thwart the twin perils of shaking and fire. In response, building heights in Manila were reduced to no more than two stories[54] and hybrid construction styles, such as the *arquitectora meztisa*, were adopted.[55] These alternative styles were said to have been strongly influenced by the Japanese artisans who lived in lightweight wood and bamboo houses in their settlement at Dilao, outside the city walls.[56] In the *arquitectora meztisa* style, above a first story of stone was a wooden upper floor of lightweight wood or lattice frames.[57] The roof was dovetailed and morticed into house posts, or *haligues*, embedded in the ground to prevent the roof collapsing should the stone walls be damaged. The stone concealed the internal wooden structure (and protected it from spreading fires). This architecture would evolve into the heavier *bahay na bato* style, which was sustained for some of the grandest Philippines houses for more than 200 years; the ground floor was constructed of stone or brick, and the upper floor of hardwood lattice walls was reached via a grand internal staircase.[58]

Recognizing the fragility of their traditional churches, the colonists imported a robust "earthquake baroque style" from Mexico.[59] The height of the nave was reduced and constructed with overthickened walls and multiple massive buttresses. At Poaoy, on the northwest coast of Luzon, the squat church, built around 1700, resembles a Mayan pyramid: it looks as if the building were located on a planet with twice the force of gravity (which is not a bad way of combating earthquake shaking).[60] Across the island, bell towers were reduced in height and the square or octagonal plan stepped inward at each level, like a toddler's stack of nesting plastic beakers.

The earthquake-resistant architecture from Manila even found its way back across the Pacific. Following the destruction of Lima, Peru, in 1746, buildings had to be either single-story or built with a second story built from quincha, a light woven-reed walling.[61] Copied from the indigenous Indians, these second stories imitated Manila's bamboo or lattice frames.

—•—

WITHIN A MONTH OF THE 1755 EARTHQUAKE, QUESTIONS WERE being asked: How should Lisbon be reconstructed? Which architect had survived the earthquake with his reputation intact? The undamaged stone arches of Lisbon's new 11-mile (18-kilometer) Águas Livres Aqueduct testified to the integrity of the work of the eighty-year-old military engineer Manuel de Maia, the aqueduct's principal engineer and designer. De Maia was tasked to recommend a scheme for the city's regeneration.[62] No rebuilding was allowed before agreement had been reached on the plans.

De Maia and his team returned the following spring with their proposals.[63] For the Baixa area—60 acres of the low-lying city center that had been obliterated by shaking and fire—he mapped out an orthogonal plan with wide streets. All buildings would be four stories high, with an internal timber "birdcage" framework with X-shaped cross bracing in every rectangle, in-filled with rubble—what was termed a "Gaiola" framework.[64] The boat builder's timber triangles had become formalized into a structured mesh. The full plans for reconstruction were published in May 1758. Landowners were given five years to rebuild or they would lose their tenure.

After the Calabria earthquakes of 1783, the government in Naples authorized the introduction of the *casa baraccata* (barracks house) design for earthquake-resistant buildings. This time the wooden cross bracing was placed on the outside of the (typically) two-story stone buildings, where it was less resistant to the weather.[65]

The cross-bracing earthquake-resistant designs in Lisbon and Calabria were independently feeding off some mother lode of insight whose roots may have gone back to sixteenth-century Constantinople. There had been trade ties between Portugal and the Ottomans for at least two centuries.[66] In Lisbon the earthquake-proof house was treated as a novel experiment and was adopted only in a single "model" district at the city's center. In contrast, in Calabria *casa baraccata* was to be used for all official reconstruction. Yet unlike the situation in Manila, the new styles were alien, not adopted by ordinary builders. Masons in

Portugal soon went back to their traditional ways and were once again raising walls out of unreinforced rubble.

By the late nineteenth century, all of these independent streams of innovation—from inserting a boat builder's wooden basket framework into a building to adding a second story of wood frame—had begun to clash with the principal urban mission of the age: to make all city buildings fireproof.

———

IN ALL OF THESE VERNACULAR EARTHQUAKE-RESISTANT BUILDING styles, the key building material was timber. Thus, the proportion of a country that was forested—that is, the local availability of timber— might then determine the innate earthquake resistance of ordinary houses. In Turkey, 26 percent of the country is forested. Haiti was 60 percent forested in 1923, but scorched-earth clearance for farming and firewood has reduced the proportion to 1.5 percent—Haiti is now, in arboreal terms, a "desert."[67]

Where wood is simply unavailable, as in the deserts of Iran, traditional single-story adobe village buildings have proven to be the most murderous anywhere on earth during earthquakes (as first identified in the 1960s by the great earthquake investigator Nicholas Ambraseys).[68] Yet the traditional buildings of Iran are also celebrated as some of the best vernacular examples of "bioclimatic architecture."[69] The deserts are scorching by day but freezing at night, especially in winter. To gain protection from searing dust and sand storms, house walls are built up to a meter thick, and the close grouping of buildings reduces wind exposure and enables them to share shade and warmth.

Design appropriate to the weather climate, however, made death traps of these same buildings in the tectonic climate of earthquakes, generated along the faults that slice through the mountains and deserts of Iran. A new layer of mud is applied to the roof dome each spring to cool the building through the baking summer sun. As the roof becomes ever heavier, it cannot endure even moderate shaking and collapses on the occupants, who are as likely to die of asphyxiation as of crush injuries. When the ancient mud-walled houses of the city of Bam were hit by a strong local earthquake at 5:26 a.m. on December 26, 2003, more than 90 percent of them collapsed (leaving a death toll of 26,000, or 30 percent of the population).[70]

The most earthquake-ridden country on the planet is Japan, which is also two-thirds forested. From that you might conclude that Japan should have the safest of all houses. Yet traditional Japanese timber houses are not particularly earthquake-resistant.[71] Their wood frames do not employ cross bracing or the rigid wooden triangles of the boat builders. The platform is raised off the ground on short, unbraced, vertical timbers, while a traditional roof of heavy tiles embedded in a layer of sand is supported on posts and lintels. It is not that Japanese architects have been unaware of how to defeat earthquake shaking: the late-eighteenth-century Jishin-den "earthquake palace" on the grounds of the Imperial Palace in Kyoto has thick timber beams and continuous foundations, while avoiding the raised floors and heavy tiled roofs that weaken most traditional Japanese buildings.[72] Yet the pursuit of earthquake resistance was not going to usurp the simplicity and openness of traditional Japanese houses, with their fragile sliding screens. Tiled roofs were designed to resist fire, a far more frequent hazard, as well as tropical downpours and gusting typhoon winds. That is why, in the 1995 Kobe earthquake, 55,000 traditional houses collapsed and another 32,000 were left wrecked: the natural resistance of wood-framed buildings was sabotaged by the weight of the heavy roofs.[73] Like an inverted pendulum, a tiled roof swings around in the shaking, cracking the wooden lintels, collapsing the house, and all too often crushing those sleeping inside.

The islanders of the Caribbean share the same conundrum. The winds from an intense hurricane can be just as dangerous to life as an earthquake. The original Spanish owners of Jamaica considered hurricanes the greater threat, but that was before the 1692 earthquake catastrophe. Almost a century later, "the dread of earthquakes" was still sufficient to motivate Jamaican colonists to build "slight houses . . . chiefly of wood."[74]

In 1690 a strong regional earthquake in the northeast Caribbean destroyed many brick buildings in Charlestown on the island of Nevis. Builders switched to wood until the 1733 Nevis hurricane, after which the local vicar, observing that "many a Life has been lost . . . by the Fall of Houses in a Storm," considered stone the better building material.[75] Over time on most Caribbean islands, just as in southern Japan, hurricane/typhoon resistance took precedence because strong cyclones were more frequent than damaging earthquakes. The seeds of the 2010 tragedy in Haiti were being sewn. With no timber and with a focus only on keeping out the wind and rain, the buildings in Port au Prince had become as dangerous in strong shaking as the domed mud-brick houses of Iran.

The choices in house construction have become like the Japanese game of "paper-scissors-stone." To every peril there is a resilient building style, but each building style makes the structure more vulnerable to another peril. Build out of stone to resist the wind, or out of mud to withstand the heat, or with a heavy tiled roof to protect against fire, and you invite earthquake demolition. Build lightly out of timber to withstand the earthquake and fire will consume your structure or hurricane winds will overturn the fragile frame. There seemed to be no alternative but to build to withstand the latest disaster, and then pray the other hazards stayed away. The notion of a building resistant to fire, earthquake, heat, and wind remained a pipe dream.

———

JUST AS BRICK BUILDINGS WERE CASUALLY IMPORTED TO EARTH-quake country, so the modern equivalent of stick houses have been constructed in the heart of cyclone territory.

In 1974 in Darwin, a city with a population of 48,000 on the tropical north coast of Australia, most houses were constructed like a box erected on sticklike stilts; they were designed for tropical living free from insects and snakes. At 10:00 p.m. on Christmas Eve, the radio station broadcast a warning about a Category 2 cyclone, christened Tracy, expected to cross the coast close to the city.[76] By dawn on Christmas Day Darwin had been almost completely erased. The small cyclone packed winds up to 150 miles per hour (240 kilometers) and scythed slowly through the city with a forward speed of only 6 miles (10 kilometers) per hour. More than half the houses in the town were destroyed, and all of those built to the latest "cyclone-resistant" standard were gone.[77] Around 70 people died and 650 were injured. The 41,000 left homeless wandered naked or in their nightclothes.

Because the Coriolis force is too weak in a band around the equator that extends about ten degrees of latitude north and south, this region is free of cyclones, and hence of strong winds. Darwin is located 12.5 degrees of latitude from the equator—not quite close enough to be protected. By contrast, the fragile architecture of Bali, with its wooden buildings missing walls and its delicate pagodas, is only possible because the island is 8.5 degrees from the equator and has not experienced high winds, at least not for the last century. But then, in November 2012, Supertyphoon Bopha hit the Philippine island of Mindanao, only 7.5 degrees from the equator, and more than 1,000 were killed.[78] The romantic wooden Balinese architectural style has been copied at resorts across the Caribbean, at latitudes between 15 and 20 degrees, where every few years the Hurricane-Wolf comes rampaging.

What would be the equivalents in our modern rich world of houses "made of straw"? Since the 1950s, a new style of residence has appeared in the United States: the mobile home (now rebranded the "manufactured" home). Mobile homes have proved to be "houses of straw" in tornadoes, getting flipped, rolled, upended, and smashed. From 1985 to 1995, more than 60 percent of the 321 people killed in their homes by twisters were in mobile homes, which housed only 6 percent of the US population during that period.[79] In a mobile home, you were more than twenty times as likely to be killed by a tornado than in permanent housing. The statistics had improved somewhat by the 2006–2011 period, when you were only five times more likely to die in a mobile home, which by then could be tied down.[80]

Mobile homes constructed after 1995 have proved to be more resilient to the wind. A well-regarded theory for what drove this improvement relates it to the 1995 repeal of the federal speed limit of 55 miles per hour, which was raised in most states to 70 miles (112 kilometers) per hour.[81] Mobile homes transported on flatbed trucks at the new speed limit were found to disintegrate during the journey. So that more homes would arrive intact at their destination, improvements had to be made in design and fabrication, and these improvements provided benefits to any mobile home owners who now see a supercell thundercloud advancing toward them. It would not make a suitable motto, but on this occasion, raising the speed limit saved lives. If we increased the speed to 100 miles (160 kilometers) per hour, the mobile home problem would be solved.

5 • RISK MADE CONCRETE

FROM ALEXANDRIA TO NEW YORK AND ON TO DUBAI, RULERS of rich cities have sustained an irrepressible urge to impress their rivals and intimidate their subjects by building bigger and taller.

One thousand years ago, churches across western Europe inherited Roman aqueduct construction techniques, arch upon arch, in the Romanesque style. When the Normans brought this design across the Channel to England, after 1066, and set about applying architectural "shock and awe" to cow the troublesome and hostile inhabitants, they built massive castles for the Norman lords and magnificent cathedrals to impose the power of their appointed bishops; these skyscrapers were two or three times higher than the Anglo-Saxon churches they replaced.[1] Within a few years of the conquest, with the invaders' colossal ambition to raise pinnacles of stone hundreds of feet in the air, thousands of English peasants had been recruited for cathedral construction as quarrymen, carters, masons, and scaffolders to work alongside stonemasons brought over from France. This was a veritable "space race" to reach for the skies.

The most architecturally challenging location for a tower was at the center of the cross-shaped plan, where the apse and choir meet the transept to create the crowning central summit of an English cathedral. To span the space, all the weight of the tower must be transferred to the four massive corner columns.

For the first 200 years, the success rate of these late-eleventh and early-twelfth-century attempts to overcome gravity was comparable to the success rate of the first US space rocket launches between 1957 and 1959—except that the effect of gravity is speeded up in the few-second trajectory of a rocket as compared with the century or two it took a 1,000-ton cathedral tower to crack through its thick stone pillars and plunge to the chancel floor.[2] In England twelve colossal cathedral building projects were under way within thirty years of the Norman landings.[3] Another four were initiated through the first decades of the twelfth century.[4]

The "half-life" of an English Norman tower proved to be somewhere between 100 and 200 years. Of the first crop of late-eleventh- and early-twelfth-century buildings, the central Norman tower at Winchester collapsed in 1202; the southwest tower at Chichester collapsed in 1210; the newly built central tower at St. Davids (in Wales) collapsed in 1220; Lincoln's central tower collapsed in 1237; and the great Norman tower at Ely lasted until 1322. At the largest cathedrals, in fact, Norman towers survived only at Norwich and Durham (although both were significantly reconstructed in the fifteenth century).

(In November 1860, almost 500 years after it was built, jagged cracks began to appear in the piers surrounding the Chichester cathedral crossing.[5] After the choir screen and altar were removed, great tree trunks were brought in to create a wooden framework to carry the colossal load. On Thursday, February 21, 1861, at 3:30 a.m., the final death throes began as one of the upper piers gave way in a series of terrifying explosions, projecting shards of shrapnel limestone across the nave before whole stones began bursting out of the columns. All the workers had withdrawn when, ten hours later, the spire and central tower collapsed into the apse.)

Faced with the early-thirteenth-century stories of tumbling Norman towers, transmitted along the "Masonic grapevine," cathedral builders began to check some of their wilder ambitions.[6] Without even knowing the cause, the news of crashes in England discouraged further high flying.

In France in the late twelfth and thirteenth centuries, cathedral builders evolved new styles of lightweight architecture with pointed arches and windows (called "Frankish" at the time and only later disparaged as "Gothic").[7] Lightweight structures were fine for handling vertical loads, as there was simply less weight to be carried. However, the mass of the thick Norman stone columns and walls served to prevent a structure from becoming pushed outward, whether by the load of a pitched roof or from storm winds.[8]

At the Church of Notre Dame Paris, during the thirteenth century, the lightweight walls started to suffer stress fractures and bulge out of line, inspiring the agile improvisation of flying buttresses, spider-leg props made to look as if they were part of the original design.[9]

As some of the largest of all structures, cathedrals were the most susceptible to the long-period ground motions of great earthquakes.[10] In Lisbon the naves of almost all the principal churches and chapels of the city collapsed on November 1, 1755. Spanish attempts to build European-style cathedrals in their colonies, as at Lima, Arequipa, Santiago, Concepcion, and Manila, were all demolished by earthquakes.

———

IN THE MIDDLE OF THE NINETEENTH CENTURY, THE CONSTRUCTION of tall buildings underwent a revolution from the application of physics. In 1866, William Rankine, engineer and physicist, articulated the concept of the "safety factor": "the ratio of the ultimate strength of the material to the maximum stress permissible" from the loads acting on a structure.[11] Engineers should work to a safety factor high enough to ensure that engineered structures, such as bridges or tall buildings, stayed standing in all anticipated physical conditions. The weight of the structure provided the first set of loads; then there were the "live loads," such as from trains passing over a bridge or the people crowded into a building; last were the infrequent extraordinary loads from strong winds or earthquakes.[12]

Instead of using traditional "assembled" building materials, such as brick and rubble walls or wooden beams, engineers switched to manufactured elements like iron and steel girders, whose strength and ability to withstand compression and tension or to resist sideways shear could be measured and predicted. Based on the physics, structural engineers could design tall structures that would remain standing indefinitely in effect. Under normal conditions, skyscrapers simply do not fall down.[13]

To resist storm winds, a load of 30 pounds per exposed square foot of the walls was assumed for the first tall buildings in New York and Chicago, with 20 pounds per square foot assumed for the calmer climate of San Francisco. In rebuilding San Francisco after 1906, engineers had no idea how to assess earthquake loads on a tall structure. Instead, they assumed that an earthquake raised the wind load to 30 pounds per square foot. Concerned with the extra cost, however, architects soon argued the assumed load back down to only half this level.

These assumptions were based on a misunderstanding of the basic difference between earthquake and wind forces. Wind attempts to push a building over, and the mass of the building and its foundations must be built to prevent that. An earthquake arrives through the foundations. When the mass of the building resists the horizontal movement through inertia, the building is left behind. How far and how fast it is left behind will determine whether it stays standing.

———

THE IDEA FOR STRENGTHENING CONCRETE WITH IRON AND STEEL rods had no single inventor but was the product of many practical artisans and engineers in France, Belgium, Britain, and America, most of whom had little interest in documenting their experiments.[14] Marc Isambard Brunel in 1825 had the original idea to interlace iron reinforcing rods through brickwork on the original Thames Tunnel.[15] New stronger Portland cement, fired at higher temperatures, was patented in England around 1850; rich in calcium silicates, it reacts with water to crystallize around the sand or gravel and create a strong artificial stone.

Take a cement paving stone and bang one edge down on something hard and solid and it will break like porcelain. Do the same with a bar of steel and you will hurt your arm. Unlike concrete, steel does not simply break when stretched or knocked. Yet steel is expensive, and it rusts when exposed to the air. So the idea emerged to unite steel's strength when pulled or knocked with the enclosing rigid properties of the concrete—yang and yin—to make a strong and resistant composite medium. Concrete and steel are also strangely compatible in how much they expand or contract with temperature.

By the start of the 1890s, this experimental material, known by its French name "ferroconcrete," had become mainstream, and the first rules for how steel and concrete should be united had been published. The composite medium seemed to have infinite potential.

Rather than devise more elaborate reinforcing to salvage brick, the solution finally emerged, like a Zen koan: keep the reinforcing but discard the brick. Instead of elaborating ways to interlace brick with steel bars, the solution was to pour a liquid into formwork shaped to create a wall, roof, or pillar and let it set as an artificial rock around the steel. A wall of concrete could be poured much faster than a wall of brick could be laid, and a reinforced-concrete building frame was far cheaper than one manufactured from steel alone.

———

THE SEVENTEENTH-CENTURY CAMPAIGN TO SWITCH CONSTRUCTION from wood and thatch to brick and tile marked the first round in a campaign to make the fire-resistant city. Yet, while brick walls provided fire-resistant shielding, inside buildings contained the same wooden beams, floors, rafters, and window frames as in their medieval ancestors.

Truly "fire-resistive" construction required that buildings be made with only incombustible materials, so that floors, roofs, and walls would all be firebreaks. Once it was learned how to build taller iron-and-steel-frame buildings, such structures were not allowed in the central business districts of the principal US cities until, for the safety of the occupants, they could be made fire-resistive. Initially, floors were constructed out of hollow brick arches between iron or steel beams. In the 1870s, a British architect, Richard Dawnay, laid a wide concrete floor, reinforced with iron bars and small joists, over a span of 20 feet (6 meters) and went on to install this novel type of fire-resistant flooring in more than 3,000 buildings.[16]

Two great city fires, in Baltimore in 1905 and San Francisco in 1906, provided the final clues in the mission to create the fireproof city. In both cities, flames from adjacent properties had gotten inside buildings believed to be fireproof through heat-shattered windows. But by 1910, once builders had removed the flammable neighbors and installed powerful sprinkler systems, supplied by rooftop tanks, the conflagrations that had consumed US city centers for more than 100 years had gone away. It was like the successful eradication of a lethal infectious disease.

IN SAN FRANCISCO BEFORE 1906, THE BRICKLAYERS UNION HAD seen the introduction of reinforced concrete as a direct threat to its members. Large quantities of concrete could be poured without having to employ the trowel skills of a Union "brickie." San Francisco was a union town, and the bricklayers used their influence to get reinforced-concrete construction banned.[17]

After the 1906 earthquake, the union's attitude contributed to the enthusiasm now lavished on the reinforced-concrete buildings that had been built in other towns around the San Francisco Bay. In Alameda, "a two story reinforced concrete building stands intact, while a brick building only 50 feet away is badly wrecked."[18] John B. Leonard wrote that "an inquiry among architects and engineers, together with my own observations, has failed to reveal any instance of failure on the part of reinforced concrete" in the whole Bay Area.[19]

The ban on reinforced-concrete (RC) construction in San Francisco was lifted ten weeks after the earthquake.[20] Within a year, there were more than seventy RC office buildings and warehouses in the city. Apart from Edward J. Brandon of the Bricklayers Union, who urged the supervisors to reject the new building code, the only opposition came from the manufacturers of the more expensive steel frames. They had a point: none of the new iron-and-steel-frame high-rise building designs were significantly damaged by the earthquake, and while several were burned out, many were later rehabilitated.

Perhaps the most neutral and informed opinion came (once again) from the young associate professor of engineering at the University of California. Charles Derleth Jr. warned of the dangers of assuming that RC construction provided a panacea; weaknesses in the way vertical and horizontal beams were interlinked in RC structures, he cautioned, could make them prone to collapse under earthquake loads.[21] His note of caution was not lost on the Japanese engineer Toshikata Sano, who returned to Japan from what he had seen in San Francisco a strong champion of properly designed RC construction. In 1915 he proclaimed that ferroconcrete was the solution to making buildings in Japan both fire- and earthquake-proof—and the answer to brick's inadequacies.[22] "In earthquake country like Japan," Sano wrote, "construction took precedent over design" while aesthetic concerns were "only women's things." His proposals proved enormously influential and led to the proliferation across Tokyo of plain, two- to five-story reinforced-concrete buildings.

Sano proposed that the earthquake forces on a structure could be represented as a horizontal acceleration.[23] This notion gave engineers a parameter that they could plug into their physics-based models of building design. In 1920 the architect Naitō Tachū calculated the earthquake loads in the design of all his new buildings and then had the good fortune to see his engineered buildings survive the 1923 earthquake.[24]

A 1920 law in Tokyo had limited buildings to 100 feet (30 meters) high. Over the next two decades, concrete cityscapes rolled out across Japan. Even up to the 1960s, there were very few buildings in Japan that reached above the sixth or eighth story.

———

BETWEEN 1910 AND 1920, THE MOST ADVENTUROUS ARCHITECTS adopted ferroconcrete to define a new aesthetic—a style that made a clean break with the traditions and ornamentation of nineteenth-century architecture.

In 1926 the Swiss French architect Le Corbusier, self-proclaimed leader of the modernist movement, set out his manifesto: "the five points for a new architecture."[25]

1. An open first floor in which the weight of the building is carried by a small number of *pilotis*, thin columns that operate like timber piles supporting a platform in the sea
2. The *free plan*, in which there is no restriction on the positions of interior walls, as they do not need to be load-bearing
3. The *free facade*, an entirely open front
4. *Strip windows*—large sheets of glass in the curtain walls
5. *Roof terraces* on the flat concrete roofs

These innovations were all facilitated by reinforced concrete, a medium that enabled exhilarating architectural freedom. No longer did a room have to have four walls, or doors and windows that occupied only one-quarter of the wall space, or walls directly above the walls on the floor below. The Villa Savoye in Poissy, constructed between 1928 and 1931, combined all five points of Le Corbusier's new "international style": a raised, white, single-story rectangular structure that had long strip windows and "floated" high off the ground on thin concrete pilotis.[26]

The new architecture would redefine how people lived. In 1922, Le Corbusier introduced his vision of the "Contemporary City": sixty-story skyscrapers, arranged on a grid, housing 3 million people, and surrounded by open spaces.[27] In 1925 he proposed that eighteen of these "Croix de Lorraine" cruciform-plan buildings replace the cluttered center of Paris north of the River Seine. In 1933 he launched his "Obus" proposal, in which the corniche at Algiers would be graced with a 9-mile-long (15-kilometer-long), fourteen-floor apartment building, housing 180,000 people, and capped with a rooftop highway.[28]

There was one small problem with Le Corbusier's new aesthetic: it was deadly in earthquakes. It took forty years for the flaw to become exposed. The only mass housing complex he did actually complete was in Marseilles, immediately after the Second World War, but by then a whole generation of his architect disciples had gone out to design and build the massive, concrete, high-rise public housing projects that came to characterize cities of the world in the 1950s and 1960s.

The role of the open floor in building collapse was first spotted in the aftermath of the Magnitude 6.5 earthquake close to Caracas, Venezuela, in 1967.[29] Four multistory apartment buildings collapsed and 240 people died. The Palace Corvin had an H-shaped plan, with two identical rectangular buildings (the verticals of the H) joined in the center by a "circulation block" of staircases. One of the two buildings had an open ground floor of columns to create space for parking, while the other building had walled apartments all the way through the ground floor. The building with the open ground-floor parking space collapsed. The other building was completely undamaged. The lesson could not have been clearer: the open floor had created a fatal weakness.

The four stories of the 1960s Olive View Hospital in Sylmar, on the northeast edge of Los Angeles, were supported by open piloti columns on the lower floors. In the 1971 San Fernando earthquake, the columns were so badly damaged that the whole building had to be demolished.[30]

Le Corbusier's first three points all referenced the open floor, straddled by his favorite pilotis. The idea of the open floor caught on, not simply for its aesthetics but because of its practicality. Elevating the building created space: both public space for pedestrians and private space for car parking, shops with their large glass facades, and reception areas in hospitals, restaurants, and hotel ballrooms. The open ground floor, made possible by reinforced concrete, became a standard functional component of urban design.

When a building with an open ground floor swings backward and forward, however, all the motion concentrates on the open floor, stressing the concrete pillars or the remaining walls, potentially all the way to the breaking point. If the pillars break, the whole building can collapse. The open story is "soft": lacking in rigidity, it is the weakest link. Engineers named this behavior the "soft story failure."

However, it took the earthquake damage in Mexico City in 1985 before the scale of the problem was recognized.[31] The city center buildings had not been designed in anticipation of strong and slow earthquake shaking. A large, long-lasting, distant earthquake off the shore of central Mexico caused the former lake basin at the heart of Mexico City to oscillate like a drum, about once every two seconds— the same resonant frequency as ten- to twenty-story buildings. As a result, 400 multistory buildings partly or completely collapsed. At the Tlatelolco apartment complex, the fifteen-story Nuevo León building pulled out of its foundations on one side and toppled to the ground like an overturned tree. At the steel-frame Conjunto Pino Suárez building, a twenty-one-story tower suffered column buckling and took out the adjacent fourteen-story tower in its fall. The most common cause of collapse was found to be inadequate linkages between columns and beams and between columns and slabs. Many buildings were over-loaded relative to the strength of their supports.

The evidence for soft story failure was now so pressing that in 1987 and 1988 it was included in the next generation of Mexican and US building codes, to be applied for new construction.[32] These codes stressed the need to check the "degree of vertical structural irregularity." Where shear walls form the main resistant elements of the upper floors of a building, they need to be continuous all the way down to the ground level; "to interrupt this load path is a fundamental error." In the Bay Area ("Loma Prieta") earthquake of 1989 in California, half of the homes that became uninhabitable were the victims of soft story damage.[33]

It was fortunate that, because he worked principally in Europe, the buildings that Le Corbusier had himself designed rarely encountered strong shaking. This was not the case, however, for the National Museum of Western Modern Art, established in Tokyo in 1959; based on one of Le Corbusier's designs, it included his familiar piloti structure of open columnar supports on the ground floor. In the early 1990s, a leading Japanese professor of earthquake engineering commented: "My apologies to Le Corbusier but the evaluation of seismic capacity of this building was terrible. [We] had to conclude that this building survived thus far only because no big earthquake had hit the building. If left untreated visitors may be in danger."[34] Unable to transform the piloti structure without ruining the design, and "because everyone admitted that this architecture was successfully meeting various emotional requirements that are deeply associated with our own time," in 1995 the Japanese added an expensive "base isolation system" beneath the building's foundations so as to prevent the vibrations of the earth from demolishing the structure.[35]

Meanwhile, as the epitome of twentieth-century modernism, buildings with open ground floors have continued to proliferate. In every city from Ashgabat, Turkmenistan, to Lima, Peru, there are now multistory offices above storefronts with thin load-bearing pillars or twenty-story tower blocks perched on stilts. In San Juan, Puerto Rico, there are fifteen-story office buildings on top of five stories of open car parking. There seems to be no place in the language of architects and town planners commissioning more and more open ground floors in their designs for the vocabulary of earthquake engineers seeking to outlaw "vertical structural irregularity."

———

BY THE 1980S, BETTER RECORDINGS OF ACTUAL EARTHQUAKE VI-brations, allied with computer modeling, had transformed the understanding of how earthquakes damage buildings. A building has a "resonant period"—the pulse at which it will naturally oscillate (like rocking a dead tree). If the earthquake is big enough and the vibrations last for tens of seconds, the vibrations may tune in to the building's natural resonant period, and then the shaking can become amplified with each vibration.[36] Moreover, the clashing resonant vibrations of adjacent short and tall buildings can smash up against one another. Close to a breaking fault, the ground can move by several meters and at speeds sufficient to threaten the elastic response of a tall building.

If the earthquake was generated by vertical movement along a fault, it will radiate vertical accelerations. As the ground lurches upward, the building is launched as if on a trampoline, only to come crashing down again, so that the whole weight of the overlying structure can be doubled on the floors below. In addition, all the individual components of the building frame will be moving, concentrating stress at the joints. A rectangle of beams will skew one way and then the other. If a floor beam is simply resting, the ledge may move enough to let it fall. Stresses will be raised where load becomes concentrated on narrow columns.

Engineers learned that there are two ways of making frame buildings earthquake-resistant. In the first, the steel or heavily reinforced concrete "moment-resisting" frame of the building is so strong, and the beams and columns so rigidly connected, that it holds together through the motions.[37] If flexed too far, the frame components are expected to buckle rather than break. The floors and walls are tied to the frame, but internal panel walls may become smashed as the frame flexes and distorts, so the panels must not be made so strong that they crack the adjacent beam. An alternative way to resist sideways forces is to build strong shearwalls: out of vertical plywood sheets in a wood frame house, or from masonry wall panels compressed within cast-in-situ reinforced concrete beams, thus creating a honeycomb of walls and beams that resists distortion, as all the components are tightly locked together.

Overall, since the lessons acquired in Mexico City in 1985, the most modern high-rise buildings have proved robust in strong shaking. No tall buildings collapsed in the 1994 Northridge, California, earthquake (although months later it was discovered that one in twenty of the rigid welded joints of steel frame buildings had broken).[38] In the 2010 Chile earthquake, only one high-rise building collapsed, after swaying so strongly that it tore off its cavernous foundations.[39]

Yet no one really knows how high-rise buildings will perform when tested in great earthquakes, especially within a few miles of a big fault rupture. The number of tall buildings continues to rise, and hundreds of them are located in coastal cities exposed to the largest earthquakes. There are more than 1,100 in Tokyo, 650 in Vancouver, 600 in Taiwan, and almost 300 each in Lima and Panama City (where the towers are particularly slender).[40]

———

THE KEY TO GETTING CONCRETE AND STEEL TO UNITE THEIR YIN-and-yang properties is "detailing."[41] Detailing defines precisely what steel reinforcing rods must be used and how they are to be arranged—the inner metal skeleton supporting the rigid concrete matrix. The twisted steel rods need to be of the right width—not too fat and not too thin—to strengthen the concrete beam or slab. They cannot be placed too close to one another or the beam could split. Bars near the edge of a beam could lead to the concrete "spalling"—breaking off in flakes. The vertical steel bars inside a column need to be bound to one another with confining stirrups so that one bar does not get pulled out of place when the beam is stressed. Where the beam is longer than the steel, the bars must be carefully overlapped and spliced. The detailing becomes most critical at junctions, where a column meets a horizontal concrete beam, or a column supports a slab, or a balcony overhangs from a wall.[42]

Today the configuration of steel rebar is specified by CAD software, which models the stresses and strains to which the concrete structure will be subject, both under the live loads in the building and under earthquake loads. The contractor then has to create the skeleton of steel bars according to the engineer's precise specification. Bending and cutting thick steel rods into the right set of lengths and angles requires a large and expensive machine. The steelwork is laid in position by the contractor, and the engineer returns to check that it has been done exactly as specified. The engineer tests whether the fresh concrete mix is the right composition and ensures that it has not started to set; then the mix is poured into the temporary shuttering, vibrated down to eliminate air pockets, and allowed to slowly set.

You get the picture! This is complicated stuff, more difficult than the most elaborate Escoffier recipe, and with far more serious consequences than a disconsolate diner if the recipe (the detailing) goes wrong.

The engineers have to check each other's work and keep detailed records. Structural engineers have spent four or five years in college to acquire strong backgrounds in mathematics and physics and experience of construction projects. Indeed, it was the challenges of working with reinforced concrete and steel that created the profession of structural engineer.

ASK ANYONE: WHAT IS THE DEADLIEST WHITE POWDER SOLD ON the street, first synthesized in the nineteenth century? *Heroin? Cocaine?* they may suggest. *Crystal meth?*

The answer? Portland cement.

Worldwide hundreds of thousands have already died and more than a million more will inevitably follow over the next forty years. Yet the majority of people entombed in their houses never bought or touched the powder, but were simply innocent secondary victims.

Since the middle of the twentieth century, the mountain roads and desert tracks of Turkey, Iran, and northern Pakistan; the jungle trails of Venezuela, Guatemala, and Ecuador; the barren steppes of Tajikistan and Azerbaijan—all have echoed to the roar of over-loaded lorries, straining uphill, stacked with bags of cement. There are now few villages in Asia or Central America that have not seen a smoke-spewing, open-backed, dust-covered truck with broken shock absorbers, dumping heavy paper sacks of cement to be sold in the local builder's yard.

Before 1960, cement was available in developing countries only for big government-financed infrastructure projects like bridges and dams. In 1947, there were four cement factories in Pakistan, producing half a million tons each year. By 2010, production was 44 million tons, a nearly hundredfold increase in sixty years. In many countries there is now a cement glut, which keeps prices low. In place of patronizing a local lime-kiln for a key building material, or digging out a supply of mud, villagers now purchase cement off some distant corporation. Yet cement has also brought modernity and globalization. Small-town builders can create five-story apartment buildings and the large shop window openings they have only previously seen in the movies.

There is only one problem with the wild architectural dreams triggered by the white powder. No one in these provincial towns knows how to build safely with cement. The same artisan builders who mortared stones or bricks to make a wall have now accommodated themselves to the new material. Steel reinforcing is a particular mystery. Steel is expensive, and most local builders have no chance of finding the equipment to bend steel rods for detailing at connections.

Throughout the twentieth century, a widening schism opened between rich and poor countries around reinforced concrete. In rich countries, concrete construction designed using the latest finite element software is supervised by qualified engineers. In developing countries there are no engineers. Anyone bright and motivated enough to become an engineer goes to college and emigrates to America or Dubai or Germany. Engineers expect to be well paid.

If reinforced concrete were no more than a formula, there would be some chance that the recipe could be followed anywhere in the world.

For laying a concrete path, it does not really matter if the aggregate is laced with sea salt or the proportion of cement is cut by half. But for an eight-story building, what is happening inside each beam and joint matters. It is impossible to understand what "detailing" accomplishes unless the designer has been trained as a structural engineer and understands about materials and forces and failure tolerance. Once the concrete is poured, the detailing is completely invisible—unless and until the building collapses. (I have seen drink cans, cigarette packets, and purely cosmetic offcuts of rebar with no concrete attached.)

After the modest February 29, 1960, earthquake at Agadir, Morocco, in which 10,000 died, J. Despeyroux, the French government chief engineer, visited the city and in his report triaged the buildings into three classes: (1) "the old or poor masonry houses"; (2) "the smaller city-like buildings, erected without any technical care"; and (3) "the Modern European Buildings." "The first two classes," he wrote, "are of no interest for our purposes."[43] In a 230-page report from the US Earthquake Engineering Research Institute on the 1972 Managua earthquake, only two were devoted to the "ordinary buildings" that were the source of almost all the 11,000 fatalities.[44] From the perspective of a structural engineer writing for other engineers, there is nothing to learn from these dangerous informal buildings. Only the "Modern European Buildings," Despeyroux proclaimed, "held any useful lessons that can be taken and applied by engineers in future buildings." Among the thousands of engineers who visit earthquake-damaged cities, almost all ask this same question: what engineering lessons can be learned? It would take orthogonal thinking to ask instead: what action(s) would most improve the construction of ordinary buildings in this country?

The lessons on building failures collected on earthquake field missions in Pakistan or Haiti today are pretty much identical to those gathered fifty years ago (so much so that structural engineers get bored witnessing them). It all comes down to bad design, bad execution, bad reinforcing, and bad concrete. The schism between the rich world and the developing world over reinforced-concrete construction has been known for seventy years. After the 1944 earthquake demolished the adobe city of San Juan in Argentina, a local judge demanded that all future construction be entrusted to engineers, "not builders with no technical knowledge or homeowners themselves."[45] To allow an untrained builder to create a building out of concrete without the attentions of a structural engineer is like giving a child a loaded automatic weapon.

You can get some idea of the impact of the great wave of concrete construction in lower- and middle-income countries by surveying what has happened in earthquakes. In the Magnitude 7.3 earthquake that hit Adapazari, Turkey, in 1967, eighty-six people died. The majority of residential buildings were of wood and stone construction. They took some damage but generally stayed standing. In a similar-sized (Magnitude 7.4) earthquake that broke thirty years later, on August 17, 1999, to the west of the 1967 shock, at Kocaeli 40 miles (60 kilometers) south of Istanbul, 115,000 buildings collapsed and 17,118 died. The fallen buildings included more than 3,000 total "pancake" collapses of unlicensed five- to seven-story concrete apartment blocks, built within the previous thirty years.[46] (Above that height an elevator would be required, inviting the attentions of an engineer.) In the 1999 Chi-Chi earthquake in Taiwan, one-third of the more than 2,000 people killed were in reinforced-concrete structures as much as ten to fifteen stories high. Only buildings above 165 feet (50 meters) in height were required to have their structure reviewed by an engineer.[47]

I HAD A MORNING MEETING IN A BALTIMORE HOTEL TO TALK TO insurers about storm risks. The plan was to leave at lunchtime to take a train to catch an afternoon flight from Newark. (I still have my unused United Airways Newark–to–San Francisco ticket from September 11, 2001.)

About 9:00 a.m., I was setting up a presentation when someone beckoned us to come and watch the TV in the hotel bar. Transfixed by what was unfolding, I recall the extraordinary moment close to 10:00 a.m. when, in the background, the South Tower of the World Trade Center began its terrible descent. The reporter, speaking to the camera, had yet to notice. The avalanche–dust-storm–squall-front surging through the canyon streets looked like the collapse of a volcanic plug.

The next day I took a train to Manhattan and slipped through the police barriers to check out how far the collateral damage had spread. The thick drifts of dust I tramped through had carpeted the streets and looked just like the aftermath of an eruption.

The collapse of the World Trade Center towers was shattering and extraordinary. People in northern Europe, the United States, and Japan go through a lifetime never witnessing a building collapse. Yet, if you are one of the 12 million inhabitants of Cairo, the collapse of a building would seem so everyday an occurrence as to be hardly worth retelling. Like car accidents, building collapses in many locales gain local headlines only when more than a handful of people have been killed.

The collapse of an eleven-story building in Alexandria in June 2012 inspired the first-ever survey of spontaneous demolition in Egypt. Over the following twelve months, almost 400 buildings collapsed in that country, killing a total of 192 people.[48] These collapses are what structural engineers call "intensity zero damage"—"intensity zero" because there was no earthquake. The toll only increases when some ground shaking is added to the mix. On October 12, 1992, a modest (Magnitude 5.9) earthquake 21 miles (35 kilometers) south of Cairo resulted in the collapse of 200 buildings in the city, including one fourteen-story building in which seventy-two died.[49] Many of these buildings would have collapsed anyway in time, but they would have done so with more crackings and grumblings in the fabric of the structure—these symptoms, which typically extend over days or weeks and indicate that a collapse is under way, serve as warnings for the inhabitants to move out ahead of the inevitable. The 1992 earthquake "harvested" these buildings early, like forest treefall in a winter storm. Almost 4,000 buildings took some structural damage; before embarking on their inevitable downward journey, they were classed as "severely damaged." Three thousand families had to be rehoused.

Why are buildings in Cairo so prone to fall? For every twenty-five buildings in Egyptian cities, only two are officially registered, and only one does not violate the city's building code in one way or another. A building may start off legal but then drop out of the system. The fourteen-story building that collapsed in the earthquake was a licensed eight-story building to which the owner had informally added six additional stories, almost doubling his rental income.

In 1999, Salah Hassaballah, the former minister of housing, claimed that three-quarters of the buildings across Egypt might collapse in the next twenty years as a result of "insufficient maintenance."[50] Ten years after the 1992 earthquake, the Ministry of Housing identified 180,000 buildings in Cairo and 2 million nationwide "on the brink of collapse."

Cairo is not alone. Many other crowded cities in the developing world suffer from "falling building sickness." In Nigeria, the city engineer's office can only keep tally of the collapses: one every fifty-two days between January 2000 and June 2007.[51] Spontaneous demolition does not discriminate: apartment buildings, houses, hotels, a mosque, and several schools have all fallen down. In one 1999 school collapse at Port Harcourt, fifty students were killed as the owner was adding extra floors during the school day.[52] But this is not just an African problem.[53] In any country without a well-enforced building code, even new buildings collapse.

Four thousand years ago, Babylon was the original crowded thriving city: space was tight within the protective city wall, and the city was beset by falling buildings. Around 1700 BC, King Hammurabi set out the responsibilities of a builder for his construction defects: "If a builder builds a house for someone, and does not construct it properly, and the house which he built falls in and kills its owner, then that builder shall be put to death."[54] Building collapse had become a hot-ticket political problem. Hammurabi's edicts are the oldest surviving "building regulations"—acknowledgment that a building is a loaded weapon for which the builder maintains the liability.

Building collapse was a problem for all ancient towns and cities. In a reflection on whether those killed accidentally are innocent, Jesus asks: "Or those eighteen, upon whom the tower in Siloam fell, and slew them, think ye that they were sinners above all men that dwelt in Jerusalem?" (Luke 13:4). The Siloam tower tragedy was evidently common knowledge to his audience. Building collapse was the most salient example of mass accidental death, just as an air crash might be to us today. Around 500 years earlier, Simonides of Ceos is said to have invented the "Art of Memory" when challenged to identify all the other diners who were crushed by a collapsed building after he alone had stepped outside of the banquet hall.

In the cities of ancient Greece and Rome, the most important civic and religious buildings—the temples and triumphal arches, the Colosseum and the Pantheon—were "overengineered": they were made more robust than was strictly necessary by builders who would have done anything to ensure that their reputation did not collapse with the structure. As a result, many were built so strongly that they remain standing today. Yet these massive public buildings were not typical of the residences of the majority of people in Rome: crowded six- to nine-story *insula* tenement buildings that were prone to collapse, just like the buildings of ancient Babylon or twenty-first-century Cairo.[55]

Beyond threatening the life of the builder, a building code requires the rule of law and only works if there are penalties when the code is ignored. Officials have to scrutinize all building plans and visit construction sites to check for compliance. Inspectors need to be vigilant and to have not only impeccable ethics but sufficient salary, so that they cannot readily be bribed. Buildings have to be torn down if constructed outside the code. All of these conditions sound possible in a rich country.

Many poorer countries have acquired building codes, but in most of them these codes are not applied. This is how it works in the informal economy: someone constructs a building without official authorization or planning approval. The builder meets an inspector in a café. Coffee is drunk and cigarettes are smoked, some money changes hands, and now there is a certificate to show that the building is "authorized" and complies with the regulations.[56]

If you do not have the capacity to borrow a building code, you are inevitably going to have problems with buildings and disasters. Corruption and earthquake casualties are both manifestations of weak governance, and in a corrupt country, construction is the most corrupt sector.[57] In 2010 Haiti, so poor and ungoverned, there was no building code, and Haiti is number 175 out of 178 on Transparency International's list of the most corrupt countries.

Spontaneous collapse reveals how the building stock will perform in a big earthquake. On November 7, 2008, a school collapsed in Pétionville near Port au Prince, leaving eighty-four dead.[58] Four days later, with the media still focused on the Pétionville story, it was reported that at least nine people were injured when a private school collapsed in the capital. Fortunately, the schoolchildren were outside at break.

In the shantytown of Cité Soleil, home to more than a quarter of a million of the poorest of the poor in Haiti, the houses have cement walls with corrugated metal or polythene roofs— scavenged materials that are too insubstantial to cause much injury in an earthquake. With a little more money, people could pay to escape damage from the frequent hurricanes by living in blockwork buildings with concrete roofs. In the absence of any controls, the poorest lived at the bottom of the steep slopes of the ravines, where the sewage flowed when it rained, while those at the top of the slope even had balconies for the view. When the slab roof of one house was liberated from a collapsing wall in the 2010 earthquake, it slid into the next house, and then so on down the slope, all of them collapsing like houses of cards. The casualties completely overwhelmed the municipal authorities.[59]

Around 30 percent of the 400,000 concrete buildings were repairable, and aid agencies brought in structural engineers to supervise repairs on 10,000 of them.[60] In the weeks following, desperate to escape from the temporary encampments, the majority of owners returned to patch up the cracks gashed through their concrete roofs and walls, wounds that will be exploited the next time the city is strongly shaken.

A plate boundary fault cuts through the hills on the edge of the city. After the 2010 earthquake, Port au Prince should have been relocated, but there was not enough government even to propose the option. Like New Orleans after Katrina, both emotionally and politically, the city is too big and has too much history and pride.

———

TENS OF MILLIONS OF FRAGILE CONCRETE BUILDINGS HAVE BEEN constructed in earthquake zones. Multistory buildings, poised on weak and unconnected supports, with all their weight suspended in the air, are weapons of mass destruction, raised blunt guillotine blades, and all it will take is the wall props moving and the concrete floors and roof beams slipping for the deadly weight of these buildings to be sent crashing down, potentially killing everyone inside. Hundreds of thousands of buildings will collapse in earthquakes over the next twenty years. Many of the people these buildings are going to kill are already living in them.

We can attribute responsibility to the slogan: "It's not the earthquake that kills you, *it's the builders*."

———

HOW WOULD WE NOW REWRITE "THE STORY OF THE THREE LITTLE Pigs and the Big Bad Wolf" to reflect earthquake construction in poor countries?

The first little pig meets a man with a load of mud bricks and rubble stones and constructs a heavy-walled traditional house. The Quake-Wolf comes along and shakes and quakes the house, and it falls down and injures the little pig.

The second little pig meets a man with a load of cement and, without reinforcement or an engineer, creates a set of concrete columns and a heavy concrete lid roof. Then, with little effort, the Quake-Wolf shakes the building to destruction, killing the little pig.

The third little pig meets a man with a load of wooden beams and branches, out of which he constructs a boat builder's frame of a half-timbered house, filled with rigid triangles. The Quake-Wolf shakes and quakes the house, but while some of the plaster panels fall out, the building does not fall down.

6 • MR. HEATH'S LITTLE BLACK BOOK

IMAGINE YOUR FATHER LOOKS AT DISASTERS FROM A BUILDER'S perspective and your mother has the eyes of a catastrophe scientist. What kind of child would you be? What insights do you bring?

We have met the scientists, architects, engineers, and builders. Now I would like to introduce another member of the "disasters academy": the insurers. They bring a new practical perspective to thinking about calamity, one based around the idea of risk.

In medieval Denmark, Germany, England, and Sweden, if a fire destroyed a house, there would be collections among all the families in a parish to help the victim rebuild.[1] However, such compensation could not be relied upon. What if there had been a poor harvest and the neighbors were broke? "Charity briefs"—collections to support victims—became so common in seventeenth-century London that the diarist Samuel Pepys, in 1661, admitted to charity brief fatigue.[2] The question arose: why not create a system in which the recoveries are guaranteed? Such a system would have to come at a price—so what price would be fair?

In 1635 the first business plan for a fire insurance system was presented to the Royal Privy Council in London.[3] For each £100 of coverage, property owners would subscribe one shilling (5 pence). The king endorsed the proposal, adding the rider that "no man be pressed to come in to subscribe, but every man left to his voluntary choice."[4]

Before the first policies could be sold, civil war broke out in England; for two decades, gunfire and siege were greater hazards than the occasional house fire. Civil war was followed by the execution of the king, the autocratic rule of Parliament, and finally, in 1660, the restoration of King Charles II.

What would catalyze fire insurance was not a better business plan but an unattended baker's oven in a house in Pudding Lane, a narrow medieval street of overhanging, wood-framed, thatched properties running down to the Thames in the heart of the City of London. The date was September 1, 1666. With the wind blowing strongly from the east, the flames spread to Thames Street and its wooden warehouses, their cellars filled with oil, tallow, and hemp. By Sunday morning, the whole neighborhood was ablaze. For four days the conflagration spread, principally to the west and north, but also back as far as the Tower of London to the east. By the time the wind turned and blew the fire back on its own embers, the charred wasteland ran one mile east-west and half a mile north-south.[5] The principal buildings of business and trade in the city, the Royal Exchange, the Customs House, and the halls of forty-four companies had all been destroyed, along with 13,000 houses. The ruined Cathedral Church of St. Paul's and eighty-seven parish churches were now skeletons of crumbling walls, ash, and rubble.

The experience of the fire in the year after the terrible plague (the last such epidemic in London) would remain seared into the memory of the inhabitants for two generations.[6] Fear is a rich culture on which to grow insurance. In the visionary plans for the new city set out by Sir Christopher Wren in 1667, there was even a site for a public "Insurance Office." In the Rebuilding Act of the same year, only 9,000 houses were licensed, and all were to be built of brick or stone, with roofs of tiles.[7] (In fact, James I had decreed back in 1605 that all new properties in the City of London were to be of brick and stone, with tiled roofs, but as with many building codes to the present day, the order was widely ignored.[8])

Head up Fish Hill close to the river in the City of London and there in the middle of the street stands "the Monument," the world's tallest—

at 210 feet (62 meters)—Roman-style Doric column mounted on a 33-foot-square (10-meter-square) plinth surmounted with stone griffins, built to celebrate the reconstruction of London after the 1666 Great Fire.[9] Completed in 1677, the Monument has an interior helical staircase that gives access to a summit platform, surmounted by a golden orb symbolizing rebirth out of fire. From the elevated viewing platform at the fire's epicenter, one could gaze across the rooftops of the reconstructed city—the late-seventeenth-century equivalent of being taken for a helicopter ride to ogle the prime real estate. The fire was history by then. The risk had drained away, and people could move on.

The first private fire insurance scheme, the "Fire Office," was launched in September 1681 by Dr. Nicholas Barbon (whose full name—Nicholas If-Jesus-Christ-Had-Not-Died-For-Thee-Thou-Hadst-Been-Damned Barbon—was shortened by his many adversaries to "Damned Barbon"). He was the son of a rabble-rousing Baptist minister in Cromwell's Parliament who, after earning a degree in medicine at the University of Leiden, became a speculative builder.[10] Barbon proposed to limit himself to selling 5,000 policies for terms up to thirty-one years.[11] As security, he offered the annual ground rents of £2,100 on his properties. Within two months, he had competition. The Corporation of London launched its own public insurance scheme, offering any term from one to 100 years and undercutting premiums from 3 shillings, 9 pennies (18 pence) per £100 for one year's coverage up to £4 per £100 "in perpetuity."

Barbon fought back, accusing the Corporation of London of an unviable business model. To run insurance in perpetuity, he claimed, "is to Spoil the Whole design; because no Security can be good where all the Profit is at first Received, and the loss is Uncertain, and Continues for ever, for the Loss being uncertain, the Security cannot be proportioned."[12]

However, the City of London insurance company fell into a dispute with the Crown that led, in 1683, to the loss of its charter. In the same year, Barbon (who claimed to have 4,000 policyholders on his books) gained a new competitor: the Friendly Society for Securing Houses from Loss by Fire, a mutual insurer in which every member paid his share of all the losses. Barbon ridiculed the Friendly Society's lack of an experienced fire brigade, as compared with his own band of "Watermen and other lusty Persons . . . in liverie with Badges" who were tasked with extinguishing fires in the properties they insured.[13]

Another mutual, the Amicable Contributorship, which became known by its badge "The Hand in Hand," arrived in 1696. Within a few years, the Hand in Hand held 7,313 policies to a value of £1.4 million.[14]

Barbon died in 1698, after which the "Fire Office" lost some of its competitive spark. In 1705 it changed its name to the "Phenix Office" and offered terms of seven years.

This first generation of insurers struggled to define the fair cost of premiums that would be adequate to pay all claims, known as the "burn cost." At first the burn cost was no more than a guess. In 1685 Barbon claimed that he was paying out losses twice as fast as he was collecting premiums. Underinsurance was rife—subscribers to the Hand in Hand insured for an average value of £192 houses that were worth £400.

For the next 200 years in the world of fire insurance, not much happened.[15] Insurance expanded to other cities and countries, each choosing its own mix of private, public, and mutual companies. The challenges remained the same: how to stay in business against a competitor who recklessly drove down prices, and how much to keep in capital reserve to pay the worst year of claims.

Insurers also wrestled with questions of "moral hazard." Life insurance had been outlawed for hundreds of years, for fear that it would incite murder.[16] A desperate homeowner might insure his property for more than it was worth, or with multiple providers, and then commit arson.[17]

FOR THE INSURERS, THE ART OF STAYING IN BUSINESS IS TO AVOID having all the losses turning up at the same time—to not have all their "eggs in the same basket." The "basket" in question turned out to be urban conflagrations. In England the forests had been cut down before the eighteenth century, and the new cities were built of brick and stone. In northern and central Europe, however, as well as in the rapidly developing Eastern cities of the United States, wooden cities were primed to burn.

The problem of the worst year of claims caught up with European insurers on a spring night in 1842. A fire in central Hamburg quickly spread through the narrow timber streets, consuming 2,000 buildings—one-quarter of the old city—to a total cost of more than $35 million.[18] The City Fire Fund (founded in 1676) exhausted its reserves. British insurers lost more than $2 million, and German insurers were "imperiled."

While the insurance payments helped rebuild the city, it was clear that in the future the risk would need to be distributed to more "baskets." And so the idea of "reinsurance" was born: a company to insure fire insurers.[19] The reinsurer could spread the risk from many cities in a national, even global, basket. Six years later, and with the help of French capital, Cologne Reinsurance was founded in 1846 in response to the Hamburg city fire. Fifteen years later, the Swiss Reinsurance Company was formed in the wake of a fire that consumed much of the Swiss town of Glarus, leaving more than 2,000 homeless.[20]

At the start of the nineteenth century, most US insurance companies only operated in a single city. When the 1835 fire in New York's business district caused $20 million of damage, twenty-three out of twenty-six local insurers went out of business, unable to pay their claims.[21] On October 9, 1871, a fire gutted the heart of Chicago, consuming 12,000 buildings. Out of the 200 insurance companies, 68 went out of business and only 40 percent of the insured losses were refunded.[22] A year later the center of Boston went up in smoke; this time thirty-two local insurers defaulted.

Faced with catastrophic urban fires, US insurers seemed incapable of offering their customers the protection they promised.[23] Insurers lazily charged the same rate whether a building was made of timber or stone, and whether it was located in a city center or a rural location.

Naked competition for price among insurers would lead them to oblivion. By the mid-1880s, insurers had established local rate-setting city "cartels" that set a floor to the premiums charged, with the argument that insurers could thereby build up their reserves to pay for the big conflagrations. The likelihood of a conflagration remained something of a guess, so underwriters mapped the location of each building they insured, to avoid writing too many in the same street or block.

In the 1890s, faced with increased competition from the factory mutual insurers and exposed to new sources of fire ignition from electricity supplies and elevator systems, US fire insurers finally embraced science. They agreed to pool their claims data so as to identify the burn costs of different building categories and to try to set premiums according to risk.[24] They also embraced initiatives in risk reduction, like the Underwriters Laboratories founded in 1894 to set safety standards around electrical products and the 1896 nonprofit National Fire Protection Association.

The strategies of diversification and rate-setting were paying off. In the 1904 Baltimore and 1906 San Francisco fires, 90 percent of the insured loss was repaid, a statistic that helped the insurance cartels resist charges of unfair price-fixing.[25] By 1910, 70 percent of burned US property was insured.

———

FOLLOWING THE SUCCESS OF THE FIRST FIRE INSURERS, THE JOURnalist Daniel Defoe speculated in 1697 that "All the Contingencies of Life might be fenc'd against . . . as Thieves, Floods by Land, Storms by Sea, Losses of all Sorts, and Death itself, in a manner, by making it up to the Survivor."[26] Defoe's idea of insuring "Floods by Land" would take more than two centuries to be realized. After fire, the next peril to be insured would be hailstone ice—first in Mecklenberg, Germany, in 1797.

On August 9, 1843, an intense hailstorm blundered across central England, obliterating crops and window-glass over a 160-mile-long swath.[27] Within a few months, the General Hail Insurance Company was launched to sell hail insurance to anxious farmers and gardeners. The business was profitable: to date, England has not seen another hailstorm of such size and intensity.

At the end of the nineteenth century, Cuthbert Heath, a buccaneering underwriter at Lloyds, saw that plain fire insurance could be turned into a multitude of risk protections, as long as someone was prepared to pay an appropriate premium. He was a pragmatic genius at identifying what this rate should be.

Born in 1859 into the heart of the English establishment (he was the son of Captain Leopold Heath, the commander of the HMS *Arrogant*), Heath was christened in honor of Cuthbert, a tenth-century English saint. He was expected to either follow the family's Royal Naval tradition or enter the Indian Civil Service. Yet childhood deafness prevented these establishment paths, and instead, at sixteen, he spent six months in France to learn the language, followed by nine months learning German, boating, and chemistry at Bonn. In 1880 he became an underwriting member at Lloyds. Standing six feet, two inches tall, he went everywhere with his black box deaf-aid, which, as his fame grew, would be carried by an honored clerk.[28]

In 1885 he delivered the first non-marine (that is, unrelated to ships and cargo) insurance contract at Lloyds, providing reinsurance for the Hand in Hand mutual fire insurance company, still in business after almost 200 years. In 1889, in response to the anxieties of the age after a spate of burglaries had terrified London society, Heath offered burglary insurance. The rates were 2 shillings, 6 pennies (12.5 pence) for £100 of coverage or 3 shilling, 4 pennies (17 pence) to include "aggravated damage." After hearing from a relative who had lost a piece of jewelry, he devised the "all risks" jewelry coverage of 10 shillings (50 pence) per £100.

———

BEFORE THE 1890S, NO ONE HAD EVER GOTTEN A PENNY OUT OF an insurer for their earthquake- or hurricane-ruined house. Heath contemplated how to price catastrophe insurance. He collected maps— including those drawn by William Redfield and William Reid—of the paths of every hurricane through the West Indies over the previous 100 years. Based on how often hurricanes had struck an island, and working with his close friend Christopher Head, Heath calculated in his little black rating book what seemed to be a realistic cost for the coverage: for St. Kitts, 12 shillings, 6 pennies (62.5 pence) per £100 for buildings worth more than £500; 17 shillings, 6 pennies (87.5 pence) for those worth between £200 and £500; and 30 shillings (150 pence) for those worth less than £200. (He had discovered that lower-priced buildings were more susceptible to loss.) He placed an "excess" of £25 (or 5 percent of the property value) on the coverage so that he would only pay claims for significant damage.[29]

Next Heath did the same for earthquakes. He paid 100 guineas to create a map of the earthquakes of India, acquired records from the Jesuits for the earthquakes of western South America, and located reports of catastrophes in China dating back more than 2,000 years. For St. Kitts, he charged 5 shillings (25 pence) for earthquake coverage and 2 shillings, 6 pennies (16 pence) for tsunami coverage. Among the highest-risk cities was San Salvador (in El Salvador), for which he charged 60 shillings (£3)—or 3 percent of the value. "The curious thing about earthquake hazards is that the inhabitants of the areas affected by them live in a state of optimism," he remarked after trying and failing to sell earthquake insurance to the inhabitants of Kingston, Jamaica, at the rate of 10 shillings (50 pence). After the 1907 Kingston earthquake, however, there was "no absence of business" at double the price.

Heath was pleased to lend his little black rating book to competitors so they would not naively undercut his rates.

———

SAN FRANCISCO HAD DONE SUCH A GOOD JOB DENYING THAT IT had an earthquake problem that almost no one bought earthquake insurance. So it was not the exotic new insurance coverages that were tested by the 1906 earthquake disaster but the most familiar kind: fire insurance.

With an investment of 600 men and 38 steamers, at an annual cost of $850,000, the San Francisco Fire Department handled an average of four incidents a day and was considered of the highest capability. The city's buildings were constructed from California Redwood, purported to be rendered uninflammable "through the absorption of sea fog moisture."[30] From 1881 to 1902, the city's fire insurers had a loss ratio of only 29 percent—they paid out $13.5 million from $47 million of accumulated insurance premiums (including $3 million in premiums for 1906). San Francisco fire risk was considered such a one-way bet that insurers undercut the agreed tariff rate so as to win business in the city. Some foreign companies chose to underwrite only in San Francisco.

In 1906, between April 18 and 21, 3,000 acres (4.7 square miles, or 12 square kilometers) and 25,000 buildings (at least 80 percent of the value of property in San Francisco, equal to $350 million) went up in smoke. The buildings were generally underinsured, but even at $235 million to $260 million, this was by far the largest insurance loss ever. To compound the catastrophe, the fire had consumed most of the original certificates of insurance as well as the local records held by the San Francisco insurance offices.[31]

On May 31, representatives from all the companies met privately in New York to agree on their strategy. There were clear grounds for refusing to pay full value: the fire had been triggered by a noncovered peril (the earthquake), which had also disabled the city's water system. Some buildings had been blown up by the army. Payment of 75 cents on the dollar was proposed and supported by sixty-eight insurers, while thirty-two voted for full compensation.[32] Someone leaked the minutes of the meeting to the *San Francisco Chronicle*, which vilified the "six-bit" (75 cents on the dollar) companies as "welchers." Recognizing the opportunity to show some leadership in a crisis, Cuthbert Heath famously sent a telegram to San Francisco commanding his agents to "pay all claims."[33] Other insurers had issued policies that explicitly excluded fires following earthquakes, or fallen buildings, and wanted to stand their ground. Those insurers that challenged full payment became involved in numerous court cases in which owners would dutifully swear that the property in question had not a tile or chimney displaced by the earthquake before the fire arrived. Arcane questions of causation were argued: Had the fire that destroyed the house been triggered by the earthquake? Or had it perhaps spread from the later "ham-and-eggs fire" at 395 Hayes Street, sparked by someone trying to cook breakfast beneath a blocked chimney? In all cases heard in the local state courts, the insurers lost.[34] Out-of-state insurers, because they could move cases to federal courts, did have some success at arguing for a reduction in their liabilities.

Twelve insurers went bankrupt. One small group of insurers—most of them German and Austrian, including the top four companies by the size of their losses ($4 million each and higher)—simply disappeared, denying all coverage.

Through the summer of 1906, as money hemorrhaged out of their accounts to pay the claims from San Francisco, European reinsurers exchanged wordings on a clause to exclude paying for damage from fires triggered by future earthquakes.[35]

What was the chance that San Francisco could experience multiple simultaneous fires, blocked streets denying access for fire equipment, no water supply, and a mortally wounded fire chief? Before 1906, such a scenario would have been considered inconceivable. Yet the agency of the earthquake had achieved all these outcomes.[36]

Reactive after a costly catastrophe, reinsurers wanted to reduce the terms of coverage. Once an event has happened, it becomes hard to argue that in reality it is extremely rare. Heath's own instinct would have been to raise the price to cover the previously unrecognized risk, but it was the reinsurers who had paid for many of these exceptional losses and who were now calling the shots.[37]

In mitigation for their actions, the reinsurers argued that science was unable to explain where earthquakes might occur or what caused them, and hence offering insurance was "tantamount to gambling."[38] More practically, as they contemplated the prospect of a catastrophe under New York or London, they knew that another "San Francisco" could put them out of business. Using their financial muscle (as every insurer now depended on reinsurance), the exclusion was included in all fire policies offered from the start of 1907 by 500 fire insurance companies worldwide.

Yet the very idea of such exclusions traduced the core principle of insurance—to offer protection for an unforeseen calamity irrespective of its cause. For the policyholder, it was immaterial whether a neighbor's fallen candle had been kicked or shaken. Their own house had gone up in smoke, and they wanted compensation. There was a deeply felt perception that insurers were not honoring their role.

———

TWO WEEKS INTO THE NEW YEAR, AT 3:25 P.M. ON JANUARY 14, 1907, an earthquake went off right underneath Kingston, Jamaica. In the space of thirty seconds, almost all the buildings in the city (many made of brick) were damaged or collapsed, leaving 800 dead. Fires broke out in the city center close to the harbor, consuming several city blocks as well as wharves and warehouses. Total damage was estimated at £2 million.[39] Scarcely anyone had bothered to buy one of Cuthbert Heath's earthquake policies. However, most of the city center commercial operations had fire insurance.

A Fire Office committee was established in London representing all the insurers, and a deputation was sent out by boat to Kingston to inform the locals that, as a result of the two-week-old "fire following earthquake" clause, fire coverage was denied. Moral outrage at the ungentlemanly conduct of the insurers ran high in Jamaica. The issue united the people of Kingston, from aristocrats to indentured workers, in the common cause of defeating the London insurers.[40]

The situation dragged on through 1907 and into May 1908, when a lengthy trial was held in Kingston: 800 policyholders sued twenty-three insurance companies with fire offices in Kingston.[41] The locals hired a high-caliber barrister from England, thirty-seven-year-old Edward George Hemmerde, Liberal Member of Parliament, who was admitted to the Colonial Bar. The whole case hinged on whether it could be shown that the fires had indeed been triggered by the earthquake. The Honorable David Corinaldi, looking down from a hill at the back of the city, swore that he had seen smoke rising from the site of the first fire before the shaking. The engineer on the Port Kingston boat newly arrived from England also testified to having seen a cloud of smoke rising in the city immediately before feeling the earthquake. Hemmerde made mincemeat of the lawyers acting for the insurers: it was said that "Hemmerde just stopped short of proving that it was the Fires that caused the Earthquake rather than the Earthquake causing the Fires."[42]

On August 4, 1908, the insurers lost the case. Accounts were finally settled on December 22 after being unsuccessfully appealed from the lower courts of Jamaica to the British Privy Council. The London insurers were compelled to pay £600,000 to cover the claims, along with £75,000 in costs. (Sixty years later, at the time of Jamaican independence, it was admitted that the fire witnesses had indulged in some 'ethically motivated' dissembling.)

Yet, even with this bruising defeat, the insurers were not about to abandon their "fire following earthquake" exclusion, even after it had been declared inadmissible for fire insurance contracts in the state by the California Senate.

Three city center business districts in the Americas (San Francisco and Valparaiso in 1906 and Kingston, Jamaica, in January 1907) had been gutted by fires triggered by earthquakes in the space of nine months. As it turned out, the hurried alarm to place exclusions in all insurance policies proved an unnecessary overreaction, at least for this geography. Except for fires in downtown Managua after an earthquake in 1972, citywide fires following earthquakes in the Americas have kept away for more than a century. Insurers could have collected billions of dollars in premiums for offering the coverage.

There was, however, one country in which fires after earthquakes remained a perennial problem—Japan. Close to midday on September 1, 1923, the Great Kantō earthquake triggered fires that consumed 212,000 houses and destroyed tens of thousands of business premises.[43] The total insured value of all the properties destroyed, as calculated by the *Osaka Daily News* on September 14, came to 2.2 billion yen, written across 291,000 policies.[44] About half this business was directly written and half was reinsured, with 46 percent of the reinsurance coming from outside Japan. Five days later, the same newspaper calculated the insurers' reserves to be less than 200 million yen—one-tenth of the total damages.

The earthquake exemption clause had been in all fire insurance contracts in Japan since the start of 1907 and was clear in stating that the fire damage in Tokyo and Yokohama would not be covered. Meanwhile, bankers, concerned for their clients who had used property as collateral, lobbied Prime Minister Gonbei Yamamoto, who expressed the hope that fire insurers would make payments; the minister of agriculture and commerce also "expected insurers to make compensation."[45]

The political heat was rising, and fire claimants were organizing angry demonstrations. The insurers eventually agreed to offer partial payment, as a gift (not acknowledging any legal responsibility), to a sum of 10 percent of their insured limits; all but the largest insurer, Tokio Marine and Fire, would require a government loan to make these payments. Foreign direct insurers refused to participate in this arrangement and instead paid back the fire premiums received for 1923, an action that stoked rising antiforeigner sentiment in Japan.

Since 1923, raging city fires have followed five or six earthquakes in Japan, but none of these would have proved ruinous to the insurance industry if the fire had been insured. In fact, there is only one city in the world where the tangible risk of fires following an earthquake could be truly beyond what the insurance industry could bear: the Tokyo megalopolis.

———

HEATH'S TELEGRAM AFTER THE SAN FRANCISCO EARTHQUAKE CREated enormous goodwill in America and over the next two decades brought his London company tremendous new business. Companies that paid their claims in full saw an 80 percent increase in premium from 1905 to 1907.

Heath was an unusually privileged pioneer. In 1907 he inherited his father's house, Anstie Grange, near Dorking Surrey, where he moved with his wife and two children. Like Downton Abbey, the property required fifty servants. Meanwhile, his oldest friend and earthquake risk collaborator, Christopher Head, was lost in the 1912 sinking of the *Titanic*.

Always on the lookout for new risks to insure, Heath reacted to a Zeppelin bomb attack on East Anglia in 1915 by estimating the number of German airships and their capacity, calculating the expected loss to properties in London, and then multiplying this number by six to set a rate of 2 shillings (10 pence) per £100. He sustained the coverage until the end of the war in 1918, moving the price up and down with the intensity of attacks, even when the Germans replaced the Zeppelins with the first aircraft bombers.[46] Perhaps Heath's most notable innovation was to use the price of insurance to incentivize risk reduction. In the midst of a smallpox outbreak in East London, he reduced the cost of his 1901 smallpox insurance to one-quarter for those insured who had been vaccinated.

Cuthbert Heath's principle that any risk is insurable at the right price became tested to the breaking point in the 1930s as aircraft bombers gained longer range and greater payloads. In 1932, Stanley Baldwin admitted, pessimistically, that "the bomber will always get through."[47]

In early 1936, the Italians attacked Ethiopia and flattened the cities of Harar and Jijiga with saturation bombing. In November 1936, aircraft from Germany and Spain bombed Madrid, then under Republican occupation. On December 4, 1936, a committee of officials from Lloyds met with the British Insurance Association to agree that all treaties renewing at the start of 1937 would exclude "War" and "Civil War" from the standard terms of fire insurance coverage, as the risk was deemed "uninsurable."[48]

The aircraft bomber was therefore the reason a government first became involved in providing property insurance. At the start of the Luftwaffe's bombing campaign in 1940, Winston Churchill prompted the creation of a British state-backed insurance scheme, called "war damage insurance," to cover bomb damage, funded through a levy on all insurance policies.[49] At the height of the 1940 Blitz, it seemed implausible that enough money would be raised to fund the damage, but funds accumulated when the raids lessened after May 1941—enough to reimburse the bomb damages of 1940 and even to make a profit from 1941 through 1943. In 1944 the arrival of the V1 and V2 weapons, with their huge radius of smashed windows, set the program back into deficit again—25,000 houses were destroyed and more than 1 million suffered some level of damage—but the scheme was restored back to surplus in 1945.

In 1944 New Zealand copied the British war damage insurance with its compulsory levy on all insureds.[50] In place of bombing raids, the principal "enemy" was earthquakes; two 1942 shocks had ruined 5,000 houses and left 10,000 fallen chimneys waiting to be repaired. The coverage was kept running after the war, and more natural perils were added. Even after its reserves were completely exhausted by the losses from the 2010 and 2011 earthquakes in Christchurch, the levy still functions today.

———

BY 1930, US INSURERS DISCOVERED, THEIR INITIATIVES TO PROMOTE fire resistance had become all too successful. Large US city conflagrations had passed into history. Unless there were additional risks to be covered, either insurance company incomes would shrink or people might cease purchasing building insurance altogether.

So the stock fire insurance companies dreamed up an "additional hazards supplemental contract" whose coverages reflected the apprehensions of the age: "tornado, explosion, riot, civil commotion and aircraft damage." In October 1930, "hail, motor vehicles and all kinds of windstorm" were added, along with "smoke damage." However, the supplement never spread its arms so wide as to include the most damaging perils: flood and earthquake.

The 1925 Santa Barbara earthquake was limited in impact and created a strong demand for an additional Californian earthquake insurance coverage. By 1928, 200 insurance companies were offering earthquake insurance, all of them desperate to understand how to calculate the risk.[51]

"Extended coverage" only became widely purchased after the September 1938 Long Island Express Hurricane; in the wake of that storm, banks began to require such coverage for mortgaged properties in coastal counties. The product took off in the 1950s, but it was not until Hurricane Betsy in 1965 that insurers (and their reinsurers) discovered just how successful their marketing had been: the property damage from a single hurricane cost insurers more than $500 million.

Actuaries were familiar with analyzing insurance losses, such as from fires, thefts, and, industrial accidents, and fitting statistical distributions of severity and frequency to their observations.[52] Yet earthquake and hurricane catastrophes were more like the American city fires that had driven hundreds of insurers bankrupt through the nineteenth century by slamming them with massive losses 100 times larger than in an ordinary year. Such statistical distributions were "fat-tailed," in that extreme events were both more common and far larger than in a normal distribution. How much insurance premium had to be collected to pay for these "fat tails"? And what was the chance that a loss might drive the company out of business? Increased competition had cut out the padding with which Cuthbert Heath had loaded his catastrophe insurance.

These were deep questions for which there did not seem to be ready answers.

7 • THE GARDEN OF
THE FORKING PATHS

JORGE LUIS BORGES, A LIBRARIAN AND POET WHO LIVED IN Buenos Aires, was experimenting with imaginary fiction and riddles, not even sure he could be a writer. His first publication was a thin book of eight strange short stories published in 1942 under the title *El Jardín de senderos que se bifurcan* (The Garden of the Forking Paths).[1]

The title story, a tale of World War I espionage, recalls the works of Ts'ui Pên, the Chinese writer and philosopher who described a world where all possible outcomes of an event or action exist alongside one another. The paths of the future continue to split and fork through time (although diverging paths sometimes serendipitously recombine). With Borges's characteristic laconic wit (and honest admission of his likely legacy given his unknown status as a writer), a letter is found from Ts'ui Pên stating that "I leave to several futures (not to all) my garden of forking paths."[2]

In the same year Borges published his short story, top physicists were working on the Manhattan Project in the quest to build an atomic bomb. Some of the problems could not be solved through applying a formula; for example, how far would a neutron travel through an array of atoms before hitting another nucleus to trigger a chain reaction?[3] (If you fire a gun in the forest while blindfolded, what is the chance you will hit a tree?) The only solution would come from testing a range of mathematical simulations. However, because this range could never contain every possibility, the tests needed to be randomized—as if generated from spins of the casino roulette wheel—to be representative. One of the physicists, Stanislaw Ulam, had an uncle who spent his time and money on the wheel in Monaco. The "Monte Carlo method" became the official term for solving a problem through random sampling.[4]

In the aftermath of the Second World War, "probabilistic thinking"—testing innumerable splitting paths of possibilities—spread like intellectual wildfire among philosophers and physicists.[5] In 1960 a mathematically trained engineer, Allin Cornell, went to Stanford University.[6] By 1964, he had completed his doctoral research, in which he explored how buildings withstand random loads, such as traffic on a bridge, gusts of wind, or the vibrations from an earthquake.[7]

After the first US nuclear power plants were built in the late 1950s, the utility companies set out ambitious plans for expansion. In 1958 northern California's Pacific Gas & Electric (PG&E) conceived a plan for the largest-ever complex of nuclear power plants, to be constructed on the Pacific coast at Bodega Bay, 60 miles north of San Francisco; this vision was announced to the public in 1961.[8] The site was provocatively placed within a few hundred yards of the 1906 18-foot (5.5 meter) rupture on the San Andreas Fault. (Alfred Hitchcock's 1963 movie *The Birds*, set in Bodega Bay, can be viewed as an allegory for the rising nuclear foreboding.) The critical cooling and control systems required to prevent a reactor from overheating had to be designed to withstand a certain level of earthquake shaking. Yet such reinforcement came at a high price, so how much protection against shaking was appropriate? This led to a deeper question as to how the shaking "hazard" from earthquakes should be calculated.

On Good Friday, March 27, 1964, a giant earthquake (the second-largest ever recorded) occurred under central Alaska; the fault, breaking for hundreds of miles, was far larger than from any previous earthquake on US territory.[9] Coastal towns south of Anchorage were permanently lowered a few feet, and a great tsunami was launched across the Pacific. Could a similar earthquake hit California? The Alaska earthquake rattled both the public and the engineering professions.[10] PG&E had already excavated the rock foundations at Bodega Bay. Detailed inspection revealed a "recent" fault break running across the site. Later in 1964, under pressure from Governor Pat Brown, the development was abandoned.[11]

Trained in thinking about probabilities and forking paths, Allin Cornell saw that for a single site, such as the location of a nuclear power plant, the "hazard" meant the ground shaking from all the potential earthquakes in the surrounding region. You would need to have a way to determine the likelihood of each of these potential earthquakes. Then, from their locations and sizes, you could calculate the strength of the vibrations at the site. Like a whisper in the ear being louder than a faraway shout, a medium-sized local earthquake might jolt the ground more fiercely than a large distant shock.

Cornell ranked the shaking at the site from all these potential earthquakes, from the most violent to the weakest vibrations, and plotted the results on a graph as the "hazard curve."[12] Hazard curves are rich in information. As we do not know which catastrophe will happen next, we have to consider all the possible forking paths, each assigned its individual chance of occurring. Hazard is not simply one big bad threat. Hazard has to be drawn in two dimensions—severity and likelihood. As the threats get worse, they become less likely.

Cornell's 1968 publication triggered a slow-burning revolution.[13] In 1976 the US Geological Survey produced the first probabilistic earthquake hazard map for California.[14] The map did not simply display where shocks had struck in the past, but showed how strongly the ground was expected to shake over the next fifty years from potential future earthquakes.[15]

If we know the exposure of buildings in the path of a hazard as well as their vulnerability to damage or injury from the hazard (for example, how much damage occurs at a certain shaking intensity), we can convert the hazard curve into a "risk curve."

Risk can be defined in many ways. For insurers, the risk curve tells them the amount they need to collect in annual premiums to pay for all their future disaster claims—the "burn cost"—as well as how much to hold in reserve to pay for a worst (once in a century) year of claims.

———

J. DOYLE DEWITT, BORN IN 1902, JOINED THE TRAVELERS INSURance Company as a claims adjuster in 1925 and then rose up through the ranks to become president. In 1952, his first presidential year, a tornado at Waco, Texas, killed 114. The following year Category 2 Hurricane Carol passed right over the Travelers headquarters in eastern Connecticut, followed less than two weeks later by Hurricane Edna, which skimmed Cape Cod.

Impressed by the impact of the weather on his bottom line, in 1955 DeWitt announced the formation of the Travelers Weather Research Center, staffed by three young scientists who had transferred from the Massachusetts Institute of Technology.[16] Among them was Don Friedman, a meteorologist with good programming skills. In 1972, inspired by Cornell, Friedman set out a manifesto for a probabilistic approach to catastrophe insurance, which he called "natural hazard simulation."[17] Instead of simply relying on what had happened in history, he proposed computer generation of synthetic histories—large sets of potential earthquakes, hurricanes, or thunderstorms. Friedman had set out the founding charter for "catastrophe modeling."

Friedman had the dream and outlined the scope, but was never able to fulfill the ambition of his 1972 manifesto.[18] The mission would need to await better analysis of past earthquakes and hurricanes as well as more powerful computers.

———

IN 1975 THE US NATIONAL WEATHER SERVICE LAUNCHED A STUDY of the threat from hurricanes and storm surges along US coastlines that set out details of the tracks, intensities, and sizes of all the historical hurricanes back to 1900.[19] In 1984 the NWS began a second, even more detailed study (published in April 1987) to model the maximum height that a hurricane storm surge could reach, all along the US East and Gulf Coasts, once every 100 years on average.[20] All the early-generation hurricane catastrophe models were based on the information contained in these two open reports.

Karen Clark graduated in 1982 from Boston College with a master's degree in business and economics.[21] She joined the Commercial Union insurance company in Boston and sat in on meetings with underwriters who wanted to write more coastal hurricane business but found themselves blocked by internal rules limiting the total value of insurance they were allowed to write in each county. Where had these rules originated? Not through any formal scientific process, she discovered, but rather by the decisions of an internal risk committee. Clark was assigned to find a better way.

She read Don Friedman's ambitious 1972 blueprint for probabilistic modeling. She found the detailed National Weather Service studies of US hurricanes. Of particular value was a 1984 publication by Friedman, who had analyzed Travelers' own claims data for three hurricanes to show the way in which building damage worsens with wind speed.[22] Clark saw how to take the 1972 recipe from Friedman, add the data and the probabilistic hurricane modeling from the National Weather Service studies, season with the all-important building damage data, and bake a catastrophe model.

In 1985, as she developed the first prototype, her business unit at Commercial Union was cut back. She put all her efforts into getting a paper on the hurricane model published by the Casualty Actuarial Society in 1986.[23] Based on simulating 2,000 years of potential storms, Clark estimated the annual cost of hurricane loss as well as the maximum loss that could be expected on average once in every 10 or 100 years.

Meanwhile, on the US West Coast, a parallel effort was already under way to explore earthquake catastrophe losses. Haresh Shah, born and educated in India, had completed his master's and PhD degrees at Stanford University, where he joined the faculty and would rise to become chairman of the Department of Civil Engineering.[24] Motivated by what he observed on field missions to the sites of devastating earthquakes in Central America and Asia, Shah attracted high-caliber engineering PhD students to Stanford from all over the world. He was in the first group of foreign experts allowed to visit the ruins of Tang-shan in September 1980.

One of the consequences of the rapprochement with China had been an invitation to a few leading Chinese engineering students to travel to the United States to undertake doctoral research. Among the first cohort was a brilliant mathematical engineer, Weimin Dong.[25] In 1985 Haresh Shah and Weimin Dong began a project to calculate the costs of earthquake damage for all the buildings in California. For the set of potential earthquakes in the state, they adopted the latest assessment from the US Geological Survey. The accumulated losses for each simulated disaster were ranked from highest to lowest so as to generate a risk curve that would show the chance of experiencing a loss above some threshold. Under Weimin Dong's lead, they developed software to perform the loss calculations for any designated set of buildings and locations.[26]

———

THE NAME "CATASTROPHE MODEL" MIGHT SUGGEST SOME HIGH-intensity video game. The initial reality was far more mundane—a standard PC interface, with tables of properties, locations, and values, outputting how much money would be lost for each simulated earthquake or hurricane. You could map what was insured, or the concentration of the losses, but insurance users were generally more interested in the risk curves that displayed financial loss against probability.

For the first time the model could provide answers to the problems that had always beset catastrophe insurers. How much should be set aside each year to pay for all the future losses, including rare catastrophes? And what was the largest loss that could be expected on average once in every 100 or 200 years? The future is latent with potential catastrophes. Since we do not know which catastrophe will occur next, we must consider a full set of forking paths.

The model contains thousands of catastrophes not experienced in the last two centuries—earthquakes in San Diego, a break in the whole of the Southern San Andreas Fault, hurricanes that hit Miami at maximum intensity and then go on to slam into New York. If an event is credible, then it needs to be in the model. Of course, the assumption is that the catastrophe modeler has full knowledge about the potential range of catastrophes and how each will cause damage and generate losses. Over the next twenty-five years, this was to remain work in progress. Time and again, modelers discovered that big catastrophes were more complex and variable than they had first believed.

After her paper was published, Karen Clark set up her own company, Applied Insurance Research (AIR), to provide a service to clients who sent in the data on their portfolios.[27] Her subsequent capability to model the loss from hurricanes was met with widespread skepticism. Clark describes telling a crowd at Lloyds of London the staggering size of potential hurricane losses and being met by silent incredulity.

In California the idea of setting up a catastrophe modeling business based on their new earthquake risk assessment software was far from the minds of Professor Haresh Shah and Dr. Weimin Dong. However, when Shah's oldest son, Hemant, who was completing a master's in engineering at Stanford, took a class that required the development of a business plan for some new piece of technology, he chose the earthquake loss modeling software. In working on the business plan, he discovered that the catastrophe model had real commercial promise, in particular with insurers.

In 1988, with $30,000 in seed money and working out of its first office—Hemant Shah's apartment in Belmont, California—Risk Management Solutions (RMS) was born.[28] Weimin Dong, the principal architect of the software, joined the enterprise. Hemant's dazzling enthusiasm connected with a small group of insurers and reinsurers who became the first patrons.

By 1991, RMS had raised more than $2 million in venture capital and a number of Haresh Shah's former PhD engineering students came to join the firm. The RMS business model right from the start was to provide the software under a licensing arrangement so that it could be run by the clients themselves, in real time, on the highest-specification PC then on the market with the Intel 80486 microprocessor.

THE LAUNCH OF TWO SEPARATE CATASTROPHE MODELING BUSI-
nesses, one on the East Coast and one on the West Coast, might have
been premature—a false dawn, becalmed in the 1980s catastrophe doldrums—if it had not been for an extraordinary run of the catastrophe
roulette wheel.

It started with a windstorm that emerged from the Bay of Biscay
into Brittany before cutting across southeast England on the balmy
autumn night of October 15–16, 1987. By dawn, under the force of
the 100-mile-per-hour wind speeds, 17 million trees had fallen, power
lines had tumbled, and all train lines in southeast England had come
to a halt, bringing London's financial center to a standstill. Insurance
companies had no contingency plans for such a storm and within weeks
found themselves paying all claims, totting up an unprecedented loss of
£1.4 billion. The following "Black Monday," as the City reopened, there
was a crash in worldwide share values.

Then, in July 1988, the North Sea Piper Alpha oil production platform caught fire and sank, taking 167 lives. The insurance cost was
£1.7 billion.

At the end of August, Hurricane Gilbert made a direct pass over
Jamaica and then intensified to a maximum Category 5 storm before
making landfall in the Yucatán Peninsula. The insurance costs were
$800 million.

Ten days before the end of the year, an explosion brought down
PanAm flight 103 over Lockerbie, Scotland, leading to more than $500
million in liability payouts.

On September 18, 1989, Hurricane Hugo, at Category 4, blasted
the US Virgin Islands before intersecting the northeast corner of Puerto
Rico. The storm traveled northwest to hit South Carolina, causing a
total insured loss of $4.2 billion.

A month later, the Magnitude 7.1 Loma Prieta earthquake, located
beneath the Santa Cruz Mountains in northern California, racked up
$960 million in insured losses.

At the end of December 1989, a modest Magnitude 5.7 earthquake
went off under the brick-built city of Newcastle, New South Wales,
bringing 1 billion Australian dollars in insurance claims for damage.

Starting on January 25, 1990, over the space of thirty-five days, eight intense windstorms emerged from the Atlantic and moved rapidly to the east across central and northern Europe, four of them strong enough to cause widespread damage in the United Kingdom, France, the Netherlands, Belgium, and Germany. The total insurance cost was more than 8 billion euros.

On September 27, 1991, Supertyphoon Mireille spread damage along the whole length of Japan from central Kyushu to western Hokkaido, creating the highest-ever insured typhoon loss, then equivalent to $6.9 billion.

In October 1991, a wildfire consumed whole neighborhoods of wealthy homes scattered across the hills of Oakland, California, generating insured losses of $1.7 billion.

Lloyds had written catastrophe business in the form of "excess of loss" contracts—as devised by Cuthbert Heath in the aftermath of the 1906 earthquake—which paid out only when the loss was above some threshold and put a cap on payments. However, individual Lloyds syndicates had taken to purchasing these same "excess of loss" reinsurance coverages for their whole account from other syndicates within the Lloyds market. For the syndicate that wrote the coverage, any losses on these contracts would be mixed in with all its other losses. And that syndicate would in turn buy a reinsurance protection from another syndicate, which might reinsure itself back with the first syndicate. Thus did the LMX (Lloyds Market Excess of Loss) Spiral emerge in an incestuous helter-skelter of risk transfer that would have impressed Jorge Luis Borges in its spontaneous and reckless symmetry.[29] The forking paths of time were reconnecting.

Piper Alpha cost Lloyds a net of $900 million but ultimately generated $15 billion in claims around the market spiral across a total of 43,000 policies as the spiral unwound. Piper Alpha had in effect been reinsured sixteen times. As fast as syndicates pushed losses out of the back door they came in through the front door as they discovered that they had repeatedly reinsured themselves.

For the whole Lloyds market, losses were rising: £510 million in 1988, £2 billion in 1989, and almost £3 billion in 1990. The unremitting attack of catastrophes, adding to escalating asbestos and pollution claims, brought the market the closest it has ever come to going out of business. However, just as the individual Lloyds name investors were taking the massive losses and fleeing their syndicates, catastrophe reinsurance prices began to rise steeply, luring new capital into the restructured market.

All these losses were as mere *amuse-bouches* to what happened in 1992. It took until the middle of August before the first hurricane of the season even formed. The vortex was labeled Andrew. After strengthening close to the Bahamas, the storm made a westerly beeline for southern Florida, intensifying dramatically and shrinking in size as it fed off the hot waters of the Gulf Stream; wind speeds were at least 165 miles (265 kilometers) per hour when it made landfall. In Dade County, 90 percent of homes were left roofless and 117,000 houses were classified as "destroyed." Initial insured loss estimates were $3 billion to $4 billion, but Karen Clark was closer to the mark at $13 billion—the final toll came in at $16 billion.

Into this battered global insurance market, with insurers uncertain how they should price their contracts or stay in business, came catastrophe models. RMS was soon busy building a hurricane model, Karen Clark's AIR was devising an earthquake model, and a third modeler, EQE Engineering Consultants, had appeared. It was fortuitous that the models had been developed in the years leading up to the run of catastrophes, for they were now available to calculate the fair price for catastrophe insurance.

In response to the high reinsurance prices, eight specialized catastrophe reinsurance companies were founded in Bermuda, and they soon captured one-quarter of the global market for catastrophe reinsurance.[30] Without any previous claims experience, these new companies based much of their US business on the output from catastrophe models.

Right from the very start, RMS identified that the problem of catastrophe risk should be understood and modeled building by building, and location by location, not based on the aggregate county-level data then received by reinsurers. As a result, through time, detailed data on all policies and all buildings became the standard for information exchange throughout the catastrophe reinsurance markets.

The agenda of catastrophe modeling would become more and more complex. An earthquake causes damage not just from vibration but also from fires triggered by the shock, from landslides, and sometimes from a tsunami. The "crazy" and long-lost eighteenth-century idea, spawned by the 1692 Port Royal disaster, that buildings are swallowed into the earth had to be rediscovered after the February 2011 earthquake in Christchurch, New Zealand, where cars sank through the tarmac and commercial fifteen-story buildings were left tilted, like the Leaning Tower of Pisa, as they settled into the liquefied ground.[31]

Catastrophe history no longer supplied just interesting anecdotes about the past, but also the raw materials for modeling the future. Disaster historians came to mine and map all the earthquakes in Italy, tsunamis in Japan, and hurricanes in Cuba, going back hundreds of years.[32]

Beyond earthquake and hurricane, there were hailstorms, tornadoes, ice storms, floods, and volcanic eruptions, not to mention secondary sources of loss from interrupted lives and broken supply chains as well as a host of economic, logistical, and political factors that pushed up the costs of the largest catastrophes.[33] And that was before risk modeling expanded to include pandemics and man-made perils like terrorism, cyber-attacks, and even war.[34] There are now hundreds of scientists, engineers, and mathematicians building catastrophe models and thousands consuming the results, in an industry that turns over more than $500 million per year.

Catastrophe models have changed the insurance industry, preventing episodes of reckless, fight-to-the-death price competition and more or less ending the tendency of insurers to be bankrupted by a disaster and then failing to pay their claims. In principle, the price charged for insurance the day after a catastrophe should not change, because the event was already included in the model. A model revision can now alter prices more than a catastrophe.

At the start of the new millennium, property insurance looked to be spreading inexorably across the world. Soon, it seemed, insurance would provide all the compensation for damage from natural catastrophes. More than $100 billion was paid out in US hurricane claims in 2004 and 2005, and $8 billion was raised from international insurance and reinsurance after the 2010 Chile earthquake (about 30 percent of the total cost of the catastrophe).

Catastrophe models helped make new markets. The World Bank commissioned catastrophe models to support the creation of new insurance systems, starting with Turkish earthquake insurance.[35] In the Caribbean, catastrophe models laid the foundation for an insurance system to rapidly refund governments after disasters.[36] The models facilitated high-interest-paying catastrophe bonds, which initially were offered to a select group of fearless investors.[37] After 2008, however, they were also bought by pension funds and banks, since it had become clear that risk analyses based on the physics of the earth and atmosphere were far more reliable than the assumptions around human herd behavior implicit in the risk of subprime mortgage markets or Russian bond defaults.

Insurance was also expanding to low-income countries. In the absence of any process to check the validity of a claim, index insurance could be based on measurements of temperature or rainfall as indicative of crop yields.[38] Micro-insurance in the Philippines brought payouts to more than 100,000 policyholders after Supertyphoon Haiyan in 2013—around $100 per claimant.[39] The pressure at the center of a storm or the magnitude of an earthquake could also be employed as a trigger for a catastrophe bond, so that payment could be settled within weeks of a disaster.

And yet, in the hot spots of US catastrophe risk, in the world's largest and richest market—the United States generates more than 60 percent of all worldwide insured catastrophe losses—insurance was encountering obstacles.[40]

Principal among these was a question of politics and ethics. What can catastrophe insurance redress when it comes to a disaster in which many people have died?

These limits became tested in the aftermath of the 9/11 attacks on the World Trade Center towers. Here was an unforeseen catastrophe for which no insurance premium had been collected, and yet insurance policies covered the majority of the losses: from building collapse and fire, from interrupted businesses, and liability for the lives and injuries of those caught up in the monstrous attack.

The traumatic political significance of 9/11 and its almost 3,000 casualties left the US government unprepared to allow the financial response to be driven by insurance compensation, and so Congress established the September 11th Victim Compensation Fund.[41] Dependents of those killed and injured were awarded a sum equivalent to the projected lost lifetime earnings of the victims (in exchange for agreeing not to sue the airlines out of existence for negligence); the average payment was $1.8 million, for a total cost of $7 billion.

Property insurers in New York City had bought plenty of reinsurance because they had a healthy fear of hurricanes. Fortuitously, therefore, the majority of the record $31.6 billion in insurance losses passed to reinsurers.[42]

The government's provision of compensation for loss of life after a diabolical terrorist attack might be seen to have introduced few precedents, but then along came a purely natural catastrophe, one for which the private and federal insurance systems were all in place to provide the coverage.

———

FIVE YEARS AFTER HURRICANE HUGO, I FIRST SAW THEM IN THE window of a real estate office in Charlotte Amalie on St. Thomas in the US Virgin Islands: advertisements for "prime Hugo coastal slab." Each picture showed a lone concrete foundation—the "slab"—located above a low cliff, with the blue Caribbean stretching to the horizon. There was no need to dress up the sales package. The house had been completely erased.

The production of slab has accelerated over the last decade. I visited Ivan slab in Grand Cayman in early 2005, wandered through whole neighborhoods of prime Katrina slab extending six blocks in from the Mississippi coast, and kicked some fine beachfront slab along the Bolivar peninsular in Texas after Ike in 2008.

However, less of this slab has passed into forced real estate sales. Unlike the aftermath of Hugo on faraway St. Croix in 1989, homeowners have gotten much better at arguing that someone should pay for their reconstruction, even if they have no flood insurance.

In the United States, wind insurance falls under a fire policy bought from a private insurer, while flood insurance is provided by a federal government agency. The system is designed to create interesting philosophical challenges after hurricane storm surges, when the building itself has disappeared.

The 2005 crop of slab claims was principally in Louisiana and Mississippi, where only one in three homeowners in the official 100-year flood zone had any flood insurance. Two weeks after Hurricane Katrina, and following the worst ratings of his presidency, President George W. Bush stood in Jackson Square in New Orleans and promised that "we will do what it takes; we will stay as long it takes, to help citizens rebuild their communities and their lives. . . . This great city will rise again."[43]

And so federal money poured in to compensate for all the uninsured losses. First in line were the Mississippi homeowners whose houses had been destroyed by the storm surge but were also situated several blocks inland, beyond the official coastal "100-year flood zone" (with more than 1 percent chance of inundation each year); these property owners had therefore not been obliged to have flood insurance.[44] To all these, ex gratia compensation was quickly agreed to, up to $150,000 per property (paid out of a federal Community Development Block Grant called "Road Home").[45] Seeing the favors being offered to their Mississippi cousins, politicians in Louisiana had successfully argued by February 2006 that the federal government should pay up to the same $150,000 threshold for more than 100,000 claimants with uninsured flood (and wind) damage in Louisiana, irrespective of whether they were in the predefined 100-year flood zone.[46] For good measure, they lumped in compensation for damages from Hurricane Rita, a later 2005 storm in western Louisiana.

Where did all the money come from? The one class of spending bill that Congress could not reject was funding to fight the wars in Iraq and Afghanistan. The first Road Home allocation of $11.5 billion for Katrina flood payments was hitched to the Defense Appropriations Act for FY2006; the second for $5.2 billion was slipped into the Emergency Supplemental Appropriations Act for Defense, the Global War on Terror, and Hurricane Recovery Act of 2006; and when even that was falling short, $3 billion was tacked on to the Department of Defense Appropriations Act for FY2008.[47]

This left one group of Katrina flood claimants without any government handouts: the coastal residents of Mississippi who lived within the 100-year flood zone and had all now lost their houses, but who had chosen not to purchase federal flood insurance. Two of the grand waterfront homes in Pascagoula, liquidated by the surge, belonged to Richard F. Scruggs, the richest US trial lawyer, and his brother-in-law, Senator Trent Lott. In the 1990s, Scruggs had won $248 billion in settlements in tobacco and asbestos lawsuits. He now proceeded to sue the insurance companies on behalf of Mississippi coast "slab" claimants, arguing that much of the damage had been caused by the insured wind, not the uninsured storm surge.[48]

The problem with insurance exclusions is how contrary they seem to natural justice. The homeowner is destitute, while the insurer has the money. After the 1906 earthquake, in the spirit of Robin Hood, owners swore that each building had been completely untouched by the shaking before the fire arrived. For the Mississippi slabs, the equivalent was to find neighbors prepared to testify that the claimant's house had been seen blowing down the street before the storm surge hit. Having won more than $100 million from the insurers, for which he personally collected $46 million in fees, Scruggs was indicted for offering $50,000 to bribe a judge to agree to a favorable settlement around the sharing of Katrina fees with another lawyer and in June 2008 was sent to jail for five years, one of the last "victims" of the hurricane.

In July 2012, President Obama signed into law a proposal for slab claims to be settled by "very sophisticated models" run by federal agencies.[49] In early 2014, seventy individuals were said to be involved in elaborating the scheme, which was still awaiting a response from Congress.[50] Never in the course of human history will so much attention be concentrated on 600 square feet of concrete and the ontological question of the role of wind or storm surge in the destruction of a vanished property. With rising sea levels, there will be no shortage of future slabs to which the "formula" will have to be applied.

AFTER THE AD 79 VESUVIUS ERUPTION, EMPEROR TITUS SENT TWO former consuls to Campania to support disaster recovery.[51] The buildings of Pompeii and Herculaneum were buried beneath dunes of volcanic ash. The consuls identified plots of land without an owner or heirs and then reallocated possession. And when that reserve was exhausted, they handed out money from the emperor's personal account.

Such was the fame of this most remarkable homeland catastrophe that many wealthy Romans came forward to offer goods and money, but whether from private citizens, cities, or kings, Titus declined all such aid, in order to demonstrate the power of the Roman state to make good the catastrophe. He also wanted to be seen, like any modern ruler, to share the pain with his suffering people, so he went to inspect the site of the disaster in the spring of AD 80. During his stay in Pompeii, a fire started in Rome, spread for three days and nights, and consumed many important public buildings and temples. Again the emperor helped fund the cost of rebuilding from his own exchequer.

In Italy paying for catastrophes has scarcely changed in 2,000 years, although today's state is not as wealthy as first-century Rome. Homeowners in Italy do not purchase catastrophe insurance for floods or earthquakes but consider it the duty of the state to compensate them for the inevitable damages that follow from living on their disaster-ridden peninsula. This is a long-held "understanding," not a contract. Following the January 1968 earthquakes in Sicily, the compensation was so generous that towns far away "imagined" that they too had experienced similar tremors.[52] After the 1980 Irpinia earthquake left 280,000 people homeless, three-quarters of almost $40 billion paid out in compensation was lost in corruption.[53] In an age of austerity, the Italian state today could not afford to compensate for another 1908 Messina earthquake or AD 79 Pompeii eruption. In 1906 the eruption of Mount Vesuvius was blamed for the state's inability to run the 1908 Olympics.[54]

Hurricane Katrina highlights how insurance compensation misses the personal touch so desired by politicians, who, like the Emperor Titus, wish to be seen as leaders dispensing funds and being thanked (and reelected) by the people. This is why President Bush sought redemption after Katrina by giving more than $18 billion to those without flood insurance, why the president of Chile dispensed $2.5 billion to the poorest uninsured homeowners after the 2010 Maule earthquake and tsunami, and why the Chinese state will never give up its role of delivering compensation after a catastrophic earthquake. Thus, a question arises: why purchase insurance when the handouts come for free?

The French have devised a particularly French compromise between a contractual insurance system and the personal but fickle intervention of politicians. The state-backed "Catastrophe Naturelle" scheme was established on July 13, 1982, after destructive floods at the end of 1981.[55] The decision as to whether the loss in a municipality will be compensated by the state as a "Cat Nat" is based on the whim of an "inter-Ministerial decree"—that is, the ministers of the interior and finance must agree with the budget minister on the compensation. Better hope an election is coming!

———

WHEN, ON THE MORNING OF APRIL 21, 1927, DESPITE DAYS OF sandbagging, the levee broke at Mound Landing outside Greenville, Mississippi, the water surged into the floodplain to create an inland sea larger than Lake Michigan, inundating 137,000 buildings and displacing five times as many people.[56] In some places water extended all the way to the horizon and remained for months, like Noah's Flood. Among the many social consequences, the abject treatment of black laborers inspired mournful ("When the Levee Breaks") blues as musicians migrated to Chicago.

The 1927 flood also ended any possibility of private flood insurance. It was not just that such a vast area and high number of properties had been inundated. The flooding was caused by the failure of the government-financed levee system. The damages were exacerbated when the city officials of New Orleans tyrannically employed 30 tons of dynamite to blow up the embankments downstream at Caernarvon so as to speed the flow of water through the city.[57] This sent the diverted river to rip up the shacks of dirt-poor sharecroppers and fishermen in St. Bernard and Plaquemines Parishes. As Gilbert White wrote in 1945: "Floods are an act of God, but flood losses are largely an act of man."[58] Mississippi River flooding in 1927 was a man-made peril and deemed uninsurable.

For the next four decades, the US government tried to cajole private insurers into offering flood insurance, but without success. After Hurricane Betsy drowned New Orleans, a Democrat-controlled Congress voted in 1968 to launch the National Flood Insurance Program.[59] To get the owners of floodplain buildings to accept the scheme, preexisting properties were "grandfathered" in and allowed cheap insurance costs in perpetuity, even if the owners extended, rebuilt, or sold the property.

As flood risk modeling became more sophisticated and "granular," it revealed the value of these subsidies.[60] A $500 reduction in insurance premium could raise property values by $10,000. Some beachfront homes enjoyed premium reductions of $5,000 or more. Finally, in July 2012, after years of argument, Republicans and Democrats, allied with vested interests on the right and left, from realtors to environmentalists, came together in a plan to end the subsidies and get everyone to pay the true costs of the risk.

Proper flood pricing, it was argued, would discourage inappropriate development and reduce the costs of future flood damage, to the benefit of all. Future sea level rise could be accommodated by revising the insurance costs. To reduce the shock, insurance price increases would be limited to a 25 percent uptick in premium each year. The so-called Biggert-Waters Act (after its two sponsors) was passed by the House of Congress overwhelmingly, by a vote of 406–22.[61]

When the 20 percent of policyholders who owned grandfathered subsidized properties saw their new insurance rates, they were horrified. For some of those on the beachfront, costs rose by a factor of four or more. The press got hold of the most dramatic increases and turned them into headlines. In 2014 the law was repealed.[62] National funds would continue to be used to subsidize people who wanted to live on the beach.

Hidden insurance subsidies for riverside and beachfront properties exist in many developed countries. Predating the risk models, these subsidies are sustained because politicians fear the strident voices of their often wealthy owners. One exception is on some of the Caribbean islands, such as the Caymans or the Bahamas, where private insurers offer a combined wind and flood insurance, a model borrowed from the United Kingdom. Insurance rates for beachfront properties can be more than 1 percent (and sometimes even 2 percent) of the value of the property each year. No local newspaper or politician would dream of campaigning to reduce the costs for the wealthy owners of beach-front houses. But charging the true risk cost is already incentivizing risk reduction on these islands, whether from building private seawalls or raising buildings on concrete stilts. Charging the technical rate for the risk is driving spontaneous adaptation.

—————

IN ADDING UP THEIR HURRICANE ANDREW LOSSES, INSURERS FOUND that the winds had been stronger and the building stock had disinte-grated far more readily than anticipated. Eight insurers went out of business.[63]

Less than eighteen months later, California was assailed by the Northridge earthquake. The first loss estimates were below $2 billion. Three months on, this had risen to $6 billion. Fifteen months later, the costs had doubled again.[64] Even lightly damaged walls proved prodigiously expensive to return to their pristine decorative state. The sprinkler system pipework collapsed in thousands of offices and stores, flooding the buildings with water; many commercial insur-ers paid out more for water spoilage than for shaking damage.[65] The Northridge earthquake cost home insurers twenty-eight times their 1993 earthquake premium, leaving several teetering on the edge of bankruptcy.

In both Florida and California, the new insurance costs calculated by the revised catastrophe models were more expensive than previously assumed. Insurers attempted to raise their prices but were blocked in doing so by state insurance regulators, both elected and politically appointed. Southeast Florida turned out to contain the greatest con-centration of insured catastrophe risk on the planet, indigestible even for global reinsurers.[66] Unable to be paid what they considered a fair price, insurers started to cancel policies in the riskiest locations, leaving homeowners to transfer to the Florida wind pools: publicly run "residual" insurers (providing coverage for all those unable to obtain private insurance), which expanded from 62,000 policies in 1992 to more than 900,000 by 1997.[67]

California insurers, not permitted to apply their requested price increases, threatened to withdraw from the state, imperiling the home-buying market.[68] In 1996 a compromise was reached: a "mini-policy" would be offered through the newly created California Earthquake Authority, with the world's most stringent 15 percent deductible.[69] As earthquake fear subsided and people recognized the cost relative to the partial compensation, the take-up rate of homeowner's earthquake insurance dropped from one in three to one in ten in 2015.

After the next big California earthquake, the large majority of people will receive no insurance compensation (unless their damaged property has the good fortune to catch fire). Among the uninsured, anyone with an earthquake-damaged house and a large mortgage will be better off handing the keys back to the bank.[70] There will be many abandoned houses and many homeowners clamoring for federal assistance, arguing the precedent of Katrina.

Wherever the catastrophe risk to US homeowners is highest, whether from flood, wind, or earthquake, insurers have failed to win the argument with politicians and the public that they must be allowed to charge the technical cost of the risk. Unless they collect enough premium to pay for the claims in their worst year, private insurers will go out of business. Public insurers can underprice the risk and then get compensated by the government when they run out of money. The National Flood Insurance Program "borrowed" $20.7 billion after Hurricane Katrina and then another $9.7 billion after Superstorm Sandy, with little prospect that the loans will be repaid.[71]

Through the government's increased contribution to losses from flooding, private insurance has been playing a diminishing role in US catastrophe compensation. After Hurricane Diane in 1955, the government paid only 6 percent of the costs, but this proportion rose to 50 percent after Katrina, and to 80 percent after Sandy.[72]

What does the US experience reveal for other countries, especially poorer countries? Catastrophe insurance can work well when impacts are impersonal—to compensate owners of hotels and factories, for instance, or even to refund damage to roads or bridges, with the premium paid by an aid agency. However, once it comes down to casualties and destroyed homes, governing politicians are unable to step back to let insurance alone determine who wins and who loses out in compensation.

One strategy would then be to split the population into two classes: the poorest, who would not consider buying property insurance, and the middle classes, who would. The Chilean government gave lump-sum compensation to the poorest 60 percent of homeowners after the 2010 Chile earthquake, funded from a temporary tax on the country's copper mines. Another 25 percent of homeowners had property insurance, as required for mortgage-holders. That left an exemplary 15 percent who received no compensation: enough to incentivize their future insurance purchase but not enough to feed mass political protests.

In the lavish compensation that followed Katrina, it was those wealthy citizens of coastal Mississippi with no flood insurance who were left "hung out to dry."

Since 1996, the Mexican government has incorporated these principles into the Fund for Natural Disasters (FONDEN), a system that compensates future disaster damage to public buildings, infrastructure, and the houses of the poorest.[73] FONDEN is funded with $1.5 billion raised each year from oil revenues. The system clearly spells out who can expect compensation, so this decision is not left to the discretion of politicians after the disaster. All other property owners need to purchase insurance. The fund is managed, and its reinsurance costed, using catastrophe models.

We will hear again from these catastrophe models, which have applications far beyond insurance. But first we will explore a different set of paths: the history of how communities and cities have been motivated to reduce their disaster risk.

8 • INTOLERABLE RISK

Wie het water deert, die het water keert. (Whom the water hurts, he the water stops.)

—Old Dutch proverb

I N TELLING THE STORY OF THE SEARCH FOR THE CURE FOR catastrophe, we have focused so far on the professionals: the scientists, the builders, the insurers, and the risk modelers. Now the curtain draws back—the scene is about to expand as we explore the strategies that societies have learned to manage their disasters. Some of those strategies have been broadly successful, while others have turned out to be misguided or impractical. We will start with some successes.

One country stands out for the way it made action on disasters core to the functioning of the state. That country is the Netherlands.

Four hundred years ago, the Dutch had mastered floods. They had come to understand that high river levels have to be guided to the sea, while sea floods need to be blocked. They had learned how to construct strong, wave-resistant embankments and where to mount secondary lines of backstop defenses. They had grown an operational system that could call out every villager to fight a dike breach, while mobilizing the ruling prince to provide the money and manpower to defend a threatened coastline. With the will, the funding, the leadership, and the communal ownership, a nation could beat disasters. The defeat of the storm surges and the elevated status given to national water management defined the Dutch nation and its entrepreneurial and consensual government. "Polder democracy" still flourishes in Holland today. In the words of the Dutch historian Herman Pleij: "The Netherlands owes its existence to the democracy of dry feet. We need each other literally in order not to drown."[1]

A thousand years ago, at the end of its journey from the Alps to the sea, the River Rhine split into three channels as it flowed through the "great bog of Europe" (as it was later derided), a vast delta of swamplands, thickets, and raised peat mires extending 50 miles (80 kilometers) inland from the North Sea coast. Apart from the coastal dunes, the land that today forms the Netherlands was completely unrecognizable then: there were no canals, windmills, or dikes, no settlement at Amsterdam, no inland Zuiderzee. The tribes who lived around the great bog huddled in their huts on dwelling mounds (*terpen*) raised above the tidal marshes and sustained themselves through fishing and trapping.[2]

Starting around AD 1000, the chief noble of the region, styling himself the Count of Holland, encouraged free peasants to create new farmland.[3] First they cut a deep ditch, fed by regularly spaced side ditches that each bounded a rented land parcel. The ditches would "bleed" the bogs, and in a generation, as the peat oxidized and the ground subsided, there would be fertile soil for growing crops or fodder for livestock. Around the same time, settlers living closer to the coast raised embankments to turn tidal salt marshes into grazing land.[4] Tens of thousands of people came to live on the drained marshlands, in farms, monasteries, and villages of single-story thatched cob houses, close to their land and their animals. Within two centuries, this fertile plain had become one of the most densely populated areas of Europe.

As the ground sank, the ditches had to be dug deeper. By the end of the twelfth century, this work required a dedicated team—the *heemraadschappen* ("water guardians"), who were elected from each village to maintain the drainage on behalf of the village.[5] They faced some daunting challenges. Runoff from rain had to be guided along the ditches to the rivers, but river floods threatened to flow back over the land. Worse, over large areas the drained bogs were sinking beneath the level of the highest tides.

In the All Saints' Day Flood of 1170, the sea surged through the Creiler forest to link up with the large freshwater Almere Lake and then would not recede; instead, the flooded area expanded over the months and years as the waves eroded the shallow layers of peat, forming a great inland sea—the Zuiderzee.[6] The Dutch settlers were forced to retreat. For the first time ships could now sail into the interior of the country, and at the end of the thirteenth century, where the River Amstel creek flowed into the new tidal sea, they built a dam and sluice to regulate the level of water in the river. The village where goods were transferred from seagoing sailing ships to inland barges was called Amster-dam.[7]

Each abbey, farm, and village was responsible for maintaining and repairing the dike that protected them on the principle cited at the beginning of this chapter: whom the water hurts, he the water stops.[8] Yet these embankments, being only high enough to protect against ordinary high water, were prone to being undermined or overtopped.

This was the beginning of a 400-year war. Decades of slow reclamation would be reversed by catastrophes when thousands of acres were lost in a single night. Through the thirteenth and fourteenth centuries, it is estimated, more than 200,000 people were drowned by storm surge floods.[9]

By 1300, the village water guardians were networked into the regional administration and by 1350 had been given the power to raise taxes.[10] The system was effective because it was ruthlessly managed. The supervisory "dike count" came to inspect every flood defense at the end of the winter and itemized the necessary repairs; returning in early autumn to check whether they had been completed, he would impose large fines and confiscate land for noncompliance.[11] The dike count might be the only source of funds for making the repairs, applying interest rates of 100 percent or more and requisitioning property when debts or fines went unpaid.

The nearest the whole system came to breakdown was at the beginning of the fifteenth century, especially at the time of the great St. Elisabeth's Day Flood of 1421.[12] In a single night, a wide new arm of the sea was carved out of the Scheldt estuary. Inland, between the Waal and the Maas Rivers, an area the size of a small county (500 square kilometers) was overwhelmed and lost; rich and densely populated lands, including forty-eight villages, were flooded so deeply that only the church spires were visible.

After the flood, defeatism took root: people were unwilling to repair dikes and disputed the response. Fortunately, the country's foreign rulers rose to the self-interested task of protecting their inheritance. Along the coast, the sea-fronting dikes were built higher and stronger.

Since the fourteenth century, people had dug peat for fuel on an industrial scale. The shallow pits became lakes, which expanded with the waves and threatened to undermine the country from within. In the early fifteenth century, a technological solution was found to this insidious problem: windmill-powered pumps that could finally reclaim land below the low tide level.[13]

In a 1565 painting by Pieter Bruegel the Elder, *The Gloomy Day* (one of the five surviving "season" pictures), the right half captures a spit of delta land embanked with sea defenses, on which people have built their houses. A winter storm is raging, ships are wrecked along the dike, and the land has partly flooded. Across the estuary there is a typical village, a cluster of thatched buildings, some half-timbered, with pink plaster walls.

The scene was painted five years before these coastal dikes were widely breached and overwhelmed in the 1570 flood, when water levels rose higher than at any time until the present day: 13.5 feet (4 meters) above sea level in places and 11.5 feet (3.5 meters) above sea level in Antwerp.[14] The flood inundated the streets of Dordrecht and Rotterdam, killing 3,000 people in the Zeeland islands, while tens of thousands of people drowned inland. Not a single island remained unflooded. Everywhere houses were washed away in the dunes, and whole streets disappeared in Scheveningen. Yet, while many dikes failed, only a few small Zeeland islands were permanently lost.

The tide of the battle with the floods was finally turned in the second half of the sixteenth century. This communal endeavor defined the new nation: "The making of new land belongs to God alone . . . for He gives to some people the wit and strength to do it." Or more brazenly:

"God made the World, but the Dutch made Holland."[15] At the end of the sixteenth century, the dike builder Andries Vierlingh described the responsibility of everyone in the village to seal a breaching dike: "I sent the drummer around to summon every person to work. . . . Those women who had no barrows carried clay in their aprons."[16]

Investment moved beyond repairing the damage caused by the last breach. Dikes were faced with timber imported from Norway, and some river dikes were lined with stone brought down the River Meuse by barge. Born in 1575, Jan Adriaanszoon, the lead engineer in the "conquest" of the Beemster Lake (an inland sea north of Amsterdam), changed his name as an act of self-promotion to Leeghwater (Low-water) and was as famous in Holland as the most victorious admiral.[17] Forty-three water-raising windmills created 17,500 acres of new fertile farmland, enriching the scheme's funders with annual rents worth 17 percent of their original investment. Amsterdam's population soared fivefold between 1578 and 1648, from 31,000 to 150,000, and was sustained by all the food grown on the newly protected farmland. A scheduled barge departed from Amsterdam to Haarlem every hour, using a network of canals that interlinked all the principal cities of the United Provinces.

By 1688, the Dutch had the highest per capita income of any northern European state.[18] The prosperity of the late-seventeenth-century Dutch Golden Age could not have been achieved without this victory over nature.

The story of Dutch flood control is the archetypal "cure for catastrophe" parable. The problem was never simply solved once and for all, but required constant vigilance in every new generation. The timber protection on dikes introduced in the seventeenth century was later found to concentrate the energy of breaking waves, eroding the supporting earth. Then, in the eighteenth century, an expensive switch to imported stone facing was required when dike timbers became riddled by the shipworm *Teredo navalis*.

In the nineteenth century, the regional water boards were combined into the national Rijkswaterstaat.[19] It took the 1953 floods, when 1,800 died, for the government to decree that the level of risk of flooding from the sea—the level of intolerable risk—should be set by statute to below one in 10,000 per year.[20] Today one-quarter of the Netherlands is below mean sea level, and another two-fifths is at or just above this level, protected by the great coastal wall of sand dunes and the defensive dike rings.

———

WHAT OTHER COUNTRY HAS REACHED THAT THRESHOLD OF INTOLerable risk and made it a societal mission to drive down the forces of destruction? One might not think the rumpled mountain landscape of Japan has anything in common with the canal-seamed plains of the Netherlands, but half the population and three-quarters of Japan's assets are situated in coastal and river floodplains, which make up only 14 percent of the land area. Japan is Holland with mountains in the middle. Typhoon-driven storm surges are at least as big as those in Holland, while in the summer in Japan, especially over the mountains, the rain can be torrential.

The first River Law, passed in 1896, required levees to be constructed along the banks of the lower channels of all the major rivers.[21] Meandering channels were straightened to help the floods flow straight out to sea. The work was completed by 1930, yet within a decade an average of 200,000 properties were being flooded each year.

Forty days after the atomic bomb was dropped on the city of Hiroshima, Typhoon Makurazaki passed over the city—the second-mostintense storm to hit Japan in modern times. The deluge drowned 2,000 survivors of the bomb, who were hiding in all that remained of their buildings—the basements.[22] In September 1947, the rainfall from Typhoon Kathleen in the Kantō Plain caused the River Tone embankment to burst, flooding the whole of eastern Tokyo for five days and drowning more than 1,000 people. Through the 1950s, 3 million properties were flooded.

The decade culminated in Japan's greatest flood disaster of all time. On September 26, 1959, a strong typhoon pushed an 11.5-foot (3.5-meter) surge tide into Ise Bay, overwhelming the defenses on the west side of the city of Nagoya and drowning more than 5,000.[23] Tens of thousands of tree trunks that had been stored for builders became wave-driven battering rams. One-fifth of the 250,000 houses in Nagoya were ruined.[24] Land subsidence from groundwater extraction left a lake one-third the size of Inner Tokyo Bay, with water up to 10 feet (3 meters) deep. It took three months to pump the water out.

The Ise Bay disaster provoked the Japanese to declare their flood risk "intolerable." The Disaster Countermeasures Basic Act, passed in 1961, created the Central Disaster Prevention Council, chaired by the prime minister.[25] In 1961 almost 8 percent of the national budget (1.5 percent of the gross domestic product) was allocated to disaster prevention. By the late 1980s, against a backdrop of rapid economic growth, a disaster management budget of 4 trillion yen (around $40 billion) still consumed 4.5 percent of the national budget (0.5 percent of GDP).

After three decades of investment in concrete flood walls and retention basins, the annual number of flooded properties fell below 40,000. By the 1990s, flood casualties were only a small fraction of those incurred in the 1950s.[26]

Yet, as with all flood walls, no protection is absolute, and on the rare occasion when they do fail—as in New Orleans—the higher the wall the deeper the flood.[27] In September 2000, after 24 inches (600 millimeters) of rainfall, the Shonai River, confined between its tall flood defenses, flowed 16 feet (5 meters) above the surrounding Nagoya suburbs. When a single section of the wall collapsed, 70,000 houses and businesses and 100,000 cars were inundated.[28]

THE CURE FOR EARTHQUAKES PROVED FAR HARDER TO FIND THAN the cure for floods. A strong city wall can keep wolves, marauders, and storm tides at bay, but no wall keeps out earthquakes. For centuries, defensive strategies were based on the latest earthquake theory, applied during reconstruction. Whatever these interventions accomplished in terms of economic renewal was eventually diminished by how little they achieved in the way of reducing risk.

If the original site of the city was doomed to disaster, why not move to a new site, innocent of bad associations? From the end of the seventeenth century, in both the Old and New Worlds, relocation became a standard Spanish colonial strategy as a remedy for a devastated city. While such moves demonstrated purposeful leadership, they often proved deeply unpopular.

There were rich opportunities to apply this geomancy after the January 1693 destruction of forty-nine cities across southeast Sicily. Among these was Noto, situated on the edge of the mountains.[29] The original Bronze Age site had been selected for its defensive qualities: the Monte Alveria plateau was incised like a maple leaf by ravines. Home to 10,000 people, the city was sustained by fifty-six churches and nineteen convents and monasteries. Then came the earthquake of January 9, 1693, which was "so horrible and ghastly that the soil undulated like the waves of a stormy sea and the mountains danced as if drunk, and the city collapsed in one miserable moment killing more than a thousand people."[30] This was the biggest earthquake in Italy's history.[31] The destruction was so widespread across Sicily that no one came to help.

Sicily was reluctantly ruled from Spain. Over the previous half-century, the province had faced uprisings and economic decline. The Spanish viceroy in Sicily appointed the duke of Camastra to the role of disaster manager. Camastra badgered the people of Noto to endorse relocation to a hilltop halfway to the coast, close to the coastal marshes. In the first summer after they moved, 3,000 died in a malaria epidemic. The survivors clamored to return to Old Noto.[32] Eventually people were coerced to stay, after watching the dressed stone from their old houses being transported to the new site in thousands of mule trains.

The buildings of New Noto started off small and squat; to ward off earthquakes they were constructed above artificial "antiseismic" caverns. Within a few decades, however, all of the supposed antiseismic provisions had been forgotten and the New Noto had become a showcase for the finest Sicilian baroque churches and palaces. The replacement buildings were far from robust: several fell in the tremors of the next three centuries, and part of the cathedral collapsed after a rainstorm in 1996.[33]

Spanish colonial administrators had another chance to apply their strategy of relocation at Concepción in the Bay of Talcahuano on the stormy coast of southern Chile. On July 8, 1730, the town's 200 buildings swayed in a distant earthquake, which was followed a few hours later by three massive sea waves that removed all the low-lying buildings by the port. Twenty-one years later, at dawn on May 25, 1751, a great wave emerged out of the shimmering darkness ten minutes after a heavy shock and destroyed the whole town. Chile's viceroy announced that the city would relocate to a site seven miles inland, on the alluvial plains of the Mocha Valley on the Bio Bio River.[34] Ten days later, a grid of streets had been drawn and work started on the crown offices and monasteries. Within a month, opposition to the move was being led by the city's bishop, José de Toro y Zambrano.[35] Even as the new city began to take shape, the ordinary fishermen and stevedores, refusing to move, were rebuilding their hovels at the old site, now named Penco. In September 1754, when the authorities attempted to evict the implacable residents, the bishop excommunicated the bailiffs. The bishop's unwavering opposition ended only with his death in 1760. Today, in memory of that forced relocation, the citizens of Concepción still refer to themselves as "Penquistas."

While the new inland site of Concepción was beyond the "tidal waves," its alluvial soils offered no refuge from shaking. In 1835 the new city was leveled in a great earthquake, and it happened once again in 1939, when 80 percent of the 15,000 adobe structures in the city collapsed.[36]

The grandest eighteenth-century city to face relocation after a disaster was in Guatemala. Conquistadors founded the city of Santiago de los Caballeros de Goathemala on July 25, 1524. The original site was relocated twice in its first twenty years—first for defensive reasons and then again after it was wiped out by a volcanic mudflow.[37] The new site prospered: it became the capital of Spanish Guatemala—a province that covered most of modern Central America—and Guatemala City was the third-largest in the Americas after Mexico City and Lima. On September 29, 1717, however, an earthquake ruined more than 3,000 buildings.[38] The city's leaders debated relocation, but instead the city was rebuilt in a bulky colonial adaptation of the latest European baroque style, with magnificent monasteries, nunneries, and churches embellished with stone carvings.

On the afternoon of July 29, 1773, the city of 40,000 was hit by another strong earthquake. Many people ran outside and were spared when the catastrophic (estimated Magnitude 7.4) main shock arrived fifteen minutes later.[39] Every building was damaged, and many had collapsed. More than 500 people were crushed by the rubble.

Within a week, the governing captain-general proposed that the city be relocated. He created a commission to review the options while strongly recommending that the new site should be in the Valle de La Ermita, 15.5 miles (25 kilometers) to the east.[40] It was initially claimed that the site was protected from earthquakes, but it was soon discovered that the two churches at La Ermita had been damaged in previous tremors. The commission chose to ignore this flaw and instead focused on the positives: the water was good, the earth was "solid," and deep ravines through the La Ermita site would create escape routes in an earthquake. Later the ravines were declared "antiseismic." After waiting more than a year for the slow exchange of letters, the choice of La Ermita was officially endorsed by the Spanish king.

In the new city, plazas were to be enlarged and streets widened, and just as at Lima after 1746, the maximum building height was set at 13 feet (4 meters). The new cathedral was to be fitted with wooden ceilings rather than vaulting. In 1776 two prototype "earthquake-proof" houses, like those at Lima, were constructed on the main square, in the hope that builders would copy them.

Terrified by the persistent aftershocks, initially people were enthusiastic about moving out of their ruined city. However, within a month the archbishop, Pedro Cortés y Larraz, and the city council, along with thousands of residents, were declaring that earthquakes occurred everywhere in their country and that the relocation proposal had been a panicked response.[41] The administration was furious. In 1776 the captain-general sent his troops to force the inhabitants to leave, but five years after the earthquake there were still 11,000 left in the old ruined city. The Spanish king, Charles III, had the archbishop expelled from Guatemala for his "scandalous, offensive and contentious opposition."[42] Without their leader, many of the remaining inhabitants were evicted and their businesses forcibly closed, until the streets of the old city were almost empty. The poor returned surreptitiously to live among the haunted ruins of what was now known as Antigua (Old) Guatemala. By 1850, it had 9,000 inhabitants.

To abandon the city was to save it. Without its earthquake, this early eighteenth-century baroque masterpiece would have been overtaken by every progressive architectural and functional fashion that has so disfigured other cities in the region, from bottling plants to bus stations, from shopping malls to six-lane highways. Instead, its architecture was preserved, fissured and brooding, bookended by one earthquake that cleared the site for the city to be built and a second that froze it in time.[43]

At the relocated site of the new Guatemala City, with its "protective ravines," little thought was given to shock-resistant buildings. Thus, earthquakes in December 1917 and January 1918 more or less destroyed the new city.[44] The archbishop had been right.

Relocation also has a political imperative. A ruler can take money and power from an urban elite whose land values will drain away once economic activity has been diverted, while enriching the landowners of the new city site, who might, as at Noto, be political patrons. Following its calamitous 1944 earthquake, the national government proposed that the city of San Juan in western Argentina should be relocated, but the old city elites defeated the move, campaigning through their control of the local press.[45]

Another elite not prepared to be dislodged were the oligarchs of the port of Galveston, Texas. In 1838 a group of investors formed the Galveston City Company to begin the development of a seaside town and port on the barrier island. The author of *Braman's Information About Texas* (1858) declared: "I should as soon think of founding a city on an iceberg as on Galveston Island, if I looked to its safety and perpetuity."[46] The town proved a huge success—by 1900, twenty-six millionaires lived in one five-block section of mansions. With its regular steamship destinations and consulates, the island had pretensions to being the Manhattan of the Gulf Coast.

However, the highest ground on the island was less than nine feet above sea level, while some buildings had thresholds only three feet above the tides. The city grew familiar with flooding in hurricanes.[47] There were three floods in 1871 alone. On one occasion, a schooner and three sloops were abandoned on the streets. After the whole island was flooded in 1875, the city established a commission to consider building a seawall, but the proposal was rejected as "too costly."

Then came the hurricane of September 8, 1900. Winds estimated at 145 miles (230 kilometers) per hour drove before them a 15-foot (4.5-meter) surge accompanied by colossal waves, turning the houses near the coast into a mass of floating timbers several stories high that acted as battering rams to scour buildings off their foundations six blocks inland.[48] An estimated 8,000 people died.

That would seem to have been a good time to relocate the city. Yet some hefty real estate values were at stake.

In January 1902, the city appointed a Board of Engineers, who were tasked to raise and protect Galveston Island. By this means, landownership would not be compromised. The plan required 3,000 buildings to be jacked up by 11 feet (3.3 meters), sand pumped beneath them, and all to be protected by a 17-foot concrete seawall.[49] The program of work took seven years to complete. The city never recovered its former status.

At the end of the twentieth century, urban relocation has come back into fashion after the 2005 earthquake in Kashmir, Pakistan, and the 2008 quake in Wenchuan, China, only now the scientific rationale is more convincing—to avoid catastrophic landslides.[50] The policy remains no less controversial.

———

INSTEAD OF FACING THE UNPOPULARITY OF RELOCATING A CITY, why not redesign it on its original site?

Destruction provides a blank canvas on which an ambitious architect can redraw the cityscape. It was the opportunity to transform the narrow winding streets of medieval London that inspired Christopher Wren's vision of a city of wide boulevards and grand piazzas after the 1666 Great Fire.[51] Time and again after catastrophes, however, the obstacles to grand design have been the same: landowners need to be bought out to make way for new boulevards, but the devastation has removed a city's income from rents and taxes.[52] There were 80,000 homeless Londoners clamoring for action, and the city's prestige as Europe's third-largest city needed to be restored. Frustrated, Wren railed against the "obstinate Adverseness of a great Part of the Citizens."[53]

Pragmatically the commission proposed a rebuilding act, which was passed by Parliament in February 1667.[54] All property owners were forced to give up a few feet of their frontage so that roads could be widened. The original geometry of the city's streets would reassert itself, like new saplings emerging on sawn stumps. By 1672, the city had been largely reconstructed on its old street plan.

Both the 1756 plans drawn up by the precocious twenty-seven-year-old Scottish architect Robert Adams for a neoclassical Lisbon and Daniel Burnham's 1906 visionary redesign of San Francisco with Parisian avenues and boulevards foundered on the same obstacles that blocked Wren: a lack of money to compensate displaced landowners.[55] It only proves possible to completely redesign a city's plan after a disaster when the majority of the landowners are either dead or dispersed. When Catania lost 16,000 of its 20,000 citizens in the 1693 Sicily earthquake, the opportunity arose to ignore the "obstinate Adverseness" of the citizenry and completely reconfigure the medieval city's plan with wide straight streets and new piazza squares (said to allow building owners to camp next to their damaged buildings in a future disaster).[56]

———

THE EARTHQUAKE OFFSHORE AT SANTA BARBARA, CALIFORNIA, AT 6:43 a.m. on Monday, June 29, 1925, had tumbled the facades of brick stores and hotels, ruining thirty-six blocks of the business district. Only the time of day limited the death toll to thirteen. The first significant earthquake in California since 1906 was generating a lot of bad publicity and threatening the vital Los Angeles tourist trade.

On the day after the earthquake, Santa Barbara community leaders met to form the Board of Public Safety and Reconstruction. As at San Francisco in 1906, the board was looking for some instant positive "spin" to counter the tales of death and destruction. There was no fire in which to shroud the earthquake. A wealthy engineer in the group, Bernhard Hoffman, successfully argued that the city should be rebuilt in the architecture he had practiced in the neighborhood of El Paseo, a village of mixed shops and restaurants imitating elements of an original

Spanish colonial building known as the "de la Guerra 1849 adobe."[57] With a flair for publicity, he christened this architecture the "Santa Barbara style." The announcement was headlined the following day in the local paper: "Spanish Architecture to Rise from Ruin." The committee listed a number of buildings that contained elements of this style and had survived the earthquake unscathed. However, there was no real evidence that this style of building was any better than others at resisting shaking damage.

Within two weeks, the Board of Public Safety and Reconstruction had created the Architectural Advisory Committee and the Architectural Board of Review, on both of which Bernhard Hoffman served.[58] "Now when everyone is absorbed in the story of our misfortune," a spokesman for the board announced, "let us surprise the balance of California and the world by turning our misfortune into a source of rejoicing." The earthquake had become the opportunity to impose a unified architectural aesthetic.

The idea of the "disaster makeover" quickly caught on. A devastating hurricane in August 1926 had stripped the tourist town of Miami Beach back to its foundations. In the reconstruction of South Beach that followed, architects designed whole blocks in Art Deco style.[59] The best remedy for the bad publicity that accompanied a disaster was for a city to be resurrected in the latest fashion.

On February 3, 1931, the town of Napier on the east coast of North Island, New Zealand, was completely destroyed by a massive earthquake situated on a fault that directly underlay the city. Based on the precedent of Santa Barbara, and perhaps showing some "California envy," a group of Napier architects campaigned to create a strong local Art Deco–influenced style and worked with the town's reconstruction committee to achieve consistency in the appearance of all the replacement buildings.[60] Out of fear of further earthquakes, the buildings were kept low—no more than two stories.

The success of the 1925–1931 aesthetic reconstruction narrative at Santa Barbara, Miami Beach, and Napier might be thought to have launched many more post-disaster imitators. Surprisingly, Napier proved to be the end of the road for this movement.[61] After the next significant earthquake, in Long Beach, California, in 1933, the reconstruction agenda moved to concerns of greater gravity, making the idea of rebuilding a city in the latest architectural fashion seem a tad decadent.

———

IN THE EARLY EVENING SHOCK, MANY NEW SCHOOL BUILDINGS, with their large roof spans and open halls, had collapsed. Damaged school buildings dominated the front pages of the local newspapers, and the head of the Long Beach School Department estimated that 6,000 children could have been killed if the earthquake had happened an hour earlier.[62] Don C. Field was the Republican state representative for the district covering Long Beach and was himself a building contractor. Within two weeks of the March 10, 1933, earthquake, he introduced a bill requiring that the design and construction of public school buildings be regulated by structural engineers acting for the state.[63] The Field Act was passed by the California State Legislature on April 10, 1933—thirty days after the earthquake.

The 1933 earthquake brought down the curtain on the long-running, business-led campaign of American "earthquake denialism." There were practical actions to be taken to withstand the earthquake threat—the mortal disease could be treated.

The Field Act focused on new construction, but if 10 percent of enrolled parents requested it, the state architect would evaluate any school building. Within a year, 333 applications had been submitted to review plans for new schools, while 1,000 had been requested by parents of children in preexisting schools. In 1939 the act was expanded to require inspection and, where needed, retrofitting for all pre-1933 school buildings. The act provided much-welcomed employment for California structural engineers throughout the Great Depression.

The proponents of California's Field Act proclaim with pride, "No student, teacher, or anyone has been killed from an earthquake in a school building since its enactment in 1933," but in fact, since 1900, no major Californian earthquake has occurred in the vicinity of a town or city during school hours.[64] The idea of declaring zero tolerance for school casualties was a brilliant initiative, but curiously, no one sought to export it or to make it a global standard.

———•———

WITH MORE EXPERIENCE OF DISASTERS THAN ANY OTHER COUNTRY, Japan has a pair of characters in its language that translate as "building back better." This is contrasted with a closely related pair meaning: "restoration to the state that existed before."[65] A catastrophe provides the opportunity to make genuine improvements to reduce the risk.

One of the earliest examples of "building back better" was London after its 1666 fire. Yet the imperative for rapid reconstruction often overtakes the ideal of "building back better," as when San Francisco completed its rebuilding in seven years, unhindered by any building code mandating earthquake-resistance, or when, after Hurricane Ivan's storm surge flooded almost the whole of Grand Cayman, buildings were reconstructed at the same elevation as before.

The first city to aim to take the time to achieve genuine "build back better" after an earthquake disaster was Messina, Sicily.[66] Because Messina's 1908 devastation was accompanied by high mortality and the subsequent dispersal of the residents, and because the city lacked the "get up and go" commercial imperative of a San Francisco or London, it was possible to contemplate a complete urban redesign. In the new plan, commissioned by the city's planning director and approved at the end of 1911, the size of the city was doubled, and the streets were widened and placed on a grid.[67] No buildings could be higher than two stories. The world's first earthquake building code required that buildings be able to withstand a sudden sideways force one-tenth of the building's weight.[68] However, within little more than thirty years, Messina had been devastated by World War II bombs and shells rather than earthquakes; after the war, all precautions about earthquakes had been forgotten, and the buildings of the city were rapidly reconstructed four to five stories high.

———•———

WHICH COUNTRY HAS MASTERED EARTHQUAKES IN THE SAME WAY the Dutch have mastered floods? Which has come closest to curing its shaking catastrophes?

In February 1835, while resting on the ground in a wood at Valdivia, Charles Darwin had the formative pleasure of experiencing the largest central Chile earthquake of the nineteenth century. A few days later, he visited the second city of Concepción; shocked by the destruction, he reflected that no civilized country could sustain or tolerate this level of repeated devastation.[69] We now know that Chile, situated alongside one of the world's fastest-moving plate boundaries, is on the earthquake front line. At the start of the twentieth century, relative to its population, Chile had some of the highest earthquake casualties of any country. Most deaths were caused by the fall of traditional adobe buildings.

On February 27, 2010, a near-repeat of Darwin's earthquake came around again: 250 miles (400 kilometers) of the plate boundary dipping down beneath the coast of central Chile broke in a Magnitude 8.8 earthquake—at the time the fifth-largest earthquake ever recorded. It was early Saturday morning, before sunrise, at the start of the last weekend of the summer holidays.

Oklahoman Will O'Donnell was sleeping on the fifteenth floor of an apartment building in Vina del Mar, on the coast north of the earthquake rupture.[70] Awakened at 3:30 a.m., he got out of bed and as the shaking became stronger and more rhythmic found himself thrown from side to side, bouncing off the opposing walls of his room. The lights went out, his desk was toppled, and plates crashed onto the floor. After ninety seconds, the shaking wound down and he looked out over a darkened city, to the cacophony of car alarms and the mad barking of hundreds of terrified dogs. There was no cell phone service. He walked down the fifteen flights of the staircase and out into the street, where he found the owner with a flashlight, surveying the base of the building.

Across the city, damage was limited to some twisted and cracked concrete where tall buildings had thrashed on their foundations. Even though the fault started to break next to the second city of Concepción and pounded the forest of skyscrapers in the inland capital of Santiago, in all the furious shaking only one tall building fell—a Concepción apartment building, not yet fully occupied, was torn off its cavernous basements.[71] Millions of people were in the zone of strongest shaking, but only a few hundred people died, half of them in the tsunami. Many of the lives lost on February 27 were the result of some oversight—like the campers on an estuary island with nowhere to evacuate to ahead of the nighttime tsunami, or those driving the Santiago toll road when the overpass ahead of them collapsed.

Fewer people died in building collapses in the Magnitude 8.8 central Chile earthquake than in the 1,000 times smaller 2009 L'Aquila earthquake in central Italy.[72] After fifty years of investment in world-class schools of engineering, and by strictly enforcing tough building codes, Chile today has some of the safest earthquake-resistant building stock in the world.

Chileans have come to fear and respect great earthquakes in the same way the Dutch fear and respect storm surge floods. Just as there is no corner of Holland entirely free from floods, so there is nowhere in Chile you can escape from shaking. All Chilean politicians expect some disaster during their period in office. Earthquake culture runs deep. Building codes are respected and followed, and developers hold a ten-year liability for building damage, with the threat of a jail term.[73] Builders know that their handiwork will be tested over the course of their working life and that this is a matter of life and death.

The response to the 2010 earthquake still left plenty of room for improvement. It was the job of the revered Chilean navy to provide a tsunami warning, but no one was on duty that night, and anyway, communication systems crashed with the loss of electrical power.[74] There still needs to be zoning to prevent development in the tsunami flood zones and a funded replacement program for the dangerous old adobe housing. Nevertheless, one day there will be a great Chilean earthquake in which nobody dies.

———

THE CARIBBEAN ISLAND OF PUERTO RICO LIES AT THE EASTERN END of the Greater Antilles, a fertile and rugged landmass 100 miles (160 kilometers) long and 40 miles (65 kilometers) wide. Without any gold or valuable minerals, the island was neglected by the Spanish colonial administrators, but then wrested away by the United States in 1898. After some relatively calm decades, on September 13, 1928, a Category 5 hurricane (known after its saint's day, San Felipe), with sustained wind speeds of more than 150 miles (240 kilometers) per hour, made landfall along the middle of the eastern end of the island and proceeded to move to the west-northwest over the capital San Juan.[75] The winds obliterated the island's fragile thatched *bohios* and one-room chattel houses, tore off the tin roofs of the estancias and parish schools, and brought trees crashing down on the hipped roofs of the town houses, leaving a tally of 25,000 houses destroyed and another 192,000 damaged.[76] Half a million people—one-third of the population—were left homeless, and more than 300 were dead. Four years later, the island was hit again, this time by the smaller (Category 4) San Ciprian hurricane, which traversed the entire length of the island from east to west, taking another 250 lives and leaving more than 75,000 homeless.[77]

Following the second storm, engineers carefully recorded which buildings survived and which ones had failed. They found that "only the heaviest construction of masonry and concrete with cemented tile roofs, came out of the zone of heaviest damage unscathed."[78] Other concrete walls with insufficient cement, with too widely spaced reinforcement, or with roofs inadequately anchored proved lethal to the occupants as well as to those downwind. Corrugated iron roofs fixed with smooth or even twisted nails, many of them installed since the 1928 storm, "were carried off like so much cardboard," while the same roofing material fixed with bolts to a properly anchored frame survived.

One catastrophe can be put down to chance. Two becomes a pattern. The construction lessons learned from San Ciprian, following in the wake of the devastation from San Felipe, came to transform the island's building stock. By the 1950s, a combination of an on-island cement industry and the marketing of the American suburban, car-owning lifestyle had encouraged the middle classes to move into estates of reinforced-concrete "bunker" houses with tiny jalousie windows.[79] Hot and confined, these houses were a total break with the traditional airy rural houses, but they were deemed "bulletproof" in the most intense hurricanes, as proved when in 1989 Category 4 Hurricane Hugo hit the island along almost the same path as San Felipe. Only nine people died.

On the island of Bermuda, the lessons had been learned from two fierce hurricanes at the beginning of the eighteenth century. Afterward, only single-story buildings with walls and roofs built out of stone were constructed.

In 1994 the Florida counties blasted by Hurricane Andrew—Broward and Miami-Dade—adopted a tough building code so that new buildings would be designed to withstand 150-mile-per-hour wind speeds. Following seven years of protracted negotiations with building industry lobbyists, however, the building code finally adopted for the rest of the state was much weaker. Even when the catastrophe was just a few counties away, the local risk was not deemed "intolerable."

How to perform a scientific experiment? Get one half of an island to apply a building code and in the other half leave the builders unsupervised. Then run the island through an intense hurricane. The experiment was performed in 1999 when Hurricane Luis pummeled the French/Dutch Caribbean island of St. Martin/Sint Maarten. The French had a building code. The Dutch did not. Buildings in the French territory were generally unscathed, while the Dutch side resembled an Alabama trailer park after a passing tornado.[80]

9 • THE DISASTER FORECAST

The press and the public will go toward the
suggestion of prediction like hogs to a trough.

—From the never-delivered retirement
speech of Charles Richter

ONCE UPON A TIME, ALL DISASTERS—STORMS, FLOODS, HUR-
ricanes, earthquakes, eruptions—arrived without warning.

Afterwards, the survivors would reflect on whether there had been
some unusual precursors. On the volcano Hekla in Iceland, the sheep
farmers noticed that the streams dried up before the start of each new
eruption.[1] Thirty-six centuries ago, the inhabitants of Akrotiri on the
Greek island of Santorini correctly interpreted the signs that a cataclysmic volcanic explosion was brewing and evacuated their town.[2]

Of all classes of catastrophe, volcanoes prove to show the earliest
premonitory signs. The question is then what action to take. A successful evacuation requires a leader willing to risk his or her reputation
and a people prepared to abandon their fields and homes. The largest
eruptions have the strongest signature, but also require retreating to
the greatest distance.

The city of St. Pierre was founded in the early seventeenth century
on the northwest lee of the island of Martinique, along a narrow coastal

shelf of land beneath the steep slopes that rise up to two mountains, one of them the highest peak on the island, 4,600-foot (1,400-meter) Mont Pelée. Through the nineteenth century, the town flourished, gaining streets of two- or three-storied, balconied houses lined with tropical trees and gardens—St. Pierre became "the little Paris of the Caribbean."[3] By 1900, the population was 26,000.

At the start of 1902, plumes of steam were spotted rising out of the ground on the flanks of Mont Pelée. The emanations increased in intensity through April, and there was a strong smell of sulfur in the city.[4] There were many small earthquakes, and the underwater cable connecting St. Pierre to Dominica and Guadeloupe mysteriously broke. On April 26, walkers visiting the summit found a lake of hot water filled from a boiling water spring on a new 50-foot (15-meter) ash cone. The local newspaper called off the picnic on the mountain planned for May 4. Then hundreds of deadly fer-de-lance snakes were spotted coming into the city.

On May 5, the crater wall containing the lake collapsed, and a hot mudflow descended the Blanche River Valley, burying the twenty-five workers at the Guerin sugar factory. People in outlying villages around the northern tip of the island started to arrive in St. Pierre, where they were housed in churches by the priests. During the night, the city's electricity gave out.

Everyone was aware that an eruption was brewing. The governor at Fort-de-France, on the south side of the island, convened a panel of "experts," who concluded that the deep valleys immediately beneath the volcano would channel the mudflow or ash cloud from any eruption directly to the sea, protecting the city. To impress the nervous citizens, on May 6 the governor and his wife arrived to stay in St. Pierre. That day an eruption of ash fell over the city, muffling the steps of people walking through the streets. Rumblings from the volcano were growing louder, intermixed with roars from avalanches of rock descending the valleys immediately beneath the volcano. People were beginning to panic. On the afternoon of May 7, the mayor requested soldiers to help keep order. Without such restraint, many people would have already left the town. A reassuring statement was published in the St. Pierre newspaper telling people not to worry. The more fearful went to the cathedral to spend the night praying.

On the bright morning of Ascension Day, May 8, at 7:52 a.m., a plug of lava blocking the mouth of the volcano suddenly burst out, releasing a foam of molten magma, ash particles, and superheated gases. As viewed from a cable-repair ship moored off the coastline, the mountainside beneath the crater suddenly ripped open, and a dense dark cloud shot out horizontally, accompanied by a second dense black cloud that soared upwards into a gigantic mushroom formation that caused darkness to descend for 25 miles around. The horizontal black cloud plunged down the western flank of the volcano, reaching the city in less than a minute. The cloud was glowing red-hot at an estimated 1,000 degrees Celsius. As it reached the city, everything in its path caught fire. Thousands of barrels of rum burst, sending streams of flames into the streets. All vegetation and buildings were incinerated over eight square miles, and all 30,000 inhabitants and visitors to the city were killed, suffocated, and burned—all except a prisoner, Ludger Sylbaris, who had been held deep underground for the night in the town's jail. The black cloud was afterwards known as a *nuée ardente*—a burning, glowing avalanche. The theory advanced by the governor's experts that the valleys descending from the volcano would protect the city failed because such an avalanche can ride over ridges as it plunges downhill.[5] The governor and his wife died trying to convince the citizens that the city was safe.

The lessons from St. Pierre are still relevant today. What is considered a "safe refuge" may simply be someone's optimistic theory, whether hurricane shelters built two feet above sea level on New Providence Island in the Bahamas or the evacuation destinations overwhelmed by the tsunami along the Tohoku coast of Japan in 2011.

After Mont Pelée erupted, no city administrator in the Lesser Antilles Islands would again dare to ignore the symptoms of an emerging eruption. However, volcanoes can be fickle: sometimes they come back to life with only explosions of superheated steam (so-called phreatic eruptions). The critical question then concerns whether the gases or ash particles reveal that fresh magma is rising, in which case the steam explosions would be preparatory to a much more catastrophic eruption.

In the second half of 1975, a series of earthquakes were recorded beneath the Grande Soufrière volcano on Basse-Terre, the southwest part of the island of Guadeloupe, sister département to Martinique.[6] The tremors increased into the early summer of 1976; then, at 8:55 a.m. on July 8, there was a large phreatic (steam) explosion at the volcano. A thick cloud laden with ash descended the mountain and plunged the town of Saint Claude, at the upper end of the city of Basse-Terre, into twenty minutes of darkness. With the folk memory of St. Pierre still strong, the people panicked: over the next two hours, 25,000 fled to the Grande Terre peninsula to the northeast of the island. On July 13, the head of the French volcanological service, Haroun Tazieff, arrived. A Polish-born and Belgian-educated former mining engineer, Tazieff was a charismatic daredevil who had made television programs about his exploits climbing down to lava lakes and standing next to fumaroles. (He had been declared one of the six most famous men in France.) He announced that, without any sign of fresh magma in the eruption on July 8, there was unlikely to be a Mont Pelée–style catastrophe involving the dreaded *nuée ardente*.[7] Tazieff returned to Paris on July 17, leaving a small monitoring team. On the 24th and 28th, further steam explosions erupted from the volcano. Meanwhile, Tazieff set off on a long-planned expedition to the volcanoes of Ecuador. In his absence, he transferred responsibility to the director of the Seismic Research Unit in Trinidad, John Tomblin, who had twenty years' experience observing Caribbean volcanoes.

Upon his arrival on the island on August 3, Tomblin declared that the volcano was capable of another Mont Pelée.[8] Back in Paris, on August 8, Claude Allègre, a very capable thirty-nine-year-old geochemist, was named head of the Institut de Physique du Globe de Paris (IPG), a position that made him Tazieff's new boss. On August 9, there was a large, explosive steam-and-ash eruption at the volcano that projected blocks weighing up to 200 pounds (100 kilograms). Tomblin wrote that there was a one-in-four chance that this would end in a magma eruption, and that it was a coin toss whether such an eruption would be cataclysmic. On August 12, when there were more explosions, a French petrologist sent to Guadeloupe, Professor Robert Brousse, made a critical announcement: contradicting Tazieff, he said that there were traces of fresh magma in the ash from the July eruption. The prefect of the island commanded that the population of Basse-Terre start evacuating; by the 15th, 76,000 people had left their homes all around the volcano.

Professor Brousse was quoted in headlines saying that the course was now irreversible: they were heading toward a great eruption that could be 30 megatons in size. The prefect upped the stakes and declared that there was only a 1-in-2,000 chance they would avoid a significant eruption.

On August 26, Claude Allègre arrived in Guadeloupe, and on the 29th Tazieff returned from Ecuador to discover he had a new boss. He immediately expressed his amazement that the "so-called" experts had termed the situation "irreversible" and declared that, from the evidence to hand, he could not see any immediate danger.

On August 30, Tomblin, Tazieff, Allègre, and other scientists made a journey to the summit of the volcano. The petrologist Brousse stayed behind, as he had forecast a significant explosive eruption on that day. At 10:30 a.m., an eruption occurred while they were standing close to the crater. Projectile blocks of up to a cubic meter were hurled into the air. Three of the party, including Tazieff, were injured by the raining stones and taken by helicopter to the hospital, but they were soon discharged. Tazieff's action-man image was burnished as he told the press it was a miracle that none of them had been killed.[9]

On September 1, Tazieff gave a press conference at which he declared that Professor Brousse, who "had never studied a volcanic eruption previously," had "panicked." If Tazieff had been around, he would never have authorized the evacuation. Now, in direct conflict with his new boss, whose job was to ensure that there was a coordinated scientific commentary, Tazieff left Guadeloupe.

Tazieff was such a celebrity that even for this level of insubordination he was hard to dismiss. On September 6, Allègre attempted to dilute Tazieff's influence by announcing that a "team of experts"—of which Tazieff could be a member—would be established to monitor the volcano. On September 9, Tazieff gave an interview to the local Guadeloupe radio station in which he described the pressure being put on him to stay silent and accused both Professor Brousse and Claude Allègre of incompetence. He also encouraged the local inhabitants to return, declaring it was safe to do so.[10]

On September 19, Tazieff was vindicated when analyses from laboratories at Los Alamos in New Mexico showed that there had been no fresh magma in the July eruption. On the 21st, the latest analyses of gases also confirmed that no new magma was rising.[11] On October 11, the prefect announced the reopening of schools and reoccupation of villages to the east of the volcano. Most people returned on October 27, the same day Tazieff was fired from his job as head of volcanology at the IPG.

Meanwhile, Tazieff had become a hero in Guadeloupe. On November 20, the consul general arranged a series of meetings—billed as "For Truth, for Science, for Guadeloupe"—at which Tazieff spoke in front of thousands of Guadeloupians. Three days later, 6,000 Guadeloupians had signed a petition demanding that Professors Brousse and Allègre be banned from any further role in monitoring volcanoes on the island and that this function be handed to Tazieff.[12]

The last village up the mountain from Basse-Terre, St. Claude, reopened on December 1. There were a couple of steam explosions early the next year, and then it was over. The evacuation had lasted three months and cost several hundred million dollars in economic disruption.

The lesson taken from Guadeloupe concerned the thanklessness of organizing an evacuation when there might not be an eruption. Now the pendulum would swing the other way. Almost inevitably, people would die because of the fear of an unnecessary evacuation. It took less than a decade for this scenario to unfold.

Through 1985, the glacier-covered 17,500-foot (5,300-meter) Nevado del Ruiz volcano in Colombia, 80 miles (130 kilometers) west of Bogotá, showed signs of reawakening.[13] After weeks of agitation, the volcano erupted shortly after 3:00 p.m. on November 13, 1985. The eruption was relatively small but generated enough heat to melt the summit glaciers and send lahar mudflows—a mix of volcanic ash and meltwater—racing down the slopes at up to one kilometer per minute and into the steep river valley ravines that led out into the surrounding plains.

A month before the eruption, hazard maps had been circulated showing that the town of Armero, in the plain just beyond the mountain, was at high risk from lahar floods.[14] Local politicians accused the scientific and civil defense agencies of damaging the local economy with their scaremongering. After the ashfall from the afternoon erup-tion, the mayor and priest of the town set out to reassure the people. When civil defense officials from other towns in the path of the lahars witnessed the arrival of the massive muddy floods and tried to alert Armero, they could not get through because the electricity was down. Later that evening, the mudflow hit the town, destroying 5,000 houses and drowning three-quarters of the 29,000 inhabitants.

The next opportunity to test evacuation procedures for a big volca-nic eruption came in 1991 on the island of Luzon in the Philippines. This time the procedure worked more or less to plan.[15] Earthquakes and steam eruptions gave several months' warning that the volcano Mount Pinatubo was coming back to life. Gas samples showed a big uptick in sulfur dioxide emissions, the signature of fresh magma rising. The swelling of the mountain was picked up by tilt meters. When, on June 7, an eruption burst 4 miles (7 kilometers) into the sky, everyone in the area, convinced that the risk was real, began formal evacuations. The presence of a nearby US airbase and a very well connected head of the Philippine volcano science agency ensured good coordination. Evacuation zones were designated at different radii around the volcano, out to almost 24 miles (40 kilometers), and were progressively depop-ulated as the eruption approached. Forty thousand people lived within 12 miles (20 kilometers) of Pinatubo, and another 370,000 lived within 24 miles. Although many people had little confidence that the govern-ment would provide them with adequate shelter and sanitation at their unknown destinations, by early June 250,000 people had been evacu-ated. The mountain exploded on June 15 in the second-largest eruption of the twentieth century. An estimated 847 were killed—mostly those who had chosen to stay in their village and then died from collapsing roofs laden with ash—but tens of thousands of lives were saved.[16]

After the success at Pinatubo, one might conclude that protect-ing people from devastating eruptions is now a problem solved. Yet in many ways Pinatubo was an ideal case. Evacuating ahead of the next big eruption in a populated region, wherever it is, may not be so straightforward. In April 2012, after scientists warned of an impending eruption of Popocatépetl in Mexico, only half the population agreed to evacuate.[17] The remainder trusted in the power of the church bells to call the faithful to prayer to calm the volcano. Fortunately the eruption was not a big one.

How would today's volcanologists handle the great 1815 eruption at Mount Tambora on the island of Sumbawa in Indonesia if that mountain had held off exploding for another two centuries? Would the evacuation begin in time? Would the evacuation destinations be set far enough away? Today there are 1.4 million people on the island of Sumbawa. On Bali and Lombok, how many people would die because of the collapse of their roofs from the weight of the ash blown by the easterly winds? When all the crops failed, would enough food and water be available to support more than 4 million inhabitants of Bali for a year or longer?

If the great 1883 eruption of Krakatoa had been delayed for 150 years, would the volcano forecasters identify tsunami as the most lethal hazard? Would people on the surrounding coasts really believe that they had to stay 100 feet (30 meters) or more above sea level?

Metropolitan Naples, home to almost 3 million people, is situated between two volcanoes: the mountain of Vesuvius broods to the east, while to the west lies the Campi Phlegraei—the 6-mile (10-kilometer)-wide caldera ("fiery fields")—centered on Pozzuoli Bay.[18] Evacuation plans exist (in principle at least) for removing the 550,000 inhabitants at greatest risk from pyroclastic avalanches in the "red zone" around Vesuvius within an assumed seventy-two-hour warning time.[19] Each of eighteen municipalities in the red zone is twinned with an Italian province expected to transport and shelter the evacuees through the emergency. The evacuation plans are far too big and complex to be tested in a practice run, and the evacuation will be triggered by a largely untested eruption forecast procedure. There are few volunteers for the role of chief forecaster: the last time Italian geophysicists became linked with an over-optimistic disaster forecast, they were successfully prosecuted for manslaughter. Any future evacuation may well be overcautious and premature. While the eruption could happen faster than anticipated, it might also start and stop, with people returning, before it starts again.

The Campi Phlegraei Vent is believed to be the source of the enormous 40,000-year-old Campanian Ignimbrite Tuff, which has a volume of 120 cubic miles (500 cubic kilometers)[20]—more than 100 times the size of the AD 79 Vesuvius eruption—and covers 2,600 square miles

(7,000 square kilometers)[21] of the Campanian Plain to the east of the Bay of Naples, where in places it is 330 feet (100 meters) thick.[22] There is no conceivable evacuation plan to handle a repeat.

Of all the places in the world with the potential for a supervolcano eruption, the most populated is the island of Kyushu in western Japan.[23] There have been seven giant eruptions there in the past 120,000 years. The latest, at Mount Aso, erupted 144 cubic miles (600 cubic kilometers) of materials, leaving a 16-by-11-mile (25-by-18-kilometer) caldera, among the largest in the world. Seven million people live in areas that could be buried meters deep in pyroclastic flow avalanches. There is no evacuation plan.

Someone should create a video game in which eruption forecasters could explore all the dimensions of their challenging role of intervening between the willful volcano and the unforgiving politicians. Catastrophic eruptions are so rare that the national officials who get charged with issuing warnings are typically novices, with no previous experience. The lead eruption forecaster will have only a single opportunity to get it right, with dire political and personal ramifications for being too early or too late or for underestimating the required evacuation distance.

It might be better if there was a global agency tasked with providing this function. Such an agency could learn much from the long-running (1995–2010) dome collapse avalanches and explosions at the Soufrière Hills volcano on the island of Montserrat, where scientists coordinated a single perspective and made the talk of eruption probabilities as everyday as the weather forecasts. We must teach people how to respond to the uncertainties of a forecast and not be like the president of Haiti in 1963—who banned a hurricane forecast for fear it might induce panic.[24]

———

AFTER SPENDING TWO MONTHS IN CALIFORNIA EXPLORING THE San Francisco earthquake, in August 1906 Fusakichi Ōmori returned to Japan to cope with some insubordination at his Tokyo department. An assistant professor of seismology who was two years younger than Ōmori, Akitsune Imamura, believed himself every bit the equal of his boss.[25] To prove the point, in 1905 Imamura published a textbook on seismology.

The same year Imamura wrote in a popular journal that sometime in the next fifty years Tokyo would be hit by a destructive earthquake in which 100,000 could die if the city once again caught fire. The Sagami Bay faults offshore to the south of the city had last generated a catastrophic earthquake in 1703. Based on recurring historical earthquakes further to the southwest, he believed that the time was approaching for a repeat.

Imamura had not checked with Ōmori before publishing his forecast. The following year Ōmori wrote an article for the same popular journal in which he scathingly compared Imamura's prediction to the folkloric legend of the fire horse—that when the astrological symbols for "fire" and "horse" were aligned, "many cities would burn." He wrote: "The theory that a large earthquake will take place in Tokyo in the near future is academically baseless and trivial."

The feud simmered for years. In 1915 Imamura arranged another public clash over his earthquake forecast for Tokyo. This time Imamura was rebuffed by his boss so badly that he had to retire from the university for months and return to his home village.

Issuing forecasts of impending earthquakes was considered very much part of the scope of Japanese seismology in this period.[26] However, as Ōmori wrote in a paper in 1920, "the repetition of destructive shocks necessarily at one and the same point is a great fallacy."[27]

Ōmori's certainty about Tokyo's earthquake potential became progressively tested. On December 8, 1921, Tokyo experienced its largest earthquake in twenty-eight years, which came close to severing the city's water supply. The shock on April 26, 1922, was even larger, damaging buildings, cutting the telephone service, and interrupting trains. Anxiety in the city was rising. To help reassure the public Ōmori publicized his official view that two successive strong earthquakes in the city were not unprecedented, but that the crisis was now over. When another earthquake occurred on January 14, 1923, he penned a scientific paper in which he asserted that "Tokyo may be assumed to be free in future from the visitation of a violent earthquake like that of 1855, as the later shock originated right under the city itself, and as destructive earthquakes do not repeat from one and the same origin, at least not in the course of 1,000 or 1,500 years."[28]

In early August 1923, Ōmori set off by boat to travel to Australia to attend the Second Pan-Pacific Science Conference. On the afternoon of September 1, he was being shown a seismic recorder in the Sydney Observatory when he saw the needle stir and then wildly swing to record a trace of a large distant earthquake. The next morning he learned that he had witnessed the signature of the earthquake that had just destroyed Yokohama and Tokyo. The initial news suggested tens of thousands of casualties.

When he was interviewed by the local Australian papers, Ōmori declared that he "thought reports of the disaster had been exaggerated." He traveled to Melbourne to embark on the *Tenyo Maru*, the first ship leaving for Tokyo. He became ill on the voyage, although he had sufficient energy to give a lecture on earthquakes to the passengers as they approached Japan. His deputy and rival Imamura had been the daily spokesperson with the Tokyo press during Ōmori's absence, and he came to meet Ōmori on the quayside when the ship arrived on October 4, more than a month after the earthquake. In a poignant and humiliating moment, Ōmori apologized for having spent twenty years scorning his deputy's earthquake forecast.

However, Ōmori was getting progressively more incapacitated and had to be hospitalized in a ward filled with earthquake victims. He was diagnosed with a brain tumor and died on November 8 at the age of fifty-five. His paper on the January 1923 earthquake discounting any prospect of Tokyo being hit by a catastrophic earthquake for 1,000 years, written before he left for Sydney, was cynically allowed to be published in the year after the earthquake. Imamura, hoping to heap further ignominy on his boss's reputation, was the likely instigator.

In an article published in 1924, Imamura wrote that he had discussed the anticipated calamity at Tokyo in great detail, "but people refused to believe me. There was even an eminent scientist who ridiculed my opinion once (in 1905) and again in 1915 as nothing other than a rumor which might cause general panic." Imamura took over Ōmori's job as professor of seismology, with a reputation that would be hard to quench in Japan—as the seismologist who had finally mastered the mysteries of earthquake forecasting. These inflated expectations have been loaded on Japanese seismologists ever since.

———

IN THE TWENTIETH CENTURY, CALIFORNIA EXPERIENCED TWO OUT-breaks of earthquake prediction fever.

Geodetic surveying after the 1906 earthquake showed that the sudden movement of up to 18 feet along the San Andreas Fault had relieved decades of accumulated strain. In 1924 the Coast and Geodetic Survey published its latest survey results for southern California: over the thirty years since the previous survey, an impressive 24 feet of movement had accumulated.[29]

Seeing the survey results, Bailey Willis, a former geology professor at Stanford University, wrote an article declaring that a major earthquake was imminent on the southern San Andreas Fault.[30] He took his forecast to the insurance industry, which was responding to the dramatic demand for earthquake insurance that followed the 1925 Santa Barbara earthquake. In response to the news, insurers raised their earthquake insurance rates for the region; in fact, some were doubling them, and one even put up the price by a factor of twenty. The Los Angeles Chamber of Commerce was outraged at this attempt to panic people into believing that their city shared the earthquake perils that blighted San Francisco.[31]

In 1927 the Coast and Geodetic Survey discovered that its earlier survey work was flawed—the 24 feet of movement had melted away. The chamber commissioned the geologist Robert Hill to write a reassuring 1928 book, *Southern California Geology and Los Angeles Earthquakes*, in which he identified and mapped the faults of the Los Angeles metropolitan area and then one by one dismissed them as "inactive" and "largely things of past geologic time."[32] Of the coast-parallel Inglewood Fault, Hill noted, "it cannot be said there is any great menace." Five years later, the Inglewood Fault ruptured in the 1933 Long Beach earthquake. Bailey Willis told a meeting of insurance industry executives in New York City that the 1933 earthquake had vindicated his prediction that "within 3, 7 or 10 years" a major earthquake could be expected, neglecting to mention that his forecast had been for a completely different fault.

This story would be echoed in the "Palmdale Bulge" saga of the 1970s, when a US Geological Survey geologist, Bob Castle, revisited old and new geodetic survey results and concluded that a region of land to the north of Los Angeles had become raised.[33] In 1976 an article in *Popular Science* asked suggestively: "What is 10 inches high in some places, covers more than 4500 square miles, and worries the hell out of laymen and professionals alike?" The Palmdale Bulge gained $2 million of earthquake prediction research funding before two scientists at UCLA identified potential errors in the survey findings, and at a 1979 science meeting there was nearly a brawl as supporters and detractors of the bulge fought over the evidence.[34] By the mid-1980s, all evidence for the Palmdale Bulge had evaporated.

The mid-1970s enthusiasm for California earthquake prediction was driven by news out of China and also by the idea that the United States was being left behind in earthquake prediction research. On the evening of February 4, 1975, a Magnitude 7.3 earthquake occurred 16 miles (25 kilometers) south of the industrial city of Haicheng in Manchuria, 380 miles (600 kilometers) northeast of Beijing. The Chinese authorities issued a press release claiming to have predicted the earthquake, saving tens of thousands of lives.[35] This story played to some potent themes: the Chinese had superior older wisdom; the Communist authorities could look after their citizens more effectively than leaders in the West; and the Chinese would lead the way in this key new area of practical science.

There had been prominent foreshocks, changes in well levels, and ground movements in the lead-up to this earthquake. There had also been a particular intuition that the larger earthquake was about to arrive, leading to the evacuation of one city. However, the Chinese were not prepared to submit their evidence to full scientific scrutiny.

The Chinese pride in their earthquake prediction prowess would last only eighteen months; then a larger and unforecasted Magnitude 7.8 earthquake occurred directly beneath the city of Tangshan.[36] In the following years, it became clear that whatever had facilitated the forecast at Haicheng was the exception and not the rule.

In 1977, when earthquake prediction enthusiasm was at its peak, Brian Brady, an expert on rock bursts in mines who worked with the geologist William Spence, based out of the US Geological Survey office in Colorado, made the bold prediction that a Magnitude 8.4 earthquake would hit Lima in late 1980. The shock would then be followed, he said, by an extraordinary Magnitude 9.2 earthquake in October or November 1981.[37] Brady and Spence's prediction was based on extrapolating the patterns seen among smaller earthquakes.

In late 1979, the news media in Peru got wind of the threatened catastrophe. In February 1980, the head of the Peruvian Red Cross appealed to the United States for 100,000 body bags. The letter was leaked to the press in Lima. As the nation seemed to march inexorably toward Armageddon, tourists cut back on their planned visits to Lima and the economy started to suffer. In January 1981, the Peruvian government asked the US National Earthquake Prediction Evaluation Council to vet the prediction. After reviewing the underlying science, the council reported that, although the possibility of an earthquake occurring on any given day could not be discounted, this particular prediction appeared to lack merit.

By April 1981, Brady had extended the window of the first great earthquake to June 28. The Peruvian authorities asked John Filson, head of the US Geological Survey's earthquake studies program, to come to Peru. Filson arrived on June 25 and soon discovered that the prediction was daily front-page news. People were leaving town, property prices had fallen, and hotel bookings were down by two-thirds. June 28 was quiet, and Filson left on the 29th, but Brady had now extended the dates of his great earthquake forecast up to July 10. When that date passed peacefully, Brady finally retracted the prediction on July 20.

Filson saw the need for more sober and scientific prediction research and was a driving force behind the program to lay a net of recording instruments to catch an earthquake at Parkfield, a rural backwater in central California. Moderate-sized Magnitude 6 earthquakes on the San Andreas Fault at Parkfield appeared to have fired off like clockwork—on average every twenty-two years all the way back to the mid-nineteenth century. The previous earthquake had been in 1966, so the instrumental trap was set for 1988.[38] The US Geological Survey seismologists gave themselves a little leeway by stating confidently that the Parkfield earthquake would strike within four years of 1988. The months passed and then the years; the prediction window came and went, the research funding drained away, and the equipment started to rust or was moved to other sites. The Parkfield prediction had become a scientific joke. The earthquake finally arrived in 2004, sixteen years late. The willful behavior of even the most regular and modest of earthquakes marked the end of significant scientific funding for California earthquake prediction.

The subject will never go away, but the likelihood that we will ever achieve reliable earthquake prediction seems lower now than it was forty years ago.[39] Only Ōmori's aftershocks (which can sometimes be bigger than the original main shock), situated around the main-shock source, with their consistent exponential decay in numbers, have proven amenable to forecasting. Many seismologists are actually quite pleased with this situation because any hint of earthquake prediction has led to a minefield of unintended consequences.

———

IT WAS AMATEUR EARTHQUAKE PREDICTION THAT WAS THE UNDOING of scientists at L'Aquila, Italy, in 2009.[40] Giampaolo Giuliani had been a technician at the Gran Sasso physics laboratory for forty years and had built four homemade radon detectors that he placed in water springs around the region. Based on the radon levels, he predicted earthquakes.

From the start of 2009, a swarm of earthquakes occurred around the city of L'Aquila, one or two on average every day, and their numbers increased through March. Giuliani started issuing predictions of specific larger earthquakes, which captured the local headlines. Faced with a rattled and fearful population, a meeting was organized in the town on March 31 between civil defense officials and national seismologists, and then a televised press conference was held by the two officials, away from the scientists and their cautions. One of the officials made the mistake of saying that the seismic situation in L'Aquila was "certainly normal," posing "no danger," and that "the scientific community continues to assure me that, to the contrary, it's a favorable situation because of the continuous discharge of energy." No one at the press conference pointed out the fragility of the town's buildings, both ancient and modern, or the fact that a swarm of tremors had preceded the last catastrophic earthquake in the city, in 1703.

Late in the evening on April 5, there was a strong shock, after which some people (mostly men) chose to spend the night outside in their cars, while others, remembering the calming official statements, stayed in their beds—to their cost. At 3:30 a.m., a Magnitude 6.3 earthquake occurred beneath the city, destroying many buildings and taking more than 300 lives. The survivors rued that they had not taken greater heed of the warnings and wished they had not believed the soothing blandishments of the officials. The scientists and civil defense officials who had attended the fateful meeting on March 31 were tried in a local court and all found guilty of manslaughter (a verdict overturned on appeal).[41]

———

PREDICTION INVOLVES FORECASTING THE SIZE, LOCATION, AND time of an earthquake. Take out the timing and we have the more general question of defining the shaking hazard. What constrains the maximum size of all potential earthquakes?

In the 1950s, Japan, with no indigenous sources of oil or gas, developed a craving for nuclear electricity. Rivers in Japan were short, their flows too intermittent and seasonal, and therefore reactor cooling would have to come from the sea. And then there was the problem of earthquakes. Most notorious was the southern coast of Honshu and Shikoku—already the site of three massive earthquakes and tsunamis in the twentieth century. In contrast, the coastline of eastern Honshu, north of Tokyo, appeared benign: there had been no large earthquakes there for at least three centuries. In the early 1960s, one of the first nuclear reactors in Japan was planned for this coastline in Fukushima Prefecture.

At the time, in July 1967, when the foundations were being dug for the site, "plate tectonics" had not even been named. By the time the reactor was operational in 1971, there was a whole new theory to explain earthquake origins.[42] The oceanic trench off northeast Japan was a classic "subduction zone" plate boundary megafault dipping down beneath the coastline.[43]

Reactor units 2 and 3 were built in 1974 and 1976. Eventually there would be ten reactors in two sites at Fukushima and a total of fourteen along this coastline, making up almost 30 percent of all the reactors in Japan. Engineers believed that the largest earthquake along this coast would be below Magnitude 8.

Through the 1980s, seismologists developed a theory for where the largest (Magnitude 9) earthquakes could and could not occur world-wide. Giant earthquakes only happened, the theory proposed, where the two sides of the subduction zone megafault were tightly locked together, a condition that required the most rapid plate motions and geologically young ocean crust.[44] The theory was taught to a whole generation of students.

For almost forty years there were no giant earthquakes. Then, on the morning of December 26, 2004, a fault started to break along a sub-duction zone to the west of northern Sumatra and continued to break north for ten minutes, by which time the rupture was 750 miles (1,200 kilometers) long and the earthquake was greater than Magnitude 9.[45] The seafloor moved tens of meters and generated a monster tsunami that overwhelmed the Sumatran city of Banda Aceh and sped across the Indian Ocean to inundate the beaches of Thailand to the east and Sri Lanka to the west. Yet this great earthquake happened in a location that the theory said was not possible—the subduction zone was neither young enough nor fast enough to be "strongly coupled."

That should have been the end of the theory. An alert should have immediately gone out to those living in all the world's subduction zones—such as the one along the Pacific coast of Japan—who were relying on the theory to protect themselves from giant earthquakes and tsunamis. Meanwhile, evidence was being uncovered to suggest that there had already been such an earthquake.

In the late ninth century, the Imperial Court of Japan was consoli-dating control over northern Honshu.[46] In the middle of the summer night of July 13 in the year AD 869, an official with the court reported a huge earthquake. As the people looked out over the ocean, a powerful glow lit up the night sky. Then, within half an hour, the ocean began to flood the land, filling the whole coastal plain of Sendai; it overwhelmed a castle at the town of Tagajo, ten miles to the east of Sendai, destroyed all the houses, and took an estimated 1,000 lives.

At the end of the 1990s, a team of geologists from Osaka City University, Tokyo University, and the local Tohoku University dug down and found traces of the destroyed town of Tagajo. By 2001, they had located the remains of many buildings of the eighth and ninth centuries, covered by sands typical of those left by a tsunami, which could be traced up to 3 miles (4.5 kilometers) inland.[47] Beneath the AD 869 tsunami sand were two earlier tsunami sand layers deposited within the past 3,000 years.

In 2007 the researchers presented a paper at a meeting of the Japanese Society of Engineering Geology, and they also talked to the press about their findings.[48] By digging trenches, they had found the same tsunami sand in marshes all along the coast, reaching several kilometers inland. The "Jogan Sanriku" tsunami, as they now called it, "may have been the strongest seismic disturbance ever to strike Japan," possibly even reaching the exalted Magnitude 9.[49] From the evidence of the earlier tsunamis, a repeat of such an earthquake was now "overdue."[50]

In 2008, after a shock close to another Japanese nuclear power plant, the Japanese nuclear regulator initiated a review of earthquake and tsunami hazards at all of the seventeen reactor sites in Japan.[51] For each site, the reviewers had to decide which was the most significant hazard. At Fukushima, they chose earthquake. Seven experts on earthquakes met twenty-two times to consider all the evidence. At the end of June 2009, a seismologist asked what would happen in a repeat of the AD 869 earthquake and mega-tsunami, but his question was rebuffed by an executive from the Tokyo Electric Power Company. At the next meeting, the earthquake and tsunami safety report for the Fukushima Daiichi nuclear power plants, declaring the safety features at the facility to be sufficient, was approved.[52]

And then, as if playing out some elemental tragedy—1,142 years after its previous incarnation but only four years after its scientific reconstruction—the colossal AD 869 earthquake and accompanying tsunami happened again. It was as if the final act of scientific reconstruction had made the whole event come back to life—the genie had come out of the bottle. This time it was not in the middle of a summer night but midafternoon on a cold late winter day, so the tsunami—50 feet (15 meters) high at Sendai, and higher to the north—was not just a black tide in the night but an event witnessed and filmed.

At the Fukushima Daiichi nuclear power complex, the vibrations caused water to slosh out of the fuel storage ponds on top of the buildings and to run in contaminated waterfalls down the stairs to the control room. Yet the tsunami was the more potent avenger. The wave came in at around 40 feet (12 meters), high above the 16-foot (5-meter) seawall protecting the site. Offsite the shaking had already broken the external power supply. The backup generators, located behind the walls in front of the plant, were knocked over by the tsunami wave, saturated in saltwater, and disconnected. (It was later admitted that, for the cost of $10,000, they could all have been located at a higher elevation.) Two reactor units were already shut down for maintenance, and a third was in cold shutdown, but reactors 1, 2, and 3 were all operating at full power. Without electricity to drive the pumps, the three reactors could not be cooled, and within a few hours the fuel rods overheated and a pool of molten fuel started to develop in the base of the reactors. Meanwhile, water decomposed to form hydrogen, which forced out seals in the reactor vessels, releasing radioactive clouds and setting off explosions.

While Fukushima was ground zero of this disaster, the tsunami walls were overwhelmed all along the coast. In some coastal towns even the evacuation destinations and disaster command posts were destroyed. At Rikuzentakata, the fire chief sent forty-five young firemen to close the tsunami gates. They all drowned.[53]

The 2011 Tohoku earthquake toppled a philosophy of overconfident mastery of the natural world. Science no longer has a theory to discriminate among the 35,000 miles (55,000 kilometers) of worldwide subduction zones. So where in the world will the next mega-tsunami happen? A safe bet is somewhere that has not been hit by such an earthquake for at least 200 years, and probably much longer. It could be in the eastern Caribbean, south of Turkey, or along the Cascadia coast in the northwest United States.

The safety of hundreds of thousands of future lives will depend on providing education and alerts about mega-tsunamis for coastlines with no recorded history of any such disaster. As in Japan, there may be strong resistance from developers and politicians to publicizing this message.

———

ONE FORM OF LIMITED EARTHQUAKE FORECASTING HAS FLOWERED in the new millennium. The initial vibrations are recorded as close as possible to the earthquake source, and then the signal is automatically read so that people farther away can be warned of the vibrations coming toward them at a speed of 2 to 4 kilometers per second.[54] For a large offshore earthquake, seafloor recorders can give tens of seconds' warning to shut down trains or dangerous equipment. The system installed in Japan after 2007 also rings all mobile phones with a sinister tone.[55] Yet where the largest earthquakes happen on land, as in California, those people located close to the source will not have sufficient time to receive an effective warning.

———

ONCE UPON A TIME, ALL CATASTROPHES—STORMS, FLOODS, HURRI-canes, earthquakes, volcanic eruptions—arrived without warning. That was before satellite observations, supercomputing, numerical weather prediction models, ensembles, Doppler radar, and Bayesian forecasting schemes. Today we have come to expect at least a week's warning for an eruption, two or three days for a hurricane, twenty-four hours for its storm surge, at least twelve hours for (faster and harder-to-forecast) intense windstorms, six hours for flash floods, twenty minutes for a tsunami, and at least five minutes for a tornado.

But the deadly earthquake remains strangely, remarkably, almost admirably, resistant to all that forecasting science has thrown at it.

10 • SAVE OUR SOULS

IT BEGINS WITHOUT WARNING, WITH A RUSH OF PURE FEAR.
An insistent force is shaking your bed. Suddenly wide awake, you fumble for the bedside light. The electricity is flickering and then fails. The room is rocking violently. You can hear objects falling from shelves and skittering across the floor.

You are in the midst of a strong earthquake.

It is totally dark.

The grinding noise is terrifying. You can feel your heart pounding. The door is only a few paces away. Should you stay or should you make a move to go?[1]

You could run from the building through the front door and hope to dodge the debris falling off the roof. Or perhaps stay inside and pray the structure of the building holds.

You have seconds to make a decision, on which your life may depend.

In an average year, tens of thousands of people face this dilemma, sometimes hundreds of thousands simultaneously.

If you live in California, you will have a simple motto in your head—"Drop, Cover, and Hold On!" Official advice is unequivocal: get under your desk if you are in school, or under a table or bed if you are at home, and hold on so you don't get shaken away. What you have most to fear is plaster and light fittings crashing on your head, followed by heavy bookcases, filing cabinets, and cupboards.[2]

But then again, walls can fail and buildings can collapse, in which case under the desk or table might not be such a smart place to hide.

Is that the sound of the beam tearing from the wall column above your head?

"Drop, Cover, and Hold On!" assumes, correctly, that most of the time the earthquake shaking will not be so strong and (at least in Chile, California, Japan, and New Zealand) the building not so weak that it will collapse.

In any earthquake, "Drop, Cover, and Hold On!" is good advice if you are situated in a modern building constructed to the building code. But what if you are somewhere else in the world, or simply in an older building?

In the middle of the day on September 1, 1923, the shaking was particularly strong on the Bund in Yokohama—a coastal street of European-style hotels, clubs, diplomatic missions, shipping offices, and lawyers' offices.[3]

Opened in 1873, the Grand Hotel was the best on the Bund, favored by the city's international adventurers and traders. Fronted with covered verandas and balconies, it would not have looked out of place on a Norwegian fjord. The wooden exterior disguised concrete columns that supported a heavy timber frame.

When the shaking started, Ensign Tommy Ryan was inside talking to a friend over a cup of tea. He assumed that this was yet another inconsequential Japanese tremor, but as the shaking became more violent and the chairs and tables began to dance he noticed that the ceiling of the lounge was creaking and sagging ominously. He leapt out of the nearest window, abandoning his friend and the teacup. A few seconds later, the entire three-story structure collapsed.

At the nearby Thomas Cook & Son office, Lois Crane, wife of the outgoing US military attaché, just got out through the front door of the building before the whole structure toppled, burying her up to the waist in debris. Her hands and head were unscathed, and she pulled herself free. She turned around and was shocked to see that all six employees had been buried beneath the rubble.

Along the street, at the brick-and-granite Yokohama United Club, all twenty regulars at the bar made a dash for the front hall. None of them made it to the street before the four-story building collapsed into a 5-foot-high (1.5-meter) pile of beams and masonry, killing all of them, along with forty Japanese employees. Remarkably, one Japanese bartender survived when a window frame collapsed around him.

In every one of the buildings along the Bund, there were similar stories of life and death, separated by the decisions of an instant. Survivors were mostly those who had already been outside or who exited really fast.

In the strong shaking of an early-twentieth-century European-style building, your best bet is to make an immediate run for the door. Similarly, in the weak precast-concrete frame buildings at Spitak, Armenia, in the 1988 earthquake, you were more than four times as likely to be injured (or die) if you remained inside.[4]

Yet, to reach safety, you have to dash for a doorway and then run the gauntlet as debris rains down from the roof. In the 1886 earthquake in Charleston, South Carolina, all those killed were outside but close to buildings, struck by falling cornices and collapsing gable walls and chimneys.[5] "At Casoletto [Calabria] the Prince and his family were dining when the first earthquake [of 1783] struck. The brother of his wife, a man renowned for presence of mind, saw a chasm appearing in the wall of the room and promptly stepped through it losing only his shoe. All the rest of the family, apart from one son, were killed in the ruins."[6]

In earthquake country, as you walk into a building, gauge its quality. In southern Italy, even today, people bolt for the street when they feel any shaking—nobody trusts their buildings.

NOW THE BUILDING HAS COLLAPSED AND YOU FIND YOURSELF trapped. You are dependent on someone coming to your assistance. Your best hope lies not with the soldiers from a base 100 miles away or even the medical personnel of your local hospital (who will be totally preoccupied with their own problems—hospital buildings are notoriously bad performers in disasters). The local police will likewise be completely overwhelmed. Instead, you are going to place your faith in a group of people who have never before worked as a team, who would never for an instant have considered the prospect of becoming the front line of disaster rescue, and who have no equipment to assist them beyond a few implements pulled from a tool box.

Who is this team of heroic volunteer frontline rescuers about to discover their extraordinary powers? Your neighbors.[7] "Neighbors" includes all those in your vicinity, your colleagues if you are at work, and your family if they live close by.

Adrenaline has kicked in, promoting wild, selfless, altruistic behavior, enough to drive men and women to venture into dangerous, partially collapsed shells of buildings to try to rescue people, even at serious risk to their own lives. This is true heroism.[8]

Within half an hour of the 1:00 p.m. Niigata, Japan, earthquake in 1964, three-quarters of those who had either escaped or been rescued were themselves engaged in rescuing other people.[9] In the 1980 Campania-Irpinia earthquake in southern Italy, nine out of ten of those rescued were extricated by people from the same town, and almost eight out of ten by people from the same building.[10]

Arriving hours after the earthquake, traditional TV news coverage misses the immediate disaster aftermath. At noon on an October Sunday in 1868, Mark Twain, standing in a San Francisco street as the buildings started to violently shake, witnessed "every door, of every house, as far as the eye could reach, . . . vomiting a stream of human beings."[11] Today, for the first time, cell-phone and security cameras capture the minutes after an urban earthquake. Crowds surge through the streets in a state of confusion and shock, while people peel off to give spontaneous assistance to those who are trapped and calling for help.

THE TANGSHAN EARTHQUAKE OF 1976 OCCURRED AT NIGHT. A quarter of a million residents pulled themselves out of the ruins of their concrete and brick apartments and then became a self-organized army of rescuers for another 300,000 people who were still buried.[12] Fingers bleeding, they tore at the rubble of tens of thousands of collapsed brick apartment buildings, while local officials urged the citizens to "Resist the Earthquake and Rescue Ourselves."

Beneath the rubble lies an invisible triage of the dead, the injured, and the trapped. The easy rescues happen quickly. Following the Irpinia earthquake in 1980, thirteen times as many people were rescued in the first day as on all the subsequent days. Postmortems showed that one-quarter to one-half of those who did not die quickly could have been saved.[13] Beneath the ruins of traditional heavy mud-wall houses in Turkey and China, fewer than half of those initially trapped are still alive after six hours. On the first day at Tangshan, four out of five of those rescued lived. By the fourth day, four out of five of those pulled out of the ruins went on to die.[14]

On TV the rescue of one more living victim is celebrated as a triumph, but the camera rarely follows the story of whether that person actually survives. In 1976 a woman trapped beneath a concrete beam pressing down on her leg for two days died within a day of being rescued. Researchers found an account by a German doctor who traveled to Messina to examine the case notes after the 1908 earthquake. Among eighty-three casualties, almost one-quarter had suffered acute pressure necrosis: a form of kidney failure.[15]

Doctors caring for soldiers during the war in southern Lebanon in 1982 learned to treat the condition by replenishing the volume of wasted muscle with fluids, keeping the metabolites correctly balanced to prevent kidney damage and acute arrhythmias.[16] The 1988 earthquake at Spitak, Armenia, provided the first successful tests of such new treatments on those pulled from beneath heavy concrete beams.[17]

<hr />

TIME AND AGAIN, THE PROSPECT OF RESCUE AFTER AN EARTHQUAKE could be ended prematurely. All it took was for oil lamps, candles, or cooking stoves to tumble, and the wooden city would catch fire and burn to the ground. San Francisco in 1906 was just another casualty in a long line of earthquake-disabled timber cities consumed by fire.

On a windless October 1989 evening, with the water mains ruptured, San Francisco's Marina District was lucky to lose only a single city block to fire, which the fire department extinguished by comman-deering a tug with pumps and half a mile of hoses. After the 1995 earthquake directly beneath the city of Kobe, fires began in the old residential section of the city and, even without any wind, consumed a square kilometer of dense wooden houses. Tumbled boilers and broken gas lines, blocked streets, disabled water mains—everything that hap-pens after an earthquake favors fire.[18]

And then it can come down to the weather alone if fires spread and unite to overwhelm firefighters and consume a city. The death toll after the 1923 earthquake in Tokyo and Yokohama was really a consequence of the ferocity of the outer typhoon winds that drove the firestorm.[19]

———

THERE WERE NO COORDINATED EARTHQUAKE RESCUES BEFORE THE twentieth century. "Bury the dead and feed the living!" commanded de Carvalho, the autocratic disaster manager of the 1755 Lisbon earth-quake. There was no call to "rescue the trapped." In the 1812 Venezu-elan earthquake, an English sea captain at the port of La Guaira close to Caracas observed: "Hundreds of suffering inhabitants . . . mixed with heaps of ruins, and many of them still yet alive with their heads out, imploring assistance from their fellow citizens, who, instead of affording them aid, were throwing themselves prostrate before images, beating their breasts, and imploring for themselves the protection of their saints."[20]

The most destructive of all mid-nineteenth-century earthquakes was at Mendoza in western Argentina. On a late summer evening, everyone was indoors after a heavy rain shower. The collapse of the thick-walled stone and adobe buildings was total. Around half of the population of 10,000 were killed outright, while another 2,000 managed to escape from the ruins. There was neither a functioning city administration nor an organized rescue mission, so that on the following day, "through whatever street one passes, nothing is heard but the shrieks and wail-ings of the victims, who lie buried alive beneath the surrounding ruins, very many having thus perished for want of organized assistance."[21]

The world has become less callous in its disregard for suffering.[22]

Standing walls create spaces when floors have only partially pancaked on one another. Strong furniture may hold up ceilings and create void space. Today the "rescuability" of victims is graded on a four-point scale, from those who are injured but not trapped, to those who are trapped by beams or rubble, and on to "void-space entrapment" and finally "the entombed."[23] Before 1970, if you found yourself "entrapped" or "entombed," you would inevitably die. Today every major country has its own rescue team. In Switzerland, for instance, 100 professional rescuers are supported by twelve canines.[24] But even today, only the most proficient, experienced, and well-equipped rescue teams have the prospect of finding and freeing the entombed.[25]

In Mexico City in 1985, many ten- to twenty-story buildings toppled in the heart of the city.[26] In one hospital, 800 doctors, nurses, and patients were in the midst of a shift change when the building collapsed. The city's administration was slow to react. Tens of thousands of people came from the undamaged suburbs to look for their relatives. Burrowing deep into the chaotic piles of debris, more than 100 rescuers died as their tunnels collapsed or the massive concrete beams shifted and compacted.

For those left under the rubble for a day or more in winter, hyperthermia can become the killer.[27] When there is too much heat, the problem is dehydration.[28] To survive for several days you need to stay warm, avoid injuries, find water, and have absolute faith that you will be discovered. When the French geologist Déodat Gratet de Dolomieu toured the ruined villages of Calabria in 1783, he talked to those who had been buried alive for three, four, or even five days. "Of all the physical evils they endured, thirst was the most intolerable; and their agony was increased by the idea that they were abandoned by their friends."[29]

—◆—

THREE DAYS AFTER THE JANUARY 14, 1907, JAMAICAN EARTHQUAKE, two American naval ships, the *Missouri* and the *Indiana*, alerted by their newly installed radio receivers, moored in Kingston Harbor and disembarked sailors who patrolled the streets, shared provisions, and brought the injured to the ship's hospital.[30] When the island's British governor, Alexander Swettenham, discovered the American presence, he was apoplectic and demanded an immediate re-embarkation and expelled the US ships.[31] The diplomatic crisis was only resolved weeks later after the governor issued a formal apology and resigned.

The incident highlighted the need for international protocols around disaster diplomacy. To attend another country's catastrophe you need an invitation. The following year the first rescuers in Messina the day after the December 28, 1908, earthquake were sailors from the Russian cruiser *Admiral Makarov*, accompanied by two naval escorts that happened to have been moored down the coast at Augusta.[32] Within days, rival fleets arrived from Britain, France, and the United States.

A catastrophe now provided the unanticipated world stage on which nations projected their international status through the strength and speed of their humanitarian missions. Kurt Waldheim, secretary-general of the United Nations, said in 1978: "Four years ago I believed that humanitarian relief was above politics. Now I know that humanitarian relief is politics."[33] The idea that a disaster creates a space that transcends national divisions goes back centuries—as when in the great hurricane of 1780 two British men-of-war were wrecked on the shores of Martinique and the French governor returned the thirty-one survivors to British Barbados under a flag of truce, noting that "in a common catastrophe, all men are brothers."[34]

In December 1988, still in the chill of the Cold War, an unprecedented humanitarian invasion of twenty-two rescue teams from twenty-one countries converged on Spitak, Armenia.[35] More powerful than any propaganda, the American and European rescuers manifested compassion and coordination up against the tragic failings of the Soviet state to protect its people.

The devastating earthquake on August 17, 1999, at the eastern end of the Sea of Marmara created the stage on which two of Turkey's estranged regional neighbors could reset their diplomatic relations. Within hours, the Greek Ministry of Foreign Affairs dispatched a rescue team accompanied by twenty-four dogs, while the Greek Secretariat of Civil Protections sent an emergency medical team. Public donations and blood banks spontaneously emerged in the principal Greek cities, and a week after the earthquake the five biggest municipalities in

Greece sent a joint aid convoy.[36] Turkish newspapers responded with headlines such as "Friendship Time" and "Help Flows in from Neighbors—Russia First, Greece the Most." When the mayor of Athens came to inspect the earthquake recovery, he was met on the tarmac by the mayor of Istanbul.

In an extraordinary piece of catastrophe theater, three weeks later, on September 7, a Magnitude 5.9 earthquake hit the northern Athens suburbs, killing 143 people and providing the perfect opportunity for reciprocity.[37] Turkey made instant pledges of aid and sent a twenty-man Turkish rescue team.

Following the August earthquake, Israel sent a field hospital to Adapazari, the most damaged town (and may have involved as many people in the accompanying PR campaign). On August 26, the *New York Times* reported that "Quake Relief Shows Israel Feels Deeply for Turkey." Dr. Claude de Ville de Goyet, chief of emergency preparedness of the Pan-American Health Organization, became so incensed by the biased reporting on the rescue operation in Turkey that he wrote to the *New York Times* and the *Washington Post* to try to force an acknowledgment that Turkish firemen and medical specialists had completed the main search-and-rescue before any foreign teams arrived on the scene, and that the international rescuers had (as is usually the case) very limited results. His critique was not published.[38]

Unlike the successful Greece-Turkey reconciliation, the post-disaster afterglow of the Turkey-Israel relationship soon faded. In March 2010, Turkey rejected an Israeli offer of earthquake aid following a modest earthquake in eastern Turkey. However, after much cajoling in December 2010, Turkey agreed to help Israel fight forest fires near Haifa, providing an opportunity for the first contacts between the Turkish leader Recep Tayyip Erdoğan and his Israeli counterpart, Benjamin Netanyahu.

These are games also played among enemies. The United States offered aid to Communist Cuba following a 1998 drought, an offer dismissed as capitalist provocation.[39] In 2005, Cuba offered copious assistance after the chaos of Katrina.[40] Along with offers from Iran and Venezuela, the proposal was quietly snubbed.

———

RESCUE TEAMS HAVE PROLIFERATED SINCE 2000. THERE ARE NOW many more national rescue teams than can be accommodated even at the largest disaster. A few days after the Haiti earthquake, five fully equipped Canadian search-and-rescue teams were waiting for the call to go to Haiti, but no call came. And a Scottish rescue team that turned up in Japan in March 2011 with no transport, logistical, or language support had to be sent back home.

Since 2001, China has maintained an on-call international search-and-rescue team for overseas missions. Yet for the leading economies, disaster assistance should be reciprocal to achieve its full diplomatic goals; after all, countries play by the same rules as children. Communist China had never allowed any other nation to come to its assistance until the Wenchuan earthquake of 2008; after taking a day to consider the matter, the Chinese conceded the diplomatic advantage of accepting help and permitted a rescue team of fifty from Japan, followed by teams from Russia, Taiwan, South Korea, and Singapore. Although not on the rescue party "A-list," the US government was asked to review its military satellite imagery to check for earthquake damage to Chinese dams.

In the Christchurch, New Zealand, earthquake of February 2011, given that almost all the 175 casualties came from the collapse of only two buildings and that the country had proficient search-and-rescue teams, it might be thought that international missions would have stayed home. After sending a team halfway around the world, the British returned, unsurprisingly, without rescuing anyone. Stranger was the unauthorized Israeli "rescue team" apprehended in Christchurch attempting to retrieve a dead Mossad agent who had been carrying several fake passports when a building fell on him.[41]

International rescue teams extricated 130 in Haiti.[42] This was a far higher total rescued than for any other recent disaster, reflecting the chaotic local rescue capacity and the vast number of partially demolished buildings. Still, 130 represented less than one-thousandth of the numbers of those who had died.

Rescue teams measure their performance in trophy numbers rescued, with intense competition between teams, as though there is a disaster Olympics. A well-publicized catastrophe today attracts between 1,000 and 2,000 international rescuers, who fly in to retrieve ten or twenty additional survivors—at a cost estimated on the order of $1 million for every life preserved.[43] For the same money, how many more lives could be saved by funding long-term medical support for those who are grievously injured, or supporting the disabled and sick, who can find themselves completely abandoned after disasters? Many disaster professionals condemn these missions as expensive, publicity-seeking distractions.[44]

However, international rescue also performs a symbolic role, manifesting the public response to help. Disaster teams train for years and are desperate to have the opportunity to save real lives and improve their skills in order to be prepared when a disaster happens close to home. The medium of television has made rescue missions focal to the creation of our "real world" disaster narratives.[45] A hurricane at least offers a few days of anticipatory buildup before the climax of landfall, but a big earthquake is a story written backwards, with the culmination occurring before the story has even gotten under way. At least for an urban earthquake disaster, by the time the TV cameras arrive there are still people to be rescued. For a hurricane, tornado, tsunami, or storm surge flood, by contrast, the rescue phase is typically completed before the news media even touch down.

The media need tales of hope and courage, but newly rescued survivors are in no state to become the human interest story (and often share no common language with those telling it). Rescue teams have therefore acted as the focal point of media coverage, establishing a codependency with TV news crews and gaining publicity in their home cities and countries. German television follows a German rescue team, while the United States follows an American team. The story remains on prime-time news as long as the rescuers stay in the foreground, manifesting solidarity and garnering donations and government promises of aid.

Rescuers and TV crews will leave the site of the disaster at the same time, even departing on the same plane. From the perspective of TV news, the catastrophe is now over. There are no visual heroics in organizing tent parks, digging latrines, extricating corpses, and tagging buildings to determine what can be salvaged.[46]

The true heroes of disasters are the larger nongovernmental organizations (NGOs): Médecins Sans Frontières (Doctors Without Borders) running field hospitals for the long term; the Red Cross and Oxfam managing camps for the homeless, bringing in water, food, and sanitation; and Save the Children caring for orphans and reuniting displaced families. All perform vital work, based on decades of experience and undertaken away from the media spotlight.

Following the 2010 Haiti earthquake, the rescue mission was called off after ten days, which is considered the limit of survival potential. On the eleventh day, Greek and French rescuers pulled a twenty-two-year-old cashier from a grocery store beneath the rubble of the Napoli Inn, where he had lived on a diet of cola, beer, and cookies. After the Irpinia, Italy, earthquake in 1980, one couple survived in the cellar beneath their ruined house for fourteen days before rescue. The most celebrated survival prodigies were the forty newborn "miracle" babies rescued after seven days from beneath the ruins of a collapsed hospital maternity unit in Juárez, Mexico, in 1985.[47] Their mothers and the maternity unit doctors and nurses had all been killed in the collapse of the building. Without food or warmth, and against all the odds, all except one of the babies had survived.

In China the period of searching for survivors is deliberately truncated. Too much focus on what has happened in an earthquake may draw attention to past building mistakes and compromises in construction quality. Three days after the 2008 Wenchuan earthquake, the office of the Front Line Propaganda Encouragement Team opened on the main street of the shattered city of Dujiangyan. Banners plastered on trucks and strung across streets declared: FIGHT THE EARTHQUAKE.[48] The following day the city's authorities, announcing the end of search efforts and a switch to debris removal, brought in the heavy excavators.

The authorities wanted the people to move on, not get paralyzed in the hope that their loved ones could still be found. A helicopter dropped leaflets over the tent city in the center of town declaring, "10,000 people—one heart! Together we will create a new city! Put your full effort into disaster rescue! Persevere to victory!" As frustration grew among survivors, Chinese premier Wen Jiabao called on officials to ensure social stability.

SENDING RESCUE TEAMS SATISFIES OUR ALTRUISTIC INSTINCTS. WE see terrible misfortune, and we want to give and will be angry if our government is not responding appropriately.

International donations continue to respond to the intensity of the media coverage and how a catastrophe holds the headlines. The 2004 Indian Ocean earthquake and the 2010 Haiti earthquake made the premier league for international funding, while 2008 Cyclone Nargis in Myanmar failed to supply the televisual stories that achieve a strong "connection" with the victims.[49] Little has changed since the eighteenth century, when the London public's generosity in giving money after a disaster (as in the 1703 windstorm, the 1755 Lisbon earthquake, or the great 1780 hurricanes in Barbados and Jamaica) was entirely driven by the level of pathos in the heartbreaking stories carried by the press. Too bad if news from the disaster was eclipsed by a headline-grabbing royal anniversary (as with the great 1897 Indian earthquake) or the Olympic Games (as with the 1976 Tangshan earthquake) or another high school shooting.[50]

And then a book could be written on the fate of all those good intentions to help after a disaster.

Following the 1755 earthquake, the British government sent ships to Lisbon from Ireland with 6,000 barrels of "good beef" and 4,000 firkins of butter. The arrival of all this free food had the potential to undermine the trade of Portuguese livestock farmers, who were otherwise unaffected by the earthquake. The ships sailed at the end of December. Delays from storms and the absence of the Portuguese king on a two-week hunting party prevented the majority of supplies from being handed over until the end of February, by which time the beef had spoiled and—if we are to believe the French ambassador—had to be dumped into Lisbon Harbor. And after the 2010 Haiti earthquake, the dispatch of a container full of secondhand shoes seriously threatened to put local tradespeople out of business.[51]

Many US orthopedic surgeons were motivated by the carnage at Port au Prince to go to Haiti to assist. Without any coordination, instructions as to what to bring (local supplies of anesthetics, for instance, soon ran out), or patient-tracking protocols, their short-lived interventions caused the hospitals run by Médecins Sans Frontières to become "overwhelmed with patients who had been left without follow-up for their amputated limbs, wounds, and fractures."[52]

Even the many agencies that went to Port au Prince to help in reconstruction found their endeavors hobbled by the absence of a sound system of land rights and official land tenure.[53] What was the point of building a permanent house for a displaced family when all too often a corrupt notary could arrive to claim that the land on which it was built belonged to a stranger? "No one cares about the land," the NGOs discovered, "until you start building on it."[54]

—

WE HAVE WANDERED A LONG WAY FROM THE ORIGINAL MOMENT OF the disaster and devoted more and more words to activities that save fewer and fewer lives—just as international earthquake rescue itself pursues the treasure hunt search for the iconic notional "last survivor": entombed, alive, and abandoned. Let's return to where we started—the moment of impact. What do we know about how disasters kill people?

In the spring of 1783, the chief physician of the Court of Naples, Giovanni Vivenzio, visited the earthquake-ruined towns of Calabria to collect the numbers of damaged buildings and take a census of the living and the dead.[55] For his survey, humanity comprised five categories: men, women, children, monks, and nuns. His statistics revealed the dangers of a cloistered life: the death rate among nuns was 13 percent, almost twice the 7 percent average for the rest of the population (while the monks' rate was 9 percent). He had discovered the inherent gender discrimination of disasters.

There are many ways in which gender affects disaster deaths.[56] Women are weaker, less likely to be taught survival skills such as swimming, and less mobile before and after childbirth. Women are expected to look after infants and the elderly and are more likely to be inside buildings (rather than sleeping outside on a hot summer night or in a car after foreshocks) or at home while the men are out at sea fishing (and therefore immune to the tsunami).

While men are more likely to die from infectious and parasitic diseases, these are not as often a source of mortality in disasters. Women are better able to cope with food shortages in famines or in refugee camps, so when more women and girls die, it must be because of how food is being allocated. The disaster gender gap is strongest where women are socially and economically disadvantaged. In addition, refugee camps can be dangerous places, with high levels of sexual violence.

A few behaviors reverse the link with gender. More men died during the deluge from 1998 Hurricane Mitch in Honduras by being washed away when they were outside in their fields or fording rivers. More men died in 2012 Typhoon Haiyan as they stayed to protect their illegal shoreline houses. (In the United States, more men die in electrical storms through playing golf or fishing.)

The most chilling discovery around gender and disasters was made from an analysis of data in the Philippines.[57] Approximately 11,000 "additional" female infants die in communities impacted by typhoons during the previous year, apparently as a result of the diminished economic resources of the affected households. This is 55 percent of the annual mortality among infant girls. While on average 750 people are killed by the direct impact of typhoons, the long-term death rate is fifteen times higher. Filipino families are large (sex selection abortion is illegal), and from the evidence some girl children are viewed as "expendable." Infant girl mortality doubles when the child has an older sister and almost doubles again where there is an older brother.

The numbers killed in a big catastrophe are never more than an informed guess. After the Haiti earthquake of 2010, bodies were collected and dumped in mass graves without detailed record-keeping. How many died? Estimates range from fewer than 80,000 to more than 300,000. We will never know the true number.

And then where do we draw a line in listing disaster casualties? Do we include those executed for looting? Or those hundreds of Koreans who were blamed for poisoning the wells and torching buildings and then lynched by crazed mobs in the mad days after the 1923 Tokyo earthquake?[58] Or those who died from cholera in the refugee camps in Haiti after 2010?[59] And should one account for years taken off lives, instead of deaths, or for all the other misfortune brought by a disaster?[60]

In well-governed countries, the estimated death toll generally falls after a disaster as those reported missing by their anxious relatives turn up in some distant town. But governments can also talk up disaster casualties—to garner media attention and aid.[61]

WHY DO WE CARE IF THOUSANDS DIE IN A DISASTER ON THE OTHER side of the earth?

After five years of lacing Indian classical music into the Beatles' eclectic repertoire, George Harrison was deeply affected by the November 12, 1970, Bangladesh cyclone. He and the world musician Ravi Shankar organized a fund-raising "Concert for Bangladesh" on August 1, 1971, at Madison Square Garden in New York. The concert gained many imitators down the years: Live Aid was held in 1985 for African famine victims, and fund-raising concerts followed Hurricane Katrina and Superstorm Sandy.

The 300,000 deaths in Bangladesh from a natural catastrophe proved to be too much for the global conscience. In December 1971, with the chords of "My Sweet Lord" and the Hare Krishna processions still ringing in the New York streets, the Bangladesh tragedy triggered a UN resolution to establish the Office of the Disaster Response Coordinator.

THE FIRST URBAN MEGA-CATASTROPHE OF THE MODERN ERA WAS AT Messina, Italy, in 1908. Only one building in fifty was left without damage. More than half the population (estimates ran from 80,000 to 130,000) died. Never had so many been suddenly killed in a single city.[62] Newspapers in Naples and Rome reported scenes of societal breakdown: "Down there, man is not the man of our anthropology."[63] Fifty thousand survivors were in a desperate state; some sheltered in wooden huts, while others were transported by boat to Naples.[64]

All the institutions of the city had collapsed, including any agency to collect the dead. As described in the Italian newspapers, Messina had been turned into 1 million tons of debris—a *cittá di morte* (city of the dead), as the Italian newspapers described it, where it might take two to three years to collect all the bodies. On January 26, Lieutenant General Francesco Mazza, sent to manage the disaster, reported that several of his troops had contracted the illusionary *infezione cadaferica* (corpse infection) from the smell.[65] Mazza proposed that the ruins be shelled by a battleship and left as a mound of rubble.[66]

Born in 1873, Giovanni Ciraolo was fortunate to survive the earthquake, but lost many friends and family in the disaster.[67] He made it his life's work to learn from everything that had happened: the chaos, the abandonment, the first responders who knew nothing about rescue. In 1909 he was elected a deputy for the neighboring mainland city of Reggio Calabria, and in 1919 he was elevated to the Senate, the same year he was appointed head of the Italian Red Cross. Based on his own traumatic experience in the earthquake, Ciraolo saw that disaster assistance should be professionalized to provide an organized defense "against the sudden furies of nature." Aid, he believed, should be a right, not the fortuitous result of charity.[68] In 1927 he convinced the League of Nations to establish the International Relief Union (l'Union Internationale de Secours, UIS). Beyond each country operating its own disaster insurance system, the scheme envisaged a formalized arrangement of mutual financial and logistical support.[69] Finally launched in 1932, the organization eventually became absorbed into the United Nations Education Scientific and Cultural Organization (UNESCO), which, since 1960, has coordinated tsunami warnings and supported disaster field missions after earthquakes.[70]

In 1984, the year the United States chose to leave UNESCO, the president of the National Academy of Sciences was the geophysicist and seismologist Frank Press, who would serve as scientific adviser to four presidents.[71] That year, Press called for an "international decade of natural hazard reduction."[72] The idea snowballed, gathering support from many countries, while the focus expanded from "hazards" to "disasters." The International Decade for Natural Disaster Reduction (IDNDR) was launched with a UN resolution at the end of 1989.[73] Each nation was tasked to identify and map its hazards and develop a strategy to reduce risk and provide disaster warnings.[74]

The IDNDR proved particularly influential in China. The Chinese People's Congress passed new laws covering earthquake and flood disaster prevention, and a ten-year goal was established by the State Council for combating earthquake disasters in the principal cities.[75]

But it would be hard to argue that the decade achieved the global disaster reduction goal featured in its title. More was being learned from dissecting actual disasters.[76] Bad outcomes were determined, researchers were discovering, not so much by the earthquake or hurricane itself as by the nature of the society affected—its inequalities, poverty, education, and preparedness. Disasters were "manifestations of unresolved development problems," and the flood or cyclone was a trigger.[77] The problem of disasters would not be solved by focusing on the hazards alone.

A successor decade titled "The Hyogo Framework for Action," launched in 2005, also promised "the substantial reduction of disaster losses."[78] By the end of the decade, more than 100 countries had established national institutions for disaster management. As the toll of disasters showed no signs of diminishing, a third initiative was launched in March 2015 at Sendai, Japan.[79] This fifteen-year effort would sharpen the focus to reduce disaster risk. Frank Press's ten-year mission had become a campaign without end.

While the earlier drafts of the 2015 Sendai Declaration proposed percentage targets for casualty reduction, the final twenty-five-page agreement limited itself to "substantially [reducing] global disaster mortality" from 2005–2015 to 2020–2030. As the earlier period was unusually catastrophe-heavy, this target has a good chance of being met, even without action. For any country, given the volatility of catastrophes, measuring progress by comparing one decade of actual disaster deaths with another may be little better than tossing a coin.

Yet the opportunity is extraordinary. Compare the casualty rates of moderate-sized earthquakes beneath cities. In the nighttime earthquake at Bam, Iran, in 2003, more than one-third of the population perished. The earthquake in the early evening of January 12, 2010, in Port au Prince, Haiti, killed one-fifth of the people in that city. In the similar-sized early-morning 1994 earthquake beneath Northridge, California, relative to the population in the zone of strong shaking, casualties were 10,000 times lower. Increased wealth can deliver dramatically improved safety.[80]

THE LUNCHBOX IS PACKED, THE SHOES ARE ON, AND THE CHILDREN have found their coats and stuffed a favorite toy animal into a pocket. It is a weekday like any other, and their Mother has kissed them good-bye. Father is walking them down the road to arrive with hundreds of other children at the school gate. This poignant scene is repeated a billion times every day all around the world. Only, on this particular day—this tragic day—the next time the mother sees her daughter she is laid out in a row in a dusty improvised morgue, surrounded by hundreds of other weeping parents.

What is the chance that the earthquake occurs during school time? About one in six—the throw of a die.[81] New Zealand has been unlucky. The February 22, 2011, Christchurch earthquake occurred in the middle of a school day. Although there was widespread damage, there were no casualties in the city's well-constructed schools. However, a foreign-language school was operating beyond the regulations in the Christchurch TV Centre, built before the most modern building codes were established.[82] The building completely collapsed, killing nine out of fifteen members of the staff and more than seventy foreign-language students.

The 1988 earthquake at Spitak in Armenia occurred at 11:41 a.m., five minutes before children would have been out of their classrooms for the lunch break. In four principal towns and fifty-eight villages, 70 percent of the Soviet-era buildings were destroyed. The official death toll was 25,000—two-thirds of them children at school or kindergarten. In Spitak and Leninakan, 105 out of 131 schools and kindergartens collapsed.[83]

In many countries, 8:52 a.m. on a Saturday would be safe for schoolchildren, but Saturday is a school day in Pakistan and classes start early. In the Magnitude 7.6 Kashmir earthquake of October 8, 2005, at the private Shaheen School in the Balakot Valley, 650 girls were trapped inside the pancaked four-story building.[84] Also completely collapsing was the Garhi Habibullah Girls High School, a symbol of aspiration and hope for the poor bright girls who came from miles around in the North-West Frontier province to be taught by twenty women teachers, the most educated and enlightened in the area, of whom only one survived.

No earthquake had ever killed so many children at school.

Three years later, a massive (Magnitude 7.9) earthquake hit southwest China at 2:28 p.m. on May 12, 2008—another school day.[85] The schools were four- or five-story precast-concrete frame structures, typical of those built in China in the 1970s and 1980s. At the Juyuan Middle School, a magnet school for the region's top students from rural areas, 900 teenagers were crushed under their school building. Troops had to stand two deep to keep parents away from the rescuers. Another 1,000 died in a school collapse in the city of Mianyang.[86] The government did everything possible to prevent investigation or discussion of what had happened.

With their large classroom ceiling spans and poor standards of construction, schools have proved to be among the most dangerous of all buildings. The government looks the other way most of the time, and people live as best they can, muddling through, avoiding regulations because they get in the way or cost money. When schools are constructed, no one connects the extra expense of proper steel reinforcing with the agony of losing so many children, possibly even their own children. The assumption is that it will not happen in the school of one's own children. And according to the probabilities, that will be the case: perhaps 100,000 of 5 million schools worldwide are in high-hazard earthquake regions, and of those, 5,000 may be assailed by a strong earthquake in the next twenty years. Building codes provide life safety at an increase of 5 to 10 percent of the building's cost.[87] How much do we value the preservation of life, in particular the lives of children?

HOW MANY PEOPLE DIE EACH YEAR ON AVERAGE FROM EARTHquakes in Italy, China, Pakistan, and the United States? Is the death rate more than for those killed by lightning or snake bites or dirty syringe needles? Are average numbers for disaster deaths rising or falling? How should we place disasters in context?

Between 1900 and 2000 in Haiti, fewer than ten people were killed by earthquakes. Then, during one evening in January 2010, more than 200,000 were killed. Starting our baseline in 1900, the annual average jumped from less than one to more than 2,000 casualties each year.

In Italy a total of more than 100,000 were killed in two earthquakes at the start of the twentieth century, so the annual average fatalities since 1900 is around 1,000. Yet, over the last thirty years, the annual average number killed by earthquakes in Italy is closer to twelve. In Portugal since 1900, only a handful of people have been killed in earthquakes. Many more have been killed by windstorms and floods. Yet start the clock in 1750 and that annual average becomes at least 100.

In the United States, some 700 people have been killed by earthquakes and tsunami since 1906—around seven each year on average. Yet FEMA predicts that 13,000 will die in Oregon, California, and Washington State when the next giant Magnitude 9 Cascadia earthquake occurs, maybe ten or a hundred years in the future.[88]

So which annual average is correct? The 1 or 100 for Portugal, the 12 or 1,000 for Italy, or the 1 or 2,000 for Haiti?

It is the pattern of long quiet periods interleaved by rare extreme disasters that makes it so difficult for humans to place catastrophes in their appropriate context. We are once again in the domain of the "fat-tailed" statistical distribution of catastrophes. For a particular country, in most decades, the number of disaster casualties is small, but every century or so a single decade may include an event in which hundreds, or thousands, or hundreds of thousands die. Although we know that the distribution of disaster casualties is fat-tailed, we don't actually know what shape it has. And without knowing the shape of the whole distribution, we cannot measure its average.

A feature of the fat-tailed distribution is that most short samples—of a decade, for example—seriously underestimate this average. But occasionally a decade contains an event like the 2010 Haiti earthquake, and then we could wildly overestimate the numbers. We would probably need at least 10,000 years of data before we had enough information by which to determine the true average. (But, of course, if we waited 10,000 years, everything would have changed by then.)

Many who work in the field of disasters call for the collection of "better data," but while more information can help resolve the small local incidents, it will not reveal the enigmatic shape of the fat-tailed distribution.

So we find ourselves with a paradox. When we want to know what priority to give something, or how to set a target to reduce it, we first measure it. Yet, from the experience of disasters, we cannot measure the true average numbers killed by earthquakes or tsunamis each year, even the average cost of catastrophe damages. What is the true average number of children killed by earthquakes each year in schools in China or Pakistan? Is that number rising or falling? From the experience of the past few decades, we simply do not know.

We have encountered this same problem before in the challenge of catastrophe insurance. What is the annual cost of all the future claims for damage from floods, storms, or earthquakes? As insurers in the 1980s found to their cost, you can't answer that question simply by adding up the costs of recent disasters.

Why not borrow the insurer's catastrophe model and reconfigure it to tell us about disaster casualties?

Following a spell of teaching in Africa, Robin Spence completed a PhD in structural engineering at Cambridge and in 1976 became a junior lecturer in the Architecture Faculty. After he saw photographs of earthquake damage to ordinary buildings in Iran and Turkey, collected by the inveterate earthquake investigator Nicholas Ambraseys, Spence was inspired to research how buildings kill and injure people. In 1980 he acquired a research student, Andrew Coburn, who pursued earthquakes in Italy, Greece, Mexico, the Philippines, Iran, and in particular Turkey, where he worked with the Ministry of Housing and Reconstruction. Coburn found that it all comes down to predicting collapse rates. If the building remains standing, you have a good chance of walking out alive.[89] Based on Spence and Coburn's work, it became possible to predict how many people would be killed and injured in a particular earthquake.[90]

Out of the human casualty catastrophe model, simulating tens of thousands of years of disasters, we can explore the shape of that elusive fat-tailed distribution, along with its annual average—"the virtual disaster lives lost." We can measure the latent casualties before the deaths are realized in a catastrophe. And we can call out the most dangerous cities in future catastrophes—cities like Beirut and Quito, Manila and Karachi.

A city could even measure its progress in reducing future fatalities without having to experience a disaster. Tokyo is the first city to promise to halve earthquake fatalities over the next decade by using a catastrophe model to test the virtual fatalities from a repeat of the 1855 Ansei Edo earthquake directly under the city.[91]

From the likelihood of earthquakes, the details of school construction, and the proportion of time children are in school, for every school we could estimate the annual number of "latent children's lives lost." The mayor could require that the annual number of latent casualties be displayed on the building. If parents knew the risk that their child could be killed, they would demand action to retrofit or replace the building—as in California.

WHY SHOULD MONEY BE SPENT ON SAVING FUTURE LIVES IN A catastrophe that may have no more than a one-in-four chance of happening during the lifetime of that building? Why should saving lives in a future earthquake deserve more attention than improvements in neonatal health or cancer treatments? We are up against an ethical problem in virtual economics. To justify this investment against others we need to know the value of saving a life.

Economists refer to the "value of a statistical life" and tease out this value from exploring preferences. How much more do people expect to be paid to compensate for a riskier job? What is the difference between the hourly rate for a driller on an oil rig and the rate for a diver, who works in more danger on the seafloor below? Or you can ask people how much should be spent on safety improvements to reduce the rates of fatal accidents.

Applying these principles, an American life works out to be worth around $7 million.[92] The Intergovernmental Panel on Climate Change

(IPCC) found that a developed country will pay fifteen times more than a developing country to avert a death resulting from climate change. These are not judgments about the worth of a life, but simply assessments of how life is intrinsically valued in different countries.

A rich country will commit up to $7 million to protect a single life. A poor country may not even know where to focus its much smaller investment.[93] And not knowing where to focus can be just as deadly as failing to deliver a tsunami warning.

11 • THE MASTER OF DISASTER

To understand why our efforts to combat disasters can seem confused, why we invest in protections in New Orleans only after the city has been flooded, I am going to share a dark secret.

Some people like disasters. This is not something we typically want to talk about. The TV news team that arrives following the earthquake does not first interview a builder rubbing his hands with glee at the prospect of all the work coming his way.

After the November 1855 earthquake and fire consumed Edo (To-kyo), while written pamphlets were prohibited by the military dictator, the field was left open for woodcut cartoonists (the original "manga" artists) to publish a daily commentary. Several of these woodcuts feature tradespeople beating at the *namazu* (giant catfish)—the source of earthquakes in Japanese folklore. In some of these cartoons, the attackers are themselves being attacked by other tradespeople who preferred that the *namazu* be left undisturbed—that the earthquakes continue.[1]

The losers from the catastrophe, the *namazu*'s attackers, included the teahouse proprietor, an eel seller, entertainers such as musicians, comedians, and storytellers, and purveyors of luxury goods, including imports and diamonds. Among those delighted by ongoing earthquakes were the carpenters, plasterers, lumber sellers, blacksmiths, roof tile merchants, physicians, and sellers of ready-to-eat meals—quite a substantial section of the economy! Elite courtesans are sometimes shown as "winners" from the earthquake (presumably from the trade brought by the thriving workmen) and at other times as losers.

Updating the cartoon, to the list of the "winners" we would now add claims assessors, disaster experts, reinsurance brokers, and risk modelers. Even insurers and reinsurers, while paying the claims, will expect to reap future premiums. We could extend this list of winners to include TV news journalists. And how about fund-raisers for the Red Cross, Oxfam, or Save the Children, organizations that raise the most money after televised disasters? The Indian journalist Palagummi Sainath called his account of the time he spent with the rural poor in India *Everyone Loves a Good Drought*, a title that highlights how disasters facilitate grandstanding by politicians and international agencies.[2]

These are all professionals who win from simply going about their honest business, but not everyone who profits from a disaster is honest.

———

THE SOCIOLOGIST CHARLES FRITZ EXPLORED WHY DISASTERS produce "such mentally healthy conditions," forcing "people to concentrate their full attention on immediate moment-to-moment needs," speeding decision-making, and facilitating "the acceptance of change."[3] Social scientists have argued that, in the presence of this consensus mentality, any looting after disasters is "minor, socially disapproved and opportunistic in nature," and more often "a myth" concocted by journalists.[4] Although the experience of a disaster is known to bring out the best in people, sometimes preexisting rage and severe inequality in a society, just as in a riot, can also find release.[5]

Following Hurricane Hugo in 1989, looting in St. Croix, the poorer of the two principal US Virgin Islands, got completely out of hand; there were reports that even police officers and other defense personnel were roaming in gangs.[6] The island's governor had to request that

1,000 troops be sent to quell the outbreak, which only cooled once everything had been removed from the stores.

As long as hurricanes and earthquakes have ruined rich cities, people have taken advantage of the disinhibition and degraded security to take what they consider to be "disaster spoils," as in a shipwreck. All it takes is one individual grabbing something and others witnessing that he is not apprehended, and looting can rapidly escalate in a chain reaction. Looting has followed almost every urban hurricane catastrophe in the United States since 1900.[7]

Once upon a time, rescue and robbery might be combined.[8] In March 1270, a violent nighttime earthquake struck the town of Dyrrachium (Durrës) on the modern coast of Albania.

> Everything inside the city collapsed, burying people in the destruction. . . . When day broke, people who lived in the surrounding area rushed into the city, using hoes and forks and every available tool, and bending low they dug to save those poor wretches who were still alive, but above all in order to pull out of the ruins all kinds of valuables; for since heirs had been buried along with goods belonging to their victims, nobody could legally claim such goods. The Albanians and their neighbors, after days spent digging up everything to be found in the earth and gathering a harvest of gold with their shovels and forks, finally left to its solitude what had once been a city, but could scarcely now be recognized as such.[9]

Opportunism can exist on both sides: "The criminal element began looting the dead, and the cold blooded commercial element began looting the living—with massive price gouging on the costs of lumber, food and ferries to the mainland," reported G. W. Ware after the 1900 Galveston hurricane.[10]

If Daniel Defoe had not been forced to abandon his tile works when he was sent to jail for sedition, he would have become rich on repairs following the Great Storm of 1703—as he grudgingly documented in his "crowdsourced" book on the calamity: the cost of tiles increased "from 21s. (£1.05) per Thousand to £6 for plain Tiles; and from 50s (£2.50) per Thousand for Pantiles, to £10."[11]

The Charleston, South Carolina, earthquake on August 31, 1886, created such demand for bricklayers that a week after the earthquake the Knights of Labor union authorized a 50-cent-per-day increase in union wages, although union bricklayers were already working for no less than $5 per day ($2 more than before the earthquake) and were soon able to command $6 to $8 per day.[12]

The greatest of all disaster inflation is for transport in the midst of a conflagration. During the 1906 San Francisco fire, Jack London witnessed a man in Union Square futilely offering $1,000 to hire a team of horses to transport a truck full of hotel trunks, which an hour later were "burning merrily."[13] In the Great Fire of London, the price of a cart rose from 10 shillings to £40.[14]

There is nothing new about opportunistic price gouging, or the civic attempts to resist it. In 1362, after a fierce Storm-Wolf windstorm spread destruction across England, King Edward III issued a proclamation requiring that prices of roofing materials should be returned to those that had prevailed before the previous Christmas. Those who disobeyed the decree were to "be taken and imprisoned, and their goods and chattels arrested and detained until further order."[15]

———

ON WHICH SIDE WOULD THE WOODCUT *NAMAZU* PRINT SHOW political leaders?

In India, the world's largest democracy, with the majority of the population involved in farming, people reward or punish politicians according to their personal disaster experiences. Memories are short. Only floods or droughts in the year leading up to an election have been found to change voting behavior.[16]

The closer to the election the greater the opportunity to win votes. Look at President Obama lavishing attention and the promise of money on Superstorm Sandy victims a week before the 2012 presidential election, for which action he gained a 68 percent approval rating.[17] Gerhard Schröder's response to the flooding in eastern Germany a few weeks before the 2002 election was widely credited with allowing him to come from behind and win a narrow victory.[18]

From an economic point of view, it can be far better to invest money to prevent disasters than to compensate people for the damage once the disaster has happened. But politically this may not be true. At the start of the new millennium, US disaster relief spending per citizen was twenty times more than spending on disaster reduction.[19] Each dollar of extra preparedness spending reduced disaster impacts by an average of $7 over a single four-year election cycle and disaster costs overall by an average of $15. With multiples of this magnitude, a politician should clearly invest in disaster reduction.

The problem is that money spent on preparedness wins no votes.[20] Voters are myopic—they reward leaders who arrive to offer aid. An ounce of prevention may technically be worth a pound of cure, but in electoral terms, an ounce of cure wins more votes than a pound of prevention.

If this is the end of the story—that disasters give political leaders the opportunity to grandstand and demonstrate their generosity—why should our leaders ever spend money on disaster preparedness? Yet there is the cautionary tale of Hurricane Katrina. Here was such egregious neglect followed by such a dismal initial disaster response that President Bush was not forgiven despite all the money that was later lavished on New Orleans and the uninsured homeowners of two states. If neglect and inaction become the story, the party in power will be blamed, however bountiful the relief.

Katrina highlights that there is a size of loss and a story of blame that politicians cannot evade. That is why they ultimately need to invest in catastrophe preparedness—if only as insurance against the accusation that they neglected to tackle the problem.

THE BIGGER THE CALAMITY THE MORE DIFFICULT IT IS FOR A LEADER to manage the aftermath. The Confucian idea that catastrophes reflect the displeasure of the gods certainly applied to George W. Bush after Hurricane Katrina.[21] In a democracy the next election provides a vent for popular displeasure. With a free press, the government is held accountable for its failings, whether in anticipating and preparing to respond to a food shortage or in disaster relief and reconstruction.[22]

An authoritarian regime, reliant on being seen to possess total control, can have its authority shattered by a catastrophe. If the catastrophe is big enough to undermine public trust, it can even provoke regime change.

The year 1976 saw the tenth anniversary of the Cultural Revolution in China. The Revolution required renouncing individuality, and intellectuals were reformed by working as peasants. Those who resisted the work and indoctrination could be killed by the young zealot thugs, the Red Guards. In the summer of 1976, the architect of the Cultural Revolution, eighty-three-year-old Mao Zedong, lay dying in a hospital, his heart failing from years of heavy smoking. Premier Zhou Enlai, who had wholeheartedly opposed the senseless activity of sending engineers and doctors to work in the fields, had died earlier that year. Yet there was another brilliant reformer in the wings: Deng Xiaoping.

Mao had appointed his chosen successor, Hua Guofeng, but it was Mao's wife, Jiang Qing of the so-called Gang of Four, who was in the news that summer, rousing the people to strengthen the individual-destroying Cultural Revolution and denouncing Deng Xiaoping as he sought to return to political power.

On July 30, a great earthquake destroyed the city of Tangshan (only 180 kilometers—100 miles—from Beijing), taking hundreds of thousands of lives.[23] Within two days of the earthquake, Hua Guofeng did something completely contrary to the self-denying ethics of the Cultural Revolution.[24] He was photographed exhibiting compassion, visiting the injured people of the ruined city, and comforting the bereaved. He had shown "concern" and expressed pity.

The Gang of Four controlled the key newspapers of the Communist Party. Headlines proclaimed that China should not become diverted by the earthquake. "There were merely several hundred thousand deaths," said Jiang Qing, quoted in an article. "So what? Denouncing Deng Xiaoping concerns 800 million people." She also cautioned: "Be alert to Deng Xiaoping's criminal attempt to exploit earthquake phobia to suppress revolution!" In August, *Red Flag* magazine published a long article devoted to "Revolutionary Optimism" and warned against negative and erroneous interpretations of the catastrophe.

Mao died in September, six weeks after the Tangshan earthquake. In Chinese history, great disasters are interpreted to portend the end of a dynasty. The earthquake was widely seen to have demonstrated the willfulness of Mao's rule.

In October, a month after Mao's death, and inspired by the popular reaction after his show of concern at Tangshan, Hua Guofeng arrested the Gang of Four, bringing the curtain down on Mao's Cultural Revolution. The reformer Deng Xiaoping was released from prison and in August 1977 elected party vice chairman. It was Deng who pioneered the reforms that turbocharged the economy and, by the year 2000, had turned China into a major world power.

Fearful that they might not survive another Tangshan-like disaster, China's rulers set about strengthening all the tens of thousands of brick apartment buildings in Beijing and other cities across China.

In 2006 I visited Tangshan to speak at a conference to commemorate the disaster's thirtieth anniversary. The city's buildings have been rebuilt in gleaming glass, chrome, and modern concrete. At the city center is a memorial park filled with flower beds and containing a great stone monument, erected on the tenth anniversary of the disaster, with four pinnacles and panels of bas relief stone carvings of stylized heroic soldiers of the People's Army, bravely and cheerfully rescuing, healing, feeding, and rehousing the grateful injured earthquake victims of Tangshan.[25] Like "the Monument" in London, the carvings relay the official narrative of the state's role in rescue and reconstruction to help overprint the initial reality—that one-quarter of the population died in the collapse of shoddy state-owned brick apartment buildings, while many survivors were left to rescue themselves.

This memorial makes no effort to commemorate the dead. For decades those who had lost loved ones could only burn paper money at street intersections to assist their lost ancestors in the afterlife, for it did not seem appropriate to mourn in front of the heroic statuary. Yet China was changing. In 2004 a private company hit upon the idea of building a granite memorial wall in Nanhu Park, on top of an abandoned coal mine, and charging people 800 to 1000 yuan ($120 to $150) to have a relative's name inscribed.[26] Even as thousands paid, others protested against this commercialization of grief, so that the municipal authorities were shamed into offering a public alternative. In 2010 the new memorial park opened, with its centerpiece: a quarter-mile-long (400-meter) black granite memorial wall, inspired by the Vietnam Veterans Memorial in Washington, DC.[27] This was the first memorial in China to attempt to list the casualties from a big natural disaster. More than 30,000 names were carved into the stone, including all 24,000 from the commercial memorial wall.

In China there is no sense that ruminating on the past will affect the future prosperity of Tangshan. Nevertheless, the deaths of all those children in the 2008 Wenchuan earthquake is still too raw, too fraught with what it revealed about the failings of the state. Those who attempted to publicize what had happened to the schools found themselves jailed. The artist Ai Weiwei commemorated the children by inscribing their names on the walls around his extraordinary sculpture *Straight*—jagged waves made out of 90 tons of straightened rods of rebar recovered from collapsed buildings in Wenchuan. For his pains, Ai Weiwei's blogs were taken down and he was placed under house arrest for months. Another of his works to commemorate the earthquake's dead children was made from 9,000 abandoned school bags arranged to make the Chinese characters for one mother's lament on losing her only child: "She lived happily for seven years in this world."

The name of every innocent civilian victim is inscribed in stone at the 9/11 memorial in New York. A poignant memorial on the seafront at Gloucester, Massachusetts, records all those who lost their lives in the offshore fisheries.[28] What is so different about disasters? Why were London and Tangshan so eager, within a decade, to create grandiose monuments to celebrate their renewal, and why did those who led the reconstruction of Galveston in 1900, San Francisco in 1906, and even New Orleans in 2005 prefer amnesia? What is that silence saying?[29]

Unlike fallen soldiers or drowned fishermen, there is nothing patriotic about losing your life in a disaster. Nonetheless, those who died in and around San Francisco on April 18, 1906, were as innocent as those who perished in the World Trade Center towers in 2001.

IN THE MID-1980S, TWO CATASTROPHES IN THE SOVIET UNION came to undermine the power and influence of the Communist state. First there was the 1985 explosion, meltdown, and release of radiation at the Chernobyl nuclear power plant. It was not just that news of the catastrophe was suppressed for several days (breaking only after radiation was detected in Sweden), but that the catastrophe revealed humiliating flaws in Soviet technology and nuclear supervision. Before Chernobyl, the state had reveled in Soviet technical superiority.

One year after his elevation to general secretary of the Communist Party of the Soviet Union, Mikhail Gorbachev used the opportunity of Chernobyl to turn up the volume on his policy of glasnost (openness). In 2006 he wrote that "the nuclear meltdown . . . was perhaps the real cause of the collapse of the Soviet Union five years later."[30]

As power leaked away from the center, a second catastrophe further undermined confidence in the Soviet state.

The original earthquake hazard map for the Soviet Union was produced at the Moscow Institute of the Physics of the Earth in 1937. Updated in 1957 and 1968, the map, like many products of the centralized Soviet state, had taken on the aura of inviolable truth.

In 1976 a Magnitude 7 earthquake occurred at the city of Gazli in the deserts of Uzbekistan and caused destruction at intensity IX when the map showed a maximum of V to VI. In 1984 the rebuilt city was once again destroyed by yet another intensity IX earthquake.[31]

It was the Spitak, Armenia, earthquake of December 7, 1988, when 25,000 died, that finally destroyed the sacred hazard map. The destruction was rated intensity X, while the map showed a maximum of only VIII. The "deconsecration" of the earthquake hazard map became a metaphor for the collapse of the Soviet state a year later. The locals had demanded the closure of a nearby nuclear power station earlier in the year. Now the plant was shut down. Soviet progress was shown to be a reckless and dangerous illusion that had offered no protection for the thousands of Armenian children killed in the collapse of Soviet-era concrete apartments and schools.

The challenge posed by catastrophes can even undermine aspiring rebel governments. The Aceh people of Indonesia had waged a separatist campaign and struggle for independence for twenty-eight years, and 13,000 had died. The Indonesian authorities had imposed military camps, deportations, and imprisonment, and no foreigners were allowed to visit the province. But after the December 26, 2004, earthquake and tsunami killed more than 150,000 people in Aceh, the myth was shattered that the province was specially favored.[32] Within days, international disaster agencies and governments demanded a ceasefire to facilitate relief.

Faced with the obliteration of its west coast cities, Aceh was completely dependent on outside support. The Indonesian president proposed "an approach of love and care, of heart and mind, and finally forgiveness." Within days, a blanket amnesty was declared, and the area was opened to relief agencies. In August 2005, the conflict officially ended. A separatist leader acknowledged: "This was the will of God—we had to accept it."[33]

The military regime in Myanmar seemed immune to all outside attempts to open up the country until Cyclone Nargis arrived on the night of May 2, 2008. When the Indian government delivered its storm forecast, the authorities in Myanmar had no way to pass on a warning to those at greatest risk. The strong southerly winds ahead of the storm drove a great surge into the myriad channels of the Ayeyarwady Delta region, drowning an estimated 140,000 and leaving more than 2 million in need of emergency aid. The administration was overwhelmed, but the authorities would not allow anyone other than locals to visit the affected areas. Some European countries suggested that refusing access could constitute a "crime against humanity." By May 17, Britain, the United States, and France had naval ships in position loaded with relief supplies, and there was talk of launching unauthorized air drops.[34] It took a meeting between UN secretary-general Ban Ki-moon and the senior Burmese general Than Shwe on May 23 finally to win international access to the devastated areas, through a coordination mechanism led by the Association of Southeast Asian Nations (ASEAN).[35] In 2012 the ASEAN secretary-general acknowledged that "Cyclone Nargis was a turning point."[36] Myanmar opened to the world because of a disaster.

Authoritarian regimes have a particular vested interest in doing something about mass-death disasters—not because they suddenly gain a humanitarian conscience, but because the catastrophe threatens their hegemony.

What if an earthquake should devastate Iran's capital city of Tehran, with its population of 12 million? Talk there of the threat of a great earthquake was inspired by the 2003 earthquake that destroyed the Iranian city of Bam, but the alarm was really raised in January 2010 by the earthquake in Port au Prince, Haiti, which was located on a fault next to the capital city and decapitated the government. The parallels with Tehran seemed all too strong.

Less than four weeks later, on February 6, the Iranian president, Mahmoud Ahmadinejad, announced that a Tehran earthquake was "imminent" and asked that one-quarter of the city's residents consider relocating. On April 20, the science minister announced that several Tehran universities would be moved away from the city.[37] A month later, the government listed 163 state agencies and state-owned companies that would be relocated, including many in the defense sector.[38] By June 2012, it was said that 100,000 people, including the family members of civil servants, had moved away.[39]

YET, AS THE EXPERIENCE AT LISBON SHOWED, A GREAT DISASTER can also provide the opportunity for a new leader to step forward to demonstrate purposeful resolve and commanding power. Herbert Hoover's role as disaster manager for the great 1927 Mississippi River flood gained him the recognition and influence to be elected US president in the 1929 election.

The government in the Dominican Republic fell in early 1930, and in the May elections the head of the armed forces, General Rafael Trujillo, was elected with 90 percent of the vote (unsurprisingly, as he was the only candidate). A few weeks into his presidency, on September 3, a Category 4 hurricane (San Zenon) made a direct hit on the capital of Santo Domingo, killing 4,000 and injuring 19,000—almost half the city of 50,000. Like de Carvalho after the 1755 earthquake, Trujillo became galvanized, issuing decrees, organizing committees, enacting new building standards for cement block construction, and creating for himself the myth that he was out on the streets in the midst of the storm and, moved by the destruction, had "drunk his own tears." Recalled in an annual commemoration ceremony, the story of how Trujillo overcame the San Zenon disaster kept the increasingly tyrannical dictator in a position of power for the next thirty years. In 1936 the reconstructed capital became Ciudad Trujillo.[40]

The leader who best learned how to harness and ride the wild catastrophe was Fidel Castro. On October 4, 1963, in the year after the Cuban Missile Crisis, when Castro was still consolidating the Communist regime, Cuba was hit by the deadliest hurricane in more than thirty years.[41] Hurricane Flora drifted over the east of the country for four days in a slow loop, producing enormous rainfall totals—over 80 inches (2 meters) in some places, as much as 1998 Mitch in Honduras. People moved onto the tops of their houses before the houses were washed away. More than 1,700 Cubans died.

The disaster had not been properly forecasted. Only two meteorologists remained in the country after the revolution. As the floods from Hurricane Flora drained away, Fidel proclaimed (echoing the words of Simón Bolívar in Caracas 150 years before): "A revolution is a force more powerful than Nature. . . . Hurricanes and all those things are trivial when compared to . . . a Revolution."[42]

The hurricane had crashed into Cuba like a wild invading army. Castro, seeing the need to neutralize the threat, bolstered the Institute of Meteorology at Havana University and elevated the Meteorological Service; in time it would be lauded like no other weather agency worldwide. (Today José Rubiera, senior professor of meteorology in Havana and a television forecaster for hurricanes, is "Cuba's weather superstar"—one of the most famous and revered people in the country.[43])

Castro (or more correctly the revolutionary government) also set up a highly proactive program of civil defense to combat hurricanes and used it as a way of proving the merits of socialism. The goal was zero fatalities. In Cuba, it was said, "the hurricane has transformed into a shared social experience . . . a source of community solidarity."[44] Che Guevara acknowledged the cooperative heroism of the people combating the hurricane and reflected that "one of our fundamental tasks . . . [is] the need to transform it into everyday practice."[45] (The Republican governor of New Jersey, Chris Christie, echoed the sentiment when in October 2013 he celebrated the purposeful and altruistic "spirit of hurricane Sandy."[46])

Keeping a self-defense force trained and mobilized against the hurricane enemy was also great preparation in case Cuba should ever be invaded by a cyclone of ships and planes from the north.[47] Cuban hurricanes are sometimes described as if they are the weapons of capitalism: they cause the most destruction to the houses of the poor, it is said, and they are now exacerbated by that "product of ravenous capitalism": climate change.[48]

Today Cuba has the most effective hurricane evacuation program in the world, though it incorporates a level of coercion only possible in a strongly regimented society. Evacuations are very carefully planned and choreographed. The entire population of coastal villages can be moved inland three days before the forecasted storm surge.[49] The civil defense force, under the direction of the secretary of the Communist Party in the affected state, is part of the military and can summon all required national resources. Troops are sent to harvest any crops considered at risk (since agricultural lands are not privately owned). Electricity supplies are cut even before the outer winds arrive. Disaster prevention is taught in primary schools, and there is a two-day hurricane drill for all citizens every year.

The toughest test came in 2008, when Cuba was struck by four hurricanes, two of them major storms.[50] Hurricane Gustav made landfall at Category 4 and crossed the western end of Cuba "like a nuclear strike," as Fidel Castro described it.[51] Hurricane Ike, which also made landfall at Category 4, ran along the whole length of the island. Throughout the season, 4.8 million people were evacuated. Remarkably, there were no casualties in Gustav and only seven in Ike. (A 2004 UN report identified the risk of dying in a hurricane as fifteen times higher in the United States than in Cuba.[52])

However, 500,000 homes were destroyed in the 2008 storms, at a cost of $10 billion, equivalent to 7.5 percent of Cuban GDP. The country already needed another 600,000 homes to house the population. Cuba has proved that it can save lives, but has been unable to harden and save properties. There is no building code or zoning to keep new development outside flood zones. The government distributed 2 million square meters of corrugated roof to patch the corrugated roofs that the storms stripped and scattered to the four winds.[53] The country has neither the cement nor the steel rebar to build safe homes for the people. And without insurance, people learn to play the system. Carlos, an inhabitant of one of Havana's poorest districts, constructed a new room for his house out of concrete blocks stolen from a state-run company and took down the supports to his dilapidated roof in advance of a hurricane, hoping that the wind would strip it clean so that he would receive a new one. Unfortunately, on this occasion, the hurricane veered away.[54]

12 • TURNING UP THE HEAT

I N AUTUMN 2000, AFTER WEEKS OF HEAVY RAIN, THE SWOLLEN River Thames flowed into Myles Allen's house in Oxford. Myles was an Oxford University physicist and junior lecturer who worked with numerical climate models that are used for weather forecasting as well as for predicting future climate. He lived with his wife and young children in a Victorian brick terrace row house, off the Botley Road. To whom, he contemplated, should he send the bill for his sodden carpets and damaged plaster? Maybe to the owners of all the coal-burning power stations, as well as to all the petrolheads (himself included) whose carbon dioxide emissions had contributed to his ruined sofa? Or perhaps this was simply a random act of fate? How could he identify the cause?

Global temperatures had been rising strongly through the 1990s. Two global reinsurers, Munich Re and Swiss Re, had been tracking the economic costs of worldwide catastrophes going back to the 1970s. Even after adjusting for inflation, the losses seemed to be rising exponentially. In 2001 the graph of accelerating catastrophe costs was displayed in the Intergovernmental Panel on Climate Change's Third

Assessment Report's technical summary. "Many of the observed trends in weather-related losses," the summary stated, "are consistent with what would be expected under climate change." After a run of fierce Atlantic windstorms in 1993, even the conservative *Financial Times* had blamed them on "Global Warming."[1]

Yet if Europeans saw the signature of climate change in every flood and storm, this was not how it seemed in North America. Since 1995, there had been more intense hurricanes in the Atlantic, but the storms had shied away from the US coastline. By March 2004, the proportion of Americans who believed that global warming was an exaggerated threat had risen five points, to 38 percent.

If the real catastrophes were not always forthcoming to make the case, there was always Hollywood. In German film director Roland Emmerich's *The Day After Tomorrow*, abrupt climate change leads to hypercanes, a surprise tsunami, and an even more unexpected (but fortunately short-lived) flash-freeze ice age. Following the film's New York premiere on May 27, 2004, Al Gore gave the climate change slide lecture he had already presented in hundreds of town hall meetings. The film producer Laurie David, who was in the audience, was so inspired by Gore's message and delivery that she set out to turn the slide show into a movie documentary. The timing was perfect. The weather gods were about to unleash a prolonged campaign of rip-roaring wild hurricane weather.

By August 2004, hurricanes had rediscovered how to reach the US coastline. (The trick is to reposition the North Atlantic anticyclonal high southwest from the Azores to Bermuda.) Nine hurricanes formed that season, six of them intense storms. Charley made landfall on the west coast of Florida on August 13, and Frances on the east coast on September 5. Hurricane Ivan devastated Grenada before intensifying to Category 5 and sending most of Grand Cayman underwater on September 11.

With a headline-grabbing maximum-intensity hurricane careering through the Caribbean, it was a good time for climate change political initiatives. In a speech on September 14, Tony Blair, the British prime minister, announced an international scientific meeting the following February during the British presidency of the G8 to answer the question: "what level of greenhouse gases in the atmosphere is self-evidently too much?"[2] (I was there, in Exeter, when the German climate scientist Hans Joachim Schellnhuber's proposal of a "guard-rail" rise in global temperatures of 2 degrees Celsius [3.6 degrees Fahrenheit] was declared to be the definition of "dangerous" climate change.[3]) On September 16, Hurricane Ivan made landfall in Alabama at Category 4, pushing a large and destructive storm surge. The total cost of Caribbean and US hurricane damages for the year approached $50 billion.

Through the spring of 2005, all the forecasts suggested that this would be another active hurricane season. However, no one had any idea what was in store.

The season began early. On July 5, Hurricane Dennis developed in the eastern Caribbean; intensifying to Category 4, it became the strongest July storm ever. A few days later, Hurricane Emily broke the record set by Dennis and reached Category 5.

On July 19, Gordon Brown, the UK chancellor of the exchequer, announced that he had asked the economist Sir Nicholas Stern to lead a major review of the economics of climate change.

On July 31, Professor Kerry Emanuel of MIT, a leading hurricane scientist, published a paper in *Nature* magazine, accompanied by a press release, announcing that "hurricanes have grown significantly more powerful and destructive over the last three decades, due in part to global warming."[4]

There had been eleven storms by the end of August. On August 12, the "K" storm emerged over the Bahamas. K was for Katrina, a storm that caused more than $80 billion of damage and the highest loss of American life in a hurricane catastrophe since 1928.

On September 16, 2005, *Science* magazine published a research paper conveying an even stronger message: "The number of storms reaching categories 4 and 5 grew from about 11 per year in the 1970s to 18 per year since 1990."[5] The "new analysis [is] sure to stir debate over whether global warming is worsening these deadly storms."

Two days after the paper was published, a new disturbance developed over the Turks and Caicos Islands. On September 21, Rita became the third-most-intense hurricane ever known in the Atlantic, prompting a mass evacuation of Houston, though it weakened down to Category 3 when it made landfall on the border between Texas and Louisiana.

A month later, on October 17, Hurricane Wilma developed southwest of Jamaica and soon became the strongest-ever Atlantic hurricane, with a central pressure of 882 millibars and 185-mile-per-hour (300-kilometer-per-hour) winds. After removing the beach and blowing out windows in Cancun hotels on the Yucatán Peninsula, the storm headed northeast, reaching southern Florida as a Category 3 storm on the 24th and crossing Miami to cause another $20 billion of damage. The season was still not over, even as the National Hurricane Center ran out of letters and switched over to the Greek alphabet—the storm Zeta arrived on December 30.

The hurricanes of 2005 caused $160 billion of damage and took more than 2,000 lives. The Atlantic season broke many records: the highest number of Category 5 storms ever, the largest number of tropical storms, and the largest number of hurricanes. Summer 2005, with its cocktail of catastrophe science and hurricane disasters, seemed proof that climate change was going to be truly apocalyptic. Early in 2006, along the coast of Dauphin Island, Alabama, I watched million-dollar beachfront houses being lifted onto giant trailers and moved inland on barges.

The Al Gore movie *An Inconvenient Truth* opened on May 26, 2006. Images from the 2004 and 2005 hurricane seasons and the mere mention of Katrina highlighted the power of these catastrophes to influence the debate.

On October 30, the 700-page Stern Review, prepared by a team of economists at HM Treasury, was published.[6] It carried the unequivocal message that, "if we don't act" (to reduce greenhouse gas emissions), "the overall costs and risks of climate change will be equivalent to losing at least 5% of global GDP each year, now and forever."[7]

The IPCC completed its fourth assessment report in 2006 and published it in early 2007. The Nobel Peace Prize of 2007 was awarded to Al Gore and to the IPCC.

Catastrophes had become enlisted to make the argument for climate change action. But what if the hurricane "publicity machine" was discontinued?

From the start of 2006, it was as if the hurricane gods had changed sides. After being pummeled with seven intense (Category 3–5) hurricanes in fifteen months, no intense hurricanes hit the US coastline for the next ten years. In the spring of 2007, a second wave of scientific publications appeared on the subject of hurricanes and climate change. Rising temperatures in all the equatorial oceans, it now seemed, would lead to stronger upper-level winds that would shear hurricanes apart before they could form. A new consensus was emerging: hurricanes were likely to be more intense, but there could also be fewer of them.[8]

The story of the rising costs of catastrophes in an era of global warming was also wilting under further scrutiny. Replacement costs increase as people build bigger houses and fill them with more possessions. Adjust the costs for the increased wealth in the path of the storms and the trend in losses disappears.[9] That is, unless we can assume that increased wealth is also invested in making properties stronger, and then a trend is back (at least up to the "high tide" of activity in 2005). However it would be difficult to argue that anyone in Louisiana was taking action to improve flood defenses or harden buildings in the years before Hurricane Katrina.[10]

We are challenged to understand that all climates contain a spectrum of extremes: heat waves and bitter freezes, monsoons and droughts, gales and doldrums. It can be a very broad spectrum. The extremes of the extremes of storms and floods have shown, so far, no simple trends. The worst-ever hurricane year for casualties was 1780.[11] The most destructive windstorm across western Europe blew through in 1703, pursued by Daniel Defoe.[12] The biggest-ever flood in central Europe occurred after eight solid days of rain in July 1342.[13] In the winter of 1861–1862, a month of persistent heavy rain, fed by an "atmospheric river" meander in the jet stream, turned the Central Valley into an inland sea 300 miles (480 kilometers) long[14] and washed away one-quarter of California's taxable real estate, sending the state bankrupt.

But there are also recent records. In October 1998, (formerly Category 5) Hurricane Mitch drifted over Honduras and for four days rained 1 to 2 feet (30 to 60 centimeters) each day.[15] Twenty-five villages on the northern slopes of the mountains simply disappeared, along with roads, electricity supplies, and water pipes. In Honduras the death toll was eventually set at 6,500, but 11,000 were missing and 1.5 million people were homeless—around 20 percent of the population. Honduras has never recovered. Some proportion of this rainfall was probably generated by warmer seas—but how much?

What would transform the argument was an idea from Myles Allen, back in Oxford, who was contemplating where to send the bill for his ruined floorboards. He decided to run global climate models with and without the increase in greenhouse gas emissions since 1950—that is, to perform climate "counterfactuals" for a parallel world that had experienced no increase in atmospheric carbon dioxide. In both the actual and counterfactual worlds, he would need to run thousands of simulated years of the climate to explore whether a particular weather extreme had become more or less likely in the model output. To match the resolution of the global climate model he needed something large and long-lasting—like a month of extreme temperatures and drought, or weeks of intense rainfall. This would take a lot of computing power, which he did not have. So he enlisted a network of tens of thousands of volunteers around the world to distribute the modeling over their idling PCs.

The first results, generated by Allen's research student Pardeep Pall, showed that the chance of the autumn 2000 floods that had flooded his Oxford house had doubled in the world of higher greenhouse gases.[16] Allen could attribute 50 percent of the cost of the floods to climate change. Within a decade, climate scientists were pursuing "attribution studies" following every climate catastrophe.[17]

In November 2013, the city of Tacloban on the Philippine island of Leyte was destroyed by Supertyphoon Haiyan, which brought the strongest cyclone wind speeds ever observed and took almost 10,000 lives, most from the storm surge.[18] A few days later, at the start of the UN climate talks in Warsaw, the Philippine delegate, Yeb Sano, gave an impassioned speech unequivocally linking the storm to climate change and the failure to agree on actions to take on greenhouse gas emissions: "To anyone who continues to deny the reality that this is climate change, I dare you to get off your ivory tower."[19]

In the developing world, it can seem that every climate extreme now gets labeled "climate change."[20] While the attribution analysis provides a tougher test of causation, it may still take months before it delivers results. Tacloban lies in a funnel-shaped bay that amplifies storm surges for intense typhoons tracking south of the town. Tacloban was devastated by typhoons in 1897 and 1912, each of which took thousands of lives.[21] So was Yeb Sano correct in his diagnosis that Haiyan's intensity was a consequence of climate change?

It seems he was. A Japanese attribution study, using a high-resolution regional climate model, found strong evidence that the maximum intensity of storms in this region has increased with preexisting warming.[22]

Environmental lawyers are following the attribution studies with great interest. If you can show that an event has doubled in probability, it may be possible to find some greenhouse gas emitters on whom to pin liability. But would the evidence withstand courtroom cross-examination and questions such as: Who exactly built this climate model? How do you know it is reliable?[23]

When a man leaves his home in Senegal, driven out by an intense Sahel drought, is he a "climate migrant" meriting compensation, perhaps even a new home, from the principal greenhouse gas emitters? Attribution studies show that the drought has doubled in probability. Does that make him one half a climate migrant? Attribution studies found that the 2007–2010 drought in Syria had been made "two to three times more likely" as a result of climate change.[24] As unemployed farmers moved to the cities, the drought was a factor in the terrible civil war that followed. This is the future in which war becomes a "threat multiplier," creating far more refugees than the drought alone.[25]

Attribution studies do not answer the question of whether a whole class of catastrophe is overall becoming more likely or more damaging. Winter 1947 in England was the coldest of the last century, with arctic conditions and a thick snowpack. In early March, a succession of Atlantic storms caused a rapid thaw, leading to the most disastrous national flooding of the past 200 years. It seems likely that such a "continental" deep-freeze winter and associated thaw floods are now less likely in a warmer world.[26] Has the disappearance of one class of severe flood been offset by an increase in the likelihood of other classes, such as prolonged episodes of autumn rain or intense summer cloudbursts? In a 2014 global review of all the evidence for worldwide changes in river flood frequency, leading IPCC authors acknowledged that, so far, there is no consistent pattern of change.[27]

Most likely Superstorm Sandy or Supertyphoon Haiyan would have formed independent of a warmer world. The extra heat in the oceans over which they traveled supplemented their landfall intensity and made them even more destructive.[28] Yet just because these storms caused more damage does not prove that overall cyclones are more damaging. Maybe one or more hurricanes have already sheared apart through stronger winds in our warmer world? Or maybe Atlantic hurricanes are recurving further offshore and failing to make landfall?

And for no disaster (so far) can we say scientifically that it could not have occurred without climate change.[29] To distinguish whether a climate extreme reflects climate change we need those attribution studies.

———

THE LARGER THREAT OF CLIMATE CHANGE LOOKING FORWARD IS not simply from stronger hurricanes or bigger floods, but from classes of irreversible tipping point catastrophes: a shutdown in the North Atlantic thermohaline circulation, a permanent dieback in the Amazon rain forest, the death of the principal coral reefs, the runaway escape of methane hydrates trapped in the permafrost, a failure of the Indian monsoon, or an acceleration in the melting of the Greenland ice cap.[30] These are not catastrophes for which we can find current examples. Look out for small headlines tucked away on obscure news websites. "Gigantic Gas Discharge Vents Discovered in the Ob Delta of Northern Siberia," "Persistent Drought in Peruvian Amazon Followed by Great Fires," or "Recent Bleaching Event on Great Barrier Reef Much Worse Than Initial Estimates."

———

SO WHAT ARE THE PRINCIPAL CLASSES OF CLIMATE EXTREMES THAT are going to be intensifying in a warmer world?

The air is scorching. It's so hot you turn to see if you are standing in the draft of a massive truck or jet engine. It is a dry itching heat, but you are sweating profusely. You're too hot to undertake any job, or even to sit outside. It's hot during the day, but most potently hot through the night, with no breeze. Without air conditioning, sleep is impossible.

Known in Latin as *dies caniculares* (the "days of the little dog"), these are the days in the calendar when the "Dog Star," Sirius, the brightest in the night sky, in the "Big Dog" constellation Canis Major, rises with the sun between July 24 and August 24 (in the Roman calendar).[31] These are the days when dogs lie panting in the shade.

We are going to see a lot of heat waves in the century ahead. We should make ourselves familiar with what to expect and learn to take precautions. The term "heat wave" does not properly capture a phenomenon that spans hundreds of miles (the size of an anticyclone), can be accompanied by a choking chemical smog, lasts for days to weeks, and brings drought, desiccation, and death to people and ecosystems over a wide area.[32] In the middle latitudes in the summer, with few hours of darkness, heat can build day by day. High temperatures lead to soil evaporation, while dry soils bake in the sun, increasing surface temperatures.

The summer 2003 European "canicule" heat wave followed the prescribed dates, from July 20 to August 20, peaking between August 10 and 12. France experienced its hottest and most persistent temperatures ever, with seven days of temperatures that were above 40 degrees Celsius (104 degrees Fahrenheit) in Auxerre, to the southeast of Paris, while high temperatures spread to all the neighboring countries. The heat shock was greatest in the north, where the heat wave brought temperatures almost 12 degrees Celsius (21 degrees Fahrenheit) hotter than the normal maximum summer temperatures.[33] As a result, no one was prepared, and no one had air conditioning.

By the middle of August, the equivalent of four nuclear power plants in France (4,000 megawatts) had to close down because the river waters were too warm for effective cooling. The French wheat harvest was down by one-fifth.

In August, Paris is closed, families gone to the beach. The roofs of the city amplify the heat. Left behind are the aged relatives, who often sleep in the hottest garret rooms under the eaves. Death rates rise with age: that summer, those under thirty-five were almost unaffected, but at the peak of the crisis, on August 12, three times as many people over age seventy-five were dying than average. At the epicenter of the impacts in the Ile de France (the greater Paris region), the death rate across all age groups peaked at nine times the average.

While "heatstroke" was the identified cause on only 3,306 French death certificates, total "excess deaths" in France were officially estimated at 14,800, and across Europe at 35,000.[34]

These deaths of the elderly and the sick had been brought forward in time, or "harvested." On average, how many months of life were lost? More than four months, or the statistics would not have shown that an additional 18,100 people died in France in 2003 than had died on average in the previous three years.[35] But less than sixteen months, because in the following year the number of deaths was 24,000 *lower* than the previous average. So the excess in 2003 was smaller than the deficit in 2004. By all accounts, the French were so shamed by what happened in the heat wave that they started looking after the elderly and the sick better than before. The heat wave changed behaviors. By the end of 2004, the French were living longer than if the canicule had not occurred. How do we account for that in our statistics on climate change mortalities?

For most mid-latitude towns and cities, the average number of extra "cold deaths" of the old and the sick in the winter exceeds the number of "heat deaths" in the summer, with the majority of deaths happening in annual cold spells. Across the northern United States, even by the end of the twenty-first century, that is likely to remain the case.[36]

The summer 2010 Russian heat wave lasted for six weeks through July and the first half of August. Temperatures exceeded 40 degrees Celsius (104 degrees Fahrenheit) across southern Russia and the Ukraine—more than 10 degrees Celsius (18 degrees Fahrenheit) higher than normal.[37] Fires set to clear vegetation spread out of control and destroyed 800 square miles (2,000 square kilometers) of countryside. Hundreds of fires moved into the underlying peat soil, consuming whole villages and creating a toxic smog even in the largest cities, where everyone was advised to wear face masks.[38] Nine million hectares of crops dried up and died, and the wheat harvest was down by one-third, with nothing left for export. At the height of the heat wave, death rates doubled in Moscow. An extra 5,000 died in July. Crazed by the heat and the smog, drunken Russians dived into pools and rivers and 2,000 drowned. An official estimate set the total "excess deaths" at 56,000. On July 30, President Dmitry Medvedev linked the crisis to climate change and demanded international action.[39]

For centuries there had never been a heat wave like the summer of 2003 in Europe or the summer of 2010 in Russia.

In December 2004, working with scientists at the UK Hadley Centre, Myles Allen showed that the chance of the 2003 heat wave across Europe had at least doubled as a result of human influence on the atmosphere.[40] Attribution studies revealed that the 2010 Russian heat wave had been made three times more likely by climate change.[41]

It is more difficult to set records for heat waves in the United States. In the 1930s, drought, combined with poor farming practices and lack of irrigation, created the 1930s Dust Bowl.[42] The barren soil turned up the temperature on scorching heat waves across the Midwest. In 1936 records were set, some of which have still to be broken, although many were finally exceeded during the 2012 heat wave.[43]

Australia, with few areas of climate-tempering forest, has always been prone to violent heat waves. Yet it is getting even hotter. In the "Angry Summer" of December 2012 to January 2013, for the first time average high temperatures across the whole country exceeded 39 degrees Celsius (102 degrees Fahrenheit).[44] In southeast Australia, the most extreme heat wave was in January 2009. On February 7, a strong northwesterly wind drew baking air out of the continent's interior and fires took off across Victoria.[45] Fallen power cables sparked one fire whose embers, blown by 60-mile-per-hour (100-kilometer-per-hour) winds, flashed from one woodland to another, overwhelming several small towns so fast that 173 died before they could escape.[46]

Heat will amplify and extend fire seasons. In October 1991, a small grass fire in the hills above Oakland, California, was whipped by strong northeasterly winds into the tree-lined hillside streets. Jumping an eight-lane freeway, the fire consumed more than 3,000 houses, while twenty-five people died.[47] There was no possibility to halt the fire until the winds had calmed. The wooden cities of Oakland and Berkeley remain at risk from a windblown firestorm emerging out of the Berkeley hills.[48]

In May 2011 in Slave Lake, Alberta, a forest fire, fanned by gale force winds, destroyed 374 properties—one-third of the town.[49] The great Chicago fire of October 8–10, 1871, also consumed one-third of the wooden city. Circumstantial evidence suggests that the fire was sparked by embers blown on strong southwesterly winds from the thousands of fires lit by settlers to clear the land. At the end of a long summer drought, it is beyond coincidence that there were four giant fires around the shores of Lake Michigan on the same day. One fire 250 miles north, at Peshtigo, burned hundreds of square miles of forest, destroyed the lumber town, and killed more than 1,500 people trapped between the fire and the lake.[50]

One thing is for sure about future warming: the heat waves will be hotter, even more frequent, and more like those in Australia. They will come not just every thirty years, but every decade, even every year.

——

EACH YEAR HIGH TIDE REACHES, ON AVERAGE, ONE-EIGHTH OF AN inch (3 millimeters) higher than the previous year. This rise is going to accelerate as the Greenland ice sheet melts and all the heat passing into the oceans expands their volume. At the last interglacial warm period, 125,000 years ago, the oceans were 16 feet (5 meters) higher. Sea level rise will be an inevitable legacy of our times.

The greatest concentration of people in a river delta is in Bangladesh, where there are already tens of thousands of climate migrants; displaced by the chronic loss of land to erosion, waves of humanity are propelled inland in the aftermath of each storm surge flood.[51] As the people come down from their raised concrete flood shelters to discover that their houses have been washed away, their only option is to catch a boat upriver, most likely to Dhaka, to find employment so as to avoid living on the street. The waves of migration that follow each storm surge will become larger and push deeper into Bangladesh and the border with Assam.[52]

Some coastal cities are already living with rapid sea level rise from land subsidence caused by groundwater extraction. Close to the shoreline, parts of Jakarta will have sunk almost 13 feet (4 meters) by 2025.[53]

In towns along the northern coast of Java, just as in Venice, people have either abandoned the ground floor of their houses or visit these rooms only at low tide.[54] In Grand Bahama, after houses in the canal estate community of Queen's Cove were flooded three times in a decade, insurance was withdrawn, mortgages became unavailable, and houses were abandoned.[55]

———

ALREADY MORE THAN HALF THE WORLD'S POPULATION LIVE IN CITies. By 2030, it will be 60 percent. We are in the era of "Catastropolis": disaster entangled with urbanization.

Cities in the rich world acquire better flood defenses and storm drains than rural areas, and the largest buildings have been designed by structural engineers. Tall buildings are anyway mostly out of reach of floods.[56] Yet even in the rich world, cities can foment risk, especially port cities that are open to the sea. When the flood defenses break, as in New Orleans in 2005 or in Nagoya, Japan, in 2000, the consequences are worse, because people in cities live as if there is no threat. Water fills the subway tunnels, the underground shopping malls, and the hospital basements where the heaviest and most expensive diagnostic scanners are situated. At the waterfront, the high price of land lures developers to reclaim the swamps, priming the land for future soil liquefaction and flooding.[57] The faster the city grows the more of the development happens outside planning controls, with informal settlements crowding over the land considered too steep or too flood-ridden for official occupation.

When Superstorm Sandy made landfall in New York and New Jersey in the early morning on October 29, 2012, it left more than 8 million customers without power, 3 million of them in New York City's five boroughs. The most surprised and least prepared were the urbanites in Lower Manhattan, where electricity cables had been laid underground to protect them from wind damage. Substations designed to survive 12.5-foot (3.8-meter) water levels blew up when the surge tide reached 14 feet (4.3 meters). The New York Stock Exchange closed for two days, the theater district was closed for three, and 6,300 patients had to be evacuated from thirty-seven New York health-care facilities.[58] Power was not fully restored to Manhattan for five days. Fortunately, power outages at the end of October are far more bearable in New York than in January or August, but the elderly and disabled were still left in dark apartments without any working elevators. Gasoline rationing continued in New York for fifteen days, while 10 billion gallons of raw and partially treated sewage spilled into the sea.

WORLDWIDE THE COASTLINE WITH THE GREATEST EXPERIENCE OF accelerated sea level rise is the "southern wild" of Louisiana, which extends as far inland as the northern shores of Lake Pontchartrain, including the city of New Orleans.[59] In areas unprotected by the levees, the Cajuns who live here watch from year to year as their orchards and cemeteries become overwhelmed by the sea and their woods die as the saltwater infiltrates tree roots. The sea level rises two-fifths to three-fifths of an inch (10 to 15 millimeters) each year, up to 6 inches (150 millimeters) every decade: 80 percent of this change reflects the land sinking rather than the sea rising. Every year another 16 square miles (40 square kilometers) of land disappears.[60]

The sinking is not new. One hundred and thirty years ago, a journalist wrote of Last Island, southeast of New Orleans: "Many and many a mile of ground has yielded to the tireless charging of Ocean's cavalry: . . . porpoises at play where of old the sugar-cane shook out its million bannerets; . . . those wan battle-grounds where the woods made their last brave stand against the irresistible invasion."[61]

Why is this region sinking so fast? The delta turns out to be a gigantic landslide, with more than 100 surface faults.[62] It is slipping inexorably into the deep waters of the Gulf of Mexico.[63]

Without massive interventions at the Old River Control Structure far to the west, in 1927 the whole Mississippi River would have diverted south along the steeper Atchafalaya channel to the sea.[64] The river at New Orleans would then have become a clogged swamp, and Morgan City would today be the "new" New Orleans. Ever-increasing amounts of money will have to be injected into both the river and the city to sustain them, but eventually most of the land will have to be let go, being too expensive and difficult to protect.[65]

TEN THOUSAND YEARS AGO, HUMANS LIVING ON THE FOOD-RICH shoreline experienced the sea rising inexorably by as much as a woman's height in her own lifetime, the water rolling miles inland on the great deltas. The sea had been rising for generations. Every decade or so, the beach camp would need to be relocated inland. We may become just as inured to the idea that the sea is inexorably rising. In the decades ahead, there will be constant renewal at the coast. The "winners" from climate change will be civil engineers and construction companies. Many airports have already been built on coastal salt marshes, like New York's John F. Kennedy International Airport. The departure board will increasingly read: DELAYED BY HIGH TIDE. Will the airport grow walls around the runways, or try to find somewhere inland to relocate? Watching their property values depreciate as people start to move to higher ground, those who live on the coast will argue for compensation for their relocation. A city like Miami cannot be protected with a wall because the reef rock on which it is built is completely porous.[66]

Insurers will emphasize "insurability," refusing to cover those properties now deemed too high-risk for wind or flood damage, while politicians talk up the "obligations" of insurance. Florida had a test drive for the climate change future after the 2004–2005 hurricane season, when "contract-terminating," "rate-hiking" insurers were identified by the press as the enemy. Insurers will need to step up to a societal role, as in agreeing to ensure that insurance remains available for the lifetime (fifty years?) of any new property that has been officially sanctioned for its location and construction quality.

A former period of climate change in Europe, the Little Ice Age, led, between 1560 and 1660, to witch hunts and ritual killings.[67] Who will be the scapegoats for future climate disasters? Coal miners and oil drillers? We could update John Wesley's imprecation that there is "no divine visitation which is likely to have so general an influence upon sinners as an earthquake" to "there is no manifestation likely to have so general an influence on climate sceptics as a succession of heat waves, intense hurricanes, or floods." After the 2004 and 2005 hurricane seasons, the proportion of Americans who disbelieved global warming dropped to its lowest-ever proportion, at 30 percent.[68] By 2010, as the intense hurricanes stayed away, that number had risen 60 percent (to 48 percent). Polling after the English floods in early 2014 showed that for one-quarter of the population the floods had strengthened their belief in "human-induced climate change."[69]

Even the Conference to the Parties (COP) of the UN Framework Convention on Climate Change is not immune to the emotional force of catastrophes. In November 2013, the devastation of Tacloban wrought by Typhoon Haiyan was widely perceived to have influenced the Warsaw COP19 to authorize the "Loss and Damage" agenda (i.e., seeking compensation for the costs of permanent loss and unstoppable climate change damage). Yet how much should countries adapt before declaring protection a lost cause? By 2100, without intervention, rising seas will largely drown four whole countries: Tuvalu, Kiribati, the Marshall Islands, and the Maldives. China has shown that political will, supplemented by giant dredgers pumping millions of tons of sand, can turn even submerged reefs into garrisoned island airports. What constitutes "sufficient adaptation" may be left to the courts as the rich world argues over their liabilities for loss and damage.

Catastrophes can make the visceral argument for action on reducing emissions more powerfully than 100 scientists and their climate projections. Until large numbers of people become seriously frightened by climate disasters, it seems we will never achieve enough on emissions reduction. Yet disasters cannot be summoned on command. We are reckless to entrust the fate of the planet to the spontaneous advocacy of catastrophes.[70]

13 • THE REMEDIES
OF DR. RESILIENCE

There have been, and will be again, many destructions
of mankind arising out of many causes; the greatest
have been brought about by the agencies of fire
and water. . . . [When there is] a great conflagration
of things upon the earth, which recurs after long
intervals; at such times those who live upon the
mountains and in dry and lofty places are more liable
to destruction than those who dwell by rivers or on the
seashore. . . . When, on the other hand the gods purge
the earth with a deluge of water, the survivors in your
country are herdsmen and shepherds who dwell on
the mountains, but those who, like you, live in cities
are carried by the rivers into the sea.

—Advice to the Greek Solon[1] from the
priests of the Temple of Neith at Sais,
Egypt (archivists of the story of Atlantis),
around 590 BC

GIRDLING THE EARTH LIKE THE SEAMS ON A SOCCER BALL, PLATE
boundaries create some of the most fertile and accommodating topography. Sediment eroded off oversteepened mountain flanks

accumulates in the well-watered plains and provides the foundation for cities like Los Angeles or Tehran. The world's best coffee, tea, coca, and marijuana is grown on the rising tectonic highlands of Java, Darjeeling, the Colombian Andes, and the Blue Mountains of Jamaica. Some of the most expensive addresses with the best views, like Beverly Hills, have been raised a meter or two at a time through the work of earthquake-generating thrust faults, just as fashionable Las Condes has been elevated above Santiago, and Beirut lifted out of the Mediterranean. Tectonics have sunk San Francisco Bay and the Gulf of Corinth. Active faults slice through Manila, Kyoto, and Jericho. Along the southern edge of the Himalayas and around the eastern flank of Tibet, beneath the rimming mountain walls, lie plate boundary faults. Active tectonics created a string of lakes along a rift through northern Turkey that passes into the Sea of Marmara. Beneath Tokyo's Kantō Plain, by far the largest in Japan, there are three tectonic plates, grinding under and over one another. Worldwide, thousands of miles of shoreline lie above subduction zones; the glamorous beach resorts of the Pacific coast of Mexico, the windswept eastern shorelines of Antigua and Barbados, the wild cliffs of Oregon—all of these coastlines will one day be swept by great tsunamis.

Cities don't find themselves in hazardous situations by chance alone. Tectonics may have created the very reason for a city's foundation: the natural harbor, the river crossing, the spring line.[2] What diabolic agency would lure all the movie studios and their star performers to locate above the same blind thrust fault in Hollywood, or get Facebook and Google to found themselves on estuarine mud midway between the tramline faults of a plate boundary?

While living on a plate boundary can bring many advantages, there is an inevitable price to pay in unpredictable earthquakes. Offshore Chile, the Pacific plate moves beneath South America at 4 inches (100 millimeters) each year, and Darwin's 1835 Concepción earthquake returned (more or less) after 165 years, in 2010.[3] The plate movement along the Cascadia subduction zone offshore Oregon and Washington State moves more slowly, at an average of around 1.5 inches (40 millimeters) each year, so we might expect the time interval between great earthquakes to be 2.5 times (1 divided by 0.4) longer in Cascadia than in Chile. Most likely we can expect the giant 1700 Cascadia earthquake to return between the years 2100 and 2200, but it could also arrive early in 2020. Yet tectonics is not clockwork, with identical repeating earthquakes, but more like a Rubik's Cube—fault segments can break in different combinations. The southern section of the Cascadia subduction zone appears to break more frequently than the rest of the zone. Southwest of Portugal, Europe collides with Africa at one-twentieth the speed of the Chilean plate boundary. The monster 1755 earthquake may not return for thousands of years.

Worldwide, one in fourteen big cities are on the plate tectonic "front line." Many of these cities are growing fast. Since 1970, in San Francisco, Los Angeles, and Tokyo, the population has increased by half again. In Karachi, Manila, Bogotá, Lima, and Tehran, there are now three to four times as many people as in 1970. Today Dhaka has ten times its 1970 population.[4] Within the frontline cities, there are 50 million to 100 million dangerous buildings at significant risk of collapsing on their occupants. Some have already fallen. In the first decade of the twenty-first century, 400,000 people were killed by buildings toppled by earthquakes.

Some cities are notoriously dangerous, like greater Kathmandu in Nepal: built on a former lake bed above a plate boundary, it is home to more than 2.5 million. Chittagong in southeast Bangladesh, with its 5 million inhabitants, is poised above a plate boundary megathrust.

In a whole other category of risk are those steamy coastal cities that lie in the path of tropical cyclones. On the east coast of Luzon Island in the Philippines, some locations have been so blitzed by the most intense typhoons that people have given up attempting to sustain a town.[5] Could that happen in Miami? The deep hot surface waters of the western Caribbean spawn Category 5 hurricanes in the vicinity of Cuba, the Caymans, Belize, and the Yucatán. The Caribbean pool feeds the torrid Gulf Stream, which hugs the coast of southeast Florida, turbocharging passing hurricanes, while keeping the Miami–Palm Beach conurbation the only frost-free enclave on the US mainland: population and danger are uniquely correlated.

It is not only water that can flood a city. The city of Goma lies in the lushest western strand of the central African rift fronting the northern shores of beautiful Lake Kivu. Twenty kilometers north lies the volcano

Nyiragongo, with a crater holding a 660-foot-diameter (200-meter) cauldron filled with red-hot magma, a satanic reservoir poised 5,000 feet (1,500 meters) above the city.

On January 17, 2002, a split in the land opened, 6 miles (10 kilometers) from the crater, pointing directly at Goma. Out of the fissure emerged 25 million cubic meters of magma, which ran in a braided river straight down the main shopping street of the city, repaving the road with craggy black lava 2 meters thick, destroying 4,500 buildings, and trapping vehicles before flowing into the lake.[6]

With our reliance on technology come new consequences and new vulnerabilities. Two hundred years ago, if the earth passed through a great eruption of plasma from the sun, an aurora would light up the night sky as far south as the Caribbean. Today the induced currents could burn out high-voltage transformers, leading to weeks of power outages. The Canadian ice storm that would once have left the forest floor strewn with branches can now bring down ice-loaded electricity transmission and distribution wires and require the evacuation of a whole city—as in January 1998. The Icelandic eruption that once would have had no more impact than to powder Scottish lakes with ash now shuts down aviation across northern Europe—as in April 2010.

EACH YEAR THE US ARMY CORPS OF ENGINEERS ESTIMATES THE flood losses that did *not* happen thanks to its dams and levees.[7] We are now at the start of the third UN-coordinated International "Decade" (now fifteen years) for Natural Disaster Reduction. What has been achieved through all those tens of billions of dollars spent worldwide on reducing disasters? What has been the product of all those institutes and agencies of disaster risk reduction? How many lives have been saved? How many livelihoods have been protected and losses prevented?

Strangely, no organization is keeping score. However, we know how to set about answering the question. As with the climate attribution studies, we can explore the counterfactuals—what would have happened with and without specific interventions, like the New Zealand building code or the Japanese tsunami walls?

We could start with the 1970 storm surge disaster that inspired George Harrison to organize the 1971 Concert for Bangladesh in New York. Thanks to a network of 2,500 raised concrete community storm surge shelters and an effective cyclone warning system, the casualties fell from 300,000 in the 1970 cyclone to an official 3,447 in a similar cyclone in 2007. More of the livestock now survives the surge tethered on artificial grazing mounds while poultry farmers have substituted ducks (which float) for chickens (which drown). Yet it is only partial progress when tens of thousands of human survivors can now return to find that their houses have been erased.

For many other disasters it is harder to demonstrate that impacts or casualties have been reduced, in large part because many disasters of the last twenty years were, for one reason or another, unexpected. Now that the world has proved to be much better prepared for disasters that have happened before—like a Bangladesh storm surge or the 2010 Chile earthquake—perhaps we should focus on why we did not anticipate many of the big catastrophes.

The reason is simple—we call it the "availability bias." We remain too much in thrall to previous disasters. Their dates—1755, 1906, 1923, 9/11—become iconic, and like generals conditioned to refight the last war, we fail to imagine what else is possible. These past events are the rare "black swans": underestimated before they happened, and that triggered overreactive responses. Even on official earthquake hazard maps, the locations of past rare large earthquakes can remain as bull's-eyes marking supposed "high hazard" because no one quite dares to relegate their significance.[8] (Maybe the hazard is everywhere else?) In Pakistan in 2005, China in 2008, and Japan in 2011, the big damaging earthquakes happened where the official hazard maps showed moderate hazard. In each case the event helped fill in a gap in the higher hazard zones. While the 2010 Haiti earthquake did occur on a known plate boundary, this hot spot was somehow missing from the official international earthquake hazard maps.[9]

The Philippines are perhaps the most disaster-impacted country of all.[10] Although the country has strong national institutions focused on taming disasters, the data on casualties and houses destroyed make it hard to demonstrate progress. Sadly, that is true of many poorer countries. As much as warning systems are implemented and flood maps are generated, the number of people and buildings in harm's way keeps rising. Even as countries set in place policies designed to limit disasters, they are all too often busy creating quantities of new risks. The flood wall lures new buildings to shelter behind it. While Florida was arguing over a building code, millions were moving to live on the coast of the Sunshine State. Sometimes, as in Haiti, it is poverty, informal settlement, and high birth rates that create risk; sometimes, as on the Malibu shoreline, it is unfettered wealth.

Since 2000, yearly worldwide disaster casualties were higher than through the 1990s, but we can't really say whether this reflects the randomness of sampling or if this is telling us something about underlying trends. An unexpected disaster in Myanmar or India takes more lives than it would have twenty-five years ago because there are more people in its path. At the same time, an average Chinese city is better built than Tangshan in 1976. And worldwide flood casualties are falling.[11]

When asked to show progress, we point at the actions taken *after* disasters—reinforcing the flood defenses in New Orleans, building the cyclone shelters in Bangladesh. Here is a paradox—it takes a disaster to reduce disaster risk. Even in terms of the counterfactuals, if the original catastrophe had not happened, people would be less prepared and casualties would be higher in the next disaster. We can only hope that the lessons also travel. If the 2004 Indian Ocean tsunami had not happened, many schoolchildren at Kamaishi would have died in 2011. We inoculate ourselves against disasters by having disasters. The bigger the disaster, the deeper the cure.

SO WHAT CHANGES DISASTER OUTCOMES? TWENTY-FIVE-PAGE INternational UN treaties or professors who teach schoolchildren self-reliance in tsunami evacuation? Top down or bottom up? Policy or culture? Is a "cure for catastrophe" like programs of mass immunization, or should we employ the metaphor of self-help medication and change our lifestyles?

After the forecast of a storm surge or eruption, the government can take the top-down initiative of arranging transportation to evacuate the people. The villagers still have to take the bottom-up action of getting on the bus. The government can provide the system to broadcast a flood warning, but people have to flee on their own initiative. In Tacloban on Leyte (in the Philippines), the poorest fishermen lived over the water, in huts supported on stilts, because the seafloor belonged to no one. Unable to demonstrate land title, the men were not prepared to abandon their homes as Haiyan's storm surge rolled toward them.[12]

Top down, the construction ministry can establish a building code. But bottom up, builders have to follow the code or it will not save lives. When will we be able to trust the walls?

We need both disaster policy and disaster culture.[13] In the example of Dutch flooding, policy and culture developed in tandem over centuries. Policy on its own does not empower people, but neither does a community's disaster culture provide building codes, storm forecasts, or flood protection schemes. Policy can be delivered by a government complying with a UN declaration, but it is much harder to change a culture.[14] How did the people of Holland or Chile come to own the collective responsibility for combating their disasters? Send in the anthropologists.

In the sixteenth century, the Dutch were "immersed" in flood culture through repeated exposure to the Water-Wolf prowling just beyond the dike. On a winter's evening, they would tell stories around the peat fire of how the villagers had sealed a breach in the teeth of a storm. In Japan it was the Zen tale of the headman burning the rice harvest to lure the villagers up the hill, a story to remind people to keep watch for all those times when the father will not be there. Around the glacier-capped volcano of Cotopaxi in Ecuador, the villagers tell children how their "grandparents" fled to high ground to escape the great eruption's lahar mudflows in 1877.[15] The neighboring towns in the valley are full of new arrivals who share no such history.

Before TV and newspapers imposed their version of "the news," elders relayed accounts of great disasters, told and retold down the generations for hundreds and sometimes even thousands of years—lessons for self-preservation when someday the disaster returned.[16]

At the port at Talcahuano in Chile, parents tell their children stories of being woken by the shaking and racing up the cliff road in the night, just as the aboriginal Onge tribesmen on Little Andaman Island in the Indian Ocean followed their ancestors' advice to flee to higher ground after feeling the great 2004 earthquake. Not all the stories will be so consistent or reliable: will the snakes that emerged from hibernation before a 1934 earthquake in Nepal turn up ahead of the next great earthquake? What of the official spiritual gatekeeper who lived high on the volcano Mount Merapi in Java? In 2010 he saw no signs of alarm, while the seismologists were warning of an eruption. When it happened, the volcano guardian was killed along with many of the villagers who revered him.

———

A HORIZONTAL LINE IS CHISELED IN THE ROCK AND NEXT TO IT THE year. We instantly know the meaning of this simplest and most profound of all forms of hazard communication—preserving the transient stain left by an exceptional flood. This brilliant shorthand for sending a hazard message to the future was invented in China more than 2,000 years ago.[17]

To anyone choosing to live near this river, or build a bridge over it, the flood mark communicates—beware! The floods can rise this high. Above all, it shows an empathy for the future, a desire to communicate with generations to come. You do not carve flood marks if you think the world is about to end, if you have no food on your table, or if you believe that catastrophic floods are a punishment from the gods.[18]

The tradition traveled to Italy, where the oldest known flood mark is from the Arco dei Banchi in Rome, recording a flood on the Tiber in AD 1277.[19] Flood marks flourished across Europe, for both river floods and storm surges, in periods of prosperity and stability.[20]

In Japan stone monuments were erected to mark the inland extent of tsunamis.[21] The oldest in southern Honshu dated back 600 years, but most of them were from the tsunamis of 1896 and 1933 on the northeast coast of Honshu. At Aneyoshi the stone reads: REMEMBER THE CA-

LAMITY OF THE GREAT TSUNAMIS. DO NOT BUILD ANY HOMES BELOW THIS POINT. One tsunami stone at Kesennuma reads as though written by Professor Katada: ALWAYS BE PREPARED FOR UNEXPECTED TSUNAMIS. CHOOSE LIFE OVER YOUR POSSESSIONS AND VALUABLES.

Central to risk culture is storytelling. The message about building materials in "The Three Little Pigs and the Big Bad Wolf" made perfect sense in its original English hazard climate. On the edge of the stormy North Atlantic, it would be dangerous to live in a straw house. As a parable for enduring faith, Jesus told a story that held the original germ for "The Three Little Pigs"—of the man who built his house on the rock and survived the storms, while the house built on sand was washed away. We can add to our disaster culture canon the tale of Tilly Smith, the English schoolgirl on a beach in Thailand who saw the sea recede and knew immediately to scream at all around her to move to higher ground.

Culture fables were collected by Aesop, a Greek slave and storyteller 2,600 years ago. Aesop became a brand, and his fable canon expanded over the centuries.[22] Fables teach us how to deal with bullies and tricksters, to avoid being consumed by arrogance or overconfidence. Beyond robbers and tyrants, there are fables with sage advice for crisis management.

In the fable of "The Boy Who Cried 'Wolf!'," the bored shepherd boy sent to guard the flock keeps crying "Wolf!"—for the fun of alerting the villagers. When the wolf does arrive, everyone ignores the boy's cries and the sheep are lost. False alarms, whether willful or overcautionary, undermine any warning system. This could equally be the Flood-Wolf in place of the original timber wolf. People died in Kamaishi and New Orleans because their previous evacuation had been unnecessary.

In "The Mountain in Labor," the mountain emits terrible noise and smoke, with trees crashing and huge rocks tumbling, as if presaging a great catastrophe. The people come to see what is happening just as a huge fissure appears in the mountain flank. As the people fall on their knees in terror, all goes quiet, bathos descends, and then out crawls a tiny squeaking mouse. (This could be the story of a volcano embarked on a benign phreatic steam eruption, as at Basse-Terre, Guadeloupe, in 1976.)

Large alarms may lead to small consequences. At the same time, if the volcano had erupted, there would be no one to tell the tale. So the fable misleads in offering any general advice. Large alarms can also lead to catastrophic consequences, as at Mont Pelée or Pinatubo.

Disaster culture not only harbors wisdom but can also provide false reassurance.

In Japan the government encouraged the belief (fostered by what happened before the 1923 disaster) that a group of wise men would emerge to forecast great earthquakes. The wise men failed to show up (or failed to be heeded) ahead of the 1995 Kobe or the 2011 Tohoku earthquakes.

Between 1869 and 1925 in California, the study of earthquakes was considered more dangerous than the earthquakes themselves. Then there was the absolute reverence afforded to the Soviet earthquake hazard map in the 1980s.

And if we are looking for powerful real-life risk fables, what of the story of Hurricane Katrina and the neglected flood walls of New Orleans? Or the tragic story of the nuclear power plants at Fukushima, the engineers who claimed that giant earthquakes there were impossible, and the painstaking reconstruction of an 1,100-year-old tsunami? These are stories to be told to children for generations to come.

And then there are fables still to be crafted. The story about the builder who acquired a load of cement and built a tall building to house many families without knowing the principles of construction—the tall building fell down in an earthquake and killed all the people. The tale of the little pig who insisted on building in brick without understanding the hazard climate. The story of the people who assumed that the only disaster to expect was the one they had already experienced.

Disaster culture focuses on what happened in the last great calamity. What if it was too long ago and the memories have been lost? There has been no big disaster for decades in the beautiful eastern Caribbean island of Barbados. And yet the island is haunted by the possibility of the most extreme hurricanes (as in 1780 or 1831) as well as the largest earthquakes and tsunamis—the island sits right on top of a plate boundary. The disaster management institutions have been established, and the island has a building code, but the code is not enforced.[23] The majority of people live in concrete block houses, but there are still plenty of traditional wooden houses, waiting to be blown away. When surveyed, islanders claim that they "know a lot" about disasters from radio and TV, but the majority also acknowledge that they are not prepared. Many have built their own houses. Complying with the building code adds costs and is not something they would spontaneously do without financial incentives. When reminded about the hurricane threat, one rescue officer replied, "Yeah, man, we get this every year, but nothing happens. Why should we take it seriously?"

To get Bajans to take disasters seriously we need to convince them that the threat is real. What would our disaster anthropologist suggest?[24] We need to activate memories the islanders do not have, simulate the vivid destruction from a great earthquake and accompanying tsunami hitting their island, or show a Category 5 hurricane blasting away all the roofs and trees. And then, to imprint these virtual memories, we would need to revive the reconstructions every year, as if these disasters had happened in the last decade.[25] But in doing this, we might scare people off the island and drive away investment in the tourist industry, on which the economy depends. We would have heard the same official arguments in the United States at the beginning of the twentieth century for denying earthquakes or avoiding the memorialization of the 1906 disaster in San Francisco. Communities can deliberately choose to foster disaster amnesia. Yet without the specter of disaster, they will not make the personal investment in reducing future risk.

REUBEN JACOB SMEED, BORN IN 1909, OBTAINED A DEGREE IN mathematics and a PhD in aeronautical engineering from Queen Mary College, London.[26] In World War II he was appointed head of research for RAF Bomber Command, where he applied statistics to minimize aircraft losses. In 1947 he moved from bombers to traffic, becoming deputy director of the Traffic and Safety Division at the Department of Scientific and Industrial Research (later to become the Transport

Research Laboratory). In this role he made some profound and surprising observations.

In 1949 Smeed proposed that during the daytime in central London the speed of traffic would always be 9 miles (14.5 kilometers) per hour.[27] This speed, he observed, was self-regulating. Any slower and some drivers would not attempt the journey or could take the Tube. Any faster and more cars would join the queues. Nine miles an hour was the borderline between tolerable and intolerable. More than sixty years later, in 2012–2013, after new daytime road pricing, traffic lights and bus lanes, one-way systems and junction layouts, the average speed of traffic in central London between 7:00 a.m. and 7:00 p.m. was 8.98 miles per hour.[28]

In the same year, 1949, Smeed discovered something similar around road traffic casualties. Taking data for 1938, the annual number of road traffic fatalities in a country could be predicted by applying a formula (specifically, a fractional power law) to the population and the number of vehicles.[29] This became known as "Smeed's Law." With the arrival of the first cars in a country, casualties per vehicle are very high. Pedestrians do not look around, the roads are potholed, and the drivers are untrained. As the number of vehicles increases the fatalities per vehicle fall consistently, even while the overall level of casualties continues to rise at a slower rate. While casualties are the consequence of billions of everyday, individual decisions and choices around speed, vehicle maintenance, fatigue, distraction, and personal protection, they can be predicted like a law of physics. For everyone who witnesses an accident and slows their driving to more carefully observe the speed limit, or buys a crash helmet after hearing of a fatality, there is a young man who drinks and speeds even faster or keeps driving while poleaxed with fatigue. Across the population, recklessness is balanced against prudence. Road traffic casualties are a thermometer of holistic risk—of what society is prepared to tolerate in death and injury in exchange for the benefits of mobility and transport.

What is the global pandemic that kills ten times more people than disasters? Why are there not charities entirely dedicated to action against this terrible scourge, with fund-raisers on every street corner? Persistent, scattered, repetitive, banal traffic accidents only attract publicity when a bus falls off a bridge or a 100-vehicle pileup occurs on a highway in the fog. India contains 1 percent of the world's vehicles but generates 10 percent of global road accident fatalities: 140,000 deaths each year, costing 1.5 percent of annual GDP. Many Indian states have laws making seat belts and motorcycle helmets compulsory, but the rules are ignored.[30]

Smeed's Law has been revisited over the decades. From the 1960s, once vehicle ownership exceeded 20 percent of the population in any country, the law was found to overpredict the casualties. By the year 2000, actual road traffic deaths in the United Kingdom, for example, had decreased to one-quarter of those predicted by the formula. The additional explanatory factor turns out to be affluence.[31] The threshold per capita income level for when a country starts to take action to reduce its traffic fatality risk was found to be $8,500 in 1985 prices (or about $18,500 in 2015). The most effective force for reducing traffic deaths is to grow a middle class, who then apply their energies to demanding reduced levels of risk. It is a virtuous cycle: reduced levels of risk expand the middle class. Rich countries have become adept at promoting safer behavior: the advertising campaigns linking condoms and HIV, seat belts and cars, have been effective. And crash testing cars shows that better safety sells.

Casualty rates in road traffic accidents turn out to be self-regulated, hovering at the boundary between acceptable and unacceptable risk, but what about disaster deaths? Traffic casualties reflect our everyday actions and reactions around traffic as well as the role taken by the state to promote safety. However, unless you are a builder, planner, or inspector, the actions that determine disaster outcomes are not part of most people's daily lives. Yet the issues are the same: Are there rules in place? How are the rules policed? Do people choose to follow the rules? Are they motivated to reduce risk?

The builder is also a driver. If he doesn't wear a seat belt, he probably ignores the building code. Moreover, in poor countries many people construct their own house. If the inspector gives a bribe to the traffic cop, he will expect to receive a payback from the builder. The jaywalking pedestrian works in the planning department. In Thailand, with the world's most dangerous traffic, the government agency in charge of disasters also oversees road safety. The risk thermometer of traffic accidents is likely to apply equally to attitudes around disaster risk, but the time it takes for action to turn into consequence can be far longer in disasters. The worst traffic death rates are in Thailand and the Dominican Republic; they are around fourteen times higher than the best rates in a country such as Sweden.[32] As we saw from the earthquake casualties, the chances of dying in an urban disaster can vary by more than a thousand between the best- and worst-performing countries. Statistical studies of the impacts of tropical cyclones have shown that wealth reduces casualties (as does increased urbanization).[33]

Concern around disasters will always follow more immediately life-sustaining concerns: getting food on the table, keeping a roof over your head, having a fire to keep warm, and being employed.

———

AFTER AN EARTHQUAKE IN THE FOOTHILLS OF NORTHERN PAKISTAN in 1974, the earthquake investigator and engineer Nicholas Ambraseys, from Imperial College London, noticed that many stone houses had horizontal wooden banding, typical of the *hatillar* village houses in Turkey. Perhaps the mountain people had been spontaneously motivated to build to resist earthquakes, using a technique that was far more sparing in its use of wood than the full wooden mesh of the boat builders?[34]

In 1980 an opportunity presented itself to test the theory. A team of six architects, engineers, and anthropologists was invited to become one of five research teams on a Royal Geographical Society expedition to the Karakoram Mountains of northern Pakistan.[35] I was with them, as a writer for *New Scientist*, as they set out to interview the inhabitants of the ancient kingdom of Hunza, 8,000 feet (2,400 meters) up in the heart of the Karakoram Mountains.[36] Had these people been motivated by the fear of earthquakes in how they chose to build their houses?

The team quickly discovered that the theory they had come to test had no merit.[37] The single-story houses of the Hunzacuts had walls constructed out of cobbles carried from the neighboring riverbed, held together with mud. Flat wooden roofs and their post supports were moved around like a tent, as they lasted longer than the rubble walls. People had concerns about schools for their daughters to make them marriageable, about a rope bridge across the gorge to get crops to market, about a proper supply of medicines, and about how to live with the noxious smoke from the central cooking and heating fire as it found its way out through a hole in the wooden roofs of their houses. It had never occurred to them to prepare for infrequent earthquakes.[38]

Six months after 2009 Cyclone Aila hammered the forested Sundarban coast of Bangladesh, villagers were interviewed about their risks. The top three were: "too salty drinking water," "pirates," and "tiger attacks."[39] Five years after the cataclysm, earthquakes are falling off the agenda at Port au Prince.[40]

What about another measure of risk—the cost of insurance? As insurance losses start to rise, unless they can otherwise limit the coverage, insurers will explore how to reduce the underlying risk, as happened toward the end of the nineteenth century for US urban fires, or in the United Kingdom after 2000 when insurers demanded that the government build more flood defenses.[41] If the cost of claims falls, insurers quietly take their foot off the brake of risk reduction. The fear that followed 9/11 led to widespread increases in the cost of property insurance, far beyond high-rise city centers, inadvertently enhancing the profitability of insurers, as the fear was not followed by higher losses.[42] Following the "Goldilocks principle," insurers want the risk to be neither too hot nor too cold.

For a rich country intent on reducing disaster risk, the agenda can be endless. In January 2013, the San Francisco Board of Supervisors launched legislation to make seismic retrofits mandatory for 3,000 "soft-story" buildings in the city (each housing an average of twenty residents). Landlords would have to post a violation "scarlet letter" on their building if they did not comply.[43] San Francisco is a sophisticated city, full of highly qualified engineers. Such an initiative is unimaginable in Kathmandu or Manila.

Meanwhile, central London's daytime traffic flows at its inevitable, self-organized 9 miles per hour. And through myriad daily choices and decisions, every society today could be said, often unwittingly, to foster its own level of disaster risk, in the same way that societies tolerate their tally of road traffic fatalities. Top-down pronouncements about risk management will fail unless they succeed in confronting and transforming the deep-rooted, and often blinkered, risk culture. The only certain way to rearrange people's risk priorities and promote catastrophe cures is by stimulating prosperity.

———

ESCAPING FROM POVERTY AND THE DAILY SEARCH FOR FOOD AND shelter allows us to focus on combating disasters.

No city is constructed so strongly that it will never suffer any damage. Most building codes only protect life, not property, so we need to cultivate resilience: the ability of individuals, communities, and cities to recover after a disaster.[44] Resilience—from the Latin *resilire* ("to bounce back")—has many definitions. The UN prefers the trinity: anticipate, absorb, reshape (or model and forecast the risk, take some repairable damage, and "build back better"). Another definition is: "Resilience is resistance, redundancy and contingency."[45] For example, the frontline defenses of Holland's resilient flood protection are the river embankments, the second line is a dike ring in case the first defenses fail, and the third line is money and resources to fund the recovery if the land is lost. Six years after the 1666 Great Fire, resilient London was rebuilt with wider streets and fire-resistant houses. Reconstruction generates boom-time economic activity and employment. And upgraded infrastructure increases economic growth.

Insurance is good for delivering on contingency, the third component of resilience—a guarantee of money when it is most required. While you could plan to set aside your own funds each year, there will always be a temptation to raid the pot you have stashed away in the bank and the disaster might come before enough money has been accumulated. Insurance guards the funds and pays out according to loss, not according to what has been paid in.

In a poor country, without insurance, all the symptoms of poverty are exacerbated after the disaster. People have no way to recover what has been lost, children are taken out of school, health problems remain untreated, roofs are left to leak. On average, natural disasters in developing countries without protections lower GDP by 2 percent, even five years later.[46] Unless the disaster has gained prime TV news coverage, the only financial support may come from overseas remittances.[47] Like Honduras after 1998 Hurricane Mitch, or Port au Prince after the 2010 earthquake, these countries and cities have been stretched beyond their elastic limit by natural disasters. The cultivation of resilience is part of the development process to escape poverty and to prevent people falling back into poverty after a disaster. "Resilient poverty" is an oxymoron.

Whenever reconstruction gets funded by international aid, the Western purse-holders will want to see that the buildings are disaster-proof. Yet a year or two of external oversight will not permanently change the local building culture. Did China transform the quality of its buildings, up to the standards of California or Chile, after the 2008 Wenchuan earthquake? China built 3,800 schools alongside housing for 1.9 million households so fast that there were many complaints about the quality.[48]

———

AROUND $80 BILLION IS SPENT EACH YEAR WORLDWIDE ON PUR-chasing catastrophe insurance. And yet insurance only spreads the costs through time and provides the funds when most needed (and makes some profit for doing this). In the end, purchasing insurance does not reduce the level of risk, or guarantee "build back better" after a disaster.[49]

In 1834, after incorporating many fire safety features into his Rhode Island wool mill, the polymath Zachariah Allen had the effrontery to ask for a premium reduction from his fire insurer. The insurer declined, claiming that it "knew nothing about his mill or apparatus."[50] So he identified neighboring mill owners who were similarly motivated to reduce their risks and in 1835 established the Providence Manufacturers Mutual Fire Insurance Company, through which they would share in each other's losses at a cost significantly below the rate for commercial insurance. Two years later, he established a second mutual insurer in Rhode Island, and the idea then became replicated in many other cities. Zachariah Allen had invented the resilience industry—a motive commercial force for risk reduction.

Challenged to pay the largest claims should a whole mill burn down, these small independent mutuals saw the benefits of achieving a larger critical mass and began to combine. However, merging with mill owners in other cities deprived them of the personal and local ability to inspect one another's facilities. A central risk inspectorate had to be established, and then a research function to identify how risk could continue to be reduced. (At this same period, risk reduction was advancing onto the agenda in Britain and the United States around lighthouses for navigation and the loading and seaworthiness of ships, as well as concerns around public health and clean water supplies.[51]) In the 1870s, the factory and mill mutuals sponsored research on fire prevention at the Massachusetts Institute of Technology in Cambridge and in the 1880s found their finest spokesperson in the Bostonian Edward Atkinson (1827–1905). A lawyer, inventor, activist, and anti-imperialist, Atkinson became an outspoken evangelist for loss prevention and better fire protection. The mill mutuals and the manufacturers' mutuals merged, and merged again, eventually to become one great mutual enterprise: Factory Mutual, for which Atkinson served as president. Still located in Johnston, Rhode Island, FM Global, as it is now known, sends out teams of engineers to identify how to drive down the level of risk below an acceptable threshold before accepting a new Fortune 1000 client to share in its club of mutuality.

The nearest to a real-life "Dr. Resilience" was John R. Freeman, born in 1855, who graduated from MIT as a civil engineer.[52] Initially an expert in hydraulics, water supplies, and rivers, he was appointed, in 1886, engineer and special inspector for the Associated Mutual Fire Insurance Companies, where he applied his knowledge of hydraulics to improve fire suppression. In 1896 he was made president and treasurer of the Manufacturers Mutual Fire Insurance Company in Providence, Rhode Island, where he remained all his life, expanding the business "fortyfold" while harnessing risk science to drive down the losses to "one fourteenth" of what they had been the year he joined. After the 1923 Tokyo earthquake, now deeply interested in how to build to withstand shaking and how to promote earthquake insurance, he linked up with the director of the Earthquake Research Institute of Japan. It was Freeman who normalized the scientific study of earthquakes in the United States and who pioneered the design and pricing of earthquake insurance, producing a 900-page compendium on earthquake hazard and risk that was published in 1932, the year of his death.

———

WE STARTED THIS STORY WITH THE JAPANESE TSUNAMI BARRIERS and the flood walls that encircle New Orleans, protections akin to those of a Roman fortress city. Around the world more and more flood walls are being built, as at the northern English garrison town of Carlisle. In January 2005, 2,000 properties were flooded in a "one-in-200-year" flood. The national Environment Agency spent £38 million on flood defenses to protect against a repeat. Then, in December 2015, the new defenses were overwhelmed, and many of the same houses inundated, by an even bigger flood. In the front rooms people had begun to decorate their Christmas trees. No one was prepared when the water arrived in the middle of the night.

A flood wall is not the same as resilience. Agencies like the UK Environment Agency or the US Army Corps of Engineers may be good at building flood defenses, but not so adept at cultivating resilience. A flood wall can be part of a culture of resilience when accompanied by regular evacuation drills, a flood warning system, and recognition that people still live in a flood zone. Over centuries the Dutch cultivated resilience precisely because they did not trust their flood defenses. Even when "protected" by a flood wall, people who live in river floodplains should make their houses resistant to flood water. They should have plans ready to move precious objects to an upper floor in the event of a flood alert. One day, in all probability, their houses will flood. By removing the more frequent smaller floods, the flood wall takes away the "risk reminders." On its own, the flood wall can even reduce the natural fortitude of people who were once familiar with smaller calamities—as we saw in the 2011 Japanese tsunami.

After they come to perceive themselves as "protected" by a flood wall, people do not want to believe that they continue to live in a floodplain, whether in New Orleans, central London, or Kamaishi. It is the irony of the flood wall that it can make us less resilient.

—

So why isn't there an industry on the scale of global catastrophe insurance that focuses on *reducing* disaster risk?

Suppose I come to your city and you agree to pay me $100,000
for every future latent disaster fatality I can prevent and $500,000 for
every public building that, thanks to my interventions, will not collapse. And I will achieve all of this without a disaster. We will have my
performance monitored objectively, using an independent catastrophe
risk auditor, so you will see whether I am succeeding. Imagine an industry composed of public associations and thriving private companies
but existing principally to reduce disaster risk, prioritizing actions that
achieve the biggest risk reduction for the investment.

Today disaster risk reduction businesses are scattered: they sell fire
alarms, tornado cellars, and solutions for retrofitting buildings, and they
consult around fragile supply chains. In the San Francisco Bay Area,
after the wake-up call of the 1989 Loma Prieta earthquake, $25 billion
was invested in upgrades to roads, bridges, and water and electricity
supplies, while retrofits to buildings received $30 billion.[53]

Welcome to the nascent catastrophe resilience industry. Only the
risks are not on everyone's balance sheet. As long as the risks are invisible, there seems to be no advantage in reducing them.

In the same way that households, companies, cities, countries, and
institutions undergo a financial audit, they will also undertake a "risk
audit" to report their key risk metrics: the risk of loss of life, or livelihoods, or money, at some key probabilities—a one-in-ten chance in a
given year versus a one-in-100, or 1 percent, chance.[54]

We then need "resilience brokers" to identify the most cost-effective
way to reduce these risks—whether by making the floors, walls, and
electricals water-resistant in anticipation of a flood or by installing a
fire sprinkler system. If it costs $1,000 to reduce a one-in-twenty-year
risk to your property by $20, it is not worth the effort. Reverse those
numbers and you should take immediate action. The broker can then
find cheaper insurance for the irreducible risks that remain.

The cost to reduce the risk of damage to your house or business
could be equivalent to several years of insurance payments, so it would

be worth taking a loan to fund the improvements. Insurers might be willing to invest in your risk reduction if they knew you would stay insuring with them. But today's insurance policies are only for a single year.[55] Is it time to resurrect one of Dr. Nicholas Barbon's 1690 multiyear insurance policies (as still offered in Japan today)?[56] Or perhaps a multiyear catastrophe "resilien-surance" bond could fund risk reduction, while also providing long-term insurance protection. For a single fee, the first London insurers also offered insurance packaged with the services of a resilience-enhancing fire brigade.

―――

IMAGINE YOU ARE THE MAYOR AND IT IS YOUR JOB TO REPORT THE city's annual disaster risk audit. A poor report will mean a worse city credit rating and could lose you the next election because you have not been making enough progress in reducing risk. In a session of the UN Human Rights Council in 2014 on indigenous peoples, it was said that "a failure [by governments and other actors] to take reasonable preventative action to reduce exposure and vulnerability and to enhance resilience, as well as to provide mitigation, is a human rights question."[57]

Tinker, tailor, soldier, sailor—we now have four new twenty-first-century professions: disaster risk modeler, risk auditor, disaster culture anthropologist, and resilience broker. They will work in tandem with the existing disaster professionals: disaster managers, flood and earthquake engineers, catastrophe insurers, and risk mappers. Just as the quantification of catastrophe risk drove a huge expansion in catastrophe insurance, it is about to drive a great industry of disaster risk reduction.

Like the Spanish colonial insistence on urban relocation, throughout history people have attempted to thwart risk without fully understanding how risk became manufactured in the first place. We still have much to learn about all the processes that grow risk, such as unplanned urbanization, overpopulation, coastification, deforestation, impoverishment, corruption, poor land zoning, weak governance, and the legacy of previous disasters.[58] The mountain of risk that was accumulating in Port au Prince should have been as obvious as a smoking volcano before the 2010 earthquake (the city was last shaken to destruction in 1770). The local UN organization was operating from one of the most dangerous large buildings in the city, the Christopher Hotel, where around 100 staff members tragically died.

New tools, new professions, and new institutions will be required in this "disaster-centric" world. Governments will have their own catastrophe models, populated with details of buildings, people, businesses, and livelihoods and modified to output metrics on casualties, damage, and economic consequences for a wide range of possible catastrophes. The civil contingencies agency will test more efficient crowdsourcing and potential bottlenecks to disaster response: collapsed hospitals, blocked roads, power outages, broken water supplies. The national disaster management agency will review the costs and benefits of alternative interventions. The finance ministry will demand to see the impact of a range of "one-in-100-year" disasters on national finances, and these numbers will be scrutinized by rating agencies exploring the risk of sovereign default or investors curious about the potential threats to sectors such as tourism. National and city governments will be expected to publish a broad set of audited disaster risk and resilience metrics.

The world could benefit from an independent and international risks agency to highlight potential hazards irrespective of whether a nest of nuclear power plants or a prestige dam project is in the vicinity. Do Japan's tsunami walls reduce casualties? Does the United States increase the risk to its citizens through its flood insurance subsidy program? What will be the tangible consequence of climate change for the economy and global security?

EARTHQUAKE ENGINEERS ARE SOME OF THE SMARTEST ON ANY ENgineering faculty. Designing structures to withstand the repeated cycles of earthquake vibration is far more challenging than simply building to withstand gravity. There is a widening gulf as earthquake engineers write ever more technical papers on highly engineered structures, even while there is a terrible hunger throughout the developing world for basic lessons in sound construction.[59]

This gap led a Californian engineer, Elizabeth Hausler Strand, to found BuildChange.[60] Strand is an expert bricklayer, a skill she learned while working summers with her mason father. Midway through a PhD in civil engineering at UC Berkeley, she saw on the news the damage to tens of thousands of unreinforced stone and adobe houses in the 2001 Gujarat earthquake and won a Fulbright Fellowship to India to study earthquake reconstruction.[61] Established in 2004, BuildChange researches local materials and traditions and identifies simple, practical, and cost-effective ways to construct earthquake-resistant houses, such as confined masonry—concrete block walls locked into a reinforced-concrete frame, cast in situ.[62] Housing serves many functions, and earthquake resistance has to be achieved alongside all the other cultural and practical requirements.

Having trained 3,000 local builders, principally in Indonesia and Haiti, within less than a decade BuildChange has a legacy of 20,000 safer houses. In a 2009 earthquake in West Sumatra, none of the BuildChange houses constructed after the 2007 earthquake were damaged.[63]

Geohazards International was the brainchild of a California seismologist, Brian Tucker.[64] This network of experts in seventy cities works to create earthquake-resistant communities, with a particular focus on improving the safety of schools.

Then there is the Global Megacities Initiative, which brings together leaders from a set of the most hazardous cities to promote disaster risk reduction.[65] Yet, for a city to participate, enough money has to be available to send officials to meetings, and the city has to host a big international meeting at least once every five years. Port au Prince did not even have the capacity to apply.

The challenge for all these initiatives is to avoid becoming, like the Gaiola buildings in the Baixa at Lisbon, a token demonstration of disaster resistance but without any embedded cultural legacy.

As identified by BuildChange, the gatekeepers standing between communities and future earthquake deaths are the ordinary builders of houses, apartments, and schools. The world needs an "engineering corps" sent out to transform building standards. *Quis custodiet ipsos custodes?* could, in this instance, be translated as: "Who will inspect the building inspectors?"

The leading frontline earthquake city, Istanbul, is harnessing rising affluence as an agent of change.[66] Since the mid-twentieth century, the North Anatolian plate boundary has unzipped from east to west in a series of destructive earthquakes all the way to the shores of the Sea of Marmara. The underwater plate boundary fault closest to the city is expected to be the next to break, in a repeat of the 1509 "Little Day of Judgment" earthquake. One study claimed that the ensuing Magnitude 7.5 earthquake would destroy 20,000 buildings, badly damage another 200,000, and kill more than 200,000 people. Another study puts the number of the dead at 60,000.[67] Most of the buildings in the city constructed in the last century were not built to withstand earthquakes. The city government has estimated that 2 million of the city's 3 million apartments could be damaged or destroyed.

Hasan Yildiz's father first constructed an illegal single-story structure in the Sumer district, part of Zeytinburnu; he later added four more floors.[68] In the 1970s and 1980s, the government legalized the building, allowing his father to sell the property to a developer, who built a neighboring five-story building in which Hasan, now in his late forties, lives on the top two floors with his family. Meanwhile, the government has surveyed all the buildings in Zeytinburnu and concluded that, along with thousands of other apartment buildings, this structure will collapse in the next big Sea of Marmara earthquake. So the offer has been made to demolish the building and swap Yildiz's apartment for a one-bedroom apartment in a new earthquake-proof block. The developer finances the exchange by receiving 50 percent of the new apartments for his own disposal.

The architect of this bold plan is a civil engineer, Metin Ilkisik. For him, the problem of earthquake-resistant housing is not one of engineering, but a "social problem and an economic problem."[69] In 2012 the Natural Disaster Law was passed, allowing the government to perform a survey and draft plans to renovate whole neighborhoods considered to be at the greatest risk. In the Zeytinburnu suburb, 2,300 buildings were put in the most dangerous category. The scheme attempts to enable everyone to benefit by raising property values as buildings are made earthquake-proof and therefore much more desirable to the educated middle classes. Since 2002, the value of apartment buildings in

Zeytinburnu has tripled. People talk about the coastal town becoming a "new Barcelona."

Only a majority of the residents need to agree for the building to be replaced, and there is no right to object to the decision once it has been taken. A single owner in an apartment building therefore cannot obstruct the process.

However, there is one catch—the new apartments are 25 percent smaller than the ones they replace. And people have grown fond of their old apartments and neighbors, so that many do not want to move. By February 2013, people had moved to 237 new apartments, but some residents were holding out, and the government was threatening that there might be no new replacement apartment at all unless they quickly accepted it. The plan is to build 60,000 earthquake-proof buildings in Zeytinburnu over five years, the government's first "transformation plan"—the big idea for reducing the population of dangerous buildings throughout Turkey. Other frontline countries are keeping a close eye on Turkey's initiative.

Istanbul illustrates how rising prosperity becomes the biggest lever for reducing earthquake casualties. With increased wealth, governments step up to their responsibilities to protect people against disasters, homeowners demand that their houses and schools be made safe, and engineers stay in their country rather than emigrate to America.

Not all is simple. What can be done about dangerous—but beautiful—heritage buildings, whether in Turkey, Chile, Italy, Iran, or Bhutan? These structures are too expensive to retrofit, but their demolition would impoverish the culture. Lives will have to be balanced against patrimony. Some of these heritage buildings, such as the rammed earth houses of Bhutan, with their ornamental wood frames, are known to be dangerous. However, the ramshackle half-timbered Srinagar buildings in Kashmir may even turn out to be inherently quake-resistant.[70] These buildings were tested in the great 2005 earthquake. The Pakistan army handed out cash grants to those who found themselves homeless and offered guidance around safe construction. In the village of Topi, only one house had survived—it was built in the half-timbered style.[71] A year later, after some campaigning, the Pakistan Buildings Ministry agreed that such construction could qualify for disaster assistance. The following year the ministry approved another wood and masonry style, *bhatar*, and by 2009, 150,000 new homes had been constructed in one or the other of these building types.[72] The vernacular half-timbered earthquake-resistant buildings—the "boat builders' houses"—are being revived.

In November 2013, a first conference was organized in Calabria in southern Italy to bring together artisans in half-timbering from across the Mediterranean so that house builders could once again confidently employ local materials to withstand earthquakes.[73] In India there is a parallel movement to revert to traditional building practices where they can be shown to provide better protection against disasters.[74]

WHAT WILL A DISASTER LOOK LIKE IN 2030?

Earthquake prediction in 2030 still remains elusive. There was one success a decade ago when an earthquake in Japan gave plenty of warning of its arrival in foreshocks and ground movements, so that people could be evacuated from Kyoto. But the following year, at Oakland, California, the people were all evacuated, the insurance companies started canceling their policies, and no earthquake came. Then a catastrophic earthquake destroyed Palermo, Sicily, without any warning, and then another at Quito. There was the Legazpi City crisis, next to the Mayon volcano in the Philippines, where tens of thousands were told to leave and then, after a few days, as nothing happened, people starting drifting back to their homes. When a month later the eruption did finally arrive, thousands were killed.

At the same time, however, every smart phone now measures the acceleration of any significant earthquake and transmits the data to the cloud, which automatically maps it as a propagating shock wave as the nearby phones count down the seconds to when the earthquake will arrive.

The world finally intervened to prevent the indiscriminate sale of cement after a quarter of a million people died from the collapse of unreinforced-concrete buildings in the great North Indian earthquake. But there is still an enormous legacy of non-engineered buildings built before the UN accord on the engineering supervision of construction. However, the Build First scheme, created in 2019, has been extraordinarily successful at getting newly qualified engineers from all around the world to work for two years in at-risk countries to teach the principles of safe construction.

Thanks to the energies of the Global Catastrophe Risk Agency, diagnostic techniques have been pioneered to determine the quality of hidden steel reinforcing so as to rapidly categorize buildings in terms of their potential for collapse. By law, a building must now display its earthquake resistance, both on the building itself and online (along with its flood hazard), so that the occupants are fully aware of the risk of continuing to live or work in it.

New "rapid retrofitting" techniques have helped make more buildings earthquake-resistant. In one, a nylon and fiberglass (or steel) net is wrapped tightly around a building (using technology first developed for wrapping hay bales) so that the outer walls cannot collapse, nor can the building move out of shape, preventing floor beams falling.[75]

Sales have been slow for the apartment-mounted, two-person steel earthquake survival box, first developed in 2018. The device requires that users sign up for the few seconds' advance warning of impending earthquake waves. Some owners of the survival box, fed up with the space it occupies, employed it for household storage and were unable to get everything out in time when the earthquake finally came. A few people had bought the Chinese bed that automatically drops the sleeper(s) into a steel box when it detects shaking even after it was found that the device could be accidentally triggered by more amatory nighttime vibrations.[76]

So the 2030 earthquake beneath the port city of Kaohsiung, Taiwan, happens without warning, around dawn, when many people are in their houses and apartments. Immediately the catastrophe response is intensively coordinated. Within minutes, drones are launched to stream images of the damage back to the control center. Those in the vicinity are directed to return images of specific buildings and streets so that a comprehensive three-dimensional picture of the building damage is quickly available.

Every year the national civil contingencies agency has simulated thousands of potential catastrophes so they can design and game the optimum response to each. This earthquake is quickly identified as simulation disaster number 6843.

In the national control center, there are already detailed digital maps of every building in the city with predictions about the occupants, the damage, and the expected casualties; this information is continually updated with data harvested and fed back from the disaster zone. All cell-phone towers in potential disaster zones have their own backup power supplies to ensure that they continue working.

Everyone in the vicinity of the earthquake has found instructions on their smart phones as to how to become a "first responder," from simple first aid to what they should attempt in terms of rescue. As a result, hundreds of injured people are rescued in the first thirty minutes; some of them would otherwise have died of their injuries. A dam has burst on the edge of town, but all those in the path of the flood have been automatically alerted according to their location.

As civil defense teams arrive, their smart phones indicate where each rescue team should focus. In China all babies are now fitted with a transponder chip at birth, so their location and vital signs can be identified by the rescuers. (Civil liberties groups in Europe and America had balked at the "big brother" surveillance implications of such a policy.) However, most people have voluntarily adopted the wristband transponder, which is triggered in an emergency. Within an hour, the 3-D map of the city includes the location of all those who are trapped and still alive. To think that only twenty years ago so much time was wasted locating the living before they could then be rescued! Now rescue can be prioritized around those whose vital signs are fading fastest.

Within five hours, the automated search robots have been delivered. Each robot spins threads of sticky carbon fiber that prevents the rubble pile from shifting as it tunnels into the debris pile, cutting through beams and concrete to find the trapped person, who is then eased onto an inflated stretcher and pulled out through the tunnel aperture.

Since all the survivors have been located from the start, all rescue is completed within two days and there is no need for international rescuers. However, the Japanese have arrived to test their latest rescue robots on the fresh piles of rubble.

———

IN 2030 THE WORLD HAS GAINED MUCH HIGHER LITERACY AROUND risk. Thanks to pressure from the Organization for Economic Cooperation and Development (OECD), in many countries risk is now in the national curriculum, with modules taught in years 4 and 9.

And because everyone is now more risk-literate, the online coverage of the disaster has been transformed from what it was only fifteen years before. Without international rescue teams to be followed, journalists have started to ask some tough questions. Did the disaster managers cry "Wolf!" or did they underestimate the threat? Why did this risk accumulate at this location? Was this event the vast legacy of dangerous twentieth-century concrete buildings, constructed without engineers, like the accumulation of bad loans on a bank's balance sheet? Was this event surprising even to the hazard scientists? Who can be held responsible? Bad builders? Weak inspectors? Rotten governance?

Even before the disaster, plans were in place for how the city would be rebuilt. "Risk-based government" is now the standard for assessing any intervention. Automated inspections ensure that every building is constructed to the "code-plus" standards, which will prevent damage in the next strong shake. Resilience loans are available from one of a number of resilience corporations, which offer householders the money to have their buildings retrofitted while locked into a ten-year reduced-rate insurance policy. As a result of their interventions, hundreds of buildings suffered only cosmetic damage. Many homeowners are now members of the self-organized, all-peril mutual insurer associations after the 2019 launch of a brilliant Facebook app that identifies hundreds of thousands of trustworthy owners prepared to team up and sustain a targeted low-risk profile. The coverage has proven far cheaper than conventional insurance policies while driving members to sustain further year-on-year reductions in risk. Through the Internet of things, the most modern buildings are now able to report their damage.

Just as in the early-twentieth-century eradication of urban conflagration risk, the campaign to remove all significant potential earthquake damage from the world's principal cities has been gathering pace. Santiago and San Francisco were two of the first cities to receive the certification back in 2024. As warranted by the Global Catastrophe Risk Agency, once reconstruction is completed in 2033, the rebuilt city will be deemed "cured" of catastrophe.

Some things, however, never change. In central London the speed of daytime traffic remains 9 miles per hour, even while there are almost no human drivers.

ACKNOWLEDGMENTS

THE IDEA FOR THIS BOOK BEGAN MORE THAN THIRTY YEARS AGO in conversations around the fire, beneath the brilliant starry skies of the precarious Karakoram Mountains, with Ian Davis, Frances D'Souza, Robin Spence, Andrew Coburn, and James Jackson. This led me to work with Geof King on the El Asnam earthquake in Algeria. There I met Tidu Maini, who was launching the consultancy Principia; he introduced me to Gordon Woo, mathematician and catastrophist, with whom I have been debating ever since. I also learned the craft of earthquake risk research from working with David Mallard, Willy Aspinall, and Scott Steedman, alongside the disaster historians Charles Melville and Emanuela Guidoboni. Nicholas Ambraseys, engineer and historian, lectured on his latest earthquake field investigation. Operation Raleigh took me to southern Chile.

The doors to the most radical of all innovations around disasters, catastrophe models, were opened for me by Haresh Shah and later by Hemant Shah and Weimin Dong, founders of Risk Management Solutions, and the first-generation catastrophe risk modelers: Charlie Scawthorn from EQE, Auguste Boissonnade, Chris Mortgat, Pane Stojanovski, and Fouad Bendimerad. In Australia, Russell Blong dissected eruptions and George Walker tested windproof buildings.

I have absorbed the behavioral economic study of insurance from Howard Kunreuther and Erwann Michel-Kerjan at the Wharton School and admired the raised profile of catastrophe insurance articulated by Rowan Douglas of Willis Towers Watson.

And I have learned firsthand from hazard scientists who have a broader social vision: Kerry Emanuel, Tom Knutson, and Gabe Vecchi, who study hurricanes; the climate scientists Myles Allen and Kevin Trenberth; the earthquake scientists Brian Atwater, Ross Stein, and Roger Bilham; and the floods expert Zbyszek Kundzewicz.

Writing for the 2011 IPCC Special Report on Managing the Risks of Extreme Events and Disasters to Advance Climate Change Adaptation (SREX) report immersed me in the social sciences perspective on disasters as articulated by Allan Lavell, Michael Oppenheimer, Susanne Moser, and David Satterthwaite. I have been privileged to work with the brilliant disaster economists Solomon Hsiang, Stephane Hallegatte, and Daniel Clarke and the team at UNISDR, led by Margareta Wahlstrom, Andrew Maskrey, and Mark Gordon.

Francis Ghesquiere on the quest for exposure data and crowdsourcing; David Alexander on disaster risk; Laurens Bouwer and Roger Pielke Jr. on disaster costs; Tom Mitchell on disasters and poverty; Mary Lou Zoback and Lauren Augustine on the politics of resilience; Laurie Johnson on disaster reconstruction; Randolph Langenbach on sleuthing wood-frame buildings; Elizabeth Hausler on training artisanal builders; Zinta Zommers on resilience and climate change; Kira Vinke on disasters and migration; and many great colleagues at RMS: Paul VanderMarck, Barbara Page, Michael Drayton, Julia Hall, Steve Jewson, Navin Peiris, Mohsen Rahnama, and many more—I have learned from all of you.

Finally, thanks to Pamela M. Henson at the Smithsonian Archives; my agents, Alex Christofi and Sophie Lambert; T. J. Kelleher of Basic Books; Sam Carter of OneWorld; massive thanks to Cynthia Buck, who brought editorial order; Helene Barthelemy and Shena Redmond; and my readers: Elizabeth Loudon, Katherine Hearn, Iain Pears, my daughter Maia, who tirelessly collated references, and my other daughter Anya, who produced the maps. An earlier version of Chapter 7 appeared in the *RMS Horizons* online client magazine.

All opinions expressed in this work are mine alone and do not reflect the perspective of any organization, association, or corporation.

For the elision of arguments and all that got lost in the economy of storytelling, I take full responsibility.

London, March 2016

NOTES

INTRODUCTION

1. Juan Kulik, "Fundaciones de los edificios asismicos," *La Ingeneria* (Buenos Aires) 855 (January 1946): 29, quoted in Mark Alan Healey, "The 'Superstition of Adobe' and the Certainty of Concrete: Shelter and Power After the 1944 San Juan Earthquake in Argentina," in *Aftershocks: Earthquakes and Popular Politics in Latin America*, edited by Jürgen Buchenau and Lyman L. Johnson (Albuquerque: University of New Mexico Press, 2009).

2. Allan Lavell and Michael Oppenheimer (coordinating lead authors), "Climate Change: New Dimensions in Disaster Risk, Exposure, Vulnerability, and Resilience," in *IPCC, 2012: Managing the Risks of Extreme Events and Disasters to Advance Climate Change Adaptation: A Special Report of Working Groups I and II of the Intergovernmental Panel on Climate Change*, edited by Chris Field et al. (Cambridge: Cambridge University Press, 2012).

CHAPTER 1: TRUST IN THE WALLS

1. National Centers for Environmental Information, National Oceanic and Atmospheric Administration (NOAA), "Great Tohoku, Japan Earthquake and Tsunami, 11 March 2011," https://www.ngdc.noaa.gov/hazard/11mar2011.html.

2. Setsuko Kamiya, "Students Credit Survival to Disaster-Preparedness Drills," *Japan Times*, June 4, 2011.

3. "Tsunami in Kamaishi City, Japan, March 11, 2011," YouTube, posted by semimaru0000, March 12, 2011, https://www.youtube.com/watch?v=M535NGr9vbo;

"Tsunami at Kamaishi Port, Iwate Prefecture," YouTube, posted by Clancy688, March 12, 2012, https://www.youtube.com/watch?v=629em0mPpUY.

4. Skeptikai, "Tsunami Survival Guide: Japanese Culture Is Not Conducive to Staying Alive," posted by Ryo, March 11, 2012, http://skeptikai.com/2012/03/11/tsunami -survival-guide-japanese-culture-is-not-conducive-to-staying-alive/.

5. John M. Glionna, "Japanese School Takes Blame for Tsunami Deaths of 74 Students," *Los Angeles Times*, January 24, 2012.

6. Public Relations Office, Government of Japan, "The 'Miracle of Kamaishi': How 3,000 Students Survived 3/11," http://mnj.gov-online.go.jp/kamaishi.html.

7. Setsuko Kamiya, "Tsunami Hero Continuing Disaster Education Efforts," *Japan Times*, May 30, 2013; Kamiya, "Students Credit Survival to Disaster-Preparedness Drills."

8. James Owen, "Tsunami Family Saved by Schoolgirl's Geography Lesson," *National Geographic News*, January 18, 2005, http://news.nationalgeographic.com/news /2005/01/0118_050118_tsunami_geography_lesson.html. Tilly Smith appeared at the United Nations in November 2005, met former president Bill Clinton (UN special envoy for tsunami relief), and read a poem on December 26, 2005, at the one-year anniversary ceremony in Khao Lak, Thailand, commemorating the tsunami. In the same month, she was named "Child of the Year" by the French magazine *Mon Quotidien*.

9. Public Relations Office, Government of Japan, "The 'Miracle of Kamaishi.'"

10. Lafcadio Hearn and Ikegami Sako, "The Tale of Hamaguchi Gohei and the Tsunami," available at SCBWI Japan Translation Group, https://ihatov.wordpress.com /2011/04/09/hamaguchi-gohei-a-living-god-by-lafcadio-hearn/ (posted by Sako Ikegami, April 9, 2011).

11. Sawaji Osamu, "Education and Disaster Reduction," *Japan Journal* 8, no. 11 (February 2012): 6–10, http://www.japanjournal.jp/home/wp-content/uploads/2012 /02/1202e_06-10_CoverStory.pdf.

12. Al Jazeera English, "Tsunami Survival Strategy Interview with Prof. Katada," Don Productions, 2012, http://vimeo.com/31601481.

13. Jun Lee, Kiichiro Hatoyama, and Hitoshi Ieda, "Formulation of Tsunami Evacuation Strategy to Designate Routes for the Car Mode—Lessons from the Three Cities in Tohoku Area, Japan," *Proceedings of the Eastern Asia Society for Transportation Studies* 9 (2013), http://easts.info/on-line/proceedings/vol9/PDF/P41.pdf.

14. Hermann M. Fritz, Jose C. Borrero, Costas E. Synolakis, Emile A. Okal, Robert Weiss, Vasily V. Titov, Bruce E. Jaffe, Spyros Foteinis, Patrick J. Lynett, I.-Chi Chan, and Philip L.-F. Liu, "Insights on the 2009 South Pacific Tsunami in Samoa and Tonga from Field Surveys and Numerical Simulations," *Earth-Science Reviews* 107 (2011): 66–75.

15. Benjamin D. Maygarden, Jill-Karen Yakubik, Ellen Weiss, Chester Peyronnin, and Kenneth R. Jones, *National Register Evaluation of New Orleans Drainage System, Orleans Parish, Louisiana* (New Orleans: Earth Search, Inc., November 1999), http://w5jgv.com /downloads/New%20Orleans%20Drainage%20History.pdf.

16. Craig E. Colten, *An Unnatural Metropolis: Wresting New Orleans from Nature* (Baton Rouge: Louisiana State University Press, 2006).

17. "Wind Driven Water Rising in New Peril to Metairie," *New Orleans States*, September 22, 1947, http://archive.oah.org/special-issues/katrina/resources/hurricanes.html.

18. US Army Corps of Engineers, New Orleans District, "History of MRGO," http://www.mvn.usace.army.mil/Missions/Environmental/MRGOEcosystemRestoration/HistoryofMRGO.aspx.

19. D. A. Goudeau and W. C. Conner, "Storm Surge over the Mississippi River Delta Accompanying Hurricane Betsy, 1965," *Monthly Weather Review* 96, no. 2 (February 1968): 118–124.

20. Anu Mittal, Director of Natural Resources and Environment, US Government Accountability Office (GAO), "Army Corps of Engineers: History of the Lake Pontchartrain and Vicinity Hurricane Protection Project: Testimony Before the Subcommittee on Energy and Water Development, Committee on Appropriations, House of Representatives" (Washington, DC: GAO, September 28, 2005).

21. Joel K. Bourne Jr., "Louisiana Wetlands," *National Geographic*, October 1, 2004.

22. David L. Johnson, "Service Assessment: Hurricane Katrina, August 23–31, 2005" (Washington, DC: US Department of Commerce, NOAA, National Weather Service, June 2006).

23. Brian Williams, "Brian Williams: We Were Witnesses," NBC News, August 28, 2006; "Hurricane Katrina Plows into Louisiana but Spares New Orleans Its Full Fury," Minnesota Public Radio, August 29, 2005.

24. American Society of Civil Engineers, Hurricane Katrina External Review Panel, *The New Orleans Hurricane Protection System: What Went Wrong and Why?* (Reston, VA: ASCE, 2007).

25. Bob Marshall, John McQuaid, and Mark Schleifstein, "For Centuries, Canals Kept New Orleans Dry. Most People Never Dreamed They Would Become Mother Nature's Instrument of Destruction," *New Orleans Times-Picayune*, January 29, 2006; Nicole T. Carter, "CRS Report for Congress: Protecting New Orleans: From Hurricane Barriers to Floodwalls" (Washington, DC: Library of Congress, Congressional Research Service, December 13, 2005).

26. Jason Berry, "Harrowing Questions, and Ethics, During Katrina" (review of *Five Days at Memorial* by Sheri Fink), *New York Times*, September 3, 2013.

27. Keith C. Heidorn, "The Saffir-Simpson Hurricane Scales," The Weather Doctor, June 30, 1999 (updated September 2013), http://www.islandnet.com/~see/weather/elements/safsimp.htm.

28. Joshua Norman, "Katrina's Dead," *Biloxi Sun Herald*, February 17, 2006.

29. Roger Yates, "When Words Save Lives: 'Storm Tsunami' v. 'Storm Surge'," Thomas Reuters Foundation, Plan International, December 4, 2013, http://news.trust.org//item/20131204083148-2anxo/.

30. Norimitsu Onishi, "Japan Revives a Sea Barrier That Failed to Hold," *New York Times*, November 2, 2011.

31. Howard E. Graham, *Meteorological Considerations Pertinent to Standard Project Hurricane, Atlantic and Gulf Coasts of the United States*. National Hurricane Research Project Report 33 (Washington, DC: US Department of Commerce, Weather Bureau, 1959). After Hurricane Betsy in 1965, the Weather Bureau revised the wind field parameters but did not change the other characteristics of the SPH; see also John Schwartz, "An Autopsy of Katrina: Four Storms, Not Just One," *New York Times*, May 29, 2006.

32. John Schwartz, "Ivor Van Heerden's 'Storm' Draws Fire at LSU," *New York Times*, May 30, 2006; Coleman Warner, "Sinking Homes Stymie Flood Survey Experts: Post-Katrina, Reliability of Elevation Maps Suspect," *New Orleans Times-Picayune*, December 5, 2005.

33. Lewis E. Link, et al., *Performance Evaluation of the New Orleans and Southeast Louisiana Hurricane Protection System: Draft Final Report of the Interagency Performance Evaluation Task Force*, vol. 1, *Executive Summary and Overview* (Washington, DC: US Army Corps of Engineers, 2007).

34. Dwight Ink, "An Analysis of the House Select Committee and White House Reports on Hurricane Katrina," *Public Administration Review* 66, no. 6 (2006): 800–807; R. B. Seed, et al., *Investigation of the Performance of the New Orleans Flood Protection Systems in Hurricane Katrina on August 29, 2005*, vol. 1, *Main Text and Executive Summary* (Berkeley, CA: Independent Levee Investigation Team, July 31, 2006), http://www .ce.berkeley.edu/projects/neworleans/report/intro&summary.pdf.

35. John Schwartz, "Vast Defenses Now Shielding New Orleans," *New York Times*, June 14, 2012; Alissa L. Miller, S. N. Jonkman, and M. van Ledden, "Risk to Life Due to Flooding in Post-Katrina New Orleans," *Natural Hazards and Earth System Science* 15, no. 1 (2015): 59–73.

36. Stéphane Hallegatte, "A Cost-Benefit Analysis of the New Orleans Flood Protection System," *American Enterprise Institute–Brookings Joint Center: Regulatory Analysis* (2006): 06–02.

37. Norimitsu Onishi, "Japan Revives a Sea Barrier That Failed to Hold," *New York Times*, November 2, 2011; David Cyranoski, "Rebuilding Japan: After the Deluge," *Nature*, March 7, 2012, http://www.nature.com/news/rebuilding-japan-after-the-deluge-1.10172.

38. "The Great Wall of Japan," *The Economist*, June 14, 2014.

CHAPTER 2: CATASTROPHE YEAR ZERO

1. The three largest, in order of size, were London, Paris, and Naples. Alvaro S. Pereira, "The Opportunity of a Disaster: The Economic Impact of the 1755 Lisbon Earthquake," *Journal of Economic History* 69, no. 2 (2009): 466–499.

2. Psalms 18:7–15; all Bible quotations are taken from *The English Standard Version Bible* (Oxford: Oxford University Press, 2009).

3. See the illustration captioned "Krak des Chevaliers," Wikipedia, http://en .wikipedia.org/wiki/Krak_des_Chevaliers#/media/File:Near_East_1135.svg (last modified March 7, 2016).

4. Kate Raphael, "The Impact of the 1157 and 1170 Syrian Earthquakes on Crusader-Muslim Politics and Military Affairs," *Geological Society of America Special Papers* 471 (2010): 59–66.

5. Ibid.

6. Emanuela Guidoboni, Filippo Bernardini, Alberto Comastri, and Enzo Boschi, "The Large Earthquake on 29 June 1170 (Syria, Lebanon, and Central Southern Turkey)," *Journal of Geophysical Research: Solid Earth (1978–2012)* 109.B7 (2004): B07304, doi:10.1029 /2003JB002523http://onlinelibrary.wiley.com/doi/10.1029/2003JB002523/pdf; Nicholas N. Ambraseys, "The 12th Century Seismic Paroxysm in the Middle East: A Historical Perspective," *Annals of Geophysics* 47, nos. 2–3 (2004).

7. William Archbishop of Tyre, *A History of Deeds Done Beyond the Sea*, vol. 2 (New York: Columbia University Press, 1943), 371.

8. Herbert Thurston, "Bells," *The Catholic Encyclopedia*, vol. 2 (New York: Robert Appleton Company, 1907), http://www.newadvent.org/cathen/02418b.htm.

9. Angelo Rocca (1612), *De Campanis Commentarium* (*A Commentary on Bells*), Rome, https://blogs.library.duke.edu/magazine/2013/01/07/for-whom-the-bell-tolls/; *The Catholic Encyclopedia*, 2:136–139; for the rite, see 31–42. See also Andrew Dickson White, "From the Prince of the Power of the Air to Meteorology. Part II. Diabolic Agency in Storms," in *A History of the Warfare of Science with Theology in Christendom* (2009), ch. 11, https://archive.org/details/historyofwarfare189701whit.

10. "Tonnerre" ("Thunder"), in *Encyclopédie Art* (1756), quoted in I. Bernard Cohen, "Franklin, Boerhaave, Newton, Boyle, and the Absorption of Heat in Relation to Color," *Isis* 46, no. 2 (1955): 99–104, note 70.

11. John L. Heilbron, *Electricity in the 17th and 18th Centuries: A Study of Early Modern Physics* (Berkeley: University of California Press, 1979), 341–342.

12. Ibid.

13. Ibid.

14. I. Bernard Cohen, *Benjamin Franklin's Science* (Cambridge, MA: Harvard University Press, 1990), 251, note 63.

15. *New York Times*, July 22, 1901.

16. G. Neilson, R. M. W. Musson, and P. W. Burton, "The 'London' Earthquake of 1580, April 6," *Engineering Geology* 20, no. 1 (1984): 113–141.

17. See, for example, Thomas Churchyards, *A Warning for the wise, a feare to the fond, a bridle to the lewde, and a glasse to the good*, or Abraham Fleming, *A bright burning beacon, forewarning all wise virgins to trim their lampes against the comming of the Bridegroome. . . . And a praier for the appeasing of Gods wrath and indignation.*

18. Within a week, the publisher and archivist Thomas Twyne had produced *A general historical catalogue of previous earthquakes*, while Arthur Golding wrote *A discourse upon the earthquake that hapned throughe this realme of Englande, and other places of Christendom.* Preempting the tabloid press was Anthony Munday's *A view of sundry examples Reporting many strunge murthers . . . What straunge and monstrous children have of late beene borne: Also a short discourse of the late earthquake the sixt of Aprill.*

19. William Shakespeare, *Henry IV: Part 1*, act 3, scene 1.

20. Kevin J. Horsburgh and Matt Horritt, "The Bristol Channel Floods of 1607: Reconstruction and Analysis," *Weather* 61, no. 10 (2006): 272–277; see also "1607 Bristol Channel Floods: 400-Year Retrospective: RMS Special Report" (London: Risk Management Solutions, 2007), http://forms2.rms.com/rs/729-DJX-565/images/fl_1607_bristol_channel_floods.pdf. The people who lived and worked on the great estuary were well aware of the causes of the flood: an exceptional tide accompanied by a wind-driven storm surge: "The ryver of Severn rose upon a sodeyn Tuesday mornyng the 20 of January beyng the full pryme day and hyghest tyde after the change of the moone," wrote the vicar of Almondsbury, John Paul. "The Sea being very tempestuously moved by the windes, overflowed his ordinary Bankes," noted Newes from Monmouthshire.

21. Two modest earthquakes had struck London in February and March 1750, presenting Wesley with the opportunity to recall the "parable" of the 1692 earthquake. "Sermon 129: The Cause and Cure of Earthquakes: A Sermon by John Wesley

First Published in the Year 1750," Wesley Center Online, http://wesley.nnu.edu/john
-wesley/the-sermons-of-john-wesley-1872-edition/sermon-129-the-cause-and-cure-of
-earthquakes/.

22. Increase Mather, "A Discourse Concerning Earthquake" (Boston, 1706), 8, in Michael G. Hall, *The Last American Puritan: The Life of Increase Mather, 1639–1723* (Middletown, CT: Wesleyan University Press, 1988), 326.

23. M. A. Baptista, J. M. Miranda, F. Chierici, and N. Zitellini, "New Study of the 1755 Earthquake Source Based on Multi-Channel Seismic Survey Data and Tsunami Modelling," *Natural Hazards and Earth System Sciences* 3 (2003): 333–340; Robert Muir-Wood and Arnaud Mignan, "A Phenomenological Reconstruction of the Mw9 November 1st 1755 Earthquake Source" (2007), in *The 1755 Lisbon Earthquake: Revisited* (Springer Netherlands, 2009), 121–146.

24. Anonymous letter from "Faro," *Gentleman's Magazine*, December 25, 1755, 563.

25. Kenneth R. Maxwell, *Pombal, Paradox of the Enlightenment* (Cambridge: Cambridge University Press, 1995).

26. "The first day of this month will be remembered throughout the centuries because of the earthquake and fires that have destroyed a large part of this city; fortunately, the safes of the royal exchequer, as well as those of many private citizens, have been recovered from the ruins"; *Gazeta de Lisboa*, no. 45 (1755), in André Belo, "Between History and Periodicity: Printed and Hand-Written News in 18th-Century Portugal," *E-journal of Portuguese History* 2, no. 2 (2005).

27. *Gentleman's Magazine*, November 29, 1755.

28. James Boswell, *Boswell's Life of Johnson*, edited by George Birkbeck Hill, vol. 1, *Life 1709–1765* (New York: Bigelow Brown & Co.), 358; *James Boswell's Life of Johnson*, vol. 9, Hester Lynch Piozzi, *Anecdotes of the Late Samuel Johnson, LL.D.* (London: John Murray, 1835), 48–49.

29. The official account was written by the Swiss Miguel Tibério Pedegache Brandão Ivo in his capacity as a correspondent of the journal *Étranger*; reprinted in T. D. Kendrick, *The Lisbon Earthquake* (London: Methuen and Co., 1955).

30. Daniel Defoe, *The Storm: Or, a Collection of the Most Remarkable Casualties and Disasters Which Happen'd in the Late Dreadful Tempest* (London: George Sawbridge and J. Nutt, 1704); Gaston R. Demarée and Robert Muir-Wood, "De 'Grote Storm van december 1703' in de Lage Landen—een stormachtige periode in de Spaanse Successieoorlog," *Jaarboek voor Ecologische Geschiedenis* (2009): 33–54.

31. Daniel Defoe, *The Lay-Man's Sermon upon the late Storm (Held Forth at an Honest Coffee-House Conventicle)* (London, 1704); see also Daniel Defoe, *The Storm* (London: Penguin Books, 2005), 86, http://www.gutenberg.org/files/36694/36694-h/36694-h.htm.

32. The questions for the viceroys were simple, direct, and to the point: "At what time? What duration? What movements were observed in floors, walls, buildings, springs and rivers? What damages and collapses had been caused? The numbers of injuries and deaths to people and animals? What other notable observations about what preceded or caused the earthquake?"

33. Mark Molesky, "The Great Fire of Lisbon," in *Flammable Cities: Urban Conflagration and the Making of the Modern World*, edited by Greg Bankoff, Uwe Lübken, and Jordan Sand (Madison: University of Wisconsin Press, 2012), 147–169; A. Carneiro and T. S. Mota, "Um Terramoto para uma vida: Francisco Luiz Pereira de Sousa" (A Life of

Earthquakes: Francisco Luiz Pereira), in O *Terramoto de 1755 Impactos Históricos* (*The Earthquake of 1755: Historical Impacts*) (Lisbon: Livros Horizonte, 2007), 127–138.

34. In 1780 a maximum-intensity hurricane hit Barbados. Admiral George Rodney visited the island and reported: "I am convinc'd that the Violence of the Wind must have prevented the Inhabitants from feeling the Earthquake which certainly attended the Storm. Nothing but an Earthquake could have occasion'd the foundations of the Strongest buildings to be rent, and so total has been the devastation that not one house or one Church, as I am well inform'd but what has been destroy'd." In a typhoon in the Bay of Bengal in October 1737 in which the water "reached 40 feet" above sea level, "20,000 Ships, Barks, Sloops, Boats and Canoes were cast away," and "300,000 perished." The colonial masters in Calcutta recognized this to be an intense storm surge, but some newspapers in London, disbelieving that a mere hurricane could be so destructive, wrote: "There was at the same time a violent earthquake, which threw down a great many houses along the river side."

35. Such as the August 25, 1618, collapse of a mountain, which had been quarried for layers of talc, onto the village of Plurs, Switzerland, killing 1,000 to 2,500 inhabitants, or the September 2, 1806, rockfall onto the village of Goldau, which killed 457 people in central Switzerland.

36. Waldo Ross, *Nuestro imaginario cultural: Simbolica literaria hispanoamericana*, Autores, Textos, y Temas 11 (Barcelona: Anthropos, 1992), 117.

37. Kendrick, *The Lisbon Earthquake*.

38. Hesiod, *Theogony: The Homeric Hymns and Homerica with an English Translation*, translated by Hugh G. Evelyn-White (Cambridge, MA: Harvard University Press, 1914), lines 664–721; see also Nonnus, *Dionysiaca*, book 13, 435ff.

39. Maxwell, *Pombal, Paradox of the Enlightenment*.

40. Robert H. Brown, "The 'Demonic' Earthquake: Goethe's Myth of the Lisbon Earthquake and Fear of Modern Change," *German Studies Review* (1992): 475–491.

41. Russell R. Dynes, "The Dialogue Between Voltaire and Rousseau on the Lisbon Earthquake: The Emergence of a Social Science View," *International Journal of Mass Emergencies and Disasters* 18, no. 1 (2000): 97–115; Russell R. Dynes, "The Lisbon Earthquake in 1755: Contested Meanings in the First Modern Disaster," in *The Lisbon Earthquake of 1755: Representations and Reactions*, edited by Theodore E. D. Braun and John B. Radner (Oxford: Voltaire Foundation, 2005), 34–49.

42. Lowell Juilliard Carr wrote in 1932: "Not every windstorm, earth-tremor, or rush of water is a catastrophe. A catastrophe is known by its works; that is to say, by the occurrence of disaster. So long as the ship rides out the storm, so long as the city resists the earth-shocks, so long as the levees hold, there is no disaster. It is the collapse of the cultural protections that constitutes the disaster proper." Lowell Juilliard Carr, "Disaster and the Sequence-Pattern Concept of Social Change," *American Journal of Sociology* (1932): 207–218.

43. "Von den Ursachen der Erderschütterungen bei Gelegenheit des Unglücks, welches die westliche Länder von Europa gegen das Ende des vorigen Jahres betroffen hat" (On the Causes of Earthquakes, on the Occasion of the Calamity That Befell the Western Countries of Europe Towards the End of Last Year); "Geschichte und Naturbeschreibung der merkwürdigsten Vorfälle des Erdbebens, welches an dem Ende des 1755sten Jahres einen grossen Teil der Erde erschüttert hat" (History and Natural Description of the Most

Noteworthy Occurrences of the Earthquake That Struck a Large Part of the Earth at the End of the Year 1755); "Fortgesetzte Betrachtung der seit einiger Zeit wahrgenommenen Erderschütterungen" (Continued Observations of the Terrestrial Convulsions That Have Been Perceived for Some Time). See translations by Olaf Reinhardt in Eric Watkins, ed., *Kant: Natural Science* (Cambridge: Cambridge University Press, 2012).

44. Dynes, "The Lisbon Earthquake in 1755."

45. "Les Tremblements de terre attribués à l'électricité," *Journal Enclyclopédique*, March 1, 1756.

46. On the origin of the word "risk," see Rolf Skjong, "Etymology of Risk: Classical Greek Origin—Nautical Expression—Metaphor for "Difficulty to Avoid in the Sea," February 25, 2005, http://research.dnv.com/skj/Papers/ETYMOLOGY-OF-RISK.pdf.

47. Howard Goodall, *The Story of Music: From Babylon to the Beatles: How Music Has Shaped Civilization* (London: Chatto and Windus, 2014), 120.

48. Ryan Nichols, "Re-evaluating the Effects of the 1755 Lisbon Earthquake on Eighteenth-Century Minds: How Cognitive Science of Religion Improves Intellectual History with Hypothesis Testing Methods," *Journal of the American Academy of Religion* 82 (2014): 970–1029.

49. Stuart McCook, "Nature, God, and Nation in Revolutionary Venezuela: The Holy Thursday Earthquake of 1812," in *Aftershocks: Earthquakes and Popular Politics in Latin America*, edited by Jürgen Buchenau and Lyman L. Johnson (Albuquerque: University of New Mexico Press, 2009), 43–69.

50. Ibid.

51. Ibid.

52. "National Pantheon of Venezuela," Wikipedia, https://en.wikipedia.org/wiki /National_Pantheon_of_Venezuela (last modified February 5, 2016).

53. McCook, "God and Nation in Revolutionary Venezuela."

54. Melvin Nava, "El Terremoto Cuatricentenario de Caracas," Venelogía, August 2, 2005, http://www.venelogia.com/archivos/627/.

55. J. D. Woodruff, et al., "Depositional Evidence for the Kamikaze Typhoons and Links to Changes in Typhoon Climatology," *Geology* 43, no. 1 (2015): 91–94.

56. Ernest Mason Satow, *Japan 1853–1864: Or, Genji Yume Monogatari* (Tokyo: Naigai Suppan Kyokai, 1905).

57. Masaru Fujimoto, "Shipwrecked Russians Lived to Tell an Epic Tale," *Japan Times*, June 1, 2003.

58. C. Veit, "Matthew Perry and the Opening of Japan," Navy and Marine Living History Association, http://www.navyandmarine.org/ondeck/1800perryjapan.htm; Rhoda Blumberg, *Commodore Perry in the Land of the Shogun* (New York: HarperCollins, 1985), 18.

59. *St. Thomas Tidende*, November 13, 1867.

60. US Department of State Archive, "Purchase of the United States Virgin Islands, 1917," http://2001-2009.state.gov/r/pa/ho/time/wwi/107293.htm; Isaac Dookhan, *A History of the Virgin Islands of the United States* (Kingston, Jamaica: Canoe Press, 1974); Erik Overgaard Pedersen, *The Attempted Sale of the Danish West Indies to the United States of America, 1865–1870* (Frankfurt: Haag & Herzhen, 1997); Charles C. Tansill, *The Purchase of the Danish West Indies* (Baltimore: Johns Hopkins University Press, 1932).

61. Roy Watlington and Shirley Lincoln, summarized by Robin Swank, "Earthquakes and Tsunamis: Prospects for the Virgin Islands," St. John Historical Society, March 7,

2008, http://stjohnhistoricalsociety.org/vol-ix-no-7-march-2008-earthquakes-tsunamis
-prospects-for-the-virgin-islands-presented-by-roy-watlington-and-shirley-lincoln
-summarized-by-robin-swank/.

62. Bret Harte, "St. Thomas: A Geographical Survey," in *The Heathen Chinee: Poems and Parodies* (London: Richard Edward King, 1888).

63. Narcisse Zahibo, et al., "The 1867 Virgin Island Tsunami," *Natural Hazards and Earth System Science* 3, no. 5 (1930): 367–376; Roy A. Watlington, "The Terrible Earthquake and Tsunami of Nov. 18, 1867," *St. Croix Source*, November 19, 2013; Aimery Caron, "The Urgency for the Acquisition of the Danish West Indies," presented to the Caribbean Genealogy Library on the occasion of the ninety-seventh anniversary of Transfer Day, March 31, 2014, http://www.rootsweb.ancestry.com/~vicgl/Caron/TransferDWI.pdf.

64. William James, "On Some Mental Effects of the Earthquake," in *Memories and Studies* (1911), 207–226, http://grammar.about.com/od/classicessays/a/WJames Earthquake_2.htm.

CHAPTER 3: CATASTROPHYSICS

1. A British planter, Christopher Jeaffreson, had been cultivating his land on St. Kitts for five years when, in 1681, a hurricane arrived and tore "downe strong stone walled houses before it . . . as well as trees and timber buildings. It left me not a house or sugar-worke standing on my plantation. It broke and twisted my sugar-canes, rooted up my Cassava, and washed the graine and new-planted puttatoes." See John C. Jeaffreson, *A Young Squire of the 17th Century, from the Papers of Christopher Jeaffreson of Dullingham House, Cambridgeshire*, vol. 1 (London, 1878), 274–280.

2. Captain Langford's "Observations of His Own Experience upon Huricanes, and Their Prognosticks," communicated by Mr. Bonavert, *The Royal Society: Philosophical Transactions* 20, nos. 236–247 (January 1, 1698): 407–416, http://rstl.royalsociety publishing.org/content/20/236-247/407.full.pdf+html.

3. Ibid.

4. William C. Redfield, "Remarks on the Prevailing Storms of the Atlantic Coast, of the North American States," *American Journal of Science and Arts* 20 (1831): 17–51.

5. Emery R. Boose, Kristen E. Chamberlin, and David R. Foster, "Landscape and Regional Impacts of Hurricanes in New England," *Ecological Monographs* 71, no. 1 (2001): 27–48.

6. Redfield, "Remarks on the Prevailing Storms of the Atlantic Coast."

7. Lee Sandlin, *Storm Kings: America's First Tornado Chasers* (New York: Vintage, 2014), 266.

8. Mark Monmonier, *Air Apparent: How Meteorologists Learned to Map, Predict, and Dramatize Weather* (Chicago: University of Chicago Press, 1999).

9. Sandlin, *Storm Kings*.

10. "Reid, William (1791–1858)," in *Dictionary of National Biography, 1885–1900*, vol. 47, edited by Robert Hamilton Vetch (London: Smith, Elder and Co., 1885–1990).

11. S. Naylor, "Log Books and the Law of Storms: Maritime Meteorology and the British Admiralty in the Nineteenth Century," *Isis* 106, no. 4 (2015): 771–797.

12. William Reid, *An Attempt to Develop a Law of Storms by Means of Facts* (London: J. Weale, 1838).

13. Stephen Taylor, *Storm and Conquest: The Battle for the Indian Ocean, 1808–1810* (London: Faber & Faber, 2012).

14. Wayne Neely, *The Great Hurricane of 1780: The Story of the Greatest and Deadliest Hurricane of the Caribbean and the Americas* (iUniverse, 2012).

15. Samuel Morison, *The European Discovery of America: The Southern Voyages, 1492–1616* (New York: Oxford University Press, 1974).

16. John Knox Laughton, "Piddington, Henry (1797–1858)," in *Dictionary of National Biography*, vol. 45 (London: Smith, Elder and Co., 1885–1990).

17. Henry Piddington, *The Sailor's Horn-book for the Law of Storms: Being a Practical Exposition of the Theory of the Law of Storms, and Its Uses to Mariners of All Classes in All Parts of the World, Shewn by Transparent Storm Cards and Useful Lessons* (London: Williams and Norgate, 1869).

18. Ibid.

19. Joseph Conrad, *Typhoon*, serialized in *Pall Mall* magazine, January–March 1902.

20. Erik H. Palmén, "On the Formation and Structure of Tropical Cyclones" (1948), *Geophysics* 3: 26–38, http://www.geophysica.fi/pdf/geophysica_1948_3_1_026_palmen .pdf.

21. John Michell, "Conjectures Concerning the Cause and Observations upon the Phaenomena of Earthquakes," *Philosophical Transactions of the Royal Society* 51 (1760): 566–634.

22. "Libro o Trattato di Pirro Ligorio (1571)," in *Di Diversi Terremoti*, vol. 28, edited by Emanuela Guidoboni (Rome: de Luca Editori d'Arte, 2005), 27, http://www .culturaimmagineroma.it/dwd/guidob.terremoti.pdf; Emanuela Guidoboni, "Riti di calamità: Terremoti a Ferrara nel 1570–74," *Quaderni Storici* 55 (1984): 107–135. The idea of engulfment has been kept alive by the phenomenon of sinkholes—particularly in Florida; see Michael Wines, "One Sinkhole Killed, and Many Others Opened, but Experts Counsel Not to Panic," *New York Times*, March 15, 2013.

23. Hotspur, in William Shakespeare, *Henry IV, Part 1*, act 3, scene 1.

24. "Von den Ursachen der Erderschütterungen bei Gelegenheit des Unglücks, welches die westliche Länder von Europa gegen das Ende des vorigen Jahres betroffen hat" (On the Causes of Earthquakes, on the Occasion of the Calamity That Befell the Western Countries of Europe Towards the End of Last Year); Immanuel Kant, *Werke* (*Works*), vol. 1, *Vorkritisch Schriften I* (*Precritical Writings I*) *1747–1756* (Berlin: Verlag von Georg Reimer, 1902).

25. Gregory Quenet, *Les Tremblements de terre aux XV11ème et VV111ème Siècles: La Naissance d'un risque* (Seyssel, France: Éditions Champ Vallon, 2005), 444.

26. Francesco Milizia, *Principii di Architettura Civile* (*Principles of Civil Architecture*), vols. 1–3 (Bassano: A spese Remondini di Venezia, 1785).

27. Emmanuel Heath, *A Full Account of the Late Dreadful Earthquake at Port Royal in Jamaica: Written in Two Letters from the Minister of that Place, from aboard the Granada in Port Royal harbour, June 22, 1692* (London: printed for Jacob Tonson, sold by R. Baldwin, 1692); Julie Yates Matlock, "The Process of Colonial Adaptation: English Responses to the 1692 Earthquake at Port Royal, Jamaica" (master's thesis, Eastern Kentucky University, 2012).

28. The sand grains, blown by the wind into the still water of the lagoon, touched at

their corners. The vibrations caused the grains to jiggle and pack together more tightly. As the space between the grains reduced, the water increased in pressure, pushing the grains apart and causing the sand to behave like a liquid.

29. Daniel Defoe, *A General History of the Pyrates* (Mineola, NY: Dover Publications, 1999); Christopher Minster, "The History of Port Royal," About Education, December 16, 2014, http://latinamericanhistory.about.com/od/historyofthecaribbean/p/The -History-Of-Port-Royal.htm

30. "Sermon 129: The Cause and Cure of Earthquakes: A Sermon by John Wesley First Published in the Year 1750," Wesley Center Online, http://wesley.nnu.edu /john-wesley/the-sermons-of-john-wesley-1872-edition/sermon-129-the-cause-and -cure-of-earthquakes/.

31. *Boston Evening-Post*, July 9, 1770.

32. Robert Muir-Wood, "Robert Mallet and John Milne: Earthquakes Incorporated in Victorian Britain," *Earthquake Engineering and Structural Dynamics* 17, no. 1 (1988): 107–142.

33. Robert Mallet, *Fourth Report upon the Facts and Theory of Earthquake Phenomena* (London: British Association for the Advancement of Science, 1858), 1–136.

34. "Robert Mallet," Wikipedia, https://en.wikipedia.org/wiki/Robert_Mallet (last modified February 15, 2016).

35. Robert Mallet, *Great Neapolitan Earthquake of 1857: The First Principles of Observational Seismology*, vol. 2 (London: Chapman and Hall, 1862).

36. W. H. Hobbs, *Earthquakes* (London: Sydney Appleton, 1908). Professor Rico, in a study of a Calabrian earthquake of 1894, found that out of thirty-three villages, in sixteen cracks pointed toward the center of the damage and in another seventeen they pointed away; see Annibale Ricco, "Terremoti el 16 Novembre 1894 in Calabria e Sicilia: Relazio Sismologica" (Earthquakes of November 16, 1894, in Calabria and Sicily: Seismological Report), *Annali del R. Ufficio Centrale Meteorologico e Geodinamico, Serie Seconda* 19, part 1 (1897).

37. Graeme J. N. Gooday and Morris F. Low, "Technology Transfer and Cultural Exchange: Western Scientists Encounter Late Tokugawa and Meiji Japan," *Osiris* 13 (1998): 99–128.

38. Muir-Wood, "Robert Mallet and John Milne," 121.

39. At the end of 1880, Ewing recorded several earthquakes using a horizontal pendulum inscribed on a smoked-glass disk. Muir-Wood, "Robert Mallet and John Milne," 124–125.

40. Bunjiro Koto, "On the Cause of the Great Earthquake in Central Japan, 1891," *Journal of the College of Science, Imperial University* 5, part 3 (1892): 295–353.

41. Ibid. The 1881 and 1883 earthquakes on the island of Ischia in Italy had been so localized and catastrophic that they were widely attributed to Aristotle's preferred cavern collapse explanation. The association of an earthquake with fault movement was offered, however, in G. K. Gilbert, "A Theory of the Earthquakes of the Great Basin, with a Practical Application," *American Journal of Science*, series 3, 27, no. 157 (1884): 49–54.

42. Gregory K. Clancey, *Earthquake Nation: The Cultural Politics of Japanese Seismicity, 1868–1930* (Berkeley: University of California Press, 2006).

43. Ōmori Fusakichi, "Notes on the Great Mino-Owari Earthquake of Oct. 28, 1891," *Publications of the Imperial Earthquake Investigation Committee I Foreign Languages*, no. 4 (1900): 13–24.

44. Finding the European intensity scale with its observations of church towers and chandeliers useless for Japan, Ōmori developed a Japanese intensity scale in seven bands; see Ōmori Fusakichi, "Preliminary Note on the Formosan Earthquake of Mar. 17, 1906," *Bulletin of the Imperial Earthquake Investigation Committee I*, no. 2 (1907): 53–69.

45. By 1906, the population of San Francisco was 372,000, and that of the Bay Area was 789,000.

46. Carl-Henry Geschwind, *California Earthquakes: Science, Risk, and the Politics of Hazard Mitigation* (Baltimore: Johns Hopkins University Press, 2001), 18; Alan E. Leviton and Michele L. Aldrich, "John Boardman Trask, Physician-Geologist in California, 1850–1879," in *Frontiers of Geological Exploration of Western North America*, edited by Alan E. Leviton, Peter U. Rodda, Ellis Yochelson, and Michele L. Aldrich (Washington, DC: American Association for the Advancement of Science, Pacific Division, 1982), 37–70.

47. "Some Facts About Earthquakes" (editorial), *Daily Alta California*, October 24, 1868.

48. University of California–Berkeley, Seismological Laboratory (BSL), "History of the BSL," http://seismo.berkeley.edu/history/; Bruce A. Bolt, "One Hundred Years of Contributions of the University of California Seismographic Stations," in *Observational Seismology: A Centennial Symposium for the Berkeley Seismographic Stations*, edited by Joe J. Litehiser (Berkeley: University of California Press, 1987), 24–50.

49. The stations were Berkeley Astronomical Observatory, Oakland Chabot Observatory, Alameda Mills College Observatory, San Jose University of the Pacific, Mount Hamilton Lick Observatory, and Carson Observatory (in Carson City, Nevada).

50. W. W. Campbell, "Edward Singleton Holden (1846–1914)," in *Biographical Memoirs* (Washington, DC: National Academy of Sciences, 1916), 347–372; UC Berkeley, "History of the BSL"; Donald E. Osterbrock, "The Rise and Fall of Edward S. Holden: Part One," *Journal for the History of Astronomy* 15, no. 2 (1984): 81; Donald E. Osterbrock, "The Rise and Fall of Edward S. Holden: Part Two," *Journal for the History of Astronomy* 15, no. 3 (1984): 151.

51. John Milne, "A Catalogue of 8,331 Earthquakes Recorded in Japan 1885–1892," *Seismological Journal of Japan* 4 (1895): 21.

52. Oscar Lewis, *George Davidson: Pioneer West Coast Scientist* (Berkeley: University of California Press, 1954).

53. Correctly, as it turned out. See "Ōmori Declares There Is No Danger of Severe Shock in Near Future," *San Francisco Chronicle*, June 6, 1906, 8.

54. "Effects of the 1906 Earthquake in San Jose," Santa Clara County Genealogy, http://www.sfgenealogy.com/santaclara/history/sc1906.htm; "Century-old Kingston Quake Monument Stands Tall," *Jamaica Gleaner*, May 28, 2015.

55. Ryan Kim, "Daly City Officials Unmoved by Quake Notoriety, Plan to Note Change of 1906 Epicenter Lacking Support," *San Francisco Chronicle*, April 11, 2004.

56. The authors of the report were Lawson and Branner; three astronomers who had been innocently housing seismological recorders at their observatories; the octogenarian George C. Davidson, who had come to San Francisco in 1850, worked on the original

geodetic survey of the state and served on the thwarted commission to research the 1868 earthquake; the distinguished US Geological Survey field geologist Grove Karl Gilbert; and Harry Fielding Reid, an earth physicist colleague of Lawson's at Johns Hopkins University.

57. Philip L. Fradkin, *Magnitude 8: Earthquakes and Life Along the San Andreas Fault* (New York: Henry Holt, 1998).

58. In 1901, when he was director of the Geological Survey, the story goes that Walcott was having breakfast with Carnegie, and Carnegie asked Walcott to tell him about James Smith, who gave the money that led to the establishment of the Smithsonian Institution. Carnegie was so impressed by Walcott's account that he eventually gave $10 million to establish the Carnegie Institution of Washington. See Ellis L. Yochelson, *Charles Doolittle Walcott, 1850–1927: A Biographical Memoir* (Washington, DC: National Academy of Sciences, 1967), http://www.nasonline.org/publications/biographical -memoirs/memoir-pdfs/walcott-charles.pdf.

59. Andrew Cowper Lawson and Harry Fielding Reid, *The California Earthquake of April 18, 1906: Report of the State Earthquake Investigation Commission in Two Volumes and Atlas*, no. 87 (Washington, DC: Carnegie Institution of Washington, 1908–1910).

60. Robert Reitherman, "The Effects of the 1906 Earthquake in California on Research and Education," *Earthquake Spectra* 22, no. S2 (April 2006): 207–236; Robert Reitherman, "Effects of Significant Earthquakes on the Development of Earthquake Engineering," paper 37, presented at the 2006 meeting of the New Zealand Society for Earthquake Engineering, http://www.nzsee.org.nz/db/2006/Paper37.pdf; Fradkin, *Magnitude 8*; Charles Derleth Jr., "The Destructive Extent of the California Earthquake of 1906: Its Effect upon Structures and Structural Materials Within the Earthquake Belt," in *The California Earthquake of 1906*, edited by David Starr Jordan (San Francisco: A. M. Robertson, 1907), 79–212; Charles Derleth Jr., "Structural Lessons on the Earthquake Disturbance," *Architects and Engineers of California* 5, no. 1 (1906);

61. Charles Derleth Jr., "Reinforced Concrete Construction: Its Proper Application in Earthquake Countries," *Journal of the Association of Engineering Societies* 38 (1907): 72–82.

62. Reitherman, "The Effects of the 1906 Earthquake."

63. Charles Walcott, letter to Charles R. Bishop, May 23, 1907, Smithsonian Institution Library.

64. Ibid.

65. In March 1910, Senator Hernando Money of Mississippi wrote to Boies Penrose: "There was great opposition in Congress to the establishment of a new Bureau."

66. US Senate, *Congressional Record*, 61st Cong., 2nd sess., parts 7–9, June 10, 1910, 7793–7794, https://archive.org/stream/congressionalrec45funit#page/n177/mode/1up.

67. A rival proposal for the Weather Bureau to undertake seismic monitoring was voted in at a meeting of the American Association for the Advancement of Science (AAAS) on the first anniversary of the San Francisco earthquake in 1907.

68. "BARS EARTHQUAKE STUDY: Controller of Treasury Says It Is Not Weather Bureau Work," *New York Times*, August 26, 1911, http://query.nytimes.com/gst/abstract .html?res=9B0DE0DB1531E233A25755C2A96E9C946096D6CF.

69. Augustan Udías and William Stauder, "The Jesuit Contribution to Seismology," in *International Handbook of Earthquake and Engineering Seismology*, vol. 81A (International

Association of Seismology and Physics of the Earth's Interior, Committee on Education, 2002), 19–27.

70. Ibid.

71. Henry M. Robinson, letter to Robert Millikan (responding to a recent publication by Bailey Willis), April 8, 1927, in Geschwind, *California Earthquakes,* 89.

72. An 80-kilogram Weichert vertical seismograph arrived at Berkeley from Germany in 1910, and the next year a 160-kilogram horizontal seismograph and an 80-kilogram Weichert vertical component seismograph were installed at the Lick Observatory.

73. Clifford W. Marsh, "San Francisco Is Burning," *The Standard,* July 7, 1906, reprinted in *Facts Concerning the Great Fire of San Francisco* (Bridgeport, CT: Marigold-Foster Printing Co., 1907), 234; Robert A. James, "Six Bits or Bust: Insurance Litigation over the 1906 San Francisco Earthquake and Fire," *Western Legal History* 24, no. 2 (2011): 127–165, https://www.pillsburylaw.com/siteFiles/Publications/SixBitsorBust InsuranceLitigation.pdf.

74. Vannevar Bush, "Biographical Memoir of John Ripley Freeman, 1855–1932," presented at the Autumn 1936 meeting of the National Academy of Sciences, http://www nasonline.org/publications/biographical-memoirs/memoir-pdfs/freeman-john.pdf.

75. "Harry Oscar Wood," Wikipedia, https://en.wikipedia.org/wiki/Harry_O._Wood (last modified November 27, 2015).

76. Geschwind, *California Earthquakes.*

77. Ibid. The British and French had been using seismic recorders to locate the enemy's big guns on the Western Front.

78. Ibid.

79. John A. Anderson had designed equipment for sensitive submarine detection; see Susan Elizabeth Hough, *Richter's Scale: Measure of an Earthquake, Measure of a Man* (Princeton, NJ: Princeton University Press, 2007).

80. Ibid.

81. Charles F. Richter, "An Instrumental Earthquake Magnitude Scale," *Bulletin of the Seismological Society of America* 25, no. 1 (1935): 1–32.

82. Charles F. Richter, *Elementary Seismology* (San Francisco: W. H. Freeman and Co., 1958).

83. Digby Diehl, *Super-Talk* (Garden City, NY: Doubleday, 1974).

84. Robert Muir-Wood, *The Dark Side of the Earth* (London: Allen & Unwin,1985).

85. Albuquerque Seismological Laboratory, "50 Years of Global Seismology," US Geological Survey Fact Sheet 2011–3065 (June 2011).

86. Bryan Isacks, Jack Oliver, and Lynn R. Sykes, "Seismology and the New Global Tectonics," *Journal of Geophysical Research* 73, no. 18 (1968): 5855–5899.

87. On plates, see Arch C. Johnston and Eugene S. Schweig, "The Enigma of the New Madrid Earthquakes of 1811–1812," *Annual Review of Earth and Planetary Sciences* 24, no. 1 (1996): 339–384; on plate tectonics, see W. Jason Morgan, "Rises, Trenches, Great Faults, and Crustal Blocks," *Journal of Geophysical Research* 73, no. 6 (1968): 1959–1982, doi:10.1029/JB073i006p01959.

88. Lucilla Benedetti, Paul Tapponier, Geoffrey C. P. King, and Luigi Piccardi, "Surface Rupture of the 1857 South Italian Earthquake?" *Terra Nova* 10, no. 4 (2002): 206–210.

89. "Interferometric Synthetic Aperture Radar," Wikipedia, https://en.wikipedia.org /wiki/Interferometric_synthetic_aperture_radar (last modified February 4, 2016).

90. Keiiti Aki, "Generation and Propagation of G Waves from the Niigata Earthquake of June 14, 1964: Part 2: Estimation of Earthquake Moment, Released Energy and Stress-Strain Drop from G Wave Spectrum," *Bulletin of the Earthquake Research Institute* 44 (1966): 73–88.

91. Shengji Wei, "Updated Result 3/11/2011 (Mw 9.0), Tohoku-oki, Japan,"Tectonics Caltech, March 11, 2011, http://www.tectonics.caltech.edu/slip_history/2011_taiheiyo-oki/; Gilles Peltzer, "Crustal Deformation Studies Using SAR Interferometry." NASA Jet Propulsion Laboratory, June 19, 2015, http://www-radar.jpl.nasa.gov/insar4crust/.

92. See, for example, "NASA/University Japan Quake Study Yields Surprises," NASA: Jet Propulsion Laboratory May 19, 2011, http://www.jpl.nasa.gov/news/news.php?feature=3006.

93. Robert Muir-Wood and Geoffrey C. P. King, "Hydrological Signatures of Earthquake Strain," *Journal of Geophysical Research* 98 (1993): 22035–22068.

94. Richard Lloyd Parry, "Japan's Hot-Spring Spas Drained by Earthquake," *Australian Times*, June 4, 2011.

95. George Plafker and J. C. Savage, "Mechanism of the Chilean Earthquakes of May 21 and 22, 1960," *Bulletin of the Geological Society of America* 81, no. 4 (April 1970): 1001–1030; George Plafker, "Surface Faults on Montague Island Associated with the 1964 Alaska Earthquake," US Geological Survey Professional Paper 543-G (1967), 41.

96. Katsuichiro Goda, Takashi Kiyota, Rama Mohan Pokhrel, Gabriele Chiaro, Toshihiko Katagiri, Keshab Sharma, and Sean Wilkinson, "The 2015 Gorkha Nepal Earthquake: Insights from Earthquake Damage Survey," *Frontiers in Built Environment*, June 22, 2015, doi:10.3389/fbuil.2015.00008.

CHAPTER 4: THE STORY OF THE THREE LITTLE PIGS

1. Henry Burstow, *Reminiscences of Horsham: Being Recollections of Henry Burstow, the Celebrated Bellringer and Songsinger* (Norwood Editions, 1975).

2. Arthur Freeman, "Phillipps, James Orchard Halliwell- (1820–1889)," in *Oxford Dictionary of National Biography* (Oxford: Oxford University Press, 2004); Charles Nicholl, "Shakespeare's Scholar Tramp," *The Guardian*, April 11, 2014.

3. "The Tale of the Three Little Pigs and the Big Bad Wolf" was included in *Nursery Rhymes and Nursery Tales* by James Orchard Halliwell-Phillipps, published in 1843.

4. Later versions of this story through the nineteenth century attempted to make the conduct of the wolf (or sometimes the fox) more credible by having him paw at each pig's house rather than blow at it.

5. William H. TeBrake, "Taming the Waterwolf: Hydraulic Engineering and Water Management in the Netherlands During the Middle Ages," *Technology and Culture* 43, no. 3 (July 2002): 475–499, http://www.yorku.ca/slater/documents/tebrake.pdf.

6. Bruno Bettelheim, "The Three Little Pigs: Pleasure Principle Versus Reality Principle," in *The Uses of Enchantment: The Meaning and Importance of Fairy Tales* (New York: Vintage Books, 1975).

7. Nathaniel Lloyd, *A History of English Brickwork* (London: H. Greville Montgomery, 1925).

8. Rand Richards, "Growing Pains (1850–1859)," in *Historic San Francisco: A Concise History and Guide* (San Francisco: Heritage House Publishers, 2007).

9. Albert Shumate, *The California of George Gordon and the 1849 Sea Voyages of His California Association: A San Francisco Pioneer Rescued from the Legend of Gertrude Atherton's First Novel* (Glendale, CA: Arthur H. Clark Co., 1976); Samuel Dickson, *Lord George Gordon: Tales of San Francisco* (Stanford, CA: Stanford University Press, 1992).

10. Walter L. Huber, "San Francisco Earthquakes of 1865 and 1868," *Bulletin of the Seismological Society of America* 20 (1930): 261–262.

11. USGS Earthquake Hazards Program, "Historic Earthquakes: Hayward, California: 1868 October 21, 15.53 UTC: Magnitude 6.8," http://earthquake.usgs.gov/earthquakes/states/events/1868_10_21.php.

12. See William H. Prescott, "Circumstances Surrounding the Preparation and Suppression of a Report on the 1868 California Earthquake," *Bulletin of the Seismological Society of America* 72, no. 6A (1982): 2389–2393.

13. Stephen Tobriner, "Weighing the Damage 1863–1869," in *Bracing for Disaster: Earthquake-Resistant Architecture and Engineering in San Francisco, 1838–1933* (Berkeley: Heyday Books, 2006), 54.

14. The admission of the distinguished surveyor George Davidson, who had been a member of the original 1868 Committee of Scientific Inquiry almost forty years earlier, was reported in 1908 by the University of California professor of geology Andrew Lawson while writing on his frustration about getting either the state of California or the city of San Francisco to fund research on the 1906 earthquake; he was quoting from a conversation with Davidson. See Oscar Lewis, *George Davidson: Pioneer West Coast Scientist* (Berkeley: University of California Press, 1954).

15. See Prescott, "Circumstances Surrounding the Preparation and Suppression of a Report. . . . "

16. Dr. Stephen Tobriner, "The Earthquake of 1868 and the Birth of Seismically Resistant Architecture and Engineering in the San Francisco Bay Area" (lecture), http://www.ncgeolsoc.org/SpeakerInfo/2009%20-%202010/DrTobriner_Jan2010_AbstBio pdf; Tobriner, *Bracing for Disaster*.

17. Conder would also be honored with a bronze statue outside the current Faculty of Engineering at Tokyo University. See Greg Clancey, *Earthquake Nation: The Cultural Politics of Japanese Seismicity, 1868–1930* (Berkeley: University of California Press, 2006), 13.

18. Ibid., 14.

19. Ibid., 12.

20. Ibid.

21. Ibid., 61.

22. Ibid., 114–115.

23. Milne and Conder independently set off to investigate the earthquake in the field and published their findings pseudonymously in the English-language newspapers. Milne took a camera and provided history's first detailed photographic record of earthquake damage.

24. Clancey, *Earthquake Nation*, 180.

25. "The San Francisco Earthquake, 1906," EyeWitness to History, 1997, http://www.eyewitnesstohistory.com/sfeq.htm.

26. "Brickmakers Opposition to Re-inforced Concrete," *Architects and Engineers of*

California 5, no. 2 (1906): 68; "Defends Use of Concrete," *San Francisco Chronicle*, June 12, 1906, 9.

27. "An Updated Map of Seattle's Brick Earthquake Risk Shows Capitol Hill Concentration," *Capitol Hill Seattle*, August 22, 2012.

28. Huixian Liu, ed., "The Great Tangshan Earthquake of 1976" (Pasadena: California Institute of Technology, Earthquake Engineering Research Laboratory, 2004).

29. Ioanna Ioannou, et al., "The 29th May 2012 Emilia Romagna Earthquake: EPICentre Field Observation Report" (London: UCL EPICentre, June 21, 2012).

30. Bigman M. Hutapea, et al., "The Mw 6.3 Java, Indonesia, Earthquake of May 27, 2006: Special Earthquake Report" (Oakland, CA: Earthquake Engineering Research Institute, 2006).

31. Otto W. Nuttli, Gilbert A. Bollinger, and Robert B. Herrmann, *The 1886 Charleston, South Carolina, Earthquake: A 1986 Perspective* (Reston, VA: US Geological Survey, 1986).

32. Roberto Meli, et al., "Seismic Design Guide for Low-Rise Confined Masonry Buildings" (Oakland, CA: Earthquake Engineering Research Institute, 2011).

33. N. N. Ambraseys and C. F. Finkel, "The Marmara Sea Earthquake of 1509," *Terra Nova* 2 (1991): 167–174; N. N. Ambraseys, "The Earthquake of 1509 in the Sea of Marmara, Turkey, Revisited," *Bulletin of the Seismological Society of America* 91, no. 6 (2001): 1397–1416, doi:10.1785/0120000305.

34. N. N. Ambraseys and C. F. Finkel, "Long-Term Seismicity of Istanbul and the Marmara Sea Region," *Terra Nova* 3 (1991): 527–539.

35. Mario Schipano, *Roma 1650–1658*, vol. 1 of *Viaggi di Pietro Della Valle il Pellegrino, La Turchia, La Persia e l'India* (*Travels of Pietro Della Valle il Pellegrino in Turkey, Persia, and India*), 3 vols. (Torino: G. Gancia, 1843).

36. Conservationtech.com: Building Conservation Technology, "Publications: Books and Articles by Randolph Langenbach on the Subject of Earthquakes and Traditional Building Construction," http://www.conservationtech.com/RL's%20resume&%20pub's /RL-publications/1-EQ-const2.htm.

37. UNESCO World Heritage Center, "Churches of Chiloé," http://whc.unesco.org /en/list/971.

38. The building in question was the Grand Hotel in San Francisco. See "South Hall and Seismic Safety at the University of California in 1870," *Chronicle of the University of California* 1, no. 1 (1998): 16.

39. For an image of a half-timbered house in Turkey next to reinforced-concrete frame construction, see http://www.ofhayrat.com/images/other/793.jpg.

40. Richard Allan, "The Beginnings of the Cretan Palaces: The Proto Palatial Period," in *Greek Architecture*, 5th ed., vol. 11, revised by Arnold Walter Lawrence (New Haven, CT: Yale University Press, 1996), 13–17.

41. Joseph Jay Deiss, "Houses of the Middle Class," in *Herculaneum: Italy's Buried Treasure* (Los Angeles: J. Paul Getty Museum, 1985).

42. Randolph Langenbach, "Rescuing the Baby from the Bathwater: Traditional Masonry as Earthquake-Resistant Construction," presented at the Eighth International Masonry Conference (2010).

43. Marisa Mazria Katz, "The Gingerbread Reclamation," *Wall Street Journal*, April 28, 2011.

44. A feature of these structures, in comparison with the half-timbering of Turkey or Kashmir, was that the interiors were lined with wooden boards, giving the structure extra strength.

45. N. N. Ambraseys and C. Finkel, *The Seismicity of Turkey and Adjacent Areas: A Historical Review, 1500–1800* (New York: John Wiley, 1996), 93. İzmir continued to be a city of wooden houses until 1922, when it was burned during a battle between Greek and Turkish forces.

46. Matthew Mulcahy, "The Port Royal Earthquake and the World of Wonders in Seventeenth-Century Jamaica," *Early American Studies: An Interdisciplinary Journal* 6, no. 2 (2008): 391–421; Matthew Mulcahy, "The Port Royal Fire of 1703," paper presented at "Disasters! A Conference on Catastrophes in History," Hagley Museum, Wilmington, DE (2011).

47. As recounted by Ebul Hasan Ali bin Muhammed, leading an ambassador's delegation from Morocco, quoted in All About Turkey, "The Map for Istanbul and Its Surroundings," http://www.adiyamanli.org/istanbul.html; see also Republic of Turkey, Ministry of Culture and Tourism, "Istanbul During the Turkish Period," http://www.kultur.gov.tr/EN,33080/istanbul-during-the-turkish-period.html.

48. B. J. Slot, "The Fires in Istanbul of 1782 and 1784 According to Maps and Reports by Dutch Diplomatic Representatives," *Güneydoğu Avrupa Araştırmaları Dergisi* 4–5 (1975–1976): 48–49, http://www.journals.istanbul.edu.tr/iugaad/article/view/1023014624.

49. Zeynep Çelik, *The Remaking of Istanbul: Portrait of an Ottoman City in the Nineteenth Century* (Berkeley: University of California Press, 1993). 49–81.

50. Istanbul Metropolitan Municipality, Istanbul Fire Brigade, "Fires in Istanbul," http://www.ibb.gov.tr/sites/itfaiye/workarea/en-us/Pages/FiresInIstanbul.aspx.

51. Greg Bankoff, "A Tale of Two Cities: The Pyro-Seismic Morphology of Nineteenth Century Manila," in Bankoff et al., *Flammable Cities*, 82–102.

52. Greg Bankoff, "Fire and Quake in the Construction of Old Manila," *Medieval History Journal* 10, nos. 1–2 (2007): 411–427, http://www2.hull.ac.uk/FASS/pdf/History-Bankoff-fire2.pdf.

53. Joseph Fayol, "Affairs in the Filipinas, 1644–1647," in *The Philippine Islands, 1493–1803*, vol. 35, edited by Emma Blair and Alexander Robertson (Cleveland: A. H. Clark, 1903–1908), 217; Bankoff, "Fire and Quake in the Construction of Old Manila."

54. Gregory Bankoff, "Living with Risk: Coping with Disasters: Hazard as a Frequent Life Experience in the Philippines," *Education About Asia* 12, no. 2 (Fall 2007): 26–29, http://www2.hull.ac.uk/FASS/pdf/History-Bankoff-Livingwithrisk2.pdf.

55. Gerard Lico, *Arkitekturang Filipino: A History of Architecture and Urbanism in the Philippines* (Manila: University of the Philippines Press, 2008); "Philippine Architecture," http://nlpdl.nlp.gov.ph:81/CC01/NLP00VM052mcd/v2/v1.pdf.

56. By 1606, there were 3,000 Japanese in the city, a number that increased after the Japanese emperor outlawed Christianity in 1614.

57. "Filipino Architecture and Its Influences: Spanish Colonial," Openthedorr, posted by Ddmdomag, April 9, 2013, https://openthedorr.wordpress.com/2013/04/09/spanish-colonial/.

58. Lico, *Arkitekturang Filipino*; "History of Architecture," http://historyofarchitecture.weebly.com/bahay-na-bato.html.

59. "Baroque Churches of the Philippines," UNESCO Information Services Section, http://www.unesco.org/archives/multimedia/?s=flvplayer&pg=33&vo=2&vl=Eng&id=185.

60. "Paoay Church," Heritage Conservation Society, July 27, 2006, https://heritage conservation.wordpress.com/2006/07/27/paoay-church/.

61. On quincha buildings, see Mark Alan Healy, "The 'Superstition of Adobe' and the Certainty of Concrete: Shelter and Power After the 1944 San Juan Earthquake in Argentina," in Buchenau and Johnson, *Aftershocks*, 100–128. Simple quincha buildings, constructed rapidly and informally after the 1944 earthquake in San Juan, Argentina, were found, against all expectations, to withstand earthquake shaking much better than the traditional thick-walled adobe construction. See Anthony Oliver-Smith, "El Terremoto de 1746 de Lima: El Modelo colonial, el desarrollo urbano y los peligros naturales," in *Historia y desastres en América Latina*, vol. 2 (Bogotá: CIESAS/Red de Estudios Sociales en Prevención de Desastres en América Latina [La Red], 1997), 2–20, http://www.desenredando.org/public/libros/1997/hydv2/hydv2_cap05-ETELP _sep-09-2002.pdf.

62. John R. Mullin, "The Reconstruction of Lisbon Following the Earthquake of 1755: A Study in Despotic Planning," Landscape Architecture and Regional Planning Faculty Publication Series, Paper 45, *Planning Perspective* 7, no. 2 (1992): 157–179.

63. Kendrick, *The Lisbon Earthquake*.

64. Rafaela Cardoso, Mário Lopes, and Rita Bento, "Earthquake Resistant Structures of Portuguese Old 'Pombalino' Buildings," Paper 3329, Thirteenth World Conference on Earthquake Engineering, Vancouver, BC, Canada (August 1–6, 2004).

65. Stephen Tobriner, "La Casa Baraccata: Earthquake-Resistant Construction in 18th-Century Calabria," *Journal of the Society of Architectural Historians* (1983): 131–138.

66. Halil İnalcık, "Devlet-i 'Aliyye," in *Osmanlı İmparatorluğu Üzerine Araştırma-lar-I. II: Beyazıd Dönemi (1481–1512): Fatih Dönemine Tepki* (Istanbul: Türkiye İş Bankası Kültür Yayınları, 2009), 129–136.

67. Library of Congress, Federal Research Division, "Dominican Republic and Haiti: Country Studies" (Washington, DC: US Government Printing Office, 2001), https:// www.loc.gov/item/2001023524/.

68. N. N. Ambraseys, "The Buyin-Zara (Iran) Earthquake of September, 1962: A Field Report," *Bulletin of the Seismological Society of America* 53, no. 4 (July 1, 1963): 705; N. Ambraseys and J. S. Tchalenko, "The Dasht-e Bayāz (Iran) Earthquake of August 31, 1968: A Field Report," *Bulletin of the Seismological Society of America* 59, no. 5 (1969): 1751–1792.

69. Parastoo Pourvahidi, "Bioclimatic Analysis of Vernacular Iranian Architecture," master's thesis, Eastern Mediterranean University (Gazimağusa, North Cyprus), January 2010, i-rep.emu.edu.tr:8080/jspui/bitstream/11129/98/1/Pourvahidi.pdf.

70. Beverley Adams, et al., "The Bam (Iran) Earthquake of December 26, 2003: Preliminary Reconnaissance Using Remotely Sensed Data and the VIEWS (Visualizing the Impacts of Earthquakes with Satellite Images) System," MCEER Earthquake Reconnaissance Investigation Report (2004): 10.

71. Stephen Tobriner, "Response of Traditional Wooden Japanese Construction," National Information Service for Earthquake Engineering (NISEE), University of California at Berkeley, http://nisee.berkeley.edu/kobe/tobriner.html (updated December 9, 1997).

72. Michio Fujioka, *Kyoto Gosho* (Tokyo: Shokokusha Publishing, 1956), 169–170.

73. Tobriner, "Response of Traditional Wooden Japanese Construction"; Heinrich Engel, *The Japanese House: A Tradition for Contemporary Architecture* (Rutland, VT: Charles E. Tuttle: 1964), 356–357.

74. Matthew Mulcahy, *Hurricanes and Society in the British Greater Caribbean, 1624–1783* (Baltimore: Johns Hopkins University Press, 2006), 126.

75. Ibid.

76. Greg J. Holland and George R. Walker, "Tracy Revisited: Historical Perspective, Synoptics, Track, and Winds," *Australian Meteorological and Oceanographic Journal* 60, no. 3 (2010): 145–154; George R. Walker, "A Review of the Impact of Cyclone Tracy on Building Regulations and Insurance," *Australian Meteorological and Oceanographic Journal* 60, no. 3 (2010): 199; Robert H. Leicester and Greg Reardon, "Impact Statistics of Tracy and an Opportunity Missed," *Australian Meteorological and Oceanographic Journal* 60, no. 3 (2010): 2079; Anthony Schofield, Craig Arthur, and Bob Cechet, "Assessing the Impacts of Tropical Cyclone Tracy on Residential Building Stock—1974 and 2008," *Australian Meteorological and Oceanographic Journal* 60, no. 3 (2010): 213.

77. George Walker, "Cyclone Tracy and the Australian Insurance Industry: The Silver Lining," *Risk Frontiers* 9, no. 3 (2010): 1–4; Colin Packham, "Cyclone Tracy and the Australian Insurance Industry: The Silver Lining, Part II," *Risk Frontiers* 9, no. 4 (2010): 1–2.

78. "Typhoon Bopha," Wikipedia, https://en.wikipedia.org/wiki/Typhoon_Bopha (last modified November 29, 2015).

79. Harold Brooks, "Mobile Home Tornado Fatalities: Some Observations," NOAA National Severe Storms Laboratory, March 25, 1997, http://www.nssl.noaa.gov/users/brooks/public_html/essays/mobilehome.html.

80. According to NOAA, 31 percent of 823 people killed in US tornadoes during that period were in mobile homes, which made up 8 percent of all housing in the United States.

81. The speed limit is as high as 70 miles per hour in Florida and most of the Eastern states, and up to 75 miles per hour in Oklahoma. See Daniel Albalate and Germà Bel, "Speed Limit Laws in America: Economics, Politics, and Geography," Working Paper 2010-02 (Barcelona: Research Institute of Applied Economics [IREA], 2010).

CHAPTER 5: RISK MADE CONCRETE

1. Eric Fernie, *The Architecture of Norman England* (Oxford: Oxford University Press, 2002).

2. Between 1957 and 1959, twenty-seven of forty-three rocket launches failed. See Dennis R. Jenkins, "Stage and a Half: The Atlas Launch Vehicle," in *To Reach the High Frontier: A History of US Launch Vehicles*, edited by Roger D. Launius and Dennis R. Jenkins (Lexington: University Press of Kentucky, 2002), 70–102.

3. At Canterbury (1070), Chichester (1075), Winchester (1079), Hereford (1079), Rochester (1080), Ely (1083), Worcester (1084), Lichfield (1085), London (1087), Lincoln (1088), Durham (1093), and Norwich (1096).

4. At Exeter (1107), St. Davids (in Pembrokeshire, Wales, 1115), Peterborough (1118), and Bristol (1140).

5. Chichester Cathedral Restoration and Development Trust, "Chichester Cathedral Spire Collapses," http://www.chichestercathedraltrust.org.uk/chichester-cathedral-spire/.

6. Paul Frankl and Paul Crossley, "The Early Gothic Period," in *Gothic Architecture*, vol. 19 (New Haven, CT: Yale University Press, 2000), 67–104.

7. Ibid.

8. The tradition of laying the axis of the chancel east-west gave the building the minimum profile facing the prevailing westerly winds, although the desire was not so much to achieve climatological optimization as simply to face Jerusalem.

9. At the cathedral at Amiens, the original thirteenth-century flying buttresses were sited too high to counteract the lateral load from the roof and a second row of stronger flying buttresses had to be inserted. When even this failed to prevent bowing and cracking in the lower walls, a massive chain of wrought-iron links was heated red-hot and tightened around the whole mezzanine level to keep the columns from further movement.

10. In Japan the large Hōkō-ji temple erected in 1589 in Kyoto was destroyed by an earthquake in 1596, then rebuilt in 1614, only to be destroyed by another earthquake in 1662.

11. William John Macquorn Rankine, *A Manual of Applied Mechanic* (London: Charles Griffin and Co., 1872).

12. Matthew Wells, *Engineers: A History of Engineering and Structural Design* (Abingdon, UK: Routledge, 2010).

13. The wind has yet to demolish a modern engineered tall building. While there have been big fires in high-rise buildings, only one such building has ever collapsed simply as a result of catching fire—the forty-seven-story 7 World Trade Center building in lower Manhattan.

14. "History of Reinforced Concrete and Structural Design," Engineer's Standpoint, November 10, 2011, http://engineerstandpoint.blogspot.com/2010/09/services.html.

15. Richard Beamish, *Memoir of the Life of Sir Marc Isambard Brunel* (Cambridge: Cambridge University Press, 2013).

16. Sara Wermiel, "The Development of Fireproof Construction in Great Britain and the United States in the Nineteenth Century," *Construction History* (1993): 3–26.

17. Geschwind, *California Earthquakes*, 28, note 31.

18. Charles W. Dickey, "Lessons of the San Francisco Earthquake and Fire," *Architect and Engineer of California* 5, no. 1 (1906).

19. John B. Leonard, "How Reinforced Concrete Stood Earthquake and Fire," *Architect and Engineer of California* 5, no. 1 (1906).

20. Edwin Duryea, et al. "The Effects of the San Francisco Earthquake of April 18th, 1906, on Engineering Constructions: Reports of a General Committee and of Six Special Committees of the San Francisco Association of Members of the American Society of Civil Engineers," *Transactions of the American Society of Civil Engineers* 59, no. 2 (1907): 264–329; Gilbert Grove Karl, Richard Lewis Humphrey, John Stephen Sewell, and Frank Soule, *The San Francisco Earthquake and Fire of April 18th, 1906, and Their Effects on Structures and Structural Materials* (Washington, DC: US Government Printing Office, 1907).

21. David Starr Jordan, John Casper Branner, Charles Derleth Jr., Stephen Taber, F. Omari, Harold W. Fairbanks, and Mary Hunter Austin, *The California Earthquake of 1906* (San Francisco: A. M. Robertson, 1907).

22. Clancey, *Earthquake Nation*, 214.

23. Jonathan Reynolds, *Maekawa Kunio and the Emergence of Japanese Modernist Architecture* (Berkeley: University of California Press, 2001).

24. Clancey, *Earthquake Nation*, 224–225.

25. Le Corbusier, *Towards a New Architecture* (London: John Rodker, 1931); Kenneth Frampton, "Corbu, Construed," *Architect* 97, no. 4 (2008): 51.

26. Andrew Kroll, "AD Classics: Villa Savoye/Le Corbusier," *ArchDaily*, October 27, 2010.

27. Gus Lubin, "Why Architect Le Corbusier Wanted to Demolish Downtown Paris," *Business Insider*, August 20, 2013.

28. When in 1934 Le Corbusier's proposals for Algiers had been rejected, he wrote: "I have been expelled, the doors have been shut in my face. I am right, I am right, I am right." See Le Corbusier, *The Radiant City: Elements of a Doctrine of Urbanism to Be Used as the Basis of Our Machine-Age Civilization* (New York: Orion Press, 1967), 260.

29. M. A. Sozen, et al., *Engineering Report on the Caracas Earthquake of 29 July 1967* (Washington, DC: National Academy of Sciences, 1968).

30. K. V. Steinbrugge, E. E. Schader, and D. F. Moran, "Building Damage in San Fernando Valley," in *San Fernando, California, Earthquake of 9 February 1971* (Sacramento: California Division of Mines and Geology, 1975), 323–353.

31. Nicole B. Trujillo, "1985 Mexico City Earthquake Summary and Lessons Learned," Wikispace, 2012, https://failures.wikispaces.com/1985+Mexico+City+Summary+%26 +Lessons+Learned.

32. Mario Ordaz and Roberto Meli, "Seismic Design and Codes in Mexico," Paper 4000, Thirteenth World Conference on Earthquake Engineering, Vancouver, BC, Canada (August 1–6, 2004).

33. L. Teresa Guevara-Perez, "'Soft Story' and 'Weak Story' in Earthquake Resistant Design: A Multidisciplinary Approach," paper presented at the World Conference on Earthquake Engineering, Lisbon (2012).

34. Tsuneo Okada, "Pursuit of Creation of Sustainable Architectural Space," *JR EAST Technical Review* 4 (2004): 2–3.

35. Toshihide Kashima, Shin Koyama, Masanori Iiba, and Izuru Okawa, "Dynamic Behavior of a Museum Building Retrofitted Using Base Isolation System," Fourteenth World Conference on Earthquake Engineering, Beijing (October 12–17, 2008), http://www.iitk.ac.in/nicee/wcee/article/14_05-06-0021.PDF.

36. Approximately an additional 0.1 second for each story of the building—thus, a ten-story building oscillates at one cycle per second. See Christopher Arnold, "Earthquake Effects on Buildings," chapter 4 in *Risk Management Series: Designing for Earthquakes: A Manual for Architects*, FEMA 454 (Washington, DC: Federal Emergency Management Agency, December 2006).

37. Ronald O. Hamburger, Helmut Krawinkler, James O. Malley, and Scott M. Adan, "Seismic Design of Steel Special Moment Frames: A Guide for Practicing Engineers," Seismic Design Technical Brief No. 2, NIST GCR 09-917-3 (Washington, DC: US Department of Commerce, National Institute of Standards and Technology [NIST], National Earthquake Hazards Reduction Program [NEHRP], 2009); Ofelia Moroni and C. Gomez, "Concrete Shear Wall Construction," Report 4, *World Housing Encyclopedia* (Earthquake Engineering Research Institute and International Association for Earthquake Engineering, 2002).

38. Robert Tremblay, et al., "Performance of Steel Structures During the 1994 Northridge Earthquake," *Canadian Journal of Civil Engineering* 22, no. 2 (1995): 338–360; Stephen A. Mahin, James O. Malley, Ronald O. Hamburger, and Michael Mahoney, "Overview of the US Program for Reduction of Earthquake Hazards in Steel Moment-Frame Structures," *Earthquake Spectra* 19 (2003): 237–254.

39. Cheng Song, Santiago Pujol, and Andrés Lepage, "The Collapse of the Alto Río Building During the 27 February 2010 Maule, Chile Earthquake," *Earthquake Spectra* 28, no. S1 (June 2012): S301–S334, http://www.earthquakespectra.org/doi /abs/10.1193/1.4000036?journalCode=eqsa; American Red Cross Multidisciplinary Team, "Report on the 2010 Chilean Earthquake and Tsunami Response," US Geological Survey, Open-File Report 2011-1053, version 1.1.0, http://pubs.usgs.gov/of/2011/1053/.

40. Shunsuke Otani, "Japanese Seismic Design of High-Rise Reinforced Concrete Buildings—An Example of Performance Based Design Code and State of Practices," Paper 5010, Thirteenth World Conference on Earthquake Engineering, Vancouver, BC, Canada (August 1–6, 2004).

41. "The Art of Detailing," PCA: America's Cement Manufacturers, http://www .cement.org/think-harder-concrete-/buildings-structures/design-aids/detailing.

42. R. I. Gilbert, "Detailing of Reinforcement in Concrete Structures," Civil and Structural Engineering Panel, Engineers Australia Sydney Division, August 28, 2012, http:// www.engineersaustralia.org.au/sites/default/files/detailing_of_reinforcement_in_concrete _structures_28_aug_2012.pdf.

43. J. Despeyroux, "The Agadir Earthquake of February 29th 1960: Behavior of Modern Buildings During the Earthquake," paper presented at the Second World Conference on Earthquake Engineering, Tokyo (1960), http://www.iitk.ac.in/nicee/wcee/article /vol.1_session5_521.pdf.

44. John F. Meehan, Henry J. Degenkolb, Donald F. Moran, Karl V. Steinbrugge, Lloyd S. Cluff, Gary A. Carver, R. B. Mathiesen, and Charles F. Knudson, *Managua, Nicaragua, Earthquake of December 23, 1972: Earthquake Engineering Research Institute (EERI) Reconnaissance Report* (Oakland, CA: EERI, May 1973).

45. Mark Alan Healey, "The 'Superstition of Adobe' and the Certainty of Concrete: Shelter and Power After the 1944 San Juan Earthquake in Argentina," in Buchenau and Johnson, *Aftershocks*, 100–128.

46. Vasile I. Marza, "On the Death Toll of the 1999 Izmit (Turkey) Major Earthquake," *European Seismological Commission Proceedings* (2004).

47. George C. Lee and Chin-Hsiung Loh, eds., *The Chi-Chi, Taiwan, Earthquake of September 21, 1999: Reconnaissance Report* (Buffalo, NY: University at Buffalo, Multidisciplinary Center for Earthquake Engineering Research, 2000).

48. "Egypt: Cairo Building Collapse Death Toll Rise to 15—Mena," AllAfrica, November 25, 2014, http://allafrica.com/stories/201411251663.html; "Why Are Buildings Collapsing in Egypt?" http://egyptbuildingcollapses.org/; "392 Buildings Collapse in One Year, 52% Due to Lack of Regulation: EIPR," *Cairo Post*, June 8, 2014, http://thecairopost .youm7.com/news/114082/inside_egypt/392-building-collapses-in-one-year-52-due-to -lack-of-regulation-eipr.

49. Hossam S. Badawi and Sherif A. Mourad, "Observations from the 12 October 1992 Dahshour Earthquake in Egypt," *Natural Hazards* 10, no. 3 (November 1994): 261–274.

50. Fatemah Farag, "Shaken, Not Stirred," *Al-Ahram Weekly*, August 29, 2002, http://www.masress.com/en/ahramweekly/22655.

51. Michael O. Ajufoh, W. A. Gumau, and Yaktor Joshua Inusa, "Curbing the Menace of Building Collapse in Nigeria," *International Letters of Natural Sciences* 15, no. 2 (2014): 168–178.

52. Olabosipo I. Fagbenle and Adedamola O. Oluwunmi, "Building Failure and Collapse in Nigeria: The Influence of the Informal Sector," *Journal of Sustainable Development* 3, no. 4 (2010): 268–276.

53. Roger Bilham, "The Seismic Future of Cities," Twelfth Annual Mallet Milne Lecture, *Bulletin of Earthquake Engineering* 7, no. 4 (2009): 839–887, doi:10.1007/s10518-009-9147-0.

54. Laws 229–233 of Hammurabi's Code of Laws (c. 1780 BC), from a stone slab discovered in 1901 and preserved in the Louvre Museum in Paris.

55. "Rome: A City of Rental Property," http://romaninsulae.weebly.com/dangers-of-living-in-an-insula.html; *The Geography of Strabo*, vol. II (Cambridge, MA: Harvard University Press/Loeb Classical Library, 1923), 235, http://penelope.uchicago.edu/Thayer/E/Roman/Texts/Strabo/5C*.html.

56. James Lewis, "Earthquake Destruction: Corruption on the Fault Line," in Transparency International, *Global Corruption Report 2005: Corruption in Construction and Post-Conflict Reconstruction* (London: Pluto Press, 2005), 23–25; Penny Green, "Disaster by Design: Corruption, Construction, and Catastrophe," *British Journal of Criminology* 45, no. 4 (July 2005): 528–546.

57. Nicholas Ambraseys and Roger Bilham, "Corruption Kills: Supplementary Materials 1: The Influence of Poverty and Corruption on the Loss of Life in Earthquakes," *Nature* 469 (January 2011): 153–155. More than 80 percent of deaths from building collapses in earthquakes in the last three decades occurred in corrupt and poor countries.

58. "Rescue Operations over for Collapsed School in Haiti," *The Guardian*, November 11, 2008.

59. Roger Bilham, "Lessons from the Haiti Earthquake," *Nature* 463 (2010): 878–879.

60. Deborah Sontag, "Two Years After Haiti Quake, Safe Housing Is a Dream for Many," *New York Times*, August 16, 2012.

CHAPTER 6: MR. HEATH'S LITTLE BLACK BOOK

1. Ilana Krausman Ben-Amos, *The Culture of Giving: Informal Support and Gift-Exchange in Early Modern England* (Cambridge: Cambridge University Press, 2008).

2. Samuel Pepys, entry of June 30, 1661, in *Diary of Samuel Pepys* (Teddington, Middlesex, UK: Echo Library, 2006).

3. Peter George Muir Dickson, *The Sun Insurance Office, 1710–1960: The History of Two and a Half Centuries of British Insurance* (Oxford: Oxford University Press, 1960), 3.

4. Ibid., 3.

5. Neil Hanson, *The Great Fire of London in That Apocalyptic Year, 1666* (Hoboken, NJ: John Wiley and Sons, 2002).

6. Alan D. Dyer, "The Influence of Bubonic Plague in England, 1500–1667," *Medical History* 22, no. 3 (1978): 308–326.

7. "Charles II, 1666: An Act for Rebuilding the City of London," in *Statutes of the Realm*, vol. 5, *1628–1680* (1819), 603–612.

8. Anthony Sutcliffe, *London: An Architectural History* (New Haven, CT: Yale University Press, 2006).

9. Christine Stevenson, "Robert Hooke: Monuments and Memory," *Art History* 28, no. 1 (2005): 43–73.

10. Becoming a builder would have made Barbon very rich if he had not chosen to ignore niceties such as planning authority for what he built, or owning the land on which his properties were developed, or providing proper foundations to his houses, some of which began to fall down soon after they were erected. See Dickson, *The Sun Insurance Office, 1710–1960*, 7–9.

11. Barbon, seeking to "avoid those Disputes which might arise about the Dimensions, Form and substantialness of Building," offered to rebuild any properties destroyed by fire. However, he soon substituted financial compensation as an alternative to "replacing the property."

12. Dickson, *The Sun Insurance Office, 1710–1960*, 8–11.

13. Ibid.

14. Ibid., 11–16.

15. Ibid., 324. See also Robin Pearson, *Insuring the Industrial Revolution: Fire Insurance in Great Britain, 1700–1850* (Aldershot, UK: Ashgate, 2004); Jennifer Anne Carlson, "The Economics of Fire Protection: From the Great Fire of London to Rural/Metro," *Economic Affairs* 25, no. 3 (2005): 39–44; Dickson, *The Sun Insurance Office, 1710–1960*, 23.

16. An exception was for ransom insurance in pirate-infested waters. See Tim Armstrong, "Slavery, Insurance, and Sacrifice in the Black Atlantic," in *Sea Changes: Historicizing the Ocean*, edited by Klein Bernhard (New York: Routledge, 2004), 167–185.

17. Robin Pearson, "Moral Hazard and the Assessment of Insurance Risk in Eighteenth- and Early Nineteenth-Century Britain," *Business History Review* 76, no.1 (May 2002): 1–35.

18. Dirk Schubert, "The Great Fire of Hamburg," in Bankoff et al., *Flammable Cities*, 212–234.

19. Originally, "reinsurance" meant exchanging part of the risk with another insurer. But insurers were not keen on sharing information or prices with their competitors. They could reinsure with an insurer in another state or country, but that was complicated to arrange. See E. W. Kopf, "Notes on the Origin and Development of Reinsurance," *Proceedings of the Casualty Actuarial Society* 16 (1929): 33–34, https://www.casact.org/pubs/proceed/proceed29/29022.pdf; David M. Holland, "Reinsurance: A Brief History," *Reinsurance News* (special issue) 65 (February 2009).

20. Peter Borscheid, David Gugerli, and Tobias Straumann, *The Value of Risk: Swiss Re and the History of Reinsurance* (Oxford: Oxford University Press, 2013).

21. Dait Baranoff, "Fire Insurance in the United States," EH.Net Encyclopedia, edited by Robert Whaples, March 16, 2008, http://eh.net/encyclopedia/fire-insurance-in-the-united-states/.

22. Sara E. Wermiel, "Did the Fire Insurance Industry Help Reduce Urban Fires in the United States in the Nineteenth Century?" In Bankoff et al., *Flammable Cities*, 235–253.

23. In 1888 the city of Sundsvall in Sweden, built of wood, burned to the ground. A group of reinsurers, Swiss Re among them, let Sweden's insurers know that there was going to be a limit in the future on losses from wooden houses, and that this limit was going to be low. Sweden began building with stone.

24. Wermiel, "Did the Fire Insurance Industry Help Reduce Urban Fires. . . . "

25. Ibid.

26. Daniel Defoe, *An Essay upon Projects* (London: Cassell & Co., 1887).

27. "The UK's Worst Convective Storm of the Last 200 Years, 9th August 1843," Severe Weather Photography from Mid-Wales," http://www.geologywales.co.uk/storms /1843.htm.

28. Antony Brown, *Cuthbert Heath: The Maker of the Modern Lloyds of London* (London: David and Charles, 1980).

29. "Loss by fire or storm" insurance was written sporadically in the late nineteenth century as an added peril to fire insurance, and it was sold until 1880 by local or farmers' mutual insurers in the Eastern United States. The first insurance that covered windstorms specifically was written in the Midwest toward the end of the century under the title of "Tornado Insurance" and continued to be written until 1930.

30. "Redwood's Claims as a Fire Resistant Substantiated," *American Lumberman* (May 26, 1906): 25.

31. In the hours between the earthquake and the fire, those who photographed a surprisingly lightly damaged city would find that their images acquired great value in later disputes with insurers. See Stephen Tobriner, "An EERI Reconnaissance Report: Damage to San Francisco in the 1906 Earthquake: A Centennial Perspective," *Earthquake Spectra* 22, no. S2 (2006): 11–41.

32. Tobriner, *Bracing for Disaster*, 193–194.

33. Lloyd's, "San Francisco Earthquake: Lloyd's and the San Francisco Earthquake, 1906," 2006, http://www.lloyds.com/lloyds/about-us/history/catastrophes-and-claims /san-francisco-1906-earthquake.

34. Robert A. James, "Six Bits or Bust: Insurance Litigation over the 1906 San Francisco Earthquake and Fire," *Western Legal History* 24, no. 2 (2011): 127–165, https:// www.pillsburylaw.com/siteFiles/Publications/SixBitsorBustInsuranceLitigation.pdf; Rene Siemens and Peter Gillon, "Lessons from the Great Fire of 1906," *Risk Management*, December 1, 2010.

35. For a list of these companies, see Tilmann Röder, *Rechtsbildung im wirtschaftlichen Weltverkehr: Das Erdbeben von San Francisco und die internationale Standardisierung von Vertragsbedingungen (1871–1914)*, vol. 206 (Frankfurt am Main: Vittorio Klostermann Verlag, 2006), 341–351.

36. Charles Scawthorn, Thomas Denis O'Rourke, and F. T. Blackburn, "The 1906 San Francisco Earthquake and Fire: Enduring Lessons for Fire Protection and Water Supply," *Earthquake Spectra* 22, no. S2 (2006): 135–158, http://scawthornporter.com/documents /06Spectra1906SFEQandFire-EnduringLessonsCRSTDOFTB.pdf.

37. Total insurance premiums collected in the city of San Francisco between January

1 and June 30, 1907, was $3,876,430, as compared with $1,606,204 during the same period in 1905.

38. Tilmann J. Röder, "The Roots of the 'New Law Merchant': How the International Standardization of Contracts and Clauses Changed Business Law," October 4, 2006, forum historiae iuris, http://www.forhistiur.de/es/2006-10-roder/.

39. "Disaster: The Earthquake of 1907," Pieces of the Past, January 14, 2002, http://old.jamaica-gleaner.com/pages/history/story0017.html.

40. The local Jamaica Cooperative, with business foresight, made a compromise agreement around paying for fire claims (thus securing by its generosity "good will and future business"): shopkeepers agreed to pay one-third of their debts plus whatever share they received from any insurance settlement.

41. David Dutton, "The Strange Case of Edward Hemmerde," *Journal of Liberal History* 69 (Winter 2010–2011): 6–16; Frederick Edwin Smith Birkenhead, "Fire and Earthquake in Jamaica," in *Famous Trials of History* (London: Hutchinson, 1926), 245–256; Ansell Hart of Newport (Manchester) Jamaica, "Monthly Comments Jamaica," *West Indies* 6, nos. 17–19 (April–June 1969).

42. *Evening Post* 76, no. 106 (October 31, 1908): 15; *London Times*, August 1, 1908.

43. Charles D. James, *The 1923 Tokyo Earthquake and Fire* (Berkeley: University of California Press, 2002).

44. Takau Yoneyama, "The Great Kanto Earthquake and the Response of Insurance Companies: A Historical Lesson on the Impact of a Major Disaster," Hitotsubashi University, 2008, https://apebhconference.files.wordpress.com/2009/09/yoneyama-20081.pdf.

45. Ibid.

46. In 1914 German reinsurers had two-thirds of the global reinsurance market, but all trade ceased with France and Britain and, after 1917, also with the United States. In its place, many new reinsurers arose in countries uninvolved in the conflict, like Denmark and Switzerland. Russian reinsurers were successful in the United States until the 1917 revolution, after which only one Russian reinsurer remained.

47. "Mr. Baldwin on Aerial Warfare—A Fear for the Future," *The Times*, November 11, 1932.

48. A. Claire Cutler, Virginia Haufler, and Tony Porter, eds., *Private Authority and International Affairs* (Albany: State University of New York Press, 1999), 207.

49. "War Damage Insurance," *Yale Law Journal* 51, no. 7 (May 1942): 1160–1174, http://www.jstor.org/stable/792291?seq=1#page_scan_tab_contents; "War Damage Bill: House of Commons Debate, 12 February 1964 vol 689 cc 431–48," Hansard 1803–2005, http://hansard.millbanksystems.com/commons/1964/feb/12/war-damage-bill.

50. "Changes to Disaster Insurance in New Zealand," *Bulletin of the New Zealand National Society for Earthquake Engineering* 26, no. 4 (1993).

51. C. T. Lowndes & Company, "About Us," http://www.ctlowndes.com/about/about.htm; *A More Detailed History of C. T. Lowndes & Company* (Charleston, SC: C. T. Lowndes & Company, 2015); Richard J. Roth Sr. and Howard Kunreuther, eds., *Paying the Price: The Status and Role of Insurance Against Natural Disasters in the United States* (Washington, DC: Joseph Henry Press, 1998).

52. Oyugi Margaret Achieng, "Actuarial Modeling for Insurance Claim Severity in Motor Comprehensive Policy Using Industrial Statistical Distributions," presented at

International Congress of Actuaries, 2010, http://www.actuaries.org/EVENTS/Congresses
/Cape_Town/Papers/Non-Life%20Insurance%20(ASTIN)/22_final%20paper_Oyugi
.pdf.

CHAPTER 7: THE GARDEN OF THE FORKING PATHS

1. Jorge Luis Borges, *El Jardín de senderos que se bifurcan* (Buenos Aires: Editorial Sur, 1941), translated as "The Garden of Forking Paths," in *Ficciones*, translated by Andrew Hurley (London: Penguin Books, 1944), 75–86, http://www.coldbacon.com/writing /borges-garden.html.

2. The book was little noticed and soon went out of print. However, Borges wrote six more enigmatic short stories, and his publisher, considering them too meager for a separate compilation, added them to the original eight stories and changed the title of the collection to *Ficciones*. The book *El Jardín de senderos que se bifurcan* disappeared, its fork in the path of history ending in oblivion. Yet Borges as a writer had taken the first steps on a path that would lead to translation and international acclaim.

3. Sharon Ghamari-Tabrizi, *The Worlds of Herman Kahn: The Intuitive Science of Thermonuclear War* (Cambridge, MA: Harvard University Press, 2009).

4. Nicholas Metropolis, "The Beginning of the Monte Carlo Method," *Los Alamos Science* 15, no. 584 (1987): 125–130.

5. At RAND in Santa Monica, California, mathematicians worked alongside economists and strategy planners, employing probabilistic methods to consider strategic options, game theory, and the likely moves of the enemy.

6. Born in 1938 at Mobridge, South Dakota, C. Allin Cornell passed away on December 14, 2007. See Robin K. McGuire, Thomas C. Hanks, and Jack W. Baker, "C. Allin Cornell (1938–2007)," *Seismological Research Letters* 79, no. 3 (2008): 382–383.

7. Carl Allin Cornell, "Stochastic Processes in Civil Engineering," PhD thesis, Department of Civil Engineering, Stanford University, 1964. Cornell took up his first academic appointment at the Massachusetts Institute of Technology as a Ford Foundation Fellow and was promoted to a faculty appointment in 1966.

8. Paula Garb, "Critical Masses: Opposition to Nuclear Power in California, 1958–1978" (book review), *Journal of Political Ecology* 6 (1999).

9. National Research Council (United States), Committee on the Alaska Earthquake, *The Great Alaska Earthquake of 1964, Part 1* (Washington, DC: National Academies, 1968).

10. Arnold J. Meltsner, "The Communication of Scientific Information to a Wider Public: The Case of Seismology in California," *Minerva* 17 (1979): 331–354, 333.

11. Richard L. Meehan, *The Atom and the Fault: Experts, Earthquakes, and Nuclear Power* (Cambridge, MA: MIT Press, 1984).

12. Robin K. McGuire, "Probabilistic Seismic Hazard Analysis: Early History." *Earthquake Engineering and Structural Dynamics* 37, no. 3 (2008): 329–338.

13. C. Allin Cornell, "Engineering Seismic Risk Analysis," *Bulletin of the Seismological Society of America* 58, no. 5 (1968): 1583–1606.

14. Sylvester Theodore Algermissen and David M. Perkins, "A Probabilistic Estimate of Maximum Ground Acceleration in Rock in the Contiguous United States," US Geological Survey, Open-File Report 76-416, 1976.

15. However, Mexican researchers were the leaders in work to combine probabilistic thinking in mapped hazards, producing a probabilistic hazard map for Mexico in 1968. See Charles Scawthorn, "A Brief History of Seismic Risk Assessment," in *Risk Assessment, Modeling, and Decision Support: Strategic Directions*, edited by Ann Bostrom, Steven French, and Sara Gottlieb (Berlin: Springer Verlag, 2008), 1–70.

16. Thomas F. Malone, "The Travelers Weather Research Center," *Weatherwise* 7, no. 6 (1954): 159.

17. Don G. Friedman, "Insurance and the Natural Hazards," *ASTIN Bulletin: International Journal for Actuarial Studies in Non-Life Insurance and Risk Theory* 7, no. 1 (1972): 4–58.

18. Don G. Friedman, "Computer Simulation in Natural Hazard Assessment," Monograph NSF-RA-E-l S-002 (Boulder: University of Colorado, Program on Technology, Environment, and Man, 1975).

19. Richard W. Schwerdt, Francis P. Ho, and Roger R. Watkins, "Meteorological Criteria for Standard Project Hurricane and Probable Maximum Hurricane Windfields, Gulf and East Coasts of the United States," NOAA Technical Report NWS 23 (Washington, DC: US Department of Commerce, National Oceanic and Atmospheric Administration, 1979).

20. Francis P. Ho, J. C. Su, K. L. Hanevich, R. J. Smith, and F. P. Richards, "Hurricane Climatology for the Atlantic and Gulf Coasts of the United States," NOAA Technical Report NWS 38 (Washington, DC: US Department of Commerce, National Oceanic and Atmospheric Administration, 1987).

21. Art Jahnke, "The Acts of God Algorithm: Why the Insurance Industry Is Headed for the Perfect Storm," *Bostonia* (2010).

22. Don G. Friedman, "Natural Hazard Risk Assessment for an Insurance Program," *Geneva Risk and Insurance Review* 9, no. 30 (January 1984): 57–128, doi:10.1057/gpp.1984.4.

23. Karen M. Clark, "A Formal Approach to Catastrophe Risk Assessment and Management," *Proceedings of the Casualty Actuarial Society* 123, no. 140 (1986): 69–92.

24. James M. Gere and Haresh C. Shah, *Terra Non Firma: Understanding and Preparing for Earthquakes* (San Francisco: W. H. Freeman & Co., 1984).

25. Weimin Dong had been director of earthquake research for the Design Institute of the Ministry of Machine Building and had visited Tangshan to study building and equipment failures within ten days of the 1976 earthquake.

26. The project was sponsored by the Aetna insurance company and Salomon investment bank. See Patricia Grossi, Weimin Dong, and Auguste Boissonnade, "Evolution of Earthquake Risk Modeling," *Risk Management* 1 (2008): 1; also presented at the Fourteenth World Conference on Earthquake Engineering, Beijing (October 12–17, 2008). A summary of their work, published in June 1988, had Weimin Dong as the lead author on the article "A Knowledge-Based Seismic Risk Evaluation System for the Insurance and Investment Industries (IRAS)"; such a system could analyze earthquake losses probabilistically on individual buildings or portfolios of buildings. See Weimin Dong, John Eup Kim, Felix S. Wong, and Haresh Shah, "A Knowledge-Based Seismic Risk Evaluation System for the Insurance and Investment Industries (IRAS)," Technical Report 5 (Stanford, CA: Stanford University, Center for Integrated Facility Management, June 1988), http://cife.stanford.edu/sites/default/files/TR005.pdf.

27. Jahnke, "The Acts of God Algorithm."

28. Thomas Starner, "Model Citizen," *Risk and Insurance* (July 1, 2003), http://www.thefreelibrary.com/Model+citizen%3A+Hemant+Shah's+youthful+exterior+belies+a+very+smart...-a0105477038.

29. Andrew Duguid, *On the Brink: How a Crisis Transformed Lloyd's of London* (London: Palgrave Macmillan, 2014); Martin Mayer and Elizabeth Luessenhop, *Risky Business: An Insider's Account of the Disaster at Lloyd's of London* (New York: Scribner, 2010).

30. Lilla Zuill, "1993 Bermuda Cat Reinsurers Celebrate 1st Decade," *Property Casualty* 360 (August 27, 2003).

31. Tonkin & Taylor Ltd., "Liquefaction Vulnerability Study," report prepared for Earthquake Commission, February 2013, http://www.eqc.govt.nz/sites/public_files/documents/liquefaction-vulnerability-study-final.pdf.

32. Emanuela Guidoboni, Alberto Comastri, and Giusto Traina, *Catalogue of Ancient Earthquakes in the Mediterranean Area up to the 10th Century* (Bologna: Istituto Nazionale di Geofisica, 1994).

33. Auguste Boissonnade, "Modeling Demand Surge," Risk Assessment and Communication Workshop, Stanford University, Risk Management Solutions (2007).

34. Gordon Woo, *Calculating Catastrophe* (London: Imperial College Press, 2011).

35. Julian Bommer, et al., "Development of an Earthquake Loss Model for Turkish Catastrophe Insurance," *Journal of Seismology* 6, no. 3 (2002): 431–446.

36. Antonio R. T. Joyette, Leonard A. Nurse, and Roger S. Pulwarty, "Disaster Risk Insurance and Catastrophe Models in Risk-Prone Small Caribbean Islands," *Disasters* 39, no. 3 (2015): 467–492.

37. Dimitris Papachristou, "Statistical Analysis of the Spreads of Catastrophe Bonds at the Time of Issue," *ASTIN Bulletin: The Journal of the International Actuarial Association* 41, no. 1 (2011): 251–277.

38. Dante O. Portula and Reynaldo Vergara, "Case Study: The Philippine Experience on Microinsurance Market Development," for the Training Program of Insurance Supervisors in Asia, organized by Access to Insurance Initiative, AITRI, GIZ-RFPI, and Toronto Center, Manila, Philippines (August 2013).

39. William Dick and Andrea Stoppa, *Weather Index-Based Insurance in Agricultural Development: A Technical Guide*, prepared for the International Fund for Agricultural Development (IFAD) and World Food Program (WFP) Weather Risk Management Facility (WRMF) (2012).

40. Angelika Wirtz, Petra Löw, Thomas Mahl, and Sibel Yildirim, "Hitting the Poor: Public-Private Partnership as an Option," in *Extreme Natural Hazards, Disaster Risks, and Societal Implications*, edited by Alik Ismail-Zadeh et al. (Cambridge: Cambridge University Press, 2014), 386–398.

41. Kenneth R. Feinberg, Camille S. Biros, Jordana Harris Feldman, Deborah E. Greenspan, and Jacqueline E. Zins, *Final Report of the Special Master for the September 11th Victim Compensation Fund of 2001*, vol. 1 (Washington, DC: US Department of Justice, n.d.), http://www.glad.org/uploads/docs/history/pdfs/walsh-victim-fund-report_(1).pdf.

42. Robert P. Hartwig, "9/11 and Insurance: The Five Year Anniversary," Insurance Information Institute, September 2006, http://www.iii.org/sites/default/files/docs/pdf/September%2011%20Anniversary.pdf.

43. Elisabeth Bumiller, "Bush Pledges Federal Role in Rebuilding Gulf Coast," *New York Times*, September 16, 2005.

44. "New Orleans Betrayed," *Washington Post*, January 29, 2006.

45. Eugene Boyd, "Community Development Block Grant Funds in Disaster Relief and Recovery," Congressional Research Service, September 21, 2011, https://www.fas .org/sgp/crs/misc/RL33330.pdf.

46. "Testimony of Paul Rainwater, Executive Director of the Louisiana Recovery Authority, Before the US House Subcommittee on Housing and Community Opportunity, August 20, 2009," Louisiana Recovery Authority, http://archives.financialservices.house .gov/media/file/hearings/111/rainwater.pdf.

47. Bruce R. Lindsay and Justin Murray, "Disaster Relief Funding and Emergency Supplemental Appropriations," Congressional Research Service, April 12, 2011, https:// www.fas.org/sgp/crs/misc/R40708.pdf; Natalie Keegan, "The Louisiana Road Home Program: Federal Aid for State Disaster Housing Assistance Programs," Congressional Research Service, July 31, 2009, https://www.hsdl.org/?view&did=714345.

48. Peter J. Boyer, "The Bribe: How the Mississippi Lawyer Who Brought Down Big Tobacco Overstepped," *The New Yorker*, May 19, 2008.

49. On July 6, 2012, the president signed into law the Consumer Option for an Alternative System to Allocate Losses (COASTAL) Act of 2012, which authorizes FEMA to arrive at a formula for settling slab claims (now known as "indeterminate losses") to be based on "very sophisticated models," for which FEMA was to submit a plan to Congress in April 2013 for an operational system by December 28, 2013.

50. "Consumer Option for an Alternative System to Allocate Losses (COASTAL) Act Project Work Plan," USACE-USGS Coordination Meeting, January 17, 2014, http:// www.iwr.usace.army.mil/Portals/70/docs/projects/2014Jan17/COASTAL_Act_Pres _17Jan.pdf. The system was first exercised for Hurricane Erika in 2015, although the storm dissipated before reaching Florida. See "Federal Coordination and Planning for Meteorological Services and Supporting Research," http://www.ofcm.gov/homepage /text/FedCoordandPlanningFY2016.pdf.

51. Cassius Dio, *Roman History*, book LXVI, sections 21–24 (Cambridge, MA: Harvard University Press/Loeb Classical Library, 1925), 305–309.

52. John Eugene Haas and Robert S. Ayre, *The Western Sicily Earthquake of 1968: A Report* (Washington, DC: National Academy of Sciences, 1969); Giacomo Parrinello, *Fault Lines: Earthquakes and Urbanism in Modern Italy* (New York: Berghahn Books, 2015).

53. Half was spent on creating "a whole new class of social millionaires in the affected region," while one-sixth went to the Camorra and one-tenth to bribe local politicians. See Antonello Caporale, "Il Terremoto Infinito: Irpinia, 20 anni dopo," *La Repubblica*, December 13, 2004; Tom Behan, "The Administrative Economy and the 1980 Earthquake," in *The Camorra: Political Criminality in Italy* (London: Routledge, 1996), 59–74.

54. "1908 Summer Olympics," Wikipedia, https://en.wikipedia.org/wiki/1908 _Summer_Olympics (last modified February 5, 2016).

55. The French "Catastrophe Naturelle" system was funded, like the UK wartime bomb damage insurance, as a uniform-percentage "solidarity" charge on all fire insurance. See Véronique Bruggeman, *Compensating Catastrophe Victims: A Comparative Law and Economics Approach* (Alphen aan Den Rijn, Netherlands: Kluwer Law International, 2010), 302–314.

56. John M. Barry, *Rising Tide: The Great Mississippi Flood of 1927 and How It Changed America* (New York: Simon & Schuster, 2007).

57. Unnecessarily, as the river had already found a shorter route to the sea upstream.

58. Gilbert White, *Human Adjustments to Floods: A Geographical Approach to the Flood Problem in the United States* (Chicago: University of Chicago, 1945).

59. American Academy of Actuaries, Flood Insurance Subcommittee, *The National Flood Insurance Program: Past, Present . . . and Future?* (Washington, DC: American Academy of Actuaries, 2011).

60. "Testimony of J. Robert Hunter, Director of Insurance, Consumer Federation of America, Before the Committee on Banking, Housing, and Urban Affairs of the United States Senate Regarding Proposals to Reform the National Flood Insurance Program," February 2, 2006, https://www.gpo.gov/fdsys/pkg/CHRG-109shrg33994/html/CHRG-109shrg33994.htm.

61. Debbie Matz, "Guidance on Biggert-Waters Flood Insurance Reform Act of 2012" (Alexandria, VA: National Credit Union Administration, April 1, 2013).

62. Andrew G. Simpson, "House Passes Flood Insurance Bill; Key Senators Sign On," *Insurance Journal News*, March 4, 2014; Bruce Alpert, "Senate Passes Bill Averting Largest Flood Insurance Increases Under Biggert-Waters," *New Orleans Times-Picayune*, March 13, 2014.

63. Lynne McChristian, "Hurricane Andrew and Insurance: The Enduring Impact of an Historic Storm" (Tampa, FL: Insurance Information Institute, August 2012), 16, http://www.iii.org/sites/default/files/paper_HurricaneAndrew_final.pdf.

64. Charles Scawthorn, "Insurance Loss Estimation: Performance After the Northridge Earthquake," *Contingencies* (September–October 1995): 26–36.

65. Philip D. LeGrone, "An Analysis of Fire Sprinkler System Failures During the Northridge Earthquake and Comparison with the Seismic Design Standard for These Systems," Paper 2136, Thirteenth World Conference on Earthquake Engineering, Vancouver, BC, Canada (August 1–6, 2004), http://www.iitk.ac.in/nicee/wcee/article/13_2136.pdf.

66. Sebastian von Dahlen and Goetz von Peter, "Natural Catastrophes and Global Reinsurance—Exploring the Linkages," *BIS Quarterly Review* (December 2012): 23–35, http://www.bis.org/publ/qtrpdf/r_qt1212e.pdf.

67. The Florida Residential Property and Casualty Joint Underwriting Association (FRCJUA) later merged into Citizens Property Insurance Corporation.

68. To obtain a mortgage required that fire insurance (but strangely, not earthquake insurance) be in place on the property.

69. Consider the impact of a $100,000 loss on a $500,000 (rebuild value) property, from which the insured would only be compensated one-quarter of outlays, or $25,000. The California Earthquake Authority was a publicly managed but privately funded agency offering limited earthquake insurance coverage.

70. Erwann O. Michel-Kerjan, "Mortgages and Disasters: A Ticking Bomb?" presented at the conference "Managing Earthquake Shake," Washington, DC, September 26, 2014, http://biotech.law.lsu.edu/blog/Erwann-Michel-Kerjan_Mortgages-and-Disasters.pdf.

71. Rawle O. King, "The National Flood Insurance Program: Status and Remaining Issues for Congress," Congressional Research Service, February 6, 2013, http://fas.org/sgp/crs/misc/R42850.pdf; W. J. T. Mitchell, ed., *Landscape and Power* (Chicago: University of Chicago Press, 2002).

72. Erwann O. Michel-Kerjan, Coping with Extreme Events and Extra-ordinary Situations (personal blog), http://erwannmichelkerjan.com/did-you-know/; Howard C. Kunreuther and Erwann O. Michel-Kerjan, *At War with the Weather: Managing Large-Scale Risks in a New Era of Catastrophes* (Cambridge, MA: MIT Press, 2009).

73. Global Facility for Disaster Reduction and Recovery (GFDRR), "FONDEN: Mexico's National Disaster Fund: An Evolving Inter-Institutional Fund for Post-Disaster Expenditures," GFDRR Disaster Risk Financing and Insurance Case Study, January 2013, https://www.gfdrr.org/sites/gfdrr.org/files/documents/Mexico_FONDEN_final _GFDRR.pdf.

CHAPTER 8: INTOLERABLE RISK

1. Herman Pleij, *Hollands Welbehagen* (*The Well-being of Holland*) (Amsterdam: Ooievaar, 1998).

2. Sophie Thasing, "On terpen from Flanders up to Frisia: Two Maritime Regions from the Last Centuries BC Until the Late Middle Ages Compared," Vlaams Institut voor de Zee, 89–96, www.vliz.be/imisdocs/publications/252971.pdf.

3. G. J. Borger, "Draining—Digging—Dredging: The Creation of a New Landscape in the Peat Areas of the Low Countries," in *Fens and Bogs in the Netherlands: Vegetation, History, Nutrient Dynamics, and Conservation,* edited by Jos T. A. Verhoeven (Dordrecht, Netherlands: Kluwer Academic, 1992), 131–171.

4. TeBrake, "Taming the Waterwolf: Hydraulic Engineering and Water Management in the Netherlands During the Middle Ages"; Daniel R. Curtis and Michele Campopiano, "Medieval Land Reclamation and the Creation of New Societies: Comparing Holland and the Po Valley, c. 800–c. 1500," *Journal of Historical Geography* 44 (2014): 93–108.

5. Salvatore Ciriacono, "Venice and Holland: Amphibious States," in *Building on Water: Venice, Holland, and the Construction of the European Landscape in Early Modern Times,* translated by Jeremy Scott (New York: Berghahn, 2006), 157–193.

6. Borger, "Draining—Digging—Dredging," 49–50.

7. Jaap-Evert Abrahamse, Menne Kosian, and Henk Weerts, "The 'Amstel Canal' in Amsterdam Canal Construction as Part of the Medieval Reclamation and Drainage System of the Western Netherlands Wilderness," EGU 2013-10767, *Geophysical Research Abstracts* 15 (2013).

8. Tim Soens, "Flood Security in the Medieval and Early Modern North Sea Area: A Question of Entitlement?" *Environment and History* 19, no. 2 (2013): 209–232.

9. M. K. E. Gottschalk, *Stormvloeden en Rivieroverstromingen in Nederland,* 3 vols. (Assen, Netherlands: Van Gorcum & Comp. NV, 1971–1977); Adriaan de Kraker, "Storminess in the Low Countries, 1390–1725," *Environment and History* 19, no. 2 (2013): 149–171.

10. Richard S. J. Tol and Andreas Langen, "A Concise History of Riverine Floods and Flood Management in the Dutch Rhine Delta," *Climate Change* 46 (2000): 357–369.

11. Ibid.

12. L. C. Geerts, "The St. Elisabeth Flood of 1421 (November 18, 1421) or the Collapse of the Hollandsche Waard," http://geerts.com/dordrecht/st-elisabeth-flood -1421.

13. Robert J. Hoeksema, *Designed for Dry Feet: Flood Protection and Land Reclamation in the Netherlands* (Reston, VA: American Society of Civil Engineers, 2006).

14. R. Glaser and H. Stangl, "Historical Floods in the Dutch Rhine Delta," *Natural Hazards and Earth System Sciences* 3, no. 6 (2003): 605–613.

15. Andries Vierlingh, *Tractae van dyckagie*, edited by J. de Hullu and A.G. Verhoeven (1920; reprint, Den Haag, the Netherlands: Martinus Nijhoff, 2008), http://dbnl.org/tekst/vier004trac01_01/vier004trac01_01.pdf.

16. Andries Vierlingh advocated a patient approach because "water will not be compelled by any force or it will return that force unto you." He wrote that it was necessary to "direct the streams from the shore without vehemence. With subtlety and sweetness you may do much at low cost." Vierlingh, *Tractaet van dyckagie*.

17. "Jan Adriaanszoon Leeghwater: Developer of a System for Creating Agricultural Land from the Sea," The Robinson Library, http://www.robinsonlibrary.com/technology/engineering/biography/leeghwater.htm (last updated February 28, 2015).

18. Simon Schama, *The Embarrassment of Riches: An Interpretation of Dutch Culture in the Golden Age* (Berkeley: University of California Press, 1988).

19. "Water Management in the Netherlands" (Rijkswaterstaat Ministry of Infrastructure and the Environment, 2011), https://staticresources.rijkswaterstaat.nl/binaries/Water%20Management%20in%20the%20Netherlands_tcm21-37646.pdf.

20. Robert Slomp, "Flood Risk and Water Management in the Netherlands: A 2012 Update" (Rijkswaterstaat Ministry of Infrastructure and the Environment, 2012).

21. Michitaro Nakai, "The Outline of the River Law," Network of Asian River Basin Organizations (NARBO), http://www.narbo.jp/narbo/event/materials/twwa03/tw03_09_01-2.pdf.

22. "Makurazaki Typhoon," Bousai Prefecture, Hiroshima Disaster Prevention (website, in Japanese), http://www.bousai.pref.hiroshima.jp.e.bq.hp.transer.com/hdis/.

23. "1959 Super Typhoon Vera: 50-Year Retrospective: RMS Special Report" (London: Risk Management Solutions, 2009), http://forms2.rms.com/rs/729-DJX-565/images/tc_1959_super_typhoon_vera.pdf.

24. Yutaka Takahasi, "Flood Management in Japan During the Last Half-Century," Working Paper 1/2011 (Singapore: Institute of Water Policy, June 2011), http://lkyspp.nus.edu.sg/iwp/wp-content/uploads/sites/3/2013/04/201106_Takahasi-IWP_WP_01.pdf; "Typhoon Vera," Wikipedia, https://en.wikipedia.org/wiki/Typhoon_Vera (last modified February 7, 2016).

25. National Land Agency, Japan, "Disaster Counter Measures Basic Act" (Act No. 223, November 15, 1961) (provisional translation), June 1997, http://www.adrc.asia/documents/law/DisasterCountermeasuresBasicAct.pdf.

26. Tom Mitchell, Debarati Guha-Sapir, Julia Hall, Emma Lovell, Robert Muir-Wood, Alastair Norris, Lucy Scott, and Pascaline Wallemacq, "Setting, Measuring and Monitoring Targets for Reducing Disaster Risk: Recommendations for Post-2015 International Policy Frameworks" (London: Overseas Development Institute, October 2014), figures 15–20, http://www.odi.org/sites/odi.org.uk/files/odi-assets/publications-opinion-files/9215.pdf.

27. Associated Programme on Flood Management (APFM), "Integrated Flood Management Case Study, Japan: Tokai Heavy Rain (September 2000)" (World Mete-

orological Organization and Global Water Partnership APFM, January 2004), http://www.apfm.info/publications/casestudies/cs_japan_full.pdf.

28. Teruko Sato, "Fundamental Characteristics of Flood Risk in Japan's Urban Areas," in *A Better Integrated Management of Disaster Risks: Toward Resilient Society to Emerging Disaster Risks in Mega-cities*, edited by S. Ikeda, T. Fukuzono, and Teruko Sato (Tokyo: Terra Scientific Publishing Company and NIED, 2006), 23–40, http://www.terrapub.co.jp/e-library/nied/pdf/023.pdf.

29. Stephen Tobriner, *The Genesis of Noto: An Eighteenth-Century Sicilian City* (Berkeley: University of California Press, 1982).

30. Ibid.; Stephen Tobriner, "Safety and Reconstruction of Noto After the Sicilian Earthquake of 1693: The Eighteenth-Century Context," in *Dreadful Visitations: Confronting Natural Catastrophe in the Age of Enlightenment*, edited by Alessa Johns (New York: Routledge, 1999): 49–80.

31. Tobriner, *The Genesis of Noto*; M. S. Barbano, et al. "Seismic History and Hazard in Some Localities of South-eastern Sicily," *Bollettino di Geofisica Teorica ed Applicata* 42, nos. 1–2 (2001): 107–120.

32. Tobriner, *The Genesis of Noto*.

33. Stephen Tobriner, "Building the Cathedral of Noto: Earthquakes, Reconstruction, and Building Practice in 18th-Century Sicily," *Construction and Building Materials* 17, no. 8 (2003): 521–532; S. Tringali, R. de Benedictis, C. Gavarini, and Rosanna La Rosa, "The Cathedral of Noto: From the Analysis of the Collapse to the Restoration and Reconstruction Project," *Proceedings of the UNESCO/ICOMOS International Millennium Congress Archi*, Paris (2000), http://www.unesco.org/archi2000/pdf/tringali.pdf.

34. David Marley, *Historic Cities of the Americas: An Illustrated Encyclopedia*, vol. 2, *North America and South America* (Santa Barbara, CA: ABC-CLIO, 2005).

35. Vicente Carvallo Goyeneche, *Descripción Histórico Geográfica del reino de Chile*, vol. 2, ch. 87, written between 1780 and 1796, published in 1875, available at Fuentes documentales y bibliográficas para el estudio de la historia de Chile, Universidad de Chile, Santiago, http://www.historia.uchile.cl/CDA/fh_complex/0,1393,SCID%253D7181%2526ISID%253D404%2526JNID%253D12,00.html.

36. "1939 Chillán Earthquake," Wikipedia, https://en.wikipedia.org/wiki/1939_Chill%C3%A1n_earthquake (last modified July 13, 2015).

37. Elizabeth Bell, *Antigua Guatemala: The City and Its Heritage* (La Antigua, Guatemala: Antigua Tours, 1999).

38. Julio Galicia Díaz, *Destrucción y traslado de la ciudad de Santiago de Guatemala*, no. 4 (Guatemala City: Editorial Universitaria, 1976).

39. "1773 Guatemala Earthquake," Wikipedia, https://en.wikipedia.org/wiki/1773_Guatemala_earthquake (last modified December 5, 2015).

40. Mauricio A. Pajon, "Building Opportunity: Disaster Response and Recovery After the 1773 Earthquake in Antigua Guatemala," PhD thesis, University of Texas at Austin, 2013 http://repositories.lib.utexas.edu/bitstream/handle/2152/21159/PAJON-DISSERTATION-2013.pdf?sequence=1; Juan González Bustillo, *Extracto, ô relacion methodica, y puntual de los autos de reconocimiento, praticado en virtud de comission del señor presidente de la real audiencia de este reino de Guatemala* (Mixco: Antonio Sánchez Cubillas, 1774), 13–14.

41. Díaz, *Destrucción y traslado*.

42. Pajon, *Building Opportunity*, 50.

43. "Antigua Guatemala," UNESCO, World Heritage Convention, http://whc.unesco.org/en/list/65.

44. Marshall H. Saville, "The Guatemala Earthquake of December, 1917, and January, 1918," *Geographical Review* 5, no. 6 (1918): 459–469.

45. Mark Alan Healey, "The 'Superstition of Adobe' and the Certainty of Concrete: Shelter and Power After the 1944 San Juan Earthquake in Argentina," in Buchenau and Johnson, *Aftershocks*, 100–128.

46. D. E. E. Braman, *Braman's Information About Texas: Carefully Prepared* (Philadelphia: J. B. Lippincott & Co., 1858).

47. Erik Larson, *Isaac's Storm: A Man, a Time, and the Deadliest Hurricane in History* (New York: Crown Publishers, 1999).

48. Ibid.

49. Jodi Wright-Gidley and Jennifer Marines, *Galveston: A City on Stilts* (Charleston, SC: Arcadia Publishing, 2008).

50. Muhammad Sadaqat, "Balakot City: A Tale of the Forgotten Town," *Express Tribune*, October 8, 2012; Zhu Ziyu, Li Ming, and Huang Shuo, "Post-Quake Reconstruction Planning and Implementation for Beichuan New Town," presented at Forty-Eighth International Society of City and Regional Planners (ISOCARP) Congress, Perm, Russia (September 10–13, 2012), http://www.isocarp.net/Data/case_studies/2149.pdf.

51. P. Abercrombie, "Wren's Plan for London After the Great Fire," *Town Planning Review* 10, no. 2 (1923): 71–78.

52. Stephen Porter, *The Great Fire of London* (Stroud, Gloucestershire, UK: The History Press, 2011).

53. Sir Christopher Wren, Christopher Wren Jr., and Stephen Wren, *Parentalia: or, Memoirs of the family of the Wrens … Chiefly of Sir Christopher Wren* (London: T. Osborn and R. Dodsley, 1750), 269.

54. "Charles II, 1670: An Additionall, Act for the rebuilding of the Citty of London, uniteing of Parishes and rebuilding of the Cathedrall and Parochiall Churches within the said City," *Statutes of the Realm*, vol. 5, *1628–1680*, edited by John Raithby (London: Great Britain Record Commission, 1819), 665–682, British History Online, http://www.british-history.ac.uk/statutes-realm/vol5/pp603-612.

55. Angela Delaforce, "The Dream of a Young Architect: Robert Adam and a Project for the Rebuilding of Lisbon in 1755," in *Portugal e o Reino Unido: A Aliança Revisitada* (Lisbon: Fundação Calouste Gulbenkian, 1995), 56–60; Robert Cherny, "Burnham Plan 1905: Historical Essay," FoundSF, http://foundsf.org/index.php?title=Burnham_Plan_1905.

56. Stefano Condorelli, "The Reconstruction of Catania After the Earthquake of 1693," *Proceedings of the Second International Congress on Construction History* 1 (2006): 799–816.

57. Named after José de la Guerra, former commandant of the Presidio in Santa Barbara (before California passed into American hands in 1846). See Neal Graffy, "The Great Santa Barbara Earthquake—The Disaster That Built a City: Day 3," *Santa Barbara Edhat*, July 1, 2010.

58. The advisory committee came up with a set of proposed new Spanish-style facades for State Street stores.

59. Steven Brooke, *Miami Beach Deco* (New York: Universe Publishing, 2011).

60. John Annabell, "Napier After the Earthquake: Reconstruction and Planning in the 1930s," *Planning Quarterly* 162 (2006): 2–7.

61. "Gibellina," SYNCHRONICITY (blog), May 10, 2009, http://synccity.blogspot .co.uk/2009/05/gibellina.html.

62. Harry O. Wood, "Preliminary Report on the Long Beach Earthquake," *Bulletin of the Seismological Society of America* 23, no: 2 (1933): 44–56; Maureen K. Fleury, "The Long Beach Earthquake 1933," May 20, 2009, http://www.suite101.com/content/the -long-beach-earthquake-1933-a118990#ixzz1AN5Xq05v; Susan Fatemi and Charles James, "The Long Beach Earthquake of 1933," National Information Service for Earthquake Engineering, University of California at Berkeley, http://nisee.berkeley.edu/long _beach/long_beach.html (updated December 8, 1997).

63. Alfred E. Alquist, "The Field Act and Public School Construction: A 2007 Perspective," California Seismic Safety Commission, February 2007, http://www.seismic .ca.gov/pub/CSSC_2007-03_Field_Act_Report.pdf.

64. National Clearinghouse for Educational Facilities (NCEF), "Earthquakes and Schools," NCEF, 2008, appendix B, http://www.ncef.org/pubs/earthquakes.pdf.

65. Shinzo Abe, statement made at the opening ceremony of the Third UN World Conference on Disaster Risk Reduction, Sendai, Japan (March 14, 2015).

66. Nicola Alessandro Pino, et al., "The 28 December 1908 Messina Straits Earthquake (Mw 7.1): A Great Earthquake Throughout a Century of Seismology," *Seismological Research Letters* 80, no. 2 (2009): 243–259.

67. Giacomo Parrinello, "The 1908 Messina Earthquake," in Parrinello, *Fault Lines*, 21–50.

68. M. S. Teramo, et al., "A Damage Scenario for the City of Messina, Italy, Using Displacement-Based Loss Assessment," presented at the Fourteenth World Conference on Earthquake Engineering, Beijing (October 12–17, 2008), http://www.iitk.ac.in/nicee /wcee/article/14_07-0023.PDF.

69. Richard V. Lee, "Darwin's Earthquake," *Revista Médica de Chile* 138 (2010): 897–901, http://www.scielo.cl/pdf/rmc/v138n7/art16.pdf.

70. Renee Salanders, "First Hand Account of Chilean Earthquake," *Oklahoma Daily*, March 1, 2010.

71. Francisco Medina, Peter I. Yanev, and Alexander P. Yanev, "The Magnitude 8.8 Offshore Maule Region Chile Earthquake of February 27, 2010: Preliminary Summary of Damage and Engineering Recommendations: A Report to the World Bank" (Berkeley: University of California, 2010).

72. D. E. Alexander, "Mortality and Morbidity Risk in the L'Aquila, Italy, Earthquake of 6 April 2009 and Lessons to Be Learned," in *Advances in Natural and Technological Hazards Research*, no. 29, *Human Casualties in Earthquakes*, edited by Robin S. Spence, Emily So, and Charles Scawthorn (Berlin: Springer, 2011).

73. Of the mortgaged residential properties in Chile, 96 percent had insurance against earthquakes in 2010. Michael Useem, Howard Kunreuther, and Erwann Michel-Kerjan, "From Nepal Quake, Lessons for the US," *Philadelphia Inquirer*, April 27, 2015.

74. "Chile Sacks Oceanography Chief over Failure to Issue Tsunami Warnings," *The Telegraph*, March 6, 2010.

75. Oliver L. Fassig, "San Felipe—The Hurricane of September 13, 1928, at San Juan, PR," *Monthly Weather Review* (September 1928): 350–352.

76. Jorge Ortiz Colom, "The Essence of Puerto Rican Historic Architecture." Academia.edu, January 24, 2003, Instituto de Cultura Puertorriqueña, http://www.academia.edu/1502878/The_Essence_of_Puerto_Rican_Historic_Architecture.

77. James R. Beverley, "Excerpts from the Thirty-Third Annual Report of the Governor of Puerto Rico (1933)," 1–6, New Deal Network, http://newdeal.feri.org/pr/pr12.htm.

78. E. J. Humphreys, ed., "West Indian Hurricanes of August and September, 1932," *Monthly Weather Review* 60, no. 9 (September 1932): 177–178, http://docs.lib.noaa.gov/rescue/mwr/060/mwr-060-09-0177.pdf.

79. Starting with the construction of rows of identical 900-square-foot concrete buildings on the old San Patricio farm south of San Juan Bay. Arq. Jorge Ortiz Colom, "The Essence of Puerto Rican Historic Architecture," P&S: Patrimonio y Sociedad, June 6, 2005, http://patrimonioysociedad.blogspot.co.uk/2005/06/essence-of-puerto-rican-historic.html.

80. Jan Geraets, "Hurricanes on Saint Martin: The Constitutional Impact of Hurricanes in the Lesser Antilles in a Comparative Perspective," master's thesis, Department of History, Leiden University (2012).

CHAPTER 9: THE DISASTER FORECAST

1. Jón Frímann, "Small Streams Around Hekla Volcano Dry Up," Earth Changes and the Pole Shift, November 29, 2010, http://poleshift.ning.com/profiles/blogs/small-streams-around-hekla.

2. Floyd W. McCoy and Grant Heiken, eds., *Volcanic Hazards and Disasters in Human Antiquity*, vol. 345 (Boulder, CO: Geological Society of America, 2000).

3. Angelo Heilprin, *Mont Pelée and the Tragedy of Martinique: A Study of the Great Catastrophes of 1902, with Observations and Experiences in the Field* (Philadelphia: J. B. Lippincott Co., 1903); Alwyn Scarth, *La Catastrophe: The Eruption of Mount Pelée, the Worst Volcanic Eruption of the Twentieth Century* (Oxford: Oxford University Press, 2002).

4. Jelle Zeilinga De Boer and Donald Theodore Sanders, "The 1902 Eruption of Mount Pelée: A Geological Catastrophe with Political Overtones," in Jelle Zeilinga De Boer and Donald Theodore Sanders, *Volcanoes in Human History: The Far-Reaching Effects of Major Eruptions* (Princeton, NJ: Princeton University Press, 2002), 186–208.

5. Alwyn Scarth, "Montagne Pelée, 1902," in Alwyn Scarth, *Vulcan's Fury: Man Against the Volcano* (New Haven, CT: Yale University Press, 1999), 156–189.

6. Basse-Terre is also the highest point in the Lesser Antilles. François Beauducel, "À Propos de la Polémique '*Soufrière 1976*,'" IPGP.fr, August 2006, http://www.ipgp.fr/~beaudu/soufriere/forum76.html.

7. Noel-Jean Bergeroux, "La Soufrière ne constitue plus un danger pour les populations environnantes," *Le Monde*, July 18, 1976, http://www.ipgp.fr/~beaudu/soufriere/1976-07-18_LeMonde.jpg.

8. "Le Processus est irréversible, nous courons à la catastrophe, déclare le professeur Brousse," *France Antilles*, August 16, 1976, http://www.ipgp.fr/~beaudu/soufriere/1976-08-16_FranceAntilles_3.jpg.

9. Dominique Pouchin, "M. Haroun Tazieff à la Guadeloupe: Il ne faut pas manquer

de sang-froid," *Le Monde*, August 31, 1976, http://www.ipgp.fr/~beaudu/soufriere/1976 -08-31_LeMonde.jpg.

10. Haroun Tazieff, "La Soufrière et la prévision volcanologique," *Le Monde*, October 6, 1976, http://www.ipgp.fr/~beaudu/soufriere/1976-10-06_LeMonde.jpg.

11. Alexander McBirney, "Obituary: Haroun Tazieff (1914–98)," *Nature* 392, no. 6675 (1998): 444.

12. Beauducel, "À Propos de la polémique."

13. Alwyn Scarth, "Nevado del Ruiz," in Scarth, *Vulcan's Fury*, 226–243.

14. Dick Thompson, "After Armero," in Dick Thompson, *Volcano Cowboys: The Rocky Evolution of a Dangerous Science* (New York: Macmillan, 2002), 180–205.

15. C. Dominik Güss and Oliver I. Pangan, "Cultural Influences on Disaster Management: A Case Study of the Mt. Pinatubo Eruption," *International Journal of Mass Emergencies and Disasters* 22, no. 2 (August 2004): 31–58, http://www.ijmed.org /articles/383/download/.

16. Alwyn Scarth, "Pinatubo, 1991," in Scarth, *Vulcan's Fury*, 254–273.

17. Tim Weiner, "Mexicans Resist Flight from 'Friendly' Volcano," *New York Times*, December 19, 2000.

18. Erik Klemetti, "World's Most Dangerous Volcano May Kill Another City," *Wired*, July 29, 2015, http://www.wired.com/2015/07/worlds-dangerous-volcano-threatens -huge-city/; S. Judenherc and A. Zollo, "The Bay of Naples (Southern Italy): Constraints on the Volcanic Structures Inferred from a Dense Seismic Survey," *Journal of Geophysical Research* 109 (2004): B10312, http://people.na.infn.it/~zollo/articoli/JGR _2004_a/2003JB002876.pdf.

19. "2001 Vesuvius Emergency Plan (Updated in 2007)," Protezione Civile, http:// www.protezionecivile.gov.it/jcms/en/view_pde.wp;jsessionid=3DDAFAE6B2D6096 A41CF68577C44324F?contentId=PDE12771.

20. B. De Vivo, G. Rolandi, P. B. Gans, A. Calvert, W. A. Bohrson, F. J. Spera, and H. E. Belkin, "New Constraints on the Pyroclastic Eruptive History of the Campanian Volcanic Plain (Italy)," *Mineralogy and Petrology* 73, no. 1 (November 2001): 47–65, http://link.springer.com/article/10.1007%2Fs007100170010; Kathryn E. Fitzsimmons, Ulrich Hambach, Daniel Veres, and Radu Iovita, "The Campanian Ignimbrite Eruption: New Data on Volcanic Ash Dispersal and Its Potential Impact on Human Evolution," *PLoS ONE* 8, no. 6 (2013): e65839, doi:10.1371/journal.pone.0065839, http://www .plosone.org/article/info%3Adoi%2F10.1371%2Fjournal.pone.0065839; Richard V. Fisher, Giovanni Orsi, Michael Ort, and Grant Heiken, "Mobility of a Large-Volume Pyroclastic Flow—Emplacement of the Campanian Ignimbrite, Italy," *Journal of Volcanology and Geothermal Research* 56 (1993): 205–220, http://volcanology.geol.ucsb .edu/camptuff.htm; Antonio Costa, et al., "Quantifying Volcanic Ash Dispersal and Impact of the Campanian Ignimbrite Super-eruption," *Geophysical Research Letters* 39 (2012), http://www.academia.edu/421040/Quantifying_volcanic_ash_dispersal_and _impact_of_the_Campanian_Ignimbrite_super-eruption.

21. John F. Hoffecker, Vance T. Holliday, M. V. Anikovich, A. A. Sinitsyn, V. V. Popov, S. N. Lisitsyn, G. M. Levkovskaya, G. A. Pospelova, Steven L. Forman, and Biagio Giaccio, "From the Bay of Naples to the River Don: The Campanian Ignimbrite Eruption and the Middle to Upper Paleolithic Transition in Eastern Europe," *Journal of Human Evolution* 55

(2008): 858–870, http://www.geos.ed.ac.uk/~nabo/meetings/glthec/materials/hoffecker/Hoffeckeretal2008.pdf.

22. John Guest, Paul Cole, Angus Duncan, and David Chester, *Volcanoes of Southern Italy* (London: Geological Society, 2003).

23. Yoshiyuki Tatsumi and Keiko Suzuki-Kamata, "Cause and Risk of Catastrophic Eruptions in the Japanese Archipelago," *Proceedings of the Japan Academy*, series B, 90 (2014): 347–352, https://www.jstage.jst.go.jp/article/pjab/90/9/90_PJA9009B-01/_pdf.

24. Laurent Dubois, *Haiti: The Aftershocks of History* (New York: Metropolitan Books, 2012), 335–336.

25. K. E. Bullen, "Imamura, Akitsune," in *Dictionary of Scientific Biography*, vol. 7 (New York: Charles Scribner's Sons, 1970–1980), 9–10.

26. In 1900 Ōmori identified the next likely earthquake locations in southern Italy (adjacent to those that had already happened): in Messina and in the Avezzano region—events that duly arrived in 1908 and 1915.

27. Charles Davison, "Fusakichi Ōmori and His Work on Earthquakes." *Bulletin of the Seismological Society of America* 14 (1924): 240–255.

28. Ōmori, "Tokyo Observations of the Strong Earthquake on Jan. 14, 1923," IEIC, *Seismological Notes*, no. 6 (Tokyo, 1924), 10.

29. Carl-Henry Geschwind, "1920s Prediction Reveals Some Pitfalls of Earthquake Forecasting," *EOS: Transactions of the American Geophysical Union*, September 2, 1997.

30. Bailey Willis, "Earthquake Risk in California," *Bulletin of the Seismological Society of America* 14 (1924): 21–23.

31. Geschwind, "1920s Prediction Reveals . . . "

32. Robert T. Hill, *Southern California Geology and Los Angeles Earthquakes, with an Introduction to the Physical Geography of the Region* (Los Angeles: Southern California Academy of Sciences, 1928).

33. Robert O. Castle, et al. "Elevation Changes Preceding the San Fernando Earthquake of February 9, 1971," *Geology* 2, no. 2 (1974): 61–66.

34. Max Wyss, "Interpretation of the Southern California Uplift in Terms of the Dilatancy Hypothesis," *Nature* 266 (1977): 805–808; Robert O. Castle, Jack P. Church, and Michael R. Elliott, "Aseismic Uplift in Southern California," *Science* 192, no. 4236 (1976): 251–253; Richard A. Kerr, "Palmdale Bulge Doubts Now Taken Seriously," *Science* 14, no. 4527 (1981): 1331–1333. "Earthquake prediction, long treated as the seismological family's weird uncle, has in the last few years become everyone's favorite nephew"; quoted in "Can We Predict the Coming California Earthquake?" *Popular Science* (November 1976): 79–82.

35. Kelin Wang, Qi-Fu Chen, Shihong Sun, and Andong Wang, "Predicting the 1975 Haicheng Earthquake," *Bulletin of the Seismological Society of America* 96, no. 3 (2006): 757–795; "China Says She Predicted Big Quake," *New York Times*, March 1, 1975.

36. Liu Huixian, et al., "The Great Tangshan Earthquake of 1976: Overview Volume" (Pasadena: California Institute of Technology, Earthquake Engineering Research Laboratory, 2002), http://authors.library.caltech.edu/26539/1/Tangshan/Overview.pdf.

37. Aberto A. Giesecke, "Case History of the Peru Prediction of 1980–81," http://www.desastres.hn/docum/crid/Septiembre-Octubre2005/CD-1/pdf/eng/doc15925/doc15925-contenido.pdf; Richard S. Olson, Bruno Podesta, and Joanne M. Nigg, *The Politics of Earthquake Prediction* (Princeton, NJ: Princeton University Press, 1989).

38. William H. Bakun, et al. "Implications for Prediction and Hazard Assessment from the 2004 Parkfield Earthquake," *Nature* 437, no. 7061 (2005): 969–974; William H. Bakun and Allan G. Lindh, "The Parkfield, California, Earthquake Prediction Experiment," *Science* 229, no. 4714 (1985): 619–624.

39. Richard A. Kerr, "Seismic Crystal Ball Proving Mostly Cloudy Around the World," *Science* 332, no. 6032 (2011): 912–913; Nicola Nosengo, "Scientists on Trial over L'Aquila Deaths," *Nature* 474, no. 7349 (2011): 15.

40. "Stephen S. Hall, "Scientists on Trial: At Fault?" *Nature News* 477, no. 7364 (2011): 264–269.

41. Nicola Nosengo "New Twists in Italian Seismology Trial: Californian Scientist Testifies Against Defendants in Quake Manslaughter Case," *Nature*, February 16, 2012, doi:doi:10.1038/nature.2012.10049.

42. W. Jason Morgan, "Rises, Trenches, Great Faults, and Crustal Blocks," *Journal of Geophysical Research* 73, no. 6 (1968): 1959–1982, doi:10.1029/JB073i006p01959.

43. Kunihiko Shimazaki, "The Giant Tsunami Had Been Foreseen, but Not Been Included in Disaster Design," translated from the Japanese by Taku Tada, *Kagaku (Science Journal)* 81, no. 10 (October 2011): 1002–1006.

44. Larry J. Ruff and Hiroo Kanamori, "Seismicity and the Subduction Process." *Physics of the Earth and Planetary Interiors* 23 (1980): 240–252.

45. Seth Stein and Emile A. Okal, "The 2004 Sumatra Earthquake and Indian Ocean Tsunami: What Happened and Why?" *The Earth Scientist* (National Earth Sciences Teachers Association) 21, no. 2 (2005): 6–11, http://www.earth.northwestern.edu/public/seth/research/nestasumatra.pdf.

46. The *Nihon Sandai Jitsuroku (The True History of Three Reigns of Japan)*, also known as *Sandai Jitsuroku*, was an official history written in AD 901 and covering the period AD 858–887.

47. Yuki Sawai, Yushiro Fujii, Osamu Fujiwara, Takanobu Kamataki, Junko Komatsubara, Yukinobu Okamura, Kenji Satake, and Masanobu Shishikura, "Marine Incursions of the Past 1,500 Years and Evidence of Tsunamis at Suijin-numa, a Coastal Lake Facing the Japan Trench," *The Holocene* 18, no. 4 (2008): 517–528.

48. "Was 869 Tohoku Quake Japan's Strongest?" *National Daily Yomi*, October 12, 2007.

49. Jogan was the era of the emperor who ruled Japan when the tsunami hit and Sanriku the name for this section of coastline.

50. K. Satake, Y. Sawai, M. Shishikura, Y. Okamura, Y. Namegaya, and S. Yamaki, "Tsunami Source of the Unusual AD 869 Earthquake Off Miyagi, Japan, Inferred from Tsunami Deposits and Numerical Simulation of Inundation," abstract T31G-03, presented at the fall 2007 meeting of the American Geophysical Union, http://adsabs.harvard.edu/abs/2007AGUFM.T31G..03S.

51. Eric Talmadge, "Quake-Damaged Nuclear Plant in Japan Shut, Leak Worse Than Thought; Auto Plants Closed," Associated Press, July 18, 2007.

52. "Japanese Nuclear Plant's Evaluators Cast Aside Threat of Tsunami," *Washington Post*, March 23, 2011.

53. S. Fraser, G. S. Leonard, I. Matsuo, and H. Murakami, "Tsunami Evacuation: Lessons from the Great East Japan Earthquake and Tsunami of March 11th 2011," GNS Science Report 2012/17, April 2012, http://crew.org/sites/default/files/SR%202012-017.pdf.

54. Lucy Birmingham, "Japan's Earthquake Warning System Explained," *Time*, March 18, 2011.

55. Tomomi Sasaki, "Japan: Not That Sound Again," Global Voices, March 14, 2011, http://globalvoicesonline.org/2011/03/14/japan-not-that-sound-again/.

CHAPTER 10: SAVE OUR SOULS

1. If you know your location is completely safe, the earthquake ride can be pleasurable, as on April 18, 1906, for Grove Karl Gilbert, who was "awakened in Berkeley . . . by a tumult of motions and noises, it was with unalloyed pleasure that I became aware that a vigorous earthquake was in progress." See Grove Karl Gilbert, "The Investigation of the California Earthquake," in Jordan et al., *The California Earthquake*, 215–261.

2. "How to Protect Yourself During an Earthquake . . . Drop, Cover, and Hold On!" Earthquake Country Alliance, http://www.earthquakecountry.org/dropcoverholdon/.

3. Joshua Hammer, *Yokohama Burning: The Deadly 1923 Earthquake and Fire That Helped Forge the Path to World War II* (New York: Simon and Schuster, 2006).

4. Following the Spitak, Armenia, earthquake of 1988, those who ran outside after the first shock suffered only one-quarter of the level of injuries of those who stayed inside. Haroutune K. Armenian, et al., "Deaths and Injuries Due to the Earthquake in Armenia: A Cohort Approach," *International Journal of Epidemiology* 26, no. 4 (1997): 806–813.

5. Otto W. Nuttli, Gilbert A. Bollinger, and Robert B. Herrmann, "The 1886 Charleston, South Carolina, Earthquake: A 1986 Perspective" (Reston, VA: US Geological Survey, 1986), http://pubs.usgs.gov/circ/1986/0985/report.pdf.

6. "Phenomena of the Great Earthquake of 1783 in Calabria and Sicily: From the Journal of a Traveller," *Blackwood's* 26, no. 160 (1829): 879–894.

7. J. Whittaker, B. McLennan, and J. Handmer, "A Review of Informal Volunteerism in Emergencies and Disasters: Definition, Opportunities, and Challenges," *International Journal of Disaster Risk Reduction* 13 (September 2015): 358–368.

8. M. O'Leary, *The First 72 Hours: A Community Approach to Disaster Preparedness* (Lincoln, NE: iUniverse Publishing, 2004); Rebecca Solnit, *A Paradise Built in Hell: The Extraordinary Communities That Arise in Disasters* (New York: Penguin, 2010).

9. Michel Lechat, "Corporal Damage as Related to Building Structure and Design, the Seed for an International Survey," presented at the International Workshop for Earthquake Epidemiology for Mitigation and Response, Baltimore (July 10–12, 1989).

10. Eric K. Noji, ed., *The Public Health Consequences of Disasters* (Oxford: Oxford University Press, 1997), 162.

11. Mark Twain, *Roughing It* (Hartford, CT: American Publishing Co., 1872), ch. 58.

12. Wang Zixing, Cui Xifu, and Liu Kerenm, "Earthquake Relief and Reconstruction of Tangshan: Disaster Relief After the Tangshan Earthquake," in *The Great Tangshan Earthquake of 1976*, vol. 3 (Pasadena: California Institute of Technology, Earthquake Engineering Laboratory, 2002), 747–837, http://authors.library.caltech.edu/26539/1/TangshanEQRept.htm.

13. A. G. Macintyre, J. A. Barbera, and E. R. Smith, "Surviving Collapsed Structure Entrapment After Earthquakes: A 'Time-to-Rescue' Analysis," *Prehospital and Disaster Medicine* 21, no. 1 (2006): 4–19.

14. Z. Sheng, "Medical Support in the Tangshan Earthquake: A Review of the Management of Mass Casualties and Certain Major Injuries," *Journal of Trauma* 27 (1987): 1130–1137.

15. The same signs were termed "muscle crush syndrome" by doctors trying to save those trapped beneath collapsed buildings in the 1940 London Blitz. See E. G. L. Bywaters, "Crushing Injury," *British Medical Journal* (November 28, 1942): 643–646.

16. I. Ashkenazi, B. Isakovich, Y. Kluger, R. Alfici, B. Kessel, and O. S. Better, "Prehospital Management of Earthquake Casualties Buried Under Rubble," *Prehospital and Disaster Medicine* 20, no. 2 (2005): 122–133.

17. Marizen Ramirez and Corinne Peek-Asa, "Epidemiology of Traumatic Injuries from Earthquakes," *Epidemiologic Reviews* 27, no. 1 (July 2005): 47–55; E. Noji, G. Kelen, H. Armenian, et al., "The 1988 Earthquake in Soviet Armenia: A Case Study," *Annals of Emergency Medicine* 19, no. 8 (1990): 891–897; S. Pocan, S. Ozkan, M. H. Us, et al., "Crush Syndrome and Acute Renal Failure in the Marmara Earthquake," *Military Medicine* 167, no. 6 (2002): 516–518.

18. Keith Porter, Lucile Jones, Dale Cox, James Goltz, Ken Hudnut, et al., "The ShakeOut Scenario: A Hypothetical Mw7.8 Earthquake on the Southern San Andreas Fault," Paper 189, CREATE Homeland Security Center Research Archive 5-2011.

19. In the Great Fire of Moscow of 1571, wind blew fire into the city, and the palace and suburbs all burned down within six hours, with casualties estimated at more than 10,000.

20. Stuart McCook, "God and Nation in Revolutionary Venezuela: The Holy Thursday Earthquake of 1812," in Buchenau and Johnson, *Aftershocks*, 43–69.

21. Quinn Dauer, "Natural Disasters and Comparative State Formation and Nation-Building: Earthquakes in Argentina and Chile (1822–1939)," Paper 764, PhD diss., Florida International University, 2012, http://digitalcommons.fiu.edu/etd/764; C. Murray, Esq., "Notice of the Occurrence of an Earthquake on the 20th of March, 1861, in Mendoza, Argentine Confederation, South America," *New York Times*, May 4, 1861; "Great and Destructive Earthquake at Mendoza, Dreadful Loss of Life and Property, from Our Own Correspondent in Valparaiso," *New York Times*, May 6, 1861; "The Great Earthquake and Subsequent Conflagration at Mendoza," *New York Times*, July 29, 1861.

22. Stephen Pinker, *The Better Angels of Our Nature: The Decline of Violence in History and Its Causes* (New York: Penguin, 2011).

23. Ramirez and Peek-Asa, "Epidemiology of Traumatic Injuries from Earthquakes"; Ashkenazi et al., "Prehospital Management of Earthquake Casualties."

24. The Swiss Agency for Development and Cooperation funds rescue teams and trains other countries, such as Jordan.

25. MacIntyre, et al., "Surviving Collapsed Structure Entrapment."

26. Larry Collins, *Technical Rescue Operations*, vol. 2, *Common Emergencies* (Tulsa, OK: Penwell Communications, 2005).

27. E. K. Noji, "The Epidemiology of Earthquakes: Implications for Vulnerability Reduction, Mitigation, and Relief," presented in part 1 of the World Health Organization (WHO) symposium "Earthquakes and People's Health," Kobe, Japan (January 27–30, 1997).

28. M. Roces, E. White, M. Dayrit, et al., "Risk Factors for Injuries Due to the 1990 Earthquake in Luzon, Philippines," *Bulletin of the World Health Organization* 70, no. 4

(1992): 509–514. Many of the 250 students and teachers trapped in the six-story Christian College in the Philippine town of Baguio in 1990 died from the heat.

29. Déodat de Dolomieu, *Mémoire sur les tremblemens de terre de la Calabre Pendant l'année 1783* (Rome: Fulgoni, 1784).

30. "Jamaica's Governor Orders American Admiral to Withdraw Forces from Kingston; Angry Commander Sails in a Hurry; Governor Swettenham Rejects American Aid to Guard Kingston," *The Daily Telegraph*, St. John, New Brunswick, January 21, 1907.

31. Stephanie Williams, "A Socialist in the West Indies," in *Running the Show: Governors of the British Empire 1857–1912* (London: Viking Press, 2011).

32. In recognition of the sailors' sacrifice, St. Petersburg and Messina became officially twinned the following year.

33. R. C. Kent, *Anatomy of Disaster Relief: The International Network in Action* (London: Pinter, 1987).

34. Sherry Johnson, *Climate and Catastrophe in Cuba and the Atlantic World in the Age of Revolution* (Chapel Hill: University of North Carolina Press, 2011).

35. Philip Taubman, "Soviet Relief Plane Crashes, Killing 78," *New York Times*, December 12, 1988.

36. Panagiotis Karkatsoulis, "Rationalism and Irrationalism in Disaster Management: The Example of Greek-Turkish Cooperation in the Aftermath of the 17.8.99 Earthquake," Sixty-Second Annual America Society for Public Administration National Conference, Newark, NJ (March 10–13, 2001), http://unpan1.un.org/intradoc/groups /public/documents/aspa/unpan000524.pdf.

37. Stephen Kinzer, "Earthquakes Help Warm Greek-Turkish Relations," *New York Times*, September 13, 1999.

38. C. de Ville de Goyet, "Stop Propagating Disaster Myths" (editorial), *Prehospital and Disaster Medicine* 14, no. 4 (1999): 213–214.

39. "US Disappointed Cuba Rejects Drought Aid," Reuters, October 1, 1998, http:// reliefweb.int/report/cuba/us-disappointed-cuba-rejects-drought-aid.

40. "Mary Murray, "Katrina Aid from Cuba? No Thanks, Says US," NBC News, September 14, 2005, http://www.nbcnews.com/id/9311876/ns/us_news-katrina_the_long _road_back/t/katrina-aid-cuba-no-thanks-says-us/#.VnMwXfmLTIU.

41. Michael Winter, "Report: Israeli Killed in NZ Quake Was Suspected Spy," *USA Today*, July 19, 2011; Derek Cheng, "Spy Claims Ridiculous, Say Israelis," *New Zealand Herald*, July 23, 2011; Sefi Krupsky, "Report: Israeli Killed in New Zealand Earthquake Was Mossad Agent," *Haaretz*, July 19, 2011.

42. Rhoda Margesson and Maureen Tuft-Morales, "Haiti Earthquake: Crisis and Response," Congressional Research Series, February 2, 2010, http://www.fas.org/sgp/crs /row/R41023.pdf.

43. Ian Davis and David Alexander, *Recovery from Disaster* (New York: Routledge, 2015), 75.

44. David Roberts, "A Lesson from Haiti: Are Search and Rescue Teams Worth It?" *Philanthropy Action*, February 26, 2010, http://philanthropyaction.com/nc/a_lesson_from _haiti_are_search_and_rescue_teams_worth_it/.

45. Zarqa S. Ali, "Media Myths and Realities in Natural Disasters," *European Journal of Business and Social Sciences* 2, no. 1 (April 2013): 125–133.

46. Pan American Health Organization (PAHO), *Management of Dead Bodies in Disaster Situations*, Disaster Manuals and Guidelines Series 5 (Washington, DC: PAHO, 2004).

47. M. Lopez and N. Leon, "Babies of the Earthquake: Follow-up Study of Their First 15 Months," *Hillside Journal of Clinical Psychiatry* 11, no. 2 (1989): 147–168.

48. Edward Cody, "Crises Cloud China's Olympic Mood as Quake Tests Party's Mettle," *Washington Post Foreign Service*, May 17, 2008; Jill Drew, "Excavators Battle Debris in China Amid Fears of Disease," *Washington Post Foreign Service*, May 17, 2008.

49. The UN special envoy to Haiti estimated that $1.6 billion had been given in relief aid and $2 billion toward reconstruction. See Bill Quigley and Amber Ramanauskas, "Haiti: Where Is the Money?—Researcher Version," January 3, 2012, http://www .haitiaction.net/News/BQ/1_4_12/1_4_12.html.

50. T. Eisensee and D. Strömberg, "News Droughts, News Floods, and US Disaster Relief," *Quarterly Journal of Economics* 122, no. 2 (2007): 693–728.

51. Matthew Collin, "How Not to Help Haiti," *Foreign Policy* (February 19, 2010), http://foreignpolicy.com/2010/02/19/how-not-to-help-haiti/.

52. "Haiti's Medical Volunteers: Helping or Harming?" Tiny Spark, October 11, 2012, http://www.tinyspark.org/podcasts/medical-volunteers/.

53. Harley F. Etienne, "Land Rights, Land Tenure, and Urban Recovery: Rebuilding Post-Earthquake Port-au-Prince and Léogâne," Oxfam America Research Backgrounder Series (2012), 40, http://www.oxfamamerica.org/static/oa4/land-rights-land-tenure-and -urban-recovery.pdf.

54. Linda O'Halloran, founder of the NGO Thinking Development, personal comment on the experience of reconstruction in Port au Prince, Haiti, November 2015.

55. Giovanni Vivenzio, *Istoria de' tremuoti avvenuti nella provincia della Calabria ulteriore e nella città de Messina nell' anno 1783: e di quanto nella Calabria fu fatto per lo suo risorgimento fino al 1787: preceduta da una teoria, ed istoria generale de' tremuoti*, vol. 1 (Nella Stamperia Regale, 1788).

56. Eric Neumayer and Thomas Plümper, "The Gendered Nature of Natural Disasters: The Impact of Catastrophic Events on the Gender Gap in Life Expectancy, 1981–2002," *Annals of the Association of American Geographers* 97, no. 3 (2007): 551–566, http://eprints.lse.ac.uk/3040/1/Gendered_nature_of_natural_disasters_(LSERO) .pdf.

57. Jesse K. Anttila-Hughes, Solomon M. Hsiang, "Destruction, Disinvestment, and Death: Economic and Human Losses Following Environmental Disaster," http://cega .berkeley.edu/assets/cega_events/49/Session_4E_Natural_Disasters.pdf.

58. "Collection of 1923 Japan Earthquake Massacre Testimonies Released," The Hankyoreh, September 3, 2013, http://www.hani.co.kr/arti/english_edition/e _international/601938.html.

59. "Epidemiological Update: Cholera," Pan American Health Organization, October 19, 2013, http://www.paho.org/hq/index.php?option=com_docman&task=doc _view&gid=23406&Itemid=.

60. Ilan Noy, "Comparing the Direct Human Impact of Natural Disasters for Two (Surprisingly Similar) Cases: The Christchurch Earthquake and Bangkok Flood in 2011," Background Paper Prepared for the 2015 Global Assessment Report on Disaster Risk

Reduction, February 2015, http://www.preventionweb.net/english/hyogo/gar/2015/en/bgdocs/Noy,%202015.pdf.

61. Kieran Corcoran, "The Landslide That Wiped Out Nearly 3,000 People: Picture Reveals How Hillside Collapsed over Afghan Village," *Daily Mail*, May 5, 2014, http://www.dailymail.co.uk/news/article-2620840/Aab-Barik-Image-shows-scale-devastation-wiped-Afghan-village-killing-2-700-leaving-thousands-homeless.html.

62. How many remains a speculation. A British Foreign Office report of May 1909 suggested that there had been 130,000 deaths. There was no body count, and many died of hunger and thirst, beyond their direct injuries.

63. As reported in *Il Tempo*, January 6, 1909.

64. "Growing Influence—Philanthropy," Encyclopedia of the New American Nation, http://www.americanforeignrelations.com/O-W/Philanthropy-Growing-influence.html#ixzz1aNFdH9e6.

65. When the body dies, the infectious diseases that lived in the body also die. The odors come from organisms that only live on dead bodies.

66. On February 1, 1909, the newspaper *Il Tempo* accused the general of demanding that a pastry chef from Palermo or Naples be sent to feed him on his command ship. See Benjamin Reilly, "Earthquakes, Messina Strait, 1908," in *Disaster and Human History: Case Studies in Nature, Society, and Catastrophe* (Jefferson, NC: McFarland, 2009). 85–92.

67. Giovanni Ciraolo Jr., "Chi siamo: La storia di un uomo eccezionale: Giovanni Ciraolo," http://www.reliefunion.com/?page_id=144.

68. Alex de Waal, *Famine Crimes: Politics and the Disaster Relief Industry in Africa* (Oxford: James Currey Publishers, 1997), 68.

69. The UIS published *Revue pour l'étude des calamités*. David D. Caron, Michael J. Kelly, and Anastasia Telesetsky, eds., *The International Law of Disaster Relief* (New York: Cambridge University Press, 2014); John F. Hutchinson, "Disasters and the International Order. II. The International Relief Union," *International History Review* 23, no. 2 (June 2001): 253–298, http://www.jstor.org/stable/40108674?seq=1#page_scan_tab_contents.

70. Peter Macalister-Smith, "The International Relief Union," *Disasters: The International Journal of Disaster Studies and Practice* 5 (1981): 147; E. M. Fournier D'Aube, "Summary of UNESCO Activities in the Field of Earthquake Engineering," Third World Conference on Earthquake Engineering, New Zealand (January 1965), http://www.iitk.ac.in/nicee/wcee/article/vol3_V-75.pdf.

71. Frank Press trained as an oceanographer but became a very successful seismologist during the field's golden age.

72. Also in 1984 there was the first International Conference on Disaster Mitigations and Response, held in Ocho Rios, Jamaica, with fifty-one participants.

73. United Nations General Assembly, "International Decade for Natural Disaster Reduction," December 11, 1987, http://www.un.org/documents/ga/res/44/a44r236.htm; United Nations General Assembly, "International Decade for Natural Disaster Reduction," December 22, 1989, http://www.un.org/documents/ga/res/42/a42r169.htm.

74. *Reducing Disasters' Toll: The United States Decade for Natural Disasters Reduction* (Washington, DC: National Academy Press, 1989), 1–40.

75. Li-Li Xie, "How Do We Evaluate IDNDR?" Paper 2818, Twelfth World Confer-

ence on Earthquake Engineering, Auckland, NZ (January 30–February 4, 2000), http://www.iitk.ac.in/nicee/wcee/article/2818.pdf.

76. Allan Lavell, "Local Level Risk Management: Concepts and Experience in Central America," paper presented at the Disaster Preparedness and Mitigation Summit, New Delhi (November 21–23, 2002), http://www.desenredando.org/public/articulos/2003 /llrmceca/llrmceca_abr-24-2003.pdf.

77. "Disasters are manifestations of unresolved development problems": #GAR15 launch March 4 #WCDRR. See Suvit Yodmani, "Disaster Risk Reduction and Vulnerability Reduction: Protecting the Poor," paper presented to the Asia and Pacific Forum on Poverty, Social Protection Workshop 6, "Protecting Communities, Social Funds, and Disaster Management," Asian Development Bank, Manila (April 5–9, 2001), http://www.pacificdisaster.net/pdnadmin/data/original/DRM_Vulnerability_Reduction.pdf; UNDP, "Reducing Disaster Risk: A Challenge for Development," 2004, http://www.preventionweb.net/files/1096_rdrenglish.pdf.

78. Hyogo was the prefecture where Kobe was situated and where in 2005, exactly ten years after the Kobe earthquake, a conference was held to launch the new decade. United Nations Office for Disaster Risk Reduction (UNISDR), "Hyogo Framework for Action 2005–2015: Building the Resilience of Nations and Communities to Disasters," 2007, http://www.unisdr.org/we/inform/publications/1037.

79. Between 2005 and 2014, over 700,000 people lost their lives, over 1.4 million were injured, and approximately 23 million were made homeless as a result of disasters. The total economic loss was more than $1.3 trillion. In addition, between 2008 and 2012, 144 million people were displaced by disasters. "Sendai Framework for Disaster Risk Reduction 2015–2030," adopted at the Third UN World Conference, Sendai, Japan, March 18, 2015, http://www.unisdr.org/files/43291_sendaiframeworkfordrren.pdf.

80. GDP per capita in California ($46,000) is 350 percent higher than in Iran ($13,000) and thirty-five times that in Haiti ($1,300).

81. Based on schools being in session for 44 out of 52 weeks per year, and for 33 out of 164 hours per week.

82. "CTV Building 'Collapsed in Seconds,'" 3 News, June 25, 2012, http://www.newshub.co.nz/nznews/ctv-building-collapsed-in-seconds-2012062505#axzz3 ugCVnDgX; "Christchurch Earthquake CTV Building Inquiry: Inquiry into the Deaths of Dr. Tamara Cvetanova and Others," Coronial Services of New Zealand, http://www.justice.govt.nz/courts/coroners-court/christchurch/ctv.

83. Sanjaya Bhatia, "Safe Schools for the Community: A Case and Tool for Disaster-Proof Schools," in *Community Disaster Recovery and Resiliency: Exploring Global Opportunities*, edited by DeMond S. Miller and Jason David Rivera (Boca Raton, FL: CRC Press, Taylor and Francis, 2011), 41–62.

84. "The Kashmir Earthquake of October 8, 2005: Impacts in Pakistan," EERI Special Earthquake Report, February 2006, http://www.ndma.gov.pk/new/aboutus /Earthquake2005.pdf.

85. Yong Chen and David C. Booth, *The Wenchuan Earthquake of 2008: Anatomy of a Disaster* (Beijing: Springer Science Press, 2011).

86. Chiun-lin Wu, Juin-Fu Chai, Chu-Chieh Jay Lin, and Fan-Ru Lin, "Reconnaissance Report of 0512 China Wenchuan Earthquake on Schools, Hospitals, and

Residential Buildings," Fourteenth World Conference on Earthquake Engineering, Beijing (October 12–17, 2008), http://www.iitk.ac.in/nicee/wcee/article/14_S31-004.pdf.

87. NEHRP Consultants, "Cost Analyses and Benefit Studies for Earthquake-Resistant Construction in Memphis, Tennessee," NIST GCR 14-917-26, prepared for US Department of Commerce, National Institute of Standards and Technology, Engineering Laboratory, 2013, http://www.nehrp.gov/pdf/NIST%20GCR%2014-917-26_CostAnalyses andBenefitStudiesforEarthquake-ResistantConstructioninMemphisTennessee.pdf.

88. Cascadia Region Earthquake Workgroup, "Cascadia Subduction Zone Earthquakes: A Magnitude 9.0 Earthquake Scenario Update," 2013, http://file.dnr.wa.gov /publications/ger_ic116_csz_scenario_update.pdf.

89. Andrew Coburn and Robin Spence, *Earthquake Protection* (Chichester, UK: John Wiley and Sons, 1992), 2–12, 74–80, 277–284.

90. "Pager—Rapid Assessment of an Earthquake's Impact," USGS Factsheet 2010-3036, US Geological Survey, http://earthquake.usgs.gov/research/pager/ (last modified September 12, 2014); Max Wyss, "Real-Time Prediction of Earthquake Casualties," International Conference, University of Karlsruhe, July 26–27, 2004, in *Proceedings: Disasters and Society—From Hazard Assessment to Risk Reduction*, edited by D. Malzahn and T. Plapp (Logos Publishers, 2004), 165–173, http://wapmerr.org/publication /Loss_prediction_Wyss_Karlsruhe.pdf.

91. "Gov't Sets Goal to Halve Victims in Possible Major Quake in Tokyo," Japan Economic Newswire, March 31, 2015.

92. W. Kip Viscusi, "The Value of Life," Discussion Paper 517, Harvard University, John M. Olin Center for Law, Economics, and Business, June 2005, http://www.law .harvard.edu/programs/olin_center/papers/pdf/Viscusi_517.pdf.

93. Roger Bilham and Vinod Gaur, "Buildings as Weapons of Mass Destruction," *Science* 341, no. 6146 (August 9, 2013): 618–619, http://www.sciencemag.org /content/341/6146/618.

CHAPTER 11: THE MASTER OF DISASTER

1. Gregory Smits, "Shaking Up Japan: Edo Society and the 1855 Catfish Picture Prints," *Journal of Social History* 39, no. 4 (Summer 2006): 1045–1078.

2. P. Sainath, *Everyone Loves a Good Drought: Stories from India's Poorest Districts* (New York: Penguin Books, 1996).

3. Charles E. Fritz, "Disasters and Mental Health: Therapeutic Principles Drawn from Disaster Studies," Historical and Comparative Disaster Series 10, University of Delaware, Disaster Research Center, 1961, http://dspace.udel.edu/bitstream/handle/19716/1325/ HC%2010.pdf?sequence=1&isAllowed=y; Rebecca Solnit, "The Uses of Disaster: Notes on Bad Weather and Good Government," *Harper's* (October 2005); Solnit, *A Paradise Built in Hell*.

4. Lauren Barsky, Joseph Trainor, and Manuel Torres, "Disaster Realities in the Aftermath of Hurricane Katrina: Revisiting the Looting Myth," Miscellaneous Report 53, Natural Hazards Center Quick Response Report 184, University of Delaware Disaster Research Center, February 2006, http://udspace.udel.edu/bitstream /handle/19716/2367/Misc%20Report%2053.pdf?sequence=1; E. L. Quarantelli and Russell Dynes, "Dissensus and Consensus in Community Emergencies," *Il Politico* 34

(1969): 276–291; E. L. Quarantelli, "Looting and Antisocial Behavior in Disasters," Preliminary Paper 205, University of Delaware, Disaster Research Center, 1994.

5. Kelly Frailing, "The Myth of a Disaster Myth: Potential Looting Should Be Part of Disaster Plans," *Natural Hazards Observer* 31, no. 4 (March 2007): 3–4, https://hazards .colorado.edu/uploads/observer/2007/mar07/mar07.pdf; Krzysztof Kaniasty and Fran H. Norris, "Social Support in the Aftermath of Disasters, Catastrophes, and Acts of Terrorism: Altruistic, Overwhelmed, Uncertain, Antagonistic, and Patriotic Communities," in *Bioterrorism: Psychological and Public Health Interventions*, edited by R. J. Ursano, A. E. Norwood, and C. S. Fullerton (Cambridge: Cambridge University Press, 2004), 200–229, http://old.impact-kenniscentrum.nl/doc/kennisbank/1000011308-1.pdf; K. Frailing and D. W. Harper, "Crime and Hurricanes in New Orleans," in *The Sociology of Katrina: Perspectives on a Modern Catastrophe*, edited by D. L. Brunsma, D. Overfelt, and J. S. Picou (Lanham, MD: Rowman & Littlefield, 2007).

6. William Branigin, "Hurricane Hugo Haunts Virgin Islands," *Washington Post*, October 31, 1989.

7. Erik Auf der Heide, "Common Misconceptions About Disasters: Panic, the 'Disaster Syndrome,' and Looting," in *The First 72 Hours: A Community Approach to Disaster Preparedness*, edited by M. O'Leary (Lincoln, NE: iUniverse Publishing, 2004); E. L. Quarantelli, "The Earliest Interest in Disasters and Crises, and the Early Social Science Study of Disasters, as Seen in a Sociology of Knowledge Perspective," University of Delaware, Disaster Research Center, 2009.

8. Emanuela Guidoboni and Alberto Comastri, *Catalogue of Earthquakes and Tsunamis in the Mediterranean Area from the 11th to the 15th Century* (Bologna: INGV-SGA, 2005), 280.

9. Georgii Pachymeris, *Relationes historicae*, vol. 7, translated by Robert Elsie (Bonn, 1835), 456–461, first published in Robert Elsie, *Early Albania: A Reader of Historical Texts, 11th–17th Centuries* (Wiesbaden, 2003), 12–13, http://www.albanianhistory.net/en /texts1000-1799/AH1267.html.

10. "Looting and Crime," The Galveston, Texas, 1900 Storm, http://ceprofs.tamu.edu /llowery/personal/songs/hurricane/thestorm/cleanup.htm; Paul Lester, *The Great Galveston Disaster, Containing a Full and Thrilling Account of the Most Appalling Calamity of Modern Time* (Gretna, LA: Pelican Publishing Co., 2000), 46.

11. "Of the Damages in the City of London and the Parts Adjacent," part 1, "Of the Effects of the Storm," in Daniel Defoe, *The Storm* (1704), edited and with an introduction by Richard Hamblyn (London: Penguin Classics, 2003), 57.

12. A. H. Olsen and K. A. Porter, "What We Know About Demand Surge: Brief Summary," *Natural Hazards Review* 12, no. 2 (2011): 62–71.

13. Jack London, "The Story of an Eyewitness," *Collier's*, May 5, 1906, reprinted at "Jack London and the Great Earthquake and Fire," Virtual Museum of the City of San Francisco, http://www.sfmuseum.org/hist5/jlondon.html.

14. Neil Hanson, *The Dreadful Judgment: The True Story of the Great Fire of London* (New York: Doubleday, 2001), 156–157.

15. "Memorials: 1362," in *Memorials of London and London Life in the 13th, 14th, and 15th Centuries*, edited by H. T. Riley (London: Longmans, Green, 1868), 306–312, reprinted at British History Online, http://www.british-history.ac.uk/no-series/ memorials-london-life/pp306-312.

16. Shawn Cole, Andrew Healy, and Eric Werker, "Do Voters Demand Responsive Governments? Evidence from Indian Disaster Relief," *Journal of Development Economics* 97 (2012): 167–181, http://myweb.lmu.edu/ahealy/papers/cole_healy_werker_2012.pdf.

17. John Cassidy, "How Much Did Hurricane Sandy Help Obama?" *The New Yorker*, November 4, 2012.

18. Geoffrey K. Roberts, "'Taken at the Flood'? The German General Election 2002," *Government and Opposition* 38, no. 1 (January 2003): 53–72; "Looking Back at the 2002 Election" DW Akademie, http://www.dw.de/looking-back-at-the-2002-election/a -1642902.

19. Andrew Healy, Neil Malhotra, "Myopic Voters and Natural Disaster Policy," *American Political Science Review* 103, no. 3 (August 2009): 387–406, http://www .ginareinhardt.com/wp-content/uploads/2012/01/Healy-Malhotra-Myopic-Voters -and-Natural-Disaster-Policy.pdf.

20. Jowei Chen, "Voter Partisanship and the Effect of Distributive Spending on Political Participation," *American Journal of Political Science* 57, no. 1 (2013): 200–217;

Andrew Healy and Neil Malhotra, "Retrospective Voting Reconsidered," *Annual Review of Political Science* 16, no. 1 (2013): 285–306; Jowie Chen, "Are Poor Voters Easier to Buy Off with Money? A Natural Experiment from the 2004 Florida Hurricane Season," lecture delivered at the American Political Science Association (APSA) meeting, Toronto (2009); Jowei Chen, "When Do Government Benefits Influence Voters' Behavior? The Effect of FEMA Disaster Awards on US Presidential Votes," 2009; Michael M. Bechtel and Jens Hainmueller, "How Lasting Is Voter Gratitude? An Analysis of the Short- and Long-Term Electoral Returns to Beneficial Policy," June 2010, http://politics.as.nyu.edu /docs/IO/16190/bechtel.pdf.

21. In the Zhou Dynasty of the first millennium BC in China, the Taoist viewpoint was developed that Heaven's disapproval of bad and corrupt rule comes through natural disasters—floods, plagues, and earthquakes. See David N. Keightley, "The Shang: China's First Historical Dynasty," in *The Cambridge History of Ancient China: From the Origins of Civilization to 221 BC*, edited by Michael Loewe and Edward L. Shaughnessy (New York: Cambridge University Press, 1999), 232–291.

22. Amarta Sen and J. H. Dreze, "Democracy as a Universal Value," *Journal of Democracy* 10 (1999): 3–17.

23. Internationally, news of the earthquake was overshadowed by the Montreal Olympics. China had not sent a team: competitive sport was a capitalist distraction.

24. It took a further three days, until August 4, for the Communist publicity machine to reveal news of his visit. See Lauri Paltemaa, "The Great Earthquake of 1976," in *Managing Flood, Famine, and Earthquake in China, 1958–1985, Tianjin* (Abingdon: Routledge, 2016), 133–179.

25. "Seismic Memorial Hall," Peking Hotels, http://ww.pekinghotels.cn/en/travel /Hebei/Seismic_Memorial_Hall_15505.html.

26. "The Tangshan Earthquake Memorial Wall," Zona Europa: EastSouthWest-North, June 4, 2006, http://www.zonaeuropa.com/20060728_1.htm.

27. Li Yanjui, "A People's Architect," *Global Times*, December 30, 2010; "Tangshan Earthquake Museum Opens: 34th Anniversary," CCTV News, July 29, 2010.

28. "Gloucester Fisherman's Memorial," Maritime History of Massachusetts, http:// www.nps.gov/nr/travel/maritime/glo.htm.

29. "Kantō Earthquake Memorial Museum," Lonely Planet, http://www.lonelyplanet
.com/japan/tokyo/sights/museums-galleries/kanto-earthquake-memorial-museum.

30. Mark Joseph Stern, "Did Chernobyl Cause the Soviet Union to Explode? The Nuclear Theory of the Fall of the USSR," *Slate*, January 25, 2013.

31. Robert Muir-Wood, "From Global Seismotectonics to Global Seismic Hazard," *Annali di Geofisica* 36 (June–July 1993): 153–168; Robert Muir-Wood, "After Armenia," *Terra Nova* 1, no. 2 (March 1989): 209–212.

32. "Aceh's Peace Agreement: Will It Hold?" *Strategic Comments* 11, no. 7 (2005): 1–2, published online October 22, 2005, doi:10.1080/1356788051174.

33. "From Tragedy Springs Peace: The Aceh Story," Fetzer Institute, October 2012, http://fetzer.org/work/projects/tragedy-springs-peace-aceh-story.

34. "Cameron Urges Aid Drops for Burma," BBC News, May 12, 2008, http://news
.bbc.co.uk/1/hi/uk_politics/7396313.stm.

35. "Cyclone Nargis, Myanmar," ASEAN Emergency Rapid Assessment Team Mission Report, May 9–18, 2008, http://reliefweb.int/report/myanmar/cyclone-nargis-myanmar
-asean-emergency-rapid-assessment-team-mission-report-09-18-may; Christopher Roberts, *ASEAN's Myanmar Crisis: Challenges to the Pursuit of a Security Community* (Singapore: Institute of Southeast Asian Security Studies, 2010).

36. Roger Mitton, "Nargis Was a Turning Point," *Myanmar Times*, February 13, 2012, http://www.mmtimes.com/index.php/in-depth/1093-nargis-was-a-turning-point
.html?limitstart=0.

37. Robin Pomeroy, "Ahmadinejad Plans Exodus to Avert Iran Quake Disaster," Reuters, April 22, 2010.

38. Ramin Mostaghim and Meris Lutz, "Iran: As Government Uses Earthquake Fears to Move Residents Out of Tehran, Temblor Injures 19," *Los Angeles Times*, July 21, 2010.

39. "Some 100,000 People Relocated from Tehran," Trend News Agency, June 17, 2012, http://en.trend.az/regions/iran/2037801.html.

40. Stuart B. Schwartz, *Sea of Storms* (Princeton, NJ: Princeton University Press, 2015), 242–251.

41. "Hurricane Flora," Wikipedia, http://en.wikipedia.org/wiki/Hurricane_Flora (last modified February 28, 2016); Hurricanes: Science and Society, "1963—Hurricane Flora," http://www.hurricanescience.org/history/storms/1960s/flora/.

42. Louis A. Pérez Jr., "In the Shadow of the Winds: Rethinking the Meaning of Hurricanes," *ReVista: Harvard Review of Latin America* (Winter 2007), http://revista.drclas
.harvard.edu/book/shadow-winds-rethinking-meaning-hurricanes.

43. Fiorella Mejia, "US-Cuban Cooperation in Defending Against Hurricanes," Center for International Policy Conference Report, August 2011, http://www.ciponline.org
/images/uploads/publications/0811_Hurricane_Conf_Report.pdf.

44. Pérez, "In the Shadow of the Winds."

45. Che Guevara, "Socialism and Man in Cuba," in *Manifesto: Three Classic Essays on How to Change the World* (Melbourne: Ocean, 2005).

46. "Chris Christie's Victory Speech, in Text and Word Cloud," Capitol Quickies, posted by John Schoonejongen, November 6, 2013, http://blogs.app.com/capitolquickies
/2013/11/06/chris-christies-victory-speech-in-text-and-word-cloud/; Schwartz, *Sea of Storms*, 337.

47. Richard Bauer, "'Ivan' Breathes New Life into the Cuban Revolution," GRID Arendal, October 1, 2004, http://www.grida.no/publications/et/ep3/page/2586.aspx.

48. *Celia Hart Santamaria*, "Cuba vs. Hurricanes: A Revolutionary Fight Against the Demon," *Climate & Capitalism*, September 9, 2008, http://climateandcapitalism .com/2008/09/09/cuba-vs-hurricanes-a-revolutionary-fight-against-the-demon/.

49. Martha Thomson and Izaskun Gaviria, *Weathering the Storm: Lessons in Risk Reduction from Cuba* (Boston: Oxfam America, 2004).

50. B. E. Aguirre and Joseph E. Trainor, "Emergency Management in Cuba: Disasters Experienced, Lessons Learned, and Recommendations for the Future," in *Comparative Emergency Management: Understanding Disaster Policies, Organizations, and Initiatives from Around the World*, edited by David A. McEntire, et al. (Washington, DC: Federal Emergency Management Agency, n.d.).

51. Marce Cameron, "After Hurricanes, Cuba Demands Lifting of US Blockade," *Direct Action for Socialism in the 21st Century* 5 (October 2008), http://directaction.org .au/issue5/after_hurricanes_cuba_demands_lifting_of_us_blockade.

52. Bureau for Crisis Prevention and Recovery–UNDP, "Reducing Disaster Risk: A Challenge for Development," PreventionWeb, 2004, http://www.preventionweb.net /english/professional/publications/v.php?id=1096.

53. Trent Hawkins, "Cuba: Rebuilding After the Hurricanes, Sustainably," *Links: International Journal of Socialist Renewal* (2008), http://links.org.au/node/840.

54. Bauer, "'Ivan' Breathes New Life. . . ."

CHAPTER 12: TURNING UP THE HEAT

1. Christopher Flavin, "Storm Warnings: Climate Change Hits the Insurance Industry," *World Watch* 7, no. 6 (November–December 1994), http://www.smartcommunities .ncat.org/articles/world-watch-storm-warnings.shtml.

2. "Avoiding Dangerous Climate Change Symposium," http://www.stabilisation2005 .com/.

3. William Nordhaus originally proposed in the 1970s that 2 degrees Celsius was the maximum rise observed over recent prehistory—and therefore that the earth had been there and returned. S. Randalls, "History of the 2 Degrees C Climate Target," *WIREs Climate Change* 1, no. 4 (2010): 598–605, doi:10.1002/wcc.62, http://discovery.ucl.ac .uk/111750/.

4. Kerry Emanuel, "Increasing Destructiveness of Tropical Cyclones over the Past 30 Years," *Nature* 436 (August 4, 2005): 686–688, doi:10.1038/nature03906; http:// www.nature.com/nature/journal/v436/n7051/abs/nature03906.html.

5. P. J. Webster, G. J. Holland, J. A. Curry, and H.-R. Chang, "Changes in Tropical Cyclone Number, Duration, and Intensity in a Warming Environment," *Science* 309 (September 16, 2005): 1844–1846.

6. William Nordhaus observed a year later: "The Review should be read primarily as a document that is political in nature and has advocacy as its purpose." William D. Nordhaus, "A Review of the Stern Review on the Economics of Climate Change," *Journal of Economic Literature* 45 (September 2007): 686–702.

7. Stern employed a grim compound 2 percent annual real increase in catastrophe

costs and a near-zero discount rate in which the estimated projections of losses in the distant future were costed straight back to the present.

8. Gabriel A. Vecchi and Brian J. Soden, "Effect of Remote Sea Surface Temperature Change on Tropical Cyclone Potential Intensity," *Nature* 450 (December 13, 2007): 1066–1070, doi:10.1038/nature06423.

9. Roger A. Pielke Jr., Joel Gratz, Christopher W. Landsea, Douglas Collins, Mark A. Saunders, and Rade Musulin, "Normalized Hurricane Damage in the United States: 1900–2005," *Natural Hazards Review* (February 2008): 29–42.

10. Francisco Estrada, W. J. Wouter Botzen, and Richard S. J. Tol, "Economic Losses from US Hurricanes Consistent with an Influence from Climate Change," *Nature Geoscience* 8 (2015): 880–884, doi:10.1038/ngeo2560.

11. "1780 Atlantic Hurricane Season," Wikipedia, https://en.wikipedia.org/wiki/1780_Atlantic_hurricane_season (last modified March 14, 2016).

12. G. R. Demaree and Robert Muir Wood, "De 'Grote Storm van 1703' in de Lage Landen-een stormachtige periode in de Spaanse successieoorlog," *Jaarboek voor Ecologische Geschiedenis* (2009): 33–54; "Great Storm of 1703," Wikipedia, https://en.wikipedia.org/wiki/Great_Storm_of_1703 (last modified January 12, 2016).

13. "St. Mary Magdalene's Flood," Wikipedia, https://en.wikipedia.org/wiki/St._Mary_Magdalene%27s_flood (last modified February 13, 2016).

14. "Great Flood of 1862," Wikipedia, https://en.wikipedia.org/wiki/Great_Flood_of_1862 (last modified March 4, 2016).

15. "Hurricane Mitch," Wikipedia, https://en.wikipedia.org/wiki/Hurricane_Mitch (last modified March 5, 2016).

16. Myles Allen, "Liability for Climate Change," *Nature* 421 (2003): 891–892, doi:10.1038/421891a; P. Pall, T. Aina, D. A. Stone, P. A. Stott, T. Nozawa, A. G. J. Hilberts, et al., "Anthropogenic Greenhouse Gas Contribution to Flood Risk in England and Wales in Autumn 2000," *Nature* 470 (February 17, 2011): 382–385, doi:10.1038/nature09762; A. L. Kay, S. M. Crooks, P. Pall, and D. A. Stone, "Attribution of Autumn/Winter 2000 Flood Risk in England to Anthropogenic Climate Change: A Catchment-Based Study," *Journal of Hydrology* 406 (2011): 97–112.

17. Friederike Otto, Rachel James, and Myles Allen, "The Science of Attributing Extreme Weather Events and Its Potential Contribution to Assessing Loss and Damage Associated with Climate Change Impacts," University of Oxford, Environmental Change Institute, 2014, https://unfccc.int/files/adaptation/workstreams/loss_and_damage/application/pdf/attributingextremeevents.pdf.

18. "Typhoon Haiyan," https://en.wikipedia.org/wiki/Typhoon_Haiyan (last modified March 13, 2016).

19. "Climate Change 'Madness' Must End, Says Philippines UN Rep Yeb Sano After Typhoon Haiyan" (video), Huffington Post UK, November 12, 2013, http://www.huffingtonpost.co.uk/2013/11/12/climate-change-typhoon_n_4258797.html.

20. Robert Winston, *Bad Ideas? An Arresting History of Our Inventions* (London: Bantam Books, 2010), 377.

21. E. Mas, J. Bricker, S. Kure, B. Adriano, C. Yi, A. Suppasri, and S. Koshimura, "Field Survey Report and Satellite Image Interpretation of the 2013 Super Typhoon Haiyan in the Philippines," *Natural Hazards and Earth System Sciences* 15 (2015): 805–816,

doi:10.5194/nhess-15–805–2015, www.nat-hazards-earth-syst-sci.net/15/805/2015/; Kim Luces, "A History of Storms: 1890s Newspaper Reveals Devastating Leyte Typhoon," GMA News Online, November 15, 2013, http://www.gmanetwork.com/news/story/335673 /scitech/science/a-history-of-storms-1890s-newspaper-reveals-devastating-leyte-typhoon.

22. Izuru Takayabu, Kenshi Hibino, Hidetaka Sasaki, Hideo Shiogama, Nobuhito Mori, Yoko Shibutani, and Tetsuya Takemi, "Climate Change Effects on the Worst-Case Storm Surge: A Case Study of Typhoon Haiyan," *Environmental Research Letters* 10, no. 6 (June 11, 2015), doi:10.1088/1748-9326/10/6/064011.

23. David Adam, "Climate Change in Court," *Nature Climate Change* 1, no. 3 (2011): 127–130; Liz Kalaugher, "Sea Level Rise Flies High," *Nature* 421 (2003): 891–892; "Environmental Research Web," February 17, 2009, http://environmentalresearchweb .org/blog/aaas-meeting/; M. R. Allen, P. Pall, D. A. Stone, P. Stott, D. Frame, S.-K. Min, T. Nozawa, and S. Yukimoto, "Scientific Challenges in the Attribution of Harm to Human Influence on Climate," *University of Pennsylvania Law Review* 155, no. 6 (2007): 1353–1400.

24. Peter H. Gleick, "Water, Drought, Climate Change, and Conflict in Syria," *Weather, Climate, and Society* 6 (2014): 331–340, doi:http://dx.doi.org/10.1175 /WCAS-D-13–00059.1.

25. Colin P. Kelley, Shahrzad Mohtadi, Mark A. Cane, Richard Seager, and Yochanan Kushnir, "Climate Change in the Fertile Crescent and Implications of the Recent Syrian Drought," *Proceedings of the National Academy of Sciences* 112, no. 11 (2015): 3241–3246, doi:10.1073/pnas.142153311, http://www.pnas.org/content/early /2015/02/23/1421533112.

26. Myles Allen, "The Scientific Basis for Climate Change Liability," in *Climate Change Liability, Transnational Law, and Practice*, edited by Richard Lord QC, Silke Goldberg, Lavanya Rajamani, and Jutta Brunnee (New York: Cambridge University Press, 2012), 21, section 2.27.

27. Zbigniew W. Kundzewicz, et al., "Flood Risk and Climate Change: Global and Regional Perspectives," *Hydrological Sciences Journal* 59, no. 1 (2014): 1–28.

28. Kevin E. Trenberth, John T. Fasullo, and Theodore G. Shepherd, "Attribution of Climate Extreme Events," *Nature Climate Change* 5 (2015): 725–730, doi:10.1038 /nclimate2657, http://www.nature.com/nclimate/journal/vaop/ncurrent/full/nclimate2657 .html.

29. With the possible exception of erosion as a result of the removal of pack ice. See David Atkinson and Peter Schweitzer, "The Arctic Coastal Margin," in *North by 2020: Perspectives on Alaska's Changing Social-Ecological Systems*, edited by Amy Lauren Lovecraft and Hajo Eicke (Fairbanks: University of Alaska Press, 2011), 217–298.

30. Hans Joachim Schellnhuber, "Tipping Elements in the Earth System," *Proceedings of the National Academy of Sciences* 106, no. 49 (2010): 20561–20563, doi:10.1073 /pnas.0911106106, http://www.pnas.org/content/106/49/20561.full.

31. "Canicule," Wikipedia, https://fr.wikipedia.org/wiki/Canicule (last modified January 28, 2016).

32. See "Heat Wave," Wikipedia, https://en.wikipedia.org/wiki/Heat_wave (last modified February 18, 2016).

33. Christoph Schär, Pier Luigi Vidale, Daniel Lüthi, Christoph Frei, Christian Häberli, Mark A. Liniger, and Christof Appenzeller, "The Role of Increasing Temperature

Variability in European Summer Heatwaves," *Nature* 427 (January 22, 2004): 332–336, doi:10.1038/nature02300.

34. Annual mortalities published by the French National Institute of Statistics, http://www.insee.fr/fr/themes/document.asp?reg_id=0&ref_id=IP1318&page=graph #graphique1; Janet Larsen, "Record Heat Wave in Europe Takes 35,000 Lives: Far Greater Losses May Lie Ahead," Earth Policy Institute, October 9, 2003, http://www.earth-policy .org/plan_b_updates/2003/update29.

35. The 2000–2002 annual average was 542,000 (ranging from 540,700 to 544,100). It was 518,100 in 2004 and 537,300 in 2005.

36. Jeff Masters, "Heat Mortality," http://www.wunderground.com/climate/heat mortality.asp; M. M. Huynen, P. Martens, D. Schram, M. P. Weijenberg, and A. E. Kunst, "The Impact of Heat Waves and Cold Spells on Mortality Rates in the Dutch Population," *Environmental Health Perspectives* 109, no. 5 (May 2001): 463–470, http:// www.ncbi.nlm.nih.gov/pmc/articles/PMC1240305/; "Cold Weather Kills Far More People Than Hot Weather," *The Lancet* (May 20, 2015), http://www.sciencedaily.com /releases/2015/05/150520193831.htm.

37. Hannah Hoag, "Russian Summer Tops 'Universal' Heatwave Index," *Nature* (October 29, 2014), http://www.nature.com/news/russian-summer-tops-universal-heatwave -index-1.16250.

38. "2010 Russian Wildfires," Wikipedia, http://en.wikipedia.org/wiki/2010_Russian _wildfires (last modified February 29, 2016).

39. Simon Shuster, "Will Russia's Heat Wave End Its Global Warming Doubts," *Time*, August 2, 2010.

40. Peter A. Stott, D. A. Stone, and M. R. Allen, "Human Contribution to the European Heatwave of 2003," *Nature* 432 (December 2, 2004): 610–614, doi:10.1038 /nature03089, http://www.nature.com/nature/journal/v432/n7017/full/nature03089.html.

41. F. E. L. Otto, N. Massey, G. J. van Oldenborgh, R. G. Jones, and M. R. Allen, "Reconciling Two Approaches to Attribution of the 2010 Russian Heat Wave," *Geophysical Research Letters* 39, no. 4 (2012): L04702, doi:10.1029/2011GL050422.

42. Karl K. Leiker, "The July 1936 Midwest Heat Wave: America's Second Worst Weather Fatality Episode: An Examination by Use of the 20th Century Reanalysis Project," presented at the Ninety-Third Annual Meeting of the American Meteorological Society, Austin, TX (January 5–10, 2013), https://ams.confex.com/ams/93Annual /webprogram/Paper221559.html.

43. Camilo Mora et al., "The Projected Timing of Climate Departure from Recent Variability," *Nature* 502 (October 10, 2013): 183–187, doi:10.1038/ nature12540; Meghan Mussoline, "Extreme Heat Wave Comes to End for Midwest, Mid-Atlantic," AccuWeather.com, July 10, 2012; http://www.accuweather.com/en/weather -news/more-than-3000-temperature-rec/67593.

44. "Angry Summer," Wikipedia, https://en.wikipedia.org/wiki/Angry_Summer (last modified March 12, 2016).

45. "Black Sunday Bushfires," Wikipedia, http://en.wikipedia.org/wiki/Black_Saturday _bushfires (last modified March 10, 2016).

46. Victorian Bushfires 2009 Research Task Force, "Victorian 2009 Bushfire Research Response: Final Report," October 2009, http://www.bushfirecrc.com/sites/default/files /managed/resource/bushfire-crc-victorian-fires-research-taskforce-final-report.pdf.

47. "The East Bay Hills Fire: Oakland-Berkeley, California," USFA-TR-060 (Washington, DC: Federal Emergency Management Agency, US Fire Administration, October 1991), http://www.usfa.fema.gov/downloads/pdf/publications/tr-060.pdf.

48. City of Berkeley, *City of Berkeley: 2014 Local Hazard Mitigation Plan*, June 1, 2014,http://www.ci.berkeley.ca.us/uploadedFiles/Fire/Level_3_-_General/2014%20 LHMP.pdf.

49. "2011 Slave Lake Wildfire," Wikipedia, http://en.wikipedia.org/wiki/2011_Slave _Lake_wildfire (last modified January 20, 2016).

50. Alasdair Wilkins, "October 8, 1871: The Night American Burned," io9, March 29, 2012, http://io9.com/5897629/october-8-1871-the-night-america-burned.

51. Maxmillan Martin, Yi hyun Kang, Motasim Billah, Tasneem Siddiqui, Richard Black, and Dominic Kniveton, "Policy Analysis: Climate Change and Migration Bangladesh," Working Paper 4, Refugee and Migratory Movements Research Unit (RM-MRU) at the University of Dhaka, and Sussex Centre for Migration Research (SCMR) at the University of Sussex, 2013, http://migratingoutofpoverty.dfid.gov.uk/files/file .php?name=wp4-ccrm-b-policy.pdf&site=354.

52. M. Zaman, "The Social and Political Context of Adjustment to Riverbank Erosion Hazard and Population Resettlement in Bangladesh," *Human Organization* 48, no. 3 (Fall 1989): 196–205. http://sfaa.metapress.com/content/v55465j651259835/fulltext .pdf?page=1.

53. Swiss Re, "Swiss Re SONAR: New Emerging Risk Insights for 2015," http:// www.swissre.com/rethinking/emerging_risks/Swiss_Re_SONAR_new_emerging_risk _insights_for_2015.html.

54. Muh Aris Marfie, Lorenz King, Junun Sartohadi, Sudrajat Sudrajat, Sri Rahaya Budiani, and Fajar Yulianto, "The Impact of Tidal Flooding on a Coastal Community in Semarang, Indonesia," *The Environmentalist* 28, no. 3 (2008): 237–248, doi:10.1007 /s10669-007-9134-4.

55. Denise Macock, "Grand Bahama Hit Hard by Storm," Tribune 242, October 29, 2012, http://www.tribune242.com/news/2012/oct/29/grand-bahama-hit-hard-storm/.

56. "Counting the Cost of Calamities," *The Economist*, January 14, 2012.

57. City of Seattle, Office of Emergency Management, *SHIVA: The Seattle Hazard Identification and Vulnerability Analysis*, April 15, 2014, http://www.seattle.gov /emergency.

58. A. A. Adalja, M. Watson, N. Bouri, K. Minton, R. C. Morhard, and E. S. Toner, "Absorbing Citywide Patient Surge During Hurricane Sandy: A Case Study in Accommodating Multiple Hospital Evacuations," *Annals of Emergency Medicine* 64, no. 1 (July 2014): 66–73, doi:10.1016/j.annemergmed.2013.12.010.

59. T. H. Dixon, F. Amelung, A. Ferretti, F. Novali, F. Rocca, R. Dokka, G. Sellall, S.-W. Kim, S. Wdowinski, and D. Whitman, "Subsidence and Flooding in New Orleans," *Nature* 441 (2006): 587–588; C. Burdeau, "Geologic Faults Cause Structures in New Orleans to Sink, Study Says," *Washington Post*, April 3, 2006.

60. Adam Wernick, "Living on Earth: Louisiana's Coastline Is Disappearing at the Rate of a Football Field an Hour," PRI, September 23, 2014, http://www.pri.org /stories/2014-09-23/louisianas-coastline-disappearing-rate-football-field-hour.

61. Lafcadio Hearn, *Chita: A Memory of Last Island* (1889).

62. Larry O'Hanlon, "New Orleans Sits Atop Giant Landslide," *Discovery News*,

March 31, 2006; Sherwood M. Gagliano, E. Burton Kemp III, Karen M. Wicker, and Kathleen S. Wiltenmuth, "Active Geological Faults and Land Change in Southeastern Louisiana: Executive Summary," prepared for US Army Corps of Engineers, New Orleans District, August 14, 2003, http://www.coastalenv.com/Executive_Summary_Active _Geological_Faults.pdf.

63. Gagliano et al., "Active Geological Faults."

64. Craig E. Colten chronicles the city's floods in *An Unnatural Metropolis: Wresting New Orleans from Nature* (Baton Rouge: Louisiana State University Press, 2005).

65. Timothy M. Kusky, "Time to Move to Higher Ground" (op-ed), *Boston Globe*, September 25, 2005; Timothy Kusky, featured on "New Orleans Is Sinking," CBS, *60 Minutes*, November 20, 2005.

66. Jeff Goodell, "Goodbye, Miami," *Rolling Stone*, June 20, 2013, http://www.rolling stone.com/politics/news/why-the-city-of-miami-is-doomed-to-drown-20130620 ?page=3.

67. Emily Oster, "Witchcraft, Weather, and Economic Growth in Renaissance Europe," *Journal of Economic Perspectives* 18, no. 1 (Winter 2004): 215–228, http://home.uchicago .edu/eoster/witchec.pdf; Christian Pfister, "Climatic Extremes, Recurrent Crises, and Witch Hunts: Strategies of European Societies in Coping with Exogenous Shocks in the Late Sixteenth and Early Seventeenth Centuries," *Medieval History Journal* 10, nos. 1–2 (2007): 33–73.

68. Frank Newport, "Global Warming Concerns Continue to Drop," Gallup: Politics, March 11, 2010, http://www.gallup.com/poll/126560/Americans-Global-Warming -Concerns-Continue-Drop.aspx.

69. "UK's Winter Floods Strengthen Belief Humans Causing Climate Change—Poll," *The Guardian*, August 27, 2014.

70. "By the time we can measure the impact, it would be extremely difficult, if not impossible, to reduce the elevated concentrations of greenhouse gases in the atmosphere." Bob Ward, *The Times of London* letters, July 4, 2012.

CHAPTER 13: THE REMEDIES OF DR. RESILIENCE

1. Plato, "Timaeus" (c. 360 BC), http://classics.mit.edu/Plato/timaeus.html.

2. M. Ibrion, H. Lein, M. Mokhtari, and F. Nadim, "At the Crossroad of Nature and Culture in Iran: The Landscapes of Risk and Resilience of Seismic Space," *International Proceedings of Economics Development and Research* 71 (2014): 38–44; J. Jackson, "Fatal Attraction: Living with Earthquakes, the Growth of Villages into Megacities, and Earthquake Vulnerability in the Modern World," *Philosophical Transactions of the Royal Society A* 364 (2006): 1911–1925.

3. Thorne Lay, "Earthquakes: A Chilean Surprise," *Nature* 471 (March 10, 2011): 174–175, doi:10.1038/471174a, http://www.nature.com/nature/journal/v471/n7337 /full/471174a.html?WT.ec_id=NATURE-20110310.

4. "South Asia Population: Urban Growth: A Challenge and an Opportunity," World Bank, 2013, http://web.worldbank.org/WBSITE/EXTERNAL/COUNTRIES /SOUTHASIAEXT/0,,contentMDK:21393869~pagePK:146736~piPK:146830 ~theSitePK:223547,00.html; "Agglomerations over 750,000," Geohive, http://www .geohive.com/earth/cy_aggmillion2.aspx.

5. Cecil Morella, "Lives of Danger, Poverty on Philippines' Typhoon Coast," *Jakarta Globe*, December 20, 2014, http://thejakartaglobe.beritasatu.com/international/lives-danger-poverty-philippines-typhoon-coast/.

6. Michael Finkel, "Nyiragongo Volcano: The Volcano Next Door," *National Geographic* (April 2011), http://ngm.nationalgeographic.com/2011/04/nyiragongo-volcano/finkel-text; P. Allard, P. Baxter, M. Halbwachs, M. Kasareka, J. C. Komorowski, and J. L. Joron, "The Most Destructive Effusive Eruption in Modern History: Nyiragongo 2003," *Geophysical Research Abstracts* 5 (2003): 11970; "Mount Nyiragongo," Wikipedia, https://en.wikipedia.org/wiki/Mount_Nyiragongo (last modified March 11, 2016).

7. James J. Comiskey, "Overview of Flood Damages Prevented by US Army Corps of Engineers Flood Control Reduction Programs and Activities," *Journal of Contemporary Water Research and Education* 130 (March 2005): 13–19, http://opensiuc.lib.siu.edu/cgi/viewcontent.cgi?article=1065&context=jcwre.

8. D. R. Burbidge, "The 2012 Australian Earthquake Hazard Map," Record 2012/071, Geoscience Australia, Canberra, 2012, http://www.ga.gov.au/metadata-gateway/metadata/record/74811/.

9. "Slide 8: Haiti Pre-Earthquake Status," in Eric Calais, "The 2010 Haiti Earthquake: Lessons for Seismic Hazard and Societal Impacts in the Caribbean," http://www.iris.edu/hq/middle_america/docs/presentations/1025/Calais_2010.pdf.

10. Greg Bankoff, *Cultures of Disaster: Society and Natural Hazards of the Philippines* (London: Routledge Curzon, 2003).

11. "Annual Disaster Statistical Review 2013: The Numbers and Trends," Centre for Research on the Epidemiology of Disasters, September 22, 2014, http://reliefweb.int/report/world/annual-disaster-statistical-review-2013-numbers-and-trends.

12. Olaf Neussner, "Assessment of Early Warning Efforts in Leyte for Typhoon Haiyan/Yolanda," 2014, Deutsche Gesellschaft für Internationale Zusammenarbeit (GIZ) GmbH, http://www.preventionweb.net/files/36860_36860gizassessmentofearlywarningyol.pdf.

13. International Federation of Red Cross and Red Crescent Societies (IFRC), *World Disasters Report 2014: Focus on Culture and Risk*, http://www.ifrc.org/Global/Documents/Secretariat/201410/WDR%202014.pdf.

14. Greg Bankoff, Terry Cannon, Fred Krüger, and E. Lisa F. Schipper, "Introduction Exploring the Links Between Culture and Disasters," in *Cultures and Disasters: Understanding Cultural Framings in Disaster Risk Reduction*, edited by Fred Krüger, et al. (London: Routledge, 2015), 1–16.

15. Olivia Cooke, Jo Gottsman, and Ryerson Christie, "Hazard Communication and Local Perception of Lahar Risk at Cotopaxi Volcano, Ecuador," Cities on Volcanoes 7, 2012, http://www.citiesonvolcanoes7.com/vistaprevia2.php?idab=498; Ryerson Christie, Olivia Cooke, Jo Gottsman, "Fearing the Knock on the Door: Critical Security Studies Insight into Limited Cooperation with Disaster Management Regimes," *Journal of Applied Volcanology* 4 (2015): 19.

16. Hilary and John Mitchell, *Te Tau Ihu o Te Waka: A History of Māori of Marlborough and Nelson* (Wellington, NZ: Huia Publishers/Wakatū Incorporation, 2004), 63; "Stories: Tsunamis," The Encyclopedia of New Zealand, http://www.teara.govt.nz/en/tsunamis/page-2; Rick Budwha, "Correlations Between Catastrophic Palaeo-Environmental Events and Native Oral Traditions of the Pacific North-West," master's thesis, Depart-

ment of Anthropology, Simon Fraser University, 2002, http://www.collectionscanada
.gc.ca/obj/s4/f2/dsk4/etd/MQ81749.pdf.

17. K. D. Pang, "Extraordinary Floods in Early Chinese History and Their Absolute Dates," *Journal of Hydrology* 96 (1987): 139–155.

18. In the AD 527 book *Shui Jung Zhu* (*Commentary on the Water Classic*), an extraordinary flood is mentioned: on the Yi River at Longmenzhen in AD 223, the water rose to a height of 45 *chih*—36 feet (10.9 meters)—the highest level since 182 BC. V. B. Sauer, "Flood Frequency Analysis with Historical Data in China," in *Hydrological Frequency Modeling: Proceedings of the International Symposium on Flood Frequency and isk Analyses*, vol. 1, edited by V. P. Singh (Dordrecht, Germany: Reidel Publishing Co., 1987), 173–182; Chen Jiaqi, "The Role of Flood-Extremes and Different Approaches in Estimating Design Floods," in *Extreme Hydrological Events: Precipitation, Floods, and Droughts* (Proceedings of the Yokohama Symposium, July 1993), International Association of Hydrological Sciences (IAHS) publication 213, 1993, http://hydrologie.org redbooks/a213/iahs_213_0201.pdf.

19. Gregory S. Aldrete, *Floods of the Tiber in Ancient Rome* (Baltimore: Johns Hopkins University Press, 2007); "Curious and Unusual: The Floods of the River Tiber," Virtual Roma 1998–2008, roma.andreapollett.com/S1/roma-c4.htm. For a photo of the inscription, reading "Tiber flood 1277," see http://www.flickr.com/photos/master _poq/3324855007/.

20. "A stone house in Wertheim, Germany, sits on the Tauber River, painted with the dates and levels of floods back to 1621"; see Jan Munza, Matthias Deutsch, et al., "Historical Floods in Central Europe and Their Documentation by Means of Floodmarks and Other Epigraphical Monuments," *Moravian Geographical Reports* 14, no. 3 (2006): 26–44. "Storm tide markers dot the North Sea coast"; see "High Level Marks," Waymarking.com, http://www.waymarking.com/cat/details.aspx?f=1&guid=e75246e7 -cc6f-4362-b3bc-fc7e20edb851&wo=True&p=3&wst=6&st=2. See also Michael Kempe, "Memories of Natural Disasters in Northern Germany from the Sixteenth Century to the Present," *Medieval History Journal* 10, nos. 1–2 (2007): 327–354.

21. Danny Lewis, "These Century-Old Stone 'Tsunami Stones' Dot Japan's Coastline," *Smithsonian*, August 31, 2015, http://www.smithsonianmag.com/smart-news /century-old-warnings-against-tsunamis-dot-japans-coastline-180956448/#zXd8HKX dHSLDbL5A.99.

22. D. L. Ashliman, "Introduction," in *Aesop's Fables*, George Stade, Consulting Editorial Director (New York: Barnes & Noble Books/Fine Creative Media, 2005), xiii–xv, xxv–xxvi; "Aesop's Fables," Wikipedia, https://en.wikipedia.org/wiki/Aesop%27s_Fables (last modified March 14, 2016).

23. Ksenia Chmutina and Lee Bosher, "Disaster Risk Reduction or Disaster Risk Production: The Role of Building Regulations in Mainstreaming DRR," *International Journal of Disaster Risk Reduction* 13 (September 2015): 10–19.

24. Anthony Oliver-Smith, "Anthropological Research on Hazards and Disasters," *Annual Review of Anthropology* 25 (1996): 303–328.

25. Rory Carroll, "How San Andreas Is Boosting California's Earthquake Industry," *The Guardian*, June 4, 2015.

26. R. J. Smeed, "Some Statistical Aspects of Road Safety Research," *Journal of the*

Royal Statistical Society. Series A (General) 112, no. 1 (1949): 1–34, doi:10.2307/2984177, JSTOR 2984177.

27. Freeman Dyson, "A Failure of Intelligence: Operational Research at RAF Bomber Command, 1943–1945 (Part II)," *MIT Technology Review* (November 1, 2006), https://www.technologyreview.com/s/406789/a-failure-of-intelligence/; "Smeed's Law," Wikipedia, https://en.wikipedia.org/wiki/Smeed%27s_law (last modified May 1, 2015).

28. "Traffic Speeds in Central London," in "Transport for London: London Streets, Performance Report Quarter 1 2012–2013," October 15, 2012, http://www.tfl.gov.uk/cdn/static/cms/documents/london-streets-performance-report-q1-2012-13.pdf.

29. The formula multiplies the number of cars in a country by the population squared, then takes the square root of the total and multiplies the result by 0.0003 to find the predicted annual number of road casualties.

30. Tom Hundley and Dan McCarey, "Not God's Will: The Fixable Crisis of Traffic Fatalities," Pulitzer Center on Crisis Reporting, August 12, 2013, http://pulitzercenter.org/reporting/worldwide-auto-fatality-safety-legislation-traffic-metro-infrastructure-pulitzer-center-initiative-roads-kill.

31. Csaba Koren and Attila Corsos, "Is Smeed's Law Still Valid? A World-wide Analysis of the Trends in Fatality Rates," *Journal of Society for Transportation and Traffic Studies* 1 (2010): 64–76, http://www.thaitransport.org/journal/index.php/Path/article/viewFile/26/31; Elizabeth Kopits and Maureen Cropper, "Traffic Fatalities and Economic Growth," *Accident Analysis and Prevention* 37, no. 1 (January 2005): 169–178.

32. World Health Organization, Global Health Observatory, "Number of Road Traffic Deaths," http://www.who.int/gho/road_safety/mortality/traffic_deaths_number/en/.

33. Laura A. Bakkensen, "Adaptation and Natural Disasters: Evidence from Global Tropical Cyclone Damages and Fatalities," September 30, 2013, http://webmeets.com/files/papers/EAERE/2013/1124/Cyclone_Adaptation.pdf; Laura Bakkensen and W. Larson, "Population Matters When Modeling Hurricane Fatalities," *Proceedings of the National Academy of Sciences* 111, no. 50 (2014): E5331–E5332.

34. Greg Bankoff, "Design by Disasters, Seismic Architecture, and Cultural Adaptation to Earthquakes," in Krüger, et al., *Cultures and Disasters*, 53–72; Jacqueline Homan and Warren J. Eastwood, "The 17 August 1999 Kocaeli (Izmit) Earthquake: Historical Records and Seismic Culture," *Earthquake Spectra* 17, no. 4 (2001): 617–634, doi:http://dx.doi.org/10.1193/1.1423654; Jacqueline Homan, "Seismic Cultures: Myth or Reality?" presented at the Second International Conference on Post-Disaster Reconstruction: Planning for Reconstruction (2004); Stephen Tobriner, "Wooden Architecture and Earthquakes in Turkey: A Reconnaissance Report and Commentary on the Performance of Wooden Structures in the Turkish Earthquakes of 17 August and 12 November 1999," http://ip51.icomos.org/iiwc/seismic/Tobriner.pdf; M. H. Boduroglu, "Rural Buildings in Turkey That Have Suffered Damages in Recent Earthquakes and Their Main Causes," *Bulletin of the International Institute of Seismology and Earthquake Engineering* 23 (1989): 369.

35. Nicholas Ambraseys, et al., "The Pattan (Pakistan) Earthquake of 28 December 1974: Field Observations," *Quarterly Journal of Engineering Geology and Hydrogeology* 14, no. 1 (1981): 1–16.

36. Robert Muir-Wood, "Hard Times in the Mountains," *New Scientist*, May 14, 1981, 411–417.

37. Ken Hewitt, *Global E-Conference on Culture and Risk: Sociocultural Settings That Influence Risk from Natural Disasters: Participants' Contributions: A Compilation,* International Centre for Integrated Mountain Development (ICIMOD) and the Mountain Forum, October 1, 2008, http://www.mtnforum.org/sites/default/files/forum/files/participants-contributions-carthreads1-2.pdf.

38. IFRC, *World Disasters Report 2014.*

39. "In-depth Recovery Needs Assessment of Cyclone Aila Affected Areas 25–31 October 2009," ActionAid, Concern WorldWide, DanChurchAid, MuslimAid, Islamic Relief, Oxfam-GB, and Save the Children-UK, http://reliefweb.int/sites/reliefweb.int/files/resources/F6603B7EF22A16B4C125768D004B1190-Full_Report.pdf.

40. Offers of $500 per year for people to move out of the camps have encouraged owners of buildings that survived to add on additional rooms.

41. Sara E. Wermiel, *The Fireproof Building: Technology and Public Safety in the Nineteenth-Century American City* (Baltimore: Johns Hopkins University Press, 2000).

42. "Profitability of Non-Life Insurers Up Post-9/11, Chubb Chief," *The Times of India/The Economic Times,* October 18, 2002, http://articles.economictimes.indiatimes.com/2002-10-18/news/27349602_1_hdfc-chubb-general-insurance-premium-income-chubb-corporation.

43. "San Francisco Is Trying Shaming to Make Its Buildings Safer from Shaking," *Los Angeles Times*/Associated Press, September 16, 2014.

44. Buildings constructed to code are designed to absorb damage—interior walls will develop diagonal cracks as a way of absorbing the energy of shaking, thereby avoiding complete failure and collapse. Following what are called "code-plus" rules, it would be possible to make buildings that suffer no damage in earthquakes.

45. Aris Papadopoulos, *Resilience, the Ultimate Sustainability: Lessons from Failing to Develop a Stronger and Safer Built Environment* (ebook), 2015, http://www.buildingresilient.com/.

46. S. Hochrainer, "Assessing Macro-economic Impacts of Natural Disasters: Are There Any?" Policy Research Working Paper 4968 (Washington, DC: World Bank, 2009).

47. Patricia Fagen, "Remittances in Crises: A Haiti Case Study," Humanitarian Policy Group Background Paper Overseas Development Institute Report, April 2006, http://www.odi.org/sites/odi.org.uk/files/odi-assets/publications-opinion-files/412.pdf.

48. "Five Years After a Quake, Chinese Cite Shoddy Reconstruction," National Public Radio, May 14, 2013, http://www.npr.org/sections/parallels/2013/05/14/183635289/Five-Years-After-A-Quake-Chinese-Cite-Shoddy-Reconstruction.

49. Although insurance can help inform people about risk and require people to take simple actions to reduce risk—as with a smoke alarm.

50. "Zachariah Allen," Wikipedia, http://en.wikipedia.org/wiki/Zachariah_Allen (last modified February 22, 2016); Amos Perry, *Memorial of Zachariah Allen: 1795–1882* (J. Wilson and Son, 1883).

51. Nicolette Jones, *The Plimsoll Sensation: The Great Campaign to Save Lives at Sea* (Boston: Little, Brown, 2006); Steven Johnson, *The Ghost Map: The Story of London's Most Terrifying Epidemic—and How It Changed Science, Cities, and the Modern World* (New York: Riverhead Books, 2006), 195–196.

52. Vannevar Bush, "Biographical Memoir of John Ripley Freeman, 1855–1932," presented at the Autumn 1935 meeting of the National Academy of Science of the United

States of America, http://www.nasonline.org/publications/biographical-memoirs/memoir-pdfs/freeman-john.pdf.

53. Mary Lou Zoback, "'Epicenters' of Resilience," *Science* 346, no. 6207 (October 17, 2014): 283, doi:10.1126/science.1261788, http://www.sciencemag.org/content/346/6207/283.full.

54. Rowan Douglas, Glen Dolcemascolo, and Rajeev Issar, "Resilience: Integrating Risks into the Global Financial System: The 1 in 100 Initiative Action Statement," United Nations Climate Summit, New York, September 2014, http://www.un.org/climatechange/summit/wp-content/uploads/sites/2/2014/09/RESILIENCE-1-in-100-initiative.pdf.

55. Howard Kunreuther and Erwann Michel-Kerjan, "Demand for Multi-Year Insurance: Experimental Evidence," Working Paper 2013–11, University of Pennsylvania, Wharton School, Risk Management and Decisions Processes Center, July 2013, http://opim.wharton.upenn.edu/risk/library/WP2013-11_Demand-for-MYI.pdf.

56. R. D. Sheldon, "Nicholas Barbon," in *Oxford Dictionary of National Biography* (Oxford: Oxford University Press, September 2004), doi:10.1093/ref:odnb/1334.

57. Elizabeth Ferris, "How Can International Human Rights Law Protect Us from Disasters?" paper presented at the annual meeting of the American Society of International Law (April 10, 2014), http://www.brookings.edu/~/media/Research/Files/Papers/2014/04/22-natural-disasters-ferris/EFerris-ASIL-Human-Rights-and-Disasters-20140410.pdf?la=en; Human Rights Council, "Promotion and Protection of the Rights of Indigenous Peoples in Disaster Risk Reduction, Prevention, and Preparedness Initiatives," United Nations General Assembly, 27th session, New York, April 28, 2014, http://www.ohchr.org/Documents/Issues/IPeoples/EMRIP/Session7/A-HRC-EMRIP-2014-2_en.pdf; Ana Gonzalez Peleaz and Sebastian von Dahlen, "Insurance Regulation for Sustainable Development: Protecting Human Rights Against Climate Risks and Natural Hazards," Cambridge Institute for Sustainable Leadership, July 2015, http://www.cisl.cam.ac.uk/publications/publication-pdfs/insurance-regulation-report.pdf.

58. "The Coast-ification of America," Affordable Housing Institute (David Smith's blog), June 15, 2007, http://affordablehousinginstitute.org/blogs/us/2007/06/the_coast_ifica.html.

59. Roger Bilham, "Lessons from the Haiti Earthquake," *Nature* 463 (February 18, 2010): 878–879, doi:10.1038/463878a.

60. Schwab Foundation for Social Entrepreneurship, "Elizabeth Hausler Strand," http://www.schwabfound.org/content/elizabeth-hausler-strand.

61. In 50 percent of developing countries, more than 30 percent of people use adobe "rammed earth" to construct their houses; 73 percent of people in India and 60 percent of people in Peru have adobe buildings. See Marcial Blondet, Gladys Villa Garcia M., and Svetlana Brzev, "Earthquake-Resistant Construction of Adobe Building: A Tutorial," contribution to the EERI/IAEE World Housing Encyclopedia, March 2003, http://www.world-housing.net/wp-content/uploads/2011/06/Adobe_Tutorial_English_Blondet.pdf.

62. Svetlana Brzev, "Earthquake-Resistant Confined Masonry Construction," National Information Center of Earthquake Engineering, Indian Institute of Technology, Kanpur, India, December 2007.

63. "You Can Keep Your Family Safe from Earthquakes: How to Build Strong and Sturdy Houses," Build Change, 2009, http://buildchange.org/tech/BC_BOOK-english.pdf.

64. Daniel Sarewitz, "World View: Brick by Brick," *Nature* 465, no. 29 (May 5, 2010), doi:10.1038/465029a.

65. Mustafa Erdik, "Earthquake Risk in Turkey," *Science* 341, no. 6147 (August 16, 2013): 724–725, doi:10.1126/science.1238945.

66. Jenna Krajeski, "A Massive Earthquake in Istanbul Is Inevitable," The Atlantic City Lab, November 2, 2012; http://www.citylab.com/housing/2012/11/massive-earthquake-istanbul-inevitable/3793/.

67. Claire Berlinski, "1 Million Dead in 30 Seconds," *City Journal* (Summer 2011), http://www.brancabika.org/0506/0506/reading/zeytinburnu.pdf; Jacob H. Pyper Griffiths, Ayhan Irfanoglu, and Santiago Pujol, "Istanbul at the Threshold: An Evaluation of the Seismic Risk in Istanbul," *Earthquake Spectra* 23, no. 1 (February 2007): 63–75, doi:http://dx.doi.org/10.1193/1.2424988.

68. Ashley Cleek, "Preparing for Earthquakes, Istanbul Rattles Its Apartment Dwellers," *The Atlantic*, March 27, 2013.

69. M. Nilay Ozeyranli Ergenc, O. Metin Ilkisik, and Murat T. Turk, "Istanbul Earthquake Risk and Mitigation Studies," Disaster Coordination Center, Istanbul Metropolitan Municipality, http://www.euromedina.org/bibliotheque_fichiers/Doc_RisksIstanbul.pdf.

70. The observations of Arthur Neve, a British visitor to Kashmir who witnessed the 1885 Kashmir earthquake, are reported in Dr. Bashir Ahmad Bilal, "Kashmir Earthquake of 1555 and 1885," Greater Kashmir, September 18, 2011, http://www.greaterkashmir.com/news/gk-magazine/kashmir-earthquake-of-1555-and-1885/104073.html.

71. Randolph Langenbach, "Rescuing the Baby from the Bathwater: Traditional Masonry as Earthquake-Resistant Construction," presented at the Eighth International Masonry Conference, Dresden (2010), https://www.yumpu.com/en/document/view/34215617/rescuing-the-baby-from-the-bathwater-conservationtech/17.

72. Kubilay Hicyilmaz, Kitendra K. Bothara, and Maggie Stephenson, "World Housing Encyclopedia: Housing Report, Dhajji Dewari," Report 146, Earthquake Engineering Research Institute and International Association for Earthquake Engineering, 2012, http://db.world-housing.net/building/146; Randolph Langenbach, "Don't Tear It Down! Preserving the Earthquake Resistant Vernacular Architecture of Kashmir, New Delhi," UNESCO/Oinfroin Media, 2009, www.traditional-is-modern.net; Randolph Langenbach, "Timber Frames and Solid Walls: Earthquake Resilient Construction from Roman Times to the Origins of the Modern Skyscraper," presented at the First International Symposium on Historic Earthquake-Resistant Timber Frames in the Mediterranean Area (HEaRT), Cosenza, Calabria, Italy (2013); Randolph Langenbach, "Rubble Stone Walls and Reinforced Concrete Frames: Heritage Structures Reveal the Hidden Truth About Risk and Resilience During the Haiti Earthquake," *ISCARSAH Newsletter* 5 (December 2013), http://iscarsah.icomos.org/images/stories/newsletter/Edition05.pdf; Randolph Langenbach, "Was Haiti in 2010 the Next Tangshan in 1976: Heritage Structures Reveal the Hidden Truth About Risk and Resilience During the Haiti Earthquake," *ISCARSAH Newsletter* 5 (2013): 10–19; IFRC, *World Disasters Report 2014*.

73. Stefania Pollone, "An Ancient Prototype of Modern Anti-seismic Wooden Framed Systems: The Case-Study of "Casa a Graticco" in the Archaeological Site of Herculaneum," https://www.academia.edu/5168385/An_ancient_prototype_of_modern_anti-seismic _wooden_framed_systems._The_case-study_of_Casa_a_Graticcio_in_the_archaeological _site_of_Herculaneum.

74. "A WiKi of Traditional Building Practices of India," Artisans in Architecture, September 18, 2009, http://aina.wikidot.com/.

75. Stephen Harris, "Fibreglass Fabric Could Protect Old Buildings from Earthquakes," The Engineer, January 8, 2013, https://www.theengineer.co.uk/fibreglass-fabric-could -protect-old-buildings-from-earthquakes/; "A 'Weightlifter's Belt' for Buildings Could Bring Quick Quake Repair," UPI Science News, January 13, 2014.

76. Ryan O'Hare, "Earthquake-proof Bed 'Swallows' You When It Senses the Ground Shaking: Mechanism Drops You and Your Mattress into a Sealed Box Full of Supplies," *Daily Mail*, December 17, 2015.

INDEX

ROBERT MUIR-WOOD is chief research officer of Risk Management Solutions. He is also a visiting professor at University College London's Institute for Risk and Disaster Reduction. He is an acknowledged international expert in the forensics of disasters and catastrophe risk modeling. He has a PhD in earth sciences from Cambridge University, where he was also a research fellow. Beyond serving as a lead author on two IPCC reports, he was a technical adviser to "Risky Business," a 2014 study sponsored by Michael Bloomberg, Henry Paulson, and Thomas Steyer that explores the future costs of climate change in the United States. Since 2007, he has been vice chair of a high-level OECD panel advising on catastrophes. He has also been a writer and journalist, was once editor of the Cambridge University student magazines *Broadsheet* and *Granta*, and has been the author of many feature articles for *New Scientist*. He was founding editor of the European earth science journal *Terra Nova*.